O9-AHW-237

THE EMOTIONAL PLAGUE

THE EMOTIONAL PLAGUE

The Root of Human Evil

CHARLES KONIA, M.D.

THE EMOTIONAL PLAGUE: The Root of Human Evil

A.C.O. Press
P.O. Box 490
Princeton, NJ 08542

ISBN-13: 978-0-9679670-3-5

DEDICATION

On more than one occasion, Dr. Elsworth Baker expressed a wish for a book to be written on the history of the emotional plague. Since this project would be an account of nearly the entire history of civilization, it would take an entire lifetime to complete. This present volume can be viewed as a "first chapter" in this enormous undertaking. It is dedicated to the memory of Elsworth Baker, M.D., who brought the science of orgonomy into the future, intact, without distortion. Without his teaching and influence, this book would never have been written.

ACKNOWLEDGMENTS

I want first to thank my best friend and love of my life, my wife, Iris, without whose support and encouragement this book would never have been written. My special thanks to the editors of the *Journal of Orgonomy*, Howard Chavis, M.D., Robert Harman, M.D., and Richard Schwartzman, D.O., for their tireless and patient assistance in taking a critical look at how the ideas were presented and for their many helpful contributions. Howard's efforts went far beyond the call of duty. Thanks also to my editors, Bud Bynack, Rebecca Schwartzman, and John Daniels. Their ability to organize and sharpen the arguments contained in this book resulted in a significant and welcome improvement. I am also indebted to Marlise Wind for her dedication to the book in its early stages and to Hilary Crist for her marketing assistance and moral support and to Jim Rossi for his valuable help in designing and producing the graphics. I would also like to express my gratitude to all those who helped make these new concepts more comprehensible to the general public, in particular Dee Apple, Ph.D., Richard Appleby and Martin Goldberg. My appreciation to Steve Rogin for his helpful suggestions on the book's design. My thanks also to Peter A. Crist, M.D., for promoting the book.

Lastly, I want to express my appreciation to all the many contributors whose generous financial donations to Project Publish made this book's publication possible. My special thanks to George Argyeas, M.D., Orson Bean, Maurice Brun, Theodota Chasapi, M.D., Edward Chastka, M.D., Howard Chavis, M.D., Deborah A. Cohen, Stephen Danforth, Steven Diab, Ruth Dingwall, Ph.D., Kathleen L. Dunlap, Steven Dunlap, Bob Fitzgerald, Marcia Futter, Jeff Freeman, Philip Heller, M.D., George Hughes, M.D., Salvatore Iacobello, M.D., Harold Konia, M.D., Eric Liden, Michael McGourty, Raymond Mero, D.O., Camilla Moore, Kenneth Noland, Josef Friedrich Puhringer, Dale Rosin, D.O., Jean and Jack Sargent, John Schleining, Contee Seely, Sylvia & George Smith, Ivan Sorenson, Wesley Szpunar, Nassos Teopoulos, M.D., Virginia Whitener, Ph.D., and Jim Wittes. And with love to my children, Brad and Andrew Konia, and Jessica and Tankut Eker, who always believed Dad could do it!

CONTENTS

PART I

Recognition of the Emotional Plague

FOREWORD

In this epic tour de force, psychiatrist Charles Konia tackles issues that have afflicted humanity throughout recorded history, offering brilliant new insights into the predicaments that people have brought upon themselves. Konia believes that emotional illness is far more severe and widespread than is realized, and he concludes that societies—for the very reason that they are shaped by emotionally damaged individuals—are themselves sick.

Time and time again, experience has proven that political solutions and social programs fail miserably. While advances in technology are enormously valuable and continue to bring us remarkable conveniences and unending distractions, people remain as dissatisfied and unhappy as ever. Why, with all of this "progress," do we still find ourselves in a world filled with violence, oppressive political regimes, religious fanaticism, racial hatred, sexual repression, child abuse, misogyny, pornography, drug and alcohol abuse, and all the other manifestations of human misery? Dr. Konia provides new insights not only to the root cause of man's predicament, but he also suggests the way out of the trap. He examines society in a radically different manner, exploring the character of the individuals who gain the power to control the lives of others.

Building on the work of Wilhelm Reich, M.D. (1897-1957) and Elsworth F. Baker, M.D. (1903-1985), Konia grounds his analysis in two key concepts—life energy and "armoring." Reich held that humans, in common with all living organisms, possess a unique biological energy. He further postulated that in man the majority of emotional illnesses, as well as many physical diseases, are the result of a block in the flow and metabolism of this life energy. Armoring refers to the actual physical contractions that form in the body in an attempt to defend itself against experiencing painful feelings and emotions. This armoring process, according to

Reich, also reduces one's vitality, the capacity for love, as well as adversely affecting sexual functioning.

Much of non-Western medicine is grounded in an acceptance that there is a life energy, and it is called by different names in virtually every culture. Reich chose to call the energy "orgone" (from the word organism) and saw it not as a mystical concept or construct, but as a real entity that could be scientifically measured and studied. Reich's ideas were radical in his day and remain so. Modern classical science, with all of its advances, has failed to recognize what should be apparent to them—that there does exist a real energy that drives life, that *is* life. Present-day science, including twenty-first-century medicine, moves forward with this central piece of the puzzle missing, but it is doing so in a strictly mechanistic fashion. Scientists and researchers world-wide cannot see life except as a combination of complex chemicals that somehow, someway in the distant past, came together to create the spark we call life. But life itself remains a complete mystery, and emotional and physical disease continues to be viewed solely in terms of chemical imbalances, genetic abnormalities, or other aberrations of a malfunctioning machine.

While classical scientists have closed their minds to the idea of a life energy—any talk of such a thing is viewed as hocus-pocus, not worthy of consideration let alone scientific investigation—Reich's ideas have continued to influence great thinking. This is evidenced here by Konia's compelling work, which moves into uncharted waters with a dynamic, scientifically based exposition of orgone energy. What Konia presents is a major paradigm shift, a wholly different approach to understanding human functioning and society's irrationality.

If Reich was correct, and armoring is the culprit, then preventing its formation must become humanity's first priority. We can only speculate when and why, in the distant past, man first began to armor. But we do know that armoring begins at the very beginning of life, in the first hours and days after birth. And we know that it forms as a defensive mechanism when the newborn's *complete* needs are not met.

The newborn baby requires far more than to be fed, diapered and clothed. She needs to have deep emotional and physical connection with her mother as soon as she enters the world. This is not possible if she cannot be with mother on an almost constant basis. She must, following delivery, remain with mother, be breast-fed on demand, have her cries promptly responded to, be touched and caressed, and have deep, open and loving eye contact with mother and others. When the newborn does not have these needs met it causes distress, and the suffering infant has only one way to handle this distress—and that is to physically contract. The long-term consequences are dire, and unless there is immediate relief, this armor remains for life. This reaction to emotional distress and pain is involuntary and occurs before any organized thought processes have formed.

Unfortunately, today's practices do not consider the complete and genuine needs of the newborn. Separating babies from their mothers in the hospital following birth, restrictive swaddling, mandating that they only be placed on their backs—an uncomfortable and unnatural position—and painful circumcision are just some of the widespread practices that cause armoring and permanent damage. Prevention rests with overcoming the universal mistaken belief that because an infant hasn't yet developed rational thought or conscious memory, there can be no lasting effects from early traumatic experiences.

As Konia so poignantly illustrates, how we treat the newborn will determine the ultimate health of the individual as well as the health of the society to which he will belong. *How we treat infants matters most of all, and therein lies the fate of our world.*

It is my great hope that Reich's pivotal ideas will be embraced and that he will, one day, join the ranks of Socrates, Aristotle, Giordano Bruno, Vesalius, Galileo, Semmelweis, Lister and virtually every other exceptional individual who broke new ground by speaking the truth. All suffered ridicule and defamation and sometimes death before their ideas were ultimately accepted.

Reich, himself, was prosecuted by the Food and Drug Administration and brought to trial, where he refused to defend his scientific discoveries in a court of law. Convicted of having failed to obey a court injunction, he was sentenced to the Lewisburg Federal Prison where he died.

We are indebted to all the individuals who carry on the legacy of Wilhelm Reich's work. They have remained committed to the idea that he was one of the major scientists of all time and that his discoveries have extraordinary potential to improve the condition of humanity. We are especially indebted to Dr. Konia for the years of labor that have gone into writing this enormously important book.

Richard Schwartzman, D.O.
Solebury, Pennsylvania
December 2007

PREFACE

Humanity is afflicted with a deadly illness, one whose existence has been apparent since the beginning of written history, and yet no one has written about it extensively until now. It permeates every area of social life, and everyone is a carrier, yet no one is aware of its existence. It is infectious and the disease can be transmitted from one person to another, yet neither the afflicted individual nor its next victim recognizes its symptoms. In fact, the disease's existence depends on its remaining hidden from awareness. Like a virulent virus, it is disintegrating the fabric of society and crippling core life functions by attacking its victims at their most vulnerable place. However, this is not a physical disease but a *bioemotional disease,* one that manifests in the realm of emotions. As it spreads from one person to another, it destroys its victims by producing confusion, uncertainty, and paralysis. Since the disease attacks emotional life, it is called the *emotional plague.*

There is nothing defamatory in this term, *emotional plague,* since it does not refer to conscious malice or moral failing. Nor can the emotional plague be trivialized, ignored, or excused as "just human nature." The world will see no genuine social improvement until the emotional plague is first recognized and then contained.

Why has this emotional plague escaped recognition? A major reason is that, until recently, we have lacked a natural scientific basis for recognizing and understanding the pathology of emotional life. To truly understand human behavior, one must know that an individual's bioemotional structure has three layers. In the *superficial layer,* the average person is restrained, polite, civil, and accommodating. This layer serves to cover the deeper, *secondary (middle) layer,* which harbors perverse impulses such as cruelty, spite, and jealousy. The secondary layer is the repository of all of humanity's destructive impulses. Beneath this secondary layer is the *biological core.* At the core, under favorable social conditions, people are decent, honest, industrious, cooperative, and capable of love. They are also capable of rational hatred. The unfortunate result of this layering is that every natural (healthy) social endeavor or emotion that originates from the biological core must, on its way to action, pass through the destructive secondary layer. There it is deflected. As a result, the original, straightforward core impulse is changed into an aberration, a malevolent, destructive force.

To comprehend the emotional plague in all its aspects, one must recognize the relationship between core impulses (primary drives) and those that result when these impulses are blocked and deflected. What causes such a block is "armor,"[1] which functions to change primary core impulses into secondary drives that are socially destructive. The source of the emotional plague is human armor. Armor is a biological condition that consists of chronic involuntary contraction of the human animal, both at the *physical level,* which manifests in contracted musculature, and at the *emotional level,* which causes a contracted, rigid character. Armor functions like a prison. It protects both the armored individual and society by blocking the breakthrough of destructive, painful, and frightening emotions and sensations. Although armor exists in humans, society and social institutions may also be referred to as "armored" because society results from and reflects the armored structure of the individuals who shape it.

Armor is produced in every new generation of infants and children through life-inimical childrearing practices. Such a process occurs at the hands of parents and social institutions that are themselves armored. Armored children grow up to armor their children, and so it goes from one generation to the next. Since society as a whole and each individual is armored to varying degrees, the scope of the emotional plague is as wide as the entire range of human activity. In armored society, the superficial and secondary layers are represented socially, but not the biological core. As a result, the communicability of the emotional plague has increased dramatically in every area of social life. An example is the world-wide increase in terrorists and terrorist sup-

---

1. See glossary.

porters. The kind and amount of social carnage carried out by ordinary civilians acting as suicide bombers—a practice considered unthinkable only a decade ago—has become commonplace.

To understand current social events, one must step outside the framework of conventional thinking. Flawed thinking is part and parcel of why things are the way they are. Hence, an understanding of armor and its effects on thought and social behavior is essential. Armor interferes with clear observation and rational thinking, and it gives rise to distorted views. The mechanistic (liberal) and the mystical (conservative) ways of thinking are a product of armor. Because scientists are themselves armored, they know nothing more of the basic functions of life than what Aristotle said in his *Poetics* twenty-five centuries ago. For example, at a 1984 symposium, possibly the first of its kind, on "The Origin and Evolution of Sex," these Darwinian statements were made: "We do not even in the least know the final cause of sexuality. The whole subject is as yet hidden in darkness. Sex is the queen of problems in evolutionary biology. Why such a thing exists at all is the largest and least ignorable and most obdurate of life's fundamental questions."[2] We will show that the life function and the sexual function are closely linked.

Sexuality remains inexplicable because one cannot understand it by means of "mechanistic materialism," the form of thinking employed by modern-day scientists. Mechanistic materialism holds to the view that nature functions as a machine. Since sexuality cannot be understood using concepts borrowed from the field of mechanics, scientists resort to teleology to fill gaps in their understanding. They postulate a purpose to explain it, such as "sex enables evolutionary gains from genetically varied offspring" or "genetic change is necessary in order for organisms to stay ahead in the never-ending race to maintain resistance to disease" or "sex has an adaptive value in its role in repairing damaged genes."[3] Teleological thinking is mystical. The phrase "in order to," used here to explain the phenomenon under investigation, only gives the *appearance* of providing a physical link between

2. Morse, C. "Why Is Sex?" *Science News*, no. 126 (September 8, 1984): 154.

3. "Is Sex Necessary? Evolutionists Are Perplexed." *New England Journal of Medicine*, no. 299 (1978): 111.

sexuality and some natural process, yet it explains nothing.

Sexuality was not clarified and placed on a scientific foundation until Wilhelm Reich discovered the energetic basis of life and the function of the orgasm. Reich understood that there are no goals in nature; rather, *nature simply functions.* From his clinical and biological observations, Reich discovered the properties of the energy that governs life. He found that it moves spontaneously and, in the human, is subjectively experienced as sensation and emotion. It periodically builds to a certain level and then under suitable conditions is discharged in the involuntary orgastic convulsion and in work. The unarmored healthy person feels the build-up as pleasurable sexual tension and the discharge is experienced as sexual gratification. Orgasm and work regulate the energy metabolism of the organism. Because armor blocks sexual excitation, it interferes with the capacity for full orgastic discharge. This results in a build-up of excess energy that can never be fully released. Over time, the sexual tension produces and fuels neurotic symptoms.

The essence of life energy is spontaneous movement. Some examples include the pulsatory movement of jellyfish, the beating of the heart, intestinal peristalsis, and the streaming movement of *living* protoplasm when observed under the microscope. When biology students are taught early on that life is exclusively based on the interaction of inert atoms and molecules and when they are not given the opportunity to observe the spontaneous motility of living protoplasm, their excitement in the subject is destroyed and they are led to conclude that a living organism is no different than a machine. In this way, mechanistic thinking is introduced into the minds of young people and an armoring process of their perceptual function begins. The restriction of bioenergetic movement due to armor results in an intolerance of sensations and the emotion of fear when spontaneous motility is experienced. Armored people cannot feel pleasurable streaming energy—especially involuntary sexual excitation and the loss of control that accompanies the orgastic convulsion—without becoming anxious. Unable to experience and discharge energy naturally, they must resort to pathological means to deal with the buildup of tension.

Armor deadens the perception of all spontaneous movements, including those arising from the environment, as well as internally arising emotions and sensations. An example of this deadening process is the way that the armored natural scientist conducts research, which is to exclude from the field of observation any natural phenomena that manifests spontaneous motility, such as the streaming motion of living protoplasm. Since armor deadens the amount and intensity of sexual feeling, the scientist must control the motion of observed natural phenomena in order to avoid being excited by the feelings generated within. This explains why scientists must view nature as a lifeless machine, one that can be controlled.

In daily life, armor also drives ordinary people to seek substitute gratification, to pursue substitute behaviors to replace unattainable, full sexual gratification. Common examples are neurotic sexual practices, drug use, excessive talking, overeating, alcoholism, sociopolitical activity, and religious practices. These will be discussed further in Part II.

Average neurotics confine these pathological methods to their personal lives. However, *individuals afflicted with the emotional plague use these same mechanisms but find it necessary to control the mores and behavior of others*—to impose their way of life on others. Such persons cannot stand unarmored expression in others because it creates intolerable longing and fills them with hatred of all that is natural in life, especially healthy sexuality. From this hatred, the plague makes its appearance, and afflicted persons are driven to thwart and destroy the life-positive expressions of healthier individuals. Some of the manifestations of unarmored life frequently targeted by plague individuals are natural sexuality; the liveliness of newborns, children, and adolescents; and spontaneous social and economic activity in democratic societies.

The destructiveness of the emotional plague is carried out through carefully planned and completely *unconscious* rationalizations that serve its end, which is to obstruct natural life. Thus, infants must be separated from their mothers at birth "to protect the health of the newborn" or "to allow the mother to rest"; male infants must be circumcised "to prevent cancer"; infants must be swaddled "to make them feel secure." On the social scene, Islam must destroy Western society "because infidels are inferior to

Muslims or they are corrupt and want to destroy Islam"; blacks and certain other minority groups deserve preferential treatment "because they have been unfairly treated in the past by whites"; pornography and obscenity are to be permitted "to protect people's First Amendment rights." Abortion should be legal "because women should be free to choose whether or not to have a child." Abortion should be illegal "because women should be responsible for the life of their unborn child." These arguments justifying the plague are honestly believed by both those afflicted and the public at large. These views are almost certain to prevail since there is always some truth in them and because people are too armored, and therefore too emotionally disturbed, to see the destructiveness that they conceal. Strip away the rationalizations, however, and the underlying hatred of unarmored life comes into view.

At this point, we have to face an objection: Why is it important to recognize the existence of the emotional plague? Why is it not enough to address human destructiveness whenever and wherever it occurs? The answer is that this approach is merely symptomatic. It does not get to the root of the problem of human destructiveness, and it makes eradication or even containment impossible. This approach is no different than that used during the Middle Ages to deal with the epidemic of the bubonic plague, which was to build walls in strategic areas to prevent the migration of people who were suspected of having the disease. Until the infectious agent, the causative bacterium, and the vector of transmission were identified, no effective method of containment was possible. Similarly, without understanding its mode of operation, the emotional plague cannot be treated. However, to understand its mode of operation, it is first necessary to recognize that the pestilence actually exists. Furthermore, without recognizing its mode of operation, it is often not possible to recognize that a socially destructive act has been perpetrated since, as we have shown, human beings are capable of rationalizing and justifying *any* socially destructive act as being for the common good.

Before we can make sense of the world, we must first ask certain questions: Why do people speak and write with abandon about falsehoods of every kind, but the truth is never revealed, accepted, or acted upon? Why are irrelevancies of every kind on vital social issues freely discussed and the essential points of the matter consistently ignored? The reason is that people are too emotionally sick to see and think clearly about their personal and social lives.

Armor also limits people's capacity to tolerate freedom. People long to be free of the restrictions of their armor, yet they are physically and emotionally unable to relinquish these restraints. Moreover, *people are unaware of the existence of armor or of being trapped in their own armored bodies.* They therefore become vulnerable to political and religious leaders who dangle the illusion of hope for greater freedom and happiness in this world or the next.

The Free World is currently engaged in a life-and-death struggle with the emotional plague as manifested in Islamic *jihad*. While most Islamic nations overtly suppress freedom, liberal Western societies covertly destroy it by indiscriminate permissiveness and license, and by undermining America's military and political efforts to contain and eradicate the destructiveness of Islamic *jihad*. The outcome of the conflict between these opposing forces is uncertain. This is partly because the West is suffering from and is weakened by its own internal struggle with the emotional plague and by the ideological conflicts between the political left and right. The Islamic pestilent individual correctly perceives this vulnerability of Western society and feels confident that the forces of *jihad* can topple it.

The diverse political and ideological groups within human society correspond to the layers of human bioemotional structure. The layer from which an ideology originates determines whether the thinking is liberal or conservative. The rational component of conservatives' thought originates from the biological core and the irrational component from the secondary layer. Liberals, on the other hand, function primarily from the superficial layer. Liberal thinking *seems* rational, but because it originates from the superficial layer, it cannot penetrate into the depths of human nature. Liberal thinking and the solutions offered for social problems are therefore idealistic. Their thought process has a well-rationalized façade that serves to suppress the secondary layer ("the beast") in armored people. Additionally, liberals often fear physical aggression and therefore cannot take appropriate, rational action in the face of a threat to their safety or even their lives.

The limitations of liberal thinking are particularly evident in matters involving national security and defense. There are some liberals who would even have us believe that America is not currently involved in a life-and-death struggle for its very survival. This denial is perceived by our enemy as appeasement. Appeasing terrorism by caving in to a terrorist's demands does not satisfy the terrorist. On the contrary, *appeasement actively promotes terrorism*. As with any other infectious disease, the only means of controlling the terrorist form of the emotional plague is to sequester or eradicate the pathogenic agent.

The depth and clearness of undistorted contact with the biological core and the environment determines one's clarity of thought. The capacity for completely rational thought presumes an absence of armor. In a relatively unarmored individual, thinking is simple and straightforward, sensing and protecting unarmored life. In armored individuals, thinking has become rigid and distorted in ways specific to that individual's character structure, and thinking therefore senses and protects *armored* life.

To evaluate a particular social issue, we must know the attendant details. The thorniest questions deal with personal responsibility and freedom. This evaluation of a social issue rests on two basic questions: Does the issue involve the expression of a core function and if so, to what extent can the core function be expressed, given the limitations due to individual and social armor. Current forms of thinking do not address these questions. However, in our era of social breakdown, the thinking and actions of the political left are more damaging than those of the right. Partly because of its mindless emphasis on promoting social change, the political left cannot maintain cohesiveness and organization of the healthy components of democratic institutions.

Irrational thinking on either side of the sociopolitical spectrum differs in kind. The rigidly moral stance of people on the political right is easily recognized. They make a clear-cut distinction between "right" and "wrong"; they believe in maintaining social traditions and the "status quo"; and they believe in the importance of personal responsibility. Examples include their requirement that women remain celibate prior to marriage and their opposition to abortion. The rigidly moral attitude of people on the left is difficult to detect and therefore more pernicious because it gives the *appearance* of flexibility and rationality. Liberals emphasize moral relativism, the importance of social change over permanence, and the belief that everyone, including the criminal and terrorist, can behave rationally and tolerate freedom once they have a little help. Examples include the belief that men and women should feel free to engage in sexual relations on a first date regardless of their degree of emotional readiness, the belief that all forms of sexual behavior are natural, and the belief that people have the right to express any idea regardless of its social consequences. Although the liberal view of allowing unconditional freedom is not seen as moralistically biased, the rigid judgment behind this attitude is as strong and tenacious as that of conservative moralism.

Because the moralistic behavior of liberals is concealed, it is more dangerous than conservative bias. Referred to as "political correctness," it is the mindless application of the same set of rules of social conduct for one and all, which will eventually reduce everyone to the lowest common denominator, lead to less individual freedom, and increase government control of society. This is because genuine freedom without personal responsibility is impossible. The absence of individual responsibility externalizes that function onto government bureaucracy. Recent decades have seen the uncritical public acceptance of liberal thinking followed by a shift in mainstream sociopolitical thinking to the left of center; in other words, the transformation from authoritarian society to *anti*-authoritarian society. In sharp contrast to the neurotic moralism of the right and left, *natural* morality is based on a solid foundation of lawful principles originating from the biological core.

The world's societies currently lack any real understanding of the underlying causes or management of the emotional plague's destructiveness. Almost every social problem becomes politicized and mired in an ideological battle between the left and the right. The solutions, bound to be merely symptomatic, are to enact legislation designed to contain or eliminate the social problem's superficial manifestations. Helpless cries of "There ought to be a law!" are common whenever a troublesome social problem arises. If the problem is big enough, social anxiety rises and public opinion pressures legislatures and politicians to "do something," which usually means enacting some form of stopgap legislation. This typically results in the installation of a new layer of bureaucracy with ever-greater restriction of individual freedom and an intensification of social armor. This sequence of events illustrates the functions of armor, which are to reduce freedom of movement and the perception of anxiety. As a result, the underlying source of the social problem is not recognized, and the social symptom is exacerbated. A recent example is the recommendation of the Presidential Commission on the September 11 attacks to install a new cabinet-level national intelligence director and a new layer of bureaucracy to police the old layers. This recommendation overlooks and obfuscates the source of the intelligence problem, namely people's characterological disturbances and political infighting that interfere with the work of intelligence personnel.

The transformation of American society that began during the second half of the twentieth century and sharply accelerated during the Vietnam War era was partly precipitated by the demand for greater sexual freedom accompanied by the breakthrough of secondary layer destructive impulses in the armored younger generation of Americans. Their hatred was directed against every possible symbol of American authority. Fueled by unfulfilled sexual longing which could not be satisfied, this breach in society resulted in greater levels of social armor, which took the form of laws mandating the protection of certain freedoms and rights; but the underlying problems—the energy source of this hatred—remained completely ignored. Unable to achieve sexual satisfaction, the younger generation who first started and then became swept up in this wave of rebellion had to fend for themselves and find a way to deal with their frustrated sexual longing. Some took drugs to numb themselves, while others became hippies, social dropouts, or leftist ideologues. Only a few were fortunate enough to survive unscathed.

Meanwhile, the emotional plague, operating below the social surface, continued to fester. The seeds of suspicion and hatred against America sowed by the leftists in the 1960s are bearing fruit today. Many of these leftist ideologues are currently in prominent positions in every area of social influence. With the fall of the Soviet Union, the world looks with mixed feelings upon America as the only remaining superpower. Since power is equated with authority, and since leftists have a covert hatred of authority, America becomes identified with the hated authority figure in the minds of the masses, which have been influenced by the left-dominated media. This anti-American bias has had disastrous consequences in the world's life-and-death battle against Islamic *jihad*. Influenced as they are by the leftist intelligentsia, many people are in danger of completely losing touch with their survival instincts.

We must see behind the social façade to understand and hopefully immobilize the emotional plague. Political solutions to social problems are an attempt to deal only with the superficial, symptomatic level of social pathology. The underlying sources of social problems can never be permanently remedied through sociopolitical, judicial, or religious activism. The only way to understand and address such problems is to gain the knowledge of how the emotional plague operates and use a method of thinking that completely differs from those employed by the left and the right. This method is called *functional energetic thinking*. It corresponds to the way nature functions and thus can be used to shed light on the emotional plague. With a clear understanding of the armored human condition and its effect on thinking and behavior, we can become aware of the existence and operation of the emotional plague, which can then lead to appropriate remedial action and prevention.

The ultimate solution to the problem of the plague's destructiveness will come when enough people are free of armor, allowing them undistorted core contact and sustained rational thought. To bring about a healthier society, our primary tasks must therefore be *armor prevention* in newborns and children and, when possible, *armor removal* in adolescents and adults.

Perhaps a little more to the "left" than the "right,"
but not one millimeter FORWARD!

—Wilhelm Reich, *Listen Little Man.*
New York: Orgone Institute Press, 1948.

PART I

RECOGNITION OF THE EMOTIONAL PLAGUE

INTRODUCTION AND ORIENTATION

The elucidation and elimination of chaotic conditions, no matter whether in a social or in an animal organism, requires scientific and practical work of long duration.
—Wilhelm Reich, *The Mass Psychology of Fascism*

Socially destructive human behavior is accelerating, and we are helpless to do anything about it. Programs aimed at social problems have not only failed in the long run but have even backfired, intensifying socially destructive activity. This destructiveness is a manifestation of what Wilhelm Reich called "the emotional plague." In *Character Analysis,* Reich defines the emotional plague as "human behavior which, on the basis of biopathic[4] character structure, makes itself felt in interpersonal, that is, social relationships and which becomes organized in corresponding social institutions" (Reich 1949a, page 252).

Today, the emotional plague manifests with particular virulence in a number of areas: fundamentalist religious movements, imperialistic war ideologies (including Islamic *jihad*), ideologically

4. Biopathy is defined in the glossary.

driven partisan politics, passive or active striving for authority, moralism, masochistic tolerance of sadistic behavior, corrupt business activity, everything subsumed under the term "racket," authoritarian bureaucracy, criminal and antisocial behavior, gossip, defamation, pornography, usury, and race hatred. The list goes on and on. The term *emotional plague* is not a metaphor to describe the underlying cause of these social phenomena. It is a biological reality of the psychic and social realms that is functionally identical to such communicable diseases as cholera, malaria, hepatitis, AIDS, and influenza. Any person can contract the illness when conditions are favorable for infection. As such, the criteria that define this pestilence are based on the same *objective diagnostic standards* that are used for any other type of medical condition. Consequently, the term *emotional plague* also has no moral connotation.

The emotional plague has afflicted human society ever since people's natural experience of themselves and their environment became distorted by armor. It survives from generation to generation largely because people are unaware of its existence and operation. This book examines, among other things, a major manifestation of the emotional plague in today's society—sociopolitical activity. This can be defined as ideologically driven political activity arising from the *displacement of intrapsychic conflicts of armored people onto the social and political sphere.* It strives to reveal the essential irrationality and destructiveness of sociopolitics and offers methods of dealing with this scourge upon humanity.

Functional Thinking and Social Phenomena

Sociology developed into an independent field of study during the nineteenth century with the emergence of the concept of society as separate from the state. Auguste Comte coined the term in 1838, as he and the other sociologists who followed attempted to understand social phenomena from the perspective of environmental forces impinging on groups of people. Herbert Spencer, for example, applied the Darwinian principle of natural selection to the development of society, while Karl Marx emphasized economic factors in social organization. Their theories reflected the materialistic worldview that assumes that natural processes are based on external factors. According to Marx, social conditions determine one's way of thinking. For example, social class determines what views a writer will express. Moreover, one cannot grow beyond one's class or free one's thoughts from the perception of class interests. Later, the principles and methods of "mechanistic materialism" crept into sociological thinking. This is a distortion of materialism that assumes that natural processes are based on material events and that these events are based on mechanical processes. Thus, under the aegis of mechanistic materialism, Emile Durkheim pioneered the use of statistical methods in sociology and Max Weber developed the working model as a tool for sociological analysis. Today, mechanistic materialism dominates in all branches of science. It views living organisms in general, and social processes in particular, as the result of external forces that mechanically impinge on humans. Exclusively focused on quantitative factors, this approach is limited and provides, at best, only a superficial comprehension of social phenomena and dysfunction.

To conduct a profound and truly meaningful investigation into any area of science, researchers must adapt their thought processes to the way nature functions. Reich defined *functional thinking* as thinking that corresponds to the way nature functions both in biological organisms and in nonliving realms. In sociology, functional thinking identifies nature's bioenergetic functions and strives to understand the origin of sociological phenomena *from the deeper biological realm.* Functionalism thus provides the deepest and most comprehensive understanding of social phenomena, including the origin of human destructiveness, because it comprehends the energetic forces that originate from *within* living organisms. These, and not external forces impinging on people, are the predominating factors determining social behavior.

Since the Age of Enlightenment, and with the change in social and political conditions that made it necessary for the masses to take charge of their own lives, opposing social groups have blamed each other for society's problems. Politics as we know it became a social force. As the political spectrum of the left and the right evolved, socialists on the left have been blaming the capitalists and others in authority on the right. In a similar fashion, those on the right have blamed the left.

Not until Wilhelm Reich's investigation of the structure and function of character and character armor did anyone focus on the *biological source of social pathology.* Reich showed that all attempts at social improvement fail not simply because of a lack of knowledge, but because of *people's mechanical way of thinking* on social issues and the resultant mysticism it induces, a form of thinking called *mechanistic-mysticism.* He went on to explain that since life is essentially not based on mechanical principals, this form of thinking cannot be used to accurately understand and describe the living in general or social functions in particular.[5]

Here is an example from a recent popular book of the mixture of mechanistic and mystical thinking that is used to explain the function of digestion.

> To extract and be able to internalize fuel and materials to run and sustain the body from something as complex as a steak is really a very difficult thing to do. You cannot simply grind up the meat and take it intravenously. First, a great deal of highly sophisticated chemistry has to take place to liberate what we need from what we eat, and then we have to transport those critical nutrients into the body. To get the necessary chemical reactions to proceed, the environment within the bowel has to be regulated, the contents of the gut have to be mixed, and the enzymes that attack foods have to be present in precisely the right concentrations. To get everything right, it is necessary to have a system of sensors in place that can detect the progress of digestion and evaluate conditions in the bowel on a moment-to-moment basis. The information derived from these sensors then has to be coordinated to assure that the internal environment within the gut will favor digestion and absorption. Beyond just nutrition, the gut also has to defend itself—and, by extension, the rest of the body—from invasion by an army of hostile germs that is forever poised to attack should the bowel ever let down its guard. Only the kind of militaristic control that a brain can exert over an organ system can assure that every element in the bowel's apparatus for digestion, absorption, and defense works well and is there when it is needed. So much nervous horsepower is involved in getting the gut to

5. See Reich (1949b) for a critique of mechanistic-mystical thinking.

> operate properly that it makes good sense for evolution to have put the requisite brain right in the organ itself. So many nerve cells have to be involved that if they were all to be controlled centrally in the head, the thickness of the interconnecting nerves would be intolerable. These cables would also be a source of danger; cut them and the digestive lifeline of the body would be severed. It is thus both safer and more convenient to let the gut look after itself. The brain in the head is also liberated to pursue things that are far more interesting than liquefying a steak.
>
> (Michael Gershon, M.D. 1999. *The Second Brain*, page 83)

Mechanical thinking and mystical thinking are opposite, distorted ways of viewing the natural world that nonetheless elicit and support each other. For example, the mechanistic scientist's hypothetical models of nature are, at best, only a distorted approximation of reality that is based on the scientist's particular armored character structure. Observations of natural processes that cannot be made to fit into this purely mechanical model are rationalized away or simply ignored. The mechanistic scientist, unable to find a physical cause, then resorts to mystical, teleological explanations of how something occurs "in order to" realize some goal, as when it is said the heart pumps blood "in order to" bring oxygen to the tissues. However, nature is not a machine, and it has no *telos*, no goal. *Nature simply functions and the function defines the goal, not the reverse.* In the above example, the heart simply functions, it pulsates. The material process, the transfer of blood gases, is a *consequence* of the function of pulsation, not its "purpose."

Mechanistic thinking in science is perfectly rational and functionally valid in the narrower domain of machines and machine technology. The value of mechanics is its usefulness in constructing tools, devices, and products that extend human function and ability. Without a precise knowledge of mechanics, one could not build bridges, aircraft, rockets, or any of the complex mechanical devices we use today. Even in the domain of mechanics, however, the construction of a machine is best determined by the human *function* for which it is designed. A poorly designed mechanical device or tool is not functional. Therefore, function determines structure. This statement is as true in the biological realm as it is in the realm of machines. However, for the mechanistic biologist, the opposite is true. The structure of a gene or biological molecule governs its function: structure determines function. The statement, chemical messengers in the brain "cause" sensation and emotion, is an example of mechanistic thinking in biology. This mechanistic notion is erroneous and gives rise to highly destructive consequences when applied to the wider and more inclusive biological (including medical), social, and psychological realms. As an example, contemporary medicine views living organisms as if they were all identical and machine-like, consisting of a countless number of replaceable parts. This view closes the door to any genuine understanding of the *energy functions* that govern life and the *origin* of disease. It ignores the fact that while all humans are alike, each organism nevertheless is unique and has different abilities and predispositions to illness. As an illustration of his lack of feeling for life, for the mechanistic clinician there is no way to be sure that babies feel anything at all because they cannot talk. In fact, the exact opposite is true: Because babies are less armored than adults, they feel much more intensely than do grownups.

As another example of mechanistic thinking in medicine, consider these divergent but equally one-sided views on the effect of mold on human health. On the one hand, the American College of Occupational and Environmental Medicine states: "Scientific evidence does not support the proposition that human health has been adversely affected by inhaled mycotoxins (from mold) in the home, school, or office environment."

On the other hand, the Institute of Medicine states: "Studies have demonstrated adverse effects—including immunotoxic, neurologic, respiratory, and dermal responses—after exposure to specific toxins, bacteria, molds, or their products."[6]

Mechanistic medicine forces facts into a previously constructed worldview. Since humans are viewed as if they were alike and no different than machines, and since all machines of the same kind function identically, the question of the effect of mold on human health should be answerable, either positively or negatively. However, since there is a great deal of variability

6. *Wall Street Journal*, "Amid Suits Over Mold, Experts Wear Two Hats," January 9, 2007.

in human reactions to toxins and other biochemical substances such as mold, it must be true that humans do *not* function mechanically. Some humans will be reactive to foreign substances but others will not. The existence of individual tendencies, ignored by mechanistic medicine, opens up the much wider field of functional thinking and the individual predisposition to disease, the realm of biological orgone energy.

The groundswell of dissatisfaction with mechanistic science is not confined to any particular group but extends across the sociopolitical spectrum to include both the left and the right. Examples are the anti-Darwinian thinking of the creationists and the throngs of alternative medicine groups that continually sprout up. Each of these quite-different groups has their own ideological agenda against mechanistic science. Most share an awareness of the limitations of the mechanical approach, but they also have a mystical bias. Disaffection with mechanistic science will continue even when it becomes clear that mysticism is not the answer to mechanism. At that time, the pendulum will once again swing to mechanism. There will be no advancement of our knowledge until it becomes clear that neither mechanism nor mysticism can adequately address humanity's medical and social problems.

We will show that the application of mechanistic or mystical thinking to natural functions is the single most important reason why all efforts at human betterment have failed. Mechanistic-mysticism results from the emotionally based disturbance in thinking of armored humans. In a vicious cycle, educators train students to apply mechanistic thinking to life processes. This, in turn, has the deadening effect of reinforcing and replicating succeeding generations of the armored individual bioemotional structure, characterized by thinking and behaving in this distorted fashion. Put simply, human thinking in its present form is incapable of effecting social improvement. This is because disturbances in the emotional life of the masses prevent them from observing and thinking about nature *as it actually functions.*

As a consequence, when mechanistic science attempts to bridge different scientific disciplines, it becomes mired in methodological problems. Attempts to interrelate separate sciences, such as biology and sociology ("sociobiology"), invariably lead to metaphysical, mystical thinking. This occurs because for mechanistic science there is no physical function that can be shown to underlie both realms. Psychology and sociology deal with elements of human behavior that are less deeply rooted in nature than biology. Applying concepts from a more superficial to a deeper realm confuses different realms of functioning. For example, in order to understand certain kinds of insect behavior, concepts, such as altruism and coercion, that belong in the superficial psychological realm are used to explain observations that belong in the deeper sociological and biological realms. This practice is an example of mystical thinking. It results in the "psychologizing" or the personification of biological process and, at the same time, passes itself off as genuine science.

It will be shown that Reich's functional approach, based on the knowledge that bioenergetic functions govern social processes, secures and integrates all the various scientific disciplines, including sociology, in their rightful place in the natural sciences. In reviewing the history of his discoveries, Reich saw that his research, based as it was in functional thinking, demonstrated a logical development from the most superficial and narrower psychological realm (psychoanalysis) to the deeper and wider sociological realm and, later, to the still deeper and wider biological realm.

His psychoanalytic investigation into the sources of neurotic behavior during the 1920s and 1930s pointed to a specific kind of pathological social organization that perpetuated human sickness. He found that at the root of all neurosis is the authoritarian (sex-negative) family structure. This insight directed Reich to investigate the sociological origins of sexual moralism. At the same time, his investigations of what he called *character armor* led into the deeper biological realm. This, in turn, brought an understanding of *muscular armor.* The discovery of muscular armor provided a biological understanding of many physical illnesses of unknown origin that have a psychic component, the so-called *psychosomatic diseases.* It opened the door to biological psychiatry which led to the development of medical orgone therapy.

The function of such armor is defensive, to protect the individual from experiencing painful, disturbing emotions and sensations. Reich learned that armor occurs in two forms, *psychic character armor* and *somatic muscular armor*. The clinical signs of armor are threefold: contraction of the voluntary muscles, respiratory inhibition, and chronic stimulation of the sympathetic branch of the autonomic nervous system. To give an everyday example, when a person is in a dentist's chair and a tooth is being drilled, a threefold response occurs that is entirely natural and involuntary: the muscles tighten, the breath is held, and there is a physical withdrawal from the source of pain. This response subsides when the traumatic situation is over; but when emotional trauma is repetitive, as too often happens in childhood, this protective response continues even after the trauma ends. It is in this way that armor becomes chronic. Unless removed, it lasts throughout the individual's life.

Reich demonstrated in both the logic of his functional method of thinking and through clinical observation that the psychic character armor and the somatic muscular armor are simultaneously antithetical and identical to each other. A "common functioning principle," as Reich called it, underlies the identity of psyche and soma and is found in the functions of a hitherto unknown form of energy. This energy, discovered and named by Reich "biological orgone energy," has been shown to govern all life processes. Thus, by penetrating into the biological realm, which is deeper and more inclusive than the social realm, it became possible to accurately explain the complex functioning of individual organisms, as well as how groups of individuals function socially. These ways of functioning will be amply demonstrated during the course of this book.

This insight made it possible, for the first time, to define manifestations of social pathology from the perspective of deeper, more inclusive biosocial functions. Healthy human societies, to the extent that they exist, spontaneously organize and function lawfully according to the principles governing biological orgone energy. However, the emotional plague interferes with or destroys these lawful relationships among individuals and groups at every level of organization in the social system. Thus, manifestations of the emotional plague are as extensive as the scope of armored human life.

Reich's functional method of thinking, his investigation of somatic functions, and his discovery of a physically demonstrable mass-free energy[7] pervading the universe and governing natural functions have provided a biological foundation for sociology. His discoveries have given humanity the opportunity to rationally understand and effectively deal with the enormous social problems it confronts. By providing an understanding of the energetic basis of human behavior and of individual sociopolitical character types, functional thinking provides a means of addressing current social problems, processes, and policies.

According to functional thinking, all the matter and material events in the universe develop from mass-free energy and its functions. Because of this orientation, functional thinking can integrate the branches of natural science according to the realms of nature that they address. These realms can be organized according to their degree of inclusiveness, as shown in the following figure.

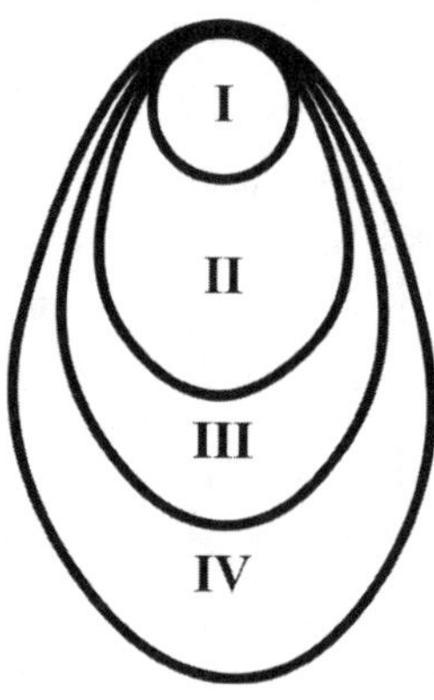

FIGURE 0.1

The superficial psychological realm (I) is based on a deeper set of sociological processes (II) which is based on the still deeper and more inclusive biological realm (III). Finally, the physical, energetic realm of orgone energy (IV) is the deepest and most inclusive of all. The different realms of nature can be grasped if one considers that biological processes can occur without psychological

---

7. The existence of a mass-free energy "filling space" has recently been demonstrated by contemporary science and thus has validated Reich's discovery of orgone energy (Lamoreaux 1997). This energy has also been shown to have a motor force (Chan et al. 2001). In 1948, Reich first succeeded in using orgone energy to power an electric motor (Reich 1949).

or sociological processes, but the opposite cannot happen. This book deals with the social sciences (including psychology, sociology, economics, and politics) and with various branches of biological science related to human functioning (such as physiology, pathophysiology, and neurophysiology).

Whether culturally based differences factor into the origins of destructive social behavior is an important question. Cultural factors originate from the superficial social layer. They are significant only insofar as they interfere with the natural development of children. However, the source of the emotional plague originates from the deeper, biological realm. Cultural differences leading to social conflict between groups of people living together are themselves symptomatic of the emotional plague.

Profound developments in science occur when a single mind perceives a deep unity from seeming disorder. This book presents such a unity, a method of scientific thought, functional thinking, and a body of knowledge discovered by Wilhelm Reich that can shed light on the destructive social processes that have plagued and baffled humanity since time immemorial. If enough people can "rethink their way of thinking" and grasp this method of thought and knowledge that is derived from it, the difficult task of reversing these destructive processes can begin.

Wilhelm Reich and Orgonomy

The science of orgonomy is based on the functional laws of orgone energy, which underlie and govern all natural phenomena. Orgonomic sociology deals with human social functioning.

Orgonomy was developed by Wilhelm Reich, M.D., who was born on March 24, 1897, in Czernowitz, Austria. After fighting in World War I, he completed studies at the Medical School of the University of Vienna. He went on to become one of Freud's most important students at a time when psychoanalytic theory was taking on recognizable form, demonstrating a remarkable grasp of emotional problems and how to address them. In fact, while still in his twenties, Reich had already made important discoveries and corrections in the psychoanalyst's understanding and treatment of neurosis. It was known, for example, that only a small part of a person's energy or libido was contained in the neurotic symptom since its elimination during psychoanalysis often produced little or no clinical improvement. Where, then, was most of the energy bound, if not in the symptom? By careful observation, Reich discovered that the energy of the neurosis is bound in the patient's *specific day-to-day characteristic attitudes and behaviors*, which the psychoanalyst often overlooked. These attitudes conceal the patient's unconscious feelings of hatred and contempt that, because they are blocked from expression, become directed at the therapist. By focusing on the negative feelings and describing these attitudes and expressions to the patient, rather than relying exclusively on the psychoanalytic technique of free association, Reich mobilized emotional responses of greater intensity and produced better results than psychoanalysts practicing Freud's method. Since he was dealing with character defenses rather than just symptoms and the content of a patient's verbal communications, Reich called his technique *character analysis.* We now know that the individual's character is the primary factor that determines human behavior and thinking.

Comparing patients who improved in therapy with those who did not, Reich found that the former, those who recovered, had developed a satisfying sexual life whereas the latter remained unsatisfied sexually. He concluded that sustained clinical improvement required that libido stasis be overcome and further prevented by adequate sexual discharge. His clinical observations led him to conclude that sexual *activity* in itself is insufficient. It is not a matter of how many times a night a man can "do it" or how many sexual partners one has. What is essential is the *capacity for complete sexual gratification.*

Thus, Reich made a crucial distinction. What is popularly called sexual "potency" and "orgasm"—*erective potency* and the capacity to ejaculate in the male, and adequate vaginal lubrication and clitoral climax in the female—differs from what he defined as *orgastic potency.* The distinction between erective and orgastic potency is essential in understanding health and disease, including the emotional plague, because the energy source that fuels this evil is the pestilent individual's inability to achieve complete orgastic discharge and gratification. Thus, a pestilent individual, such as an Osama bin Laden, can have sexual relations with many women and have numerous offspring but he is, nevertheless, orgastically impotent. It is exactly this impotence that provides the fuel for his hatred and murderous behavior, cleverly concealed behind a mystical, Christ-like façade. Culture aside, the fact that he has many wives indicates the orgastic disturbance. For someone who is potent, one mate is sufficient.

To be considered orgastically potent, individuals require the regular and complete pleasurable discharge of energy with *involuntary convulsions* of the body's total musculature, accompanied by a *temporary suspension of consciousness*, and followed by total relaxation and a tender, grateful attitude toward one's partner. When this capacity is disturbed, as it more or less is in all armored persons, the result is a condition that Reich called *orgastic impotence*. The function of characterological and muscular armor is to bind energy that otherwise would be available for sexual discharge and gratification. To the degree that characterological and muscular armor are present, the capacity for orgastic gratification is correspondingly disturbed.

These considerations illuminate Reich's findings that sexual satisfaction corresponds to the completeness of energy discharge in the orgastic convulsion and that the *quantity* of energy discharged is functionally identical to the *qualitative* intensity of sexual satisfaction. Because he observed that someone who develops truly adequate sexual release cannot maintain a neurosis, he concluded that neuroses are rooted in blocked energy. Reich thus developed a standard of health based on the individual's capacity for unrestricted charge and discharge that he called *sex economy*.

Focusing on the physical, energetic aspects of sexual functioning, Reich came to view Freud's "libido" not as a metaphor but as a real physical energy. Electrophysiological research with human subjects during various emotional states supported Reich's energetic view of biological activity (Reich 1934). By measuring the bioelectrical charge at the surface of the skin, he discovered that there are two directions to the flow of energy. During states of rage and anxiety, bioelectric skin potential drops. During states of pleasurable excitation, the skin potential rises. From these experiments Reich was able to conclude that the experience of anxiety and pleasure arises from the perception of energy movement in the organism, but in opposite directions: *inward in anxiety* and *outward in pleasure. For the first time in the history of natural science the subjective realm of emotions and sensations was taken out of the province of metaphysics and objectified and quantified.*

In living organisms energy is accumulated through the intake of food and air, as well as absorbed directly through the skin. Energy is discharged by physical activity and work, metabolism, emotional expression, excretion, the process of thinking, and its transformation into body heat, which radiates into the environment. In the usual course of events, more energy is taken in than is used. Thus, to maintain a state of energy balance, excess energy must be discharged at more or less regular intervals. This occurs through the orgastic convulsion and is what Reich termed the *function of the orgasm.* As previously described, the genital orgasm includes the ability to experience pleasurable streaming and to surrender to the involuntary orgastic convulsion.

Through his clinical investigation, Reich found that the overwhelming majority of the population are armored and suffer from sexual disturbance. He therefore focused his attention on social factors that determine sexual disturbance. He noted that in authoritarian societies the child is not permitted to function in accord with its natural instincts. From the moment of birth, the natural needs of the infant and the infant's spontaneous expression are thwarted at every turn. This was true in Reich's time and remains so today. The newborn is treated roughly, is almost always separated from its mother at birth, is placed on regimented feedings and sleep schedules, is often swaddled, and crying goes unheeded. Growing children are subjected to parental control, such as the prevention of pleasurable genital exploration and play, and they are barraged with prohibitions by well-meaning parents and parent surrogates. This requires children to hold back feelings and expression. Children accomplish this by inhibiting breathing and tightening muscles. Sustained over time, these contractions become involuntary and give rise to a state of chronic muscle tension and respiratory inhibition, a condition that Reich termed *armor.* Armored persons are disturbed in their capacity for full orgastic discharge. Excess bioenergy that is not discharged is bound in armor, and these persons cannot tolerate the loss of voluntary control that accompanies orgasm. *This disturbance is at the basis of every neurotic symptom and form of behavior.* Chronic armor is almost universal, so when I speak about "humans" or "people" in this book I am referring to armored people.

The repressive, authoritarian approach to childrearing that predominated prior to around 1960 stands in contrast to its exact opposite, the anti-authoritarian, permissive upbringing of the last few decades. This approach amounts to parental abdication of a constructive role in guiding and disciplining the child. Such a permissive attitude and lack of rational parental guidance produces intense anxiety and anger in the child and adolescent, resulting in a continuation of early patterns of disordered behavior such as disrespect, inconsiderateness, selfishness, brattiness, defiance of rational authority, and aimlessness that are prevalent today. This form of childrearing is more damaging to children than the overly structured, disciplined, authoritarian upbringing of past times. The failure to guide and to curb the child's neurotic behavior is partially responsible for the generalized disintegration of the family and of social institutions and customs characteristic of modern society.

While still leading Freud's training seminar for psychoanalytic therapy, Reich began researching the social cause of the neurosis, which he continued at mental hygiene clinics in Vienna from 1928 through 1930, at which point he moved to Berlin. He continued to teach and lecture within the Psychoanalytic Institute and in various workers' organizations. He became the leading physician in the mental hygiene and sex consultation centers of various liberal and socialist organizations in Germany. He also took an active part in social and political education and in organizations of young men and women of the working class, as well as academic youth. He lectured, wrote pamphlets and articles, and organized clinics and advisory centers for mental hygiene and sexual counseling. Because of the political turmoil of the time, this activity often put Reich at great personal risk. However, this same activity furnished him with abundant data for his scientific research into the origin of neurosis. His lectures were very popular and outdrew political rallies organized by the Communist Party, to their dismay.

Even so, the social implications of Reich's work offer no solace for anyone engaged in conventional partisan politics. As he wrote in *People in Trouble*:

> Nothing remains standing of the old political concepts which one finds in my early sociological writings. They perished, morally and factually, together with the organizations under whose influence they came into my writings . . . the exclusion of political party concepts is no regression to academic socially disinterested natural science; entirely on the contrary, it is a gigantic step *forward* from the realm of political irrationality out into the rational thought world of natural work-democracy . . . I would like to reject any responsibility for attempts to exploit in a party political way, my earlier party connections of more than fourteen years ago. I would have to protest at once, publicly, if anyone wished to exploit my name or my works for the support of socialistic, communistic, parliamentarian, or any other kind of *power politics. I have never had and do not have anything to do with power politics.*
>
> (Reich 1953b, page xviii; italics in the original)

Even in his work most laden with Marxist rhetoric, *Masses and State,* published in the early 1930s and privately circulated to select colleagues to warn them of dangerous authoritarian developments in the Soviet Union, Reich identified the inner emotional helplessness of people as *the* significant cause of their social problems. As his thinking developed, he came to understand that the armored condition is what impairs people's capacity to be free and responsible, that armored people long to be free, and that this longing renders them vulnerable to the "freedom peddlers" or "salvation peddlers" on both sides of the political spectrum. Freedom peddlers are politicians and others on the political left who promise freedom and a socialistic "heaven on Earth" to the gullible mass individual. Salvation peddlers are mystical leaders on the political right who promise religious salvation.

Reich's investigation of the authoritarian family's role in causing neurosis and his desire to prevent this neurosis in the masses led to his early association with communist movements in the 1930s. At that time, he mistakenly believed that he and the communists were fighting for the same social goals. His involvement with the Communist Party displeased Freud, as did Reich's emphasis of the importance of the orgasm function in regulating energy economy. Because of these differences, in 1934, the leaders of the International Psychoanalytic Association (IPA) expelled Reich from that organization. This decision had, and continues to have, profound and lasting effects on the direction and practice of psychiatry and medicine.[8]

In addition to being opposed to Reich's sociopolitical ideas, Freud and his followers were biophysically unable to grasp the truth and import of Reich's energetic, biological theories and his revolutionary discoveries. As a consequence, they remained stuck in the realm of psychology. Unable to comprehend new functional energetic principles and therefore unable to effectively apply characteranalytic technique or the orgasm theory to their clinical practice, psychoanalysts could not follow the logical development of Reich's work from the more superficial psychological realm to the deeper, more inclusive sociological and biological realms.

According to Reich, his expulsion from the IPA had a positive and liberating effect. His thinking and research were no longer bound by psychoanalytic formulations and ideas, which by definition are limited to the psychological realm. For psychoanalysis, however, and all that has developed from it into present-day psychiatry, Reich's expulsion had a profound damaging effect that continues to this day. The expulsion kept Reich's contribution of character analysis, as well as his later discoveries, from being fully incorporated into the developing body of psychoanalytic and psychiatric knowledge. Instead of having an effective and practical technique of therapy to access the underlying bioenergetic disturbance of the neurotic character, psychoanalysis and all subsequent non-pharmacological therapies remain largely focused on the psychological and mired in mechanistic-mystical thinking.

The consequences for psychiatry have been devastating. Power and influence in the profession have shifted between those who believe in the mechanistic, chemical causation of mental disease and those who believe illnesses are a result of environmental ("psychosocial") factors. Without Reich's unifying understanding of bioenergetic pulsation and the cause of emotionally based physical diseases due to chronic armoring, psychiatry lacks a *functional* bridge to connect these two divergent views.

In the early 1950s, following the final disillusionment with

8. See "Editor's Page: A Fateful Event." *Journal of Orgonomy* 29(2): 97–99, 1995.

the structure-based biological approach of Emil Kraepelin, which ignored environmental and psychodynamic factors in the etiology of emotional illness in favor of organic factors, psychiatry turned to psychoanalysis. Its dominance was relatively brief, for its practical and clinical limitations in the treatment of neurosis in general and of psychosis in particular soon became apparent. With their prominent somatic symptoms, depressive and anxiety disorders proved difficult to treat with psychoanalysis. The discovery of neuroleptic medication in the late 1950s ushered in the current era of psychopharmacology, molecular biology, and the "medicalization" of psychiatry. "Chemical imbalance" in the brain was invoked to explain emotional symptoms and virtually every psychiatric illness. This idea led to the notion that if psychiatric disturbances result from chemical imbalance, then emotional factors must not be important.[9] Psychoanalytic technique could not stand up to the practical therapeutic promise of medication therapy. This promise, however, has not been realized. Despite some relief of troubling symptoms, people's problems still remain, and this current "magic bullet" has fallen short of its goal. Moreover, medications have significant, troubling, and severe side effects, almost always including emotional deadening and disturbed sexual functioning.

The divergent perspectives of the two therapeutic approaches, psychological and chemical, will continue for the foreseeable future and have become structuralized in patient care today. The psychiatrist, as physician, has been relegated to dispensing psychotropic medication, while the nonphysician psychologist or social worker counsels the patient and attempts to address the emotional and psychological aspects of the individual's illness. Neither approach speaks to the bioemotional factors that are at the source of humanity's problems. Both evade the essential, the underlying *bioenergetic* basis of psychic *and* somatic processes.

The problems and limitations of contemporary psychiatry can largely be traced to 1934 when the International Psychoanalytic Association rejected Reich's pivotal discoveries of the functions of

9. That there are biochemical and neurophysiological "imbalances" in the brain associated with emotional illness goes without saying. These imbalances arise *as a result* of an underlying disturbance in the emotional life of the individual. The energetic function of the bioemotional disturbance *determines* the type of structural biochemical imbalance—not the other way around, as mechanistic science asserts.

character and orgasm. These ideas were rejected not on any rational basis, but because psychoanalysts and psychiatrists could not grasp their validity and use them practically.

Today, millions of people are dissatisfied with the current pharmacological approach to treating emotional illness and other physical disorders. They are turning away from conventional medicine and seeking alternative treatment for what ails them. Medical orgonomy offers an understanding and treatment of the neuroses and functional psychoses but also provides the deeper, more comprehensive understanding of human illness and health sought by so many.

Meanwhile, the unacknowledged misappropriation of Reich's discoveries continues unabated. The torrent of body therapies and "Reichian" therapies, the misuse of characteranalytic technique, the "new" eye-movement therapy, the practice of "mindfulness" and so on, as well as the host of self-help "how-to" books that have inundated the market (including, for example, titles such as *Feel the Fear and Do It Anyway*) all remind us of Reich's prediction that his discoveries would be misappropriated piecemeal, without any comprehension of the underlying energetic principles on which they are based, and without acknowledgement or credit given to the originator. Without a functional energetic approach, the fragmented use of Reich's discoveries cannot produce lasting improvement, and the individual's level of functioning will remain as before.

In addition to pursuing social research and his extensive psychoanalytic practice, Reich found time to write and publish many seminal articles and books. Among these are several books that are of basic importance in medicine, sociology, and psychiatry. These include *The Function of the Orgasm*, *The Cancer Biopathy*, *Character Analysis*, and *The Mass Psychology of Fascism*.

Reich's elucidation of the bioemotional basis of fascism and his warning that, because of the psychic structure of the average human being, fascism is liable to engulf both the workers and the middle classes, made him dangerous to both the communists, who excluded him from their party, and the Nazis, who tried to imprison him shortly after coming to power.

It was at this time that Reich came to the inescapable conclusion that it is futile to attempt to improve social conditions by any kind of political activity.[10] He also realized that since social problems are *biologically* rooted, armored people are unable to respond significantly to superficial counseling. Like Freud, who saw the problem of humanity in destructive forces in the unconscious depths, Reich understood that the human condition could not be altered simply through sociopolitical activity. However, unlike Freud's pessimistic view, Reich's clinical investigation into neurosis discovered that this social situation is not hopeless. When armor was dissolved in his patients, their character changed fundamentally. From these clinical experiences he concluded that, to reduce and ultimately prevent human suffering and destructiveness, it is necessary to alleviate or prevent armoring in the masses of humanity.

When the Nazis threatened to imprison Reich, he escaped from Germany to Denmark, where he was not allowed to remain long, most likely due to pressure on Danish authorities from Nazi Germany. He then moved to Sweden, but was soon expelled and then moved to Norway. He stayed there until 1939, when he received an invitation from the New School of Social Research in New York to lecture on medical psychology. In spite of great tribulation, Reich made some of his most important discoveries during these years.

In Norway, Reich began research into the origin of life itself and into biogenesis. These investigations revealed that all matter, when heated to incandescence and made to swell by being plunged into water, forms microscopic, pulsatory and mobile vesicles that Reich called "bions" (Reich 1979). He concluded that bions represent a transitional stage between the nonliving and living realms of nature. Further investigation led to the discovery of a highly energetic form of bion that he called the "SAPA-bion," for SAnd PAcket, since he discovered these vesicles by experimenting with sand. In 1939, he discovered the same energy in the atmosphere that he had observed earlier in SAPA-bion cultures. Reich termed this energy *orgone.*

Soon after Reich came to America, around 1940, a group of physicians gathered around him, seeking therapy and training. In 1950, he transferred almost all of his research to Maine, where

10. These historical events are fully documented by Reich (1953).

he founded a center, Orgonon, for the further study of orgone energy. Just before his death in 1957, Reich appointed Elsworth F. Baker, M.D. to be in charge of the future of his new science, which he called *orgonomy*. Of all of Reich's students, Baker most profoundly and clearly grasped the significance of Reich's discoveries and teachings. One of Baker's most important contributions to orgonomy was his identification of the eyes as an erogenous zone. Baker's other important discovery was the delineation of the sociopolitical character types based on the pattern of bodily armor, making comprehensible the biophysical basis of differences in sociopolitical thinking and behavior. The importance of sociopolitical characterology is that it provides a natural scientific way to understand social pathology.

Having studied with Baker for a quarter century, I can attest that he carried out his responsibility to the fullest. In 1967, he published *Man in the Trap*, a book that is the text for the didactic seminar for medical orgonomists-in-training given by the American College of Orgonomy. One function of the College, founded by Baker in 1968, is to set and maintain the highest standard of excellence in the selection and training of future medical orgonomists.

I first became acquainted with orgonomy as a young violinist trying to master the technical difficulties of the instrument. Despite having the finest teacher and technical expertise, I was missing something, an unknown factor that had a very powerful and negative effect on my playing. I also noticed this "something" was also missing in other students who could play the instrument faultlessly and who trained with the same teacher. There was something at work in each individual, something characteristic of that person, which impeded fullest execution. One violinist showed an absence of emotional expression; another used vibrato excessively in a forced, obtrusive fashion. These characteristics remained constant for each individual.

I developed an avid interest in Freud and read his writings, but his ideas were unrelated to the problem I faced. Then, when I was fortunate enough to come across *Character Analysis* by Reich, the missing factor became immediately evident. Here is the passage that impressed me:

> It is from the plasmatic emotions of the chest that most emotional expressive movements of the arms and hands originate. These limbs are, biophysically speaking, extensions of the chest segment. In the artist who is capable of freely developing his longings, the emotion of the chest is directly extended into identical emotions and expressive movements of the arms and hands. This is true for the violinist and pianist as well as the painter. In the dancer, the main expressive movements derive from the total organism. (Reich 1949a, page 377)

I immediately understood that it must be the energy in the chest that is blocked by armor. The concepts of energy and armor became real physical entities to me. In the presence of armor, emotional energy from the chest that enables reaching out (toward the world), particularly *longing,* cannot move freely into the arms and hands to find its musical expression. This was the basis of my limitations in musical execution. Although technical correctness is a prerequisite to good playing, I saw that so long as armor was present in the chest segment, technical expertise in and of itself would not enable full expression of the music's emotion.

With these ideas in mind, I entered therapy with a medical orgonomist. As armor was removed in therapy, my playing improved dramatically. I became so impressed by the power of medical orgonomy that I lost interest in pursuing a musical career. I decided to become a physician so I could study the science of medical orgonomy.

After finishing medical school, I entered therapy with Baker, and I soon began attending his didactic and clinical seminars. After about ten years of training, I began instructing the younger physicians. In 1983, Baker asked me to organize a diagnostic seminar that was to be added to the didactic and clinical seminars already in progress.

It gradually became evident in these early seminars that training physicians to practice medical orgone therapy was only part of the knowledge orgonomic medicine had to offer. The body of sociological knowledge is large, gathered through decades of clinical and field work, and can be of great value to people engaged in a variety of endeavors, not only physicians and psychologists, but also social workers, teachers, and others involved in helping people in different ways. With this in mind, I began adding to a book I was writing on medical orgone therapy that dealt with social and political problems resulting from the emotional illness of the masses. The present volume, which is to be used as the text for a course given to medical and nonmedical health care professionals, is the outcome of this effort.

The Emotional Plague

The material contained in this book, as discovered by Reich, illustrates the sharp distinction between Reich's unarmored perceptual apparatus and way of thinking and the perceptual and cognitive functioning of armored humans. Any scientific inquiry depends on how the investigator perceives the world. This goes to the root of the investigative process itself. Contrary to popular belief, there is no such thing as neutral or purely objective observation. The act of observing has the immediate effect of producing bioenergetic movement and a subjective response, and corresponding physical change, in the observer. Therefore, the state of the observer is critical regarding the outcome of the investigation. This phenomenon is well known in quantum physics: an act of measurement produces a change in the measuring system. The fact that this phenomenon must be accounted for on the subatomic scale of observation, but for all practical purposes is typically ignored in making gross measurements in everyday life, only emphasizes the importance of the dynamic interaction between the process of observation and the process under observation. Indeed, the accuracy of the perceptual events occurring in the observer on a molecular level must be considered whenever one evaluates any act of observation or measurement. The type of movement, or response, depends entirely on the character structure of the observer. To the extent that the observer is not armored, perception is free of distortion. From accurate perception, the observer gains a view of the world that correctly reflects reality. This objective sense of the world leads to behavior or action that is harmonious with the natural world, not one that is in conflict with it. Put in another way, the behavior and action of the unarmored observer will not be destructive. If, however, perception is disturbed because of armor, the world will be misperceived and misunderstood. The observing or investigative process gives rise to a contradiction between the process of observation (the observer) and the process under observation (the observed world), and this often results in destructive social consequences.

Understandably, because of their armored structure, mechanistic natural scientists attempt to bypass the role of the observer in the process of observation. One way that they try to eliminate the subjective influence of the observer is by relying exclusively on quantitative statistical data and by relying on double-blind studies. However, this still cannot eliminate the subjective element involved in *interpreting* the data. Distorted as it is in the armored scientist, the interpretive process is forced into the framework of a preconceived mechanistic-materialistic system of thinking. The result ensures a mechanical world picture of "space" as empty, filled with nothing but atoms and molecules and their interactions.

In preparing the field of observation, the mechanistic scientist always makes certain that the observed phenomenon will conform to the preconceived framework of mechanistic thinking. The mechanistic biologist, for example, regularly disrupts or kills the biological specimen before observing it, although dead tissue has none of the functional energetic properties of living protoplasm. The tendency of the mechanistic biologist to chemically fix living tissue or the mechanistic physicist, sociologist, or economist to use a working model that is solely influenced by external forces is based on his terror of observing and understanding that *spontaneous movement* is one of the essential characteristics of life. It is impossible to see the pulsatory nature of life while looking through an electron or light microscope at fixed and stained specimens. Those who have never observed living tissue under the light microscope, which includes most biologists, will never appreciate the profound *qualitative* differences between living and nonliving protoplasm. Those who have never observed an unarmored infant cannot truly know the profound biophysical difference between a healthy baby and an armored one.

Until Reich's crucial discoveries of biological orgone energy, the perceptions arising from this energy's spontaneous movement in living systems, and the effect of armor in distorting such perceptions, objective and scientific exploration of the qualitative differences in the worldview of unarmored and armored individuals was impossible. These discoveries are especially important for the investigation of the emotional plague carrier, the individual who habitually carries and spreads the emotional pestilence to others. These discoveries made it possible to bring the emotional plague into sharp focus. It is now possible to penetrate the dense fog surrounding the source of human irrationality and the destructiveness that follows in its wake and to find ways to eliminate them.

Reich emphasized that it is incorrect to simply equate emotional plague activity with political reaction or politics in general. This is because he distinguished between rational and appropriate social or political activity and emotional plague behavior. Rational political behavior deals, among other things, with the administration of the state. It also serves to preserve and protect what exists of healthy life in an otherwise armored society and not the neurotically based special interests of individuals, groups, or institutions that function to destroy it. Emotional plague behavior in politics is the opposite of rational political behavior: It is an attempt by an individual, group, or institution, for whatever reason, to wreak havoc on rational work and governance and to quash the lives of others through destructive social activity.

Armored thought and behavior are not, in themselves, manifestations of the emotional plague, although they can facilitate its spread through the operation of public opinion. Likewise, not all socially destructive acts between individuals constitute emotional plague activity. One characteristic that distinguishes the destructiveness of the emotional plague from other socially destructive behavior is *that the stated reason for the emotional plague behavior is never congruent with the real motive.* The real motive is always obscured and replaced by a seemingly altruistic, well-intentioned, or moral motive. Since the emotional plague individual has a high energy level, he makes demands—for example, sexual asceticism or conversion to Islam—not only to satisfy his own needs, as does the ordinary neurotic, but primarily "*for the good of others.*" Thus, plague carriers fight against other people's ways of living, even when, in reality, these ways do not affect them at all. Small differences in ways of life or in ideas are perceived as threats that often give rise to the impulse to control others. The level of control can vary from letting others know what they should or should not say or do to denying them to the right to live.

Another distinguishing feature of the emotional plague behavior from other socially destructive behavior is its *contagiousness.*

Its deadliness lies in the ease of communicability from one individual or group to another and from one generation to the next. It begins with the armoring process in infancy, childhood and adolescence between parents and their offspring; continues throughout the individual's life in irrational adult interactions; and spreads to others through the process of identification by carriers of the plague. Reich coined the terms *familitis* and *socialitis* to designate these highly infectious neurotic social interactions. As with other contagious diseases, the process occurs without either the carrier or the victim being aware of what is happening. In the past authoritarian era, the infection was transmitted primarily from parent to child. In our current anti-authoritarian society, children and adolescents also can function as carriers of infection. Examples of this are children blaming their parents when they are being rationally disciplined in an effort to evoke guilt in the parent or behaving provocatively toward authority figures to incite a reaction of rage in them.

Transmission from person to person often occurs through existing social organizations, which become centers of public opinion. Under the guise of freedom of the press, the news media is increasingly becoming a carrier of the plague. The strictly formal parliamentarian functioning of the United Nations is an example of politics at its worst. Fundamentalist religious organizations on the right and political organizations on the left are also particularly vulnerable. The co-opting of the National Organization for Women (NOW) by leftist ideologues Gloria Steinem and Patricia Ireland is another example (Bruce 2001). The emotional plague can exist in organized form, as in social institutions, or in unorganized social interactions among individuals. It can occur locally in civil strife or globally in world wars. It can be present in chronic or acute forms. When the attack happens, it seems to come out of nowhere. It takes its victims by complete surprise.

The emotional plague is an endemic disease of armored humans, who constitute the enormous reservoir of carriers at large. Tragically, the masses of humanity are as ignorant of the emotional plague today as they were of organisms carrying infectious diseases in centuries past. Just as the Black Death attacked the physical body, the emotional plague paralyzes the emotional life of the individual. The destructiveness of the plague resides in its ability to strike every armored individual at his or her weakest, most vulnerable point. This occurs partly because every manifestation of the emotional plague, no matter how irrational or destructive, contains a germ of truth to which the victim of the plague is vulnerable. Failure to recognize and acknowledge this germ of truth in the irrational makes it difficult if not impossible to effectively deal with the emotional plague. However, if the existence and operation of the emotional plague can be recognized and understood in the same way that other endemic and epidemic diseases are recognized and dealt with, humanity's social pathologies would resolve over time.

It is possible to objectively determine the occurrence of an emotional plague attack by recognizing its effects on the victim. The emotional plague attack results in confusion and paralysis when plague victims think, believe, or feel that whatever they do in response to being attacked is wrong.

Since infectious diseases are defined by the presence of an identifiable pathogenic agent such as a virus or a bacterium, and since there is no disease-producing microorganism in the case of the emotional plague, is it correct to view it as a true infectious disease? The answer is that all infectious diseases are based on the bioenergetic interaction between two living energy systems: the host organism and the invading pathogen. This becomes evident if one considers that if the pathogen is killed, the host's infection is eliminated. In the case of the emotional plague, it is not a microorganism but an armored human being who functions as the infecting vector. The pestilent individual functions exactly as a disease-carrying bacteria or virus in the case of an infectious illness. Moreover, as with medical infections, exposure to the pestilence can, under certain circumstances, confer some degree of immunity to future attacks on the victim. The ability of the emotional plague to induce confusion and paralysis in the victim, its virulence, is because it reactivates repressed unresolved conflicts. If victims can re-experience and work through these conflicts in their personal lives, they become partially immunized to future attack.

The past sadistic, authoritarian social order and the current masochistic, permissive, anti-authoritarian social order derive their enormous virulence from the genital frustration of the masses, and this is the energy source of the emotional plague. Today, masochistic tolerance of socially destructive behavior by certain individuals and groups on the political left (freedom-peddlers, "progressive" activists, and social minority "leaders") has almost entirely replaced the expression of overt sadism of the past authoritarian social order upheld by the political right. The predominant emotional plague behavior in today's anti-authoritarian society is passive, helpless, masochistic tolerance of the sadistic behavior of psychopaths and other criminals throughout the world by the left-indoctrinated masses.[11] Together, these masochistic and sadistic behavioral manifestations of the emotional plague have encouraged further destructive behavior and ensured continued human suffering.

The target of the plague is not only the lives of ordinary people. Throughout history, average people have reacted typically with deep anxiety and irrational hatred toward exceptional individuals. These plague attacks happened for two reasons: (1) Because their discoveries and ideas threatened to bring people into deeper contact with life and natural functions; and (2) Because their ideas threatened popular mechanistic-mystical thinking and beliefs that were in vogue. Such was the intensity of these sick reactions that the lives of these individuals were often threatened. Consider the long list of great men who were in conflict with the emotional pestilence: Socrates was martyred for defending the importance of "freedom of thought"; Plato was banished and sold as a slave for his reformist ideas; Aristotle went into exile for fear of being persecuted for regarding prayer and sacrifice as useless; Galileo Galilei incurred the wrath of the Church for his observations of the heliocentric solar system; Giordano Bruno was burned at the stake for his belief that the universe is infinite; Christopher Columbus was regarded as a mad adventurer and demigod: He was brought back in chains from one of his expeditions to America; William Tyndale was burned at the stake for translating the Bible from Latin into English, thus making it available to the common man; Andreas Vesalius, who corrected the anatomical views of his predecessor, Galen, by studying human anatomy was accused of murder and denounced to

11. An example is the eulogizing praise and tribute paid by heads of state world-wide following the death of the terrorist, Yasser Arafat.

the Inquisition; William Harvey, who discovered the circulation of the blood, met with difficulties in overcoming the persistent belief in the theories of Galen; Ignaz Semmelweis, who tried to introduce aseptic technique in the delivery room, was ridiculed for his medical practices; Freud, the discoverer of infantile sexuality, was accused of being a reprobate; Halton Arp, whose revolutionary findings on the redshift of quasars and certain galaxies shook the foundations of modern cosmology, was denied the use of observatory telescope time to do research—the list goes on and on. These destructive attacks have nothing to do with rational differences of opinion, nor are they accidental, unusual events or relics of the past. They are deeply rooted in the armored human bioemotional structure, the malignancy of which manifests in emotional plague attacks on people who shed light on the world through knowledge, which is a core function of life.

A current example of the effect of the emotional plague in sociopolitics appears in Shelby Steele's account of the public response to his lectures at various universities across the country. Among other things, Steele accused African-American leaders of practicing a politics of victim-focused racial identity that stifled black advancement more than racism itself did. When he was criticized in turn by "a virtual militia of angry black students . . . a mixture of decorum and fear silenced the decent people" who might have defended his right to his views in the face of his critics' attempts to shame him: "The goal of [this] shaming was never to win an argument with me; it was to make a *display* of shame that would make *others* afraid for themselves." This, Steele says, exemplifies "a kind of licensing process"—Steele's intuitive grasp of the emotional plague—that makes it possible for "blacks and whites to have contempt for the black conservative" (Steele 1998, page 5).

Neither Left nor Right

This book is founded on the sociological and medical writings of Wilhelm Reich and Elsworth F. Baker. My unique contributions to this body of knowledge include identifying *social armor* as the common functioning principle of the two fundamental forms of armored human thought, mechanistic materialism, and mysticism. Social armor is manifested in the varying degrees of restriction in the flow of social and economic activity. Some examples in order of degrees of rigidity are formal democracy (as distinguished from work-democracy, seen later), and the various "isms" as they pertain to governmental organization such as socialism, totalitarianism, fascism, and communism. I have also distinguished between the *authoritarian social order* that existed until the second half of the twentieth century and its transformation into the *anti-authoritarian social order* that emerged in the following decades. I have identified a specific manifestation of anxiety, *social anxiety*, resulting from this transformation of society. I have defined the various *forms of human work* based on their origination from the various strata of the armored human bioemotional structure—the biological core, secondary layer, and façade. This clarification is essential if the destructiveness of current social and economic work-related problems is to be effectively addressed. What is generally called corruption or organized crime is one example of work activity originating from the destructive secondary layer. I have also introduced the application of orgonometry, which is a system of thought that is closely aligned with natural processes, to provide an understanding of social and economic interactions. With the tool of orgonometry, I have demonstrated that the work function is the biological basis of human economic activity. Thus, economics has been taken out of the sphere of ideas and placed in the realm of the natural sciences.

Among this book's intended contributions is to show that sociopolitical characterology (the sociopolitical character structure of people) is the all-important determining factor of current and historical social events. I will employ characteranalytic principles to provide an understanding of pathological social interactions for the diagnosis and treatment of social disorders. These principles will be discussed during the course of this book. The assignment of a sociopolitical character diagnosis to individuals participating in social processes is necessary to make sense of all the destructive irrationality that is happening in today's world. Most importantly, it is necessary to distinguish between the true liberal character and the pseudo-liberal character. Without making this critical distinction, there is no way out of the impasse resulting from the seemingly irreconcilable ideological differences between the political left and the right that is tearing America apart. The use of sociopolitical character diagnosis does not have a defamatory connotation in the description of social behavior any more than psychiatric diagnosis does in the clinical description of individual behavior or medical diagnosis does in medicine.

Part One introduces functional thinking and the biological origin of social organization. Since all social activity is based on biological functions, the reader must be able to think in a manner corresponding to these functions if he or she is to grasp the energetic processes underlying human behavior. Chapter 1 explains the bioenergetic basis of social processes. It also provides a functional energetic perspective of armor, the origin of human destructiveness, and the measures humans have developed to cope with armor and its destructive consequences. Cognitive distortions are shown to be a product of the individual's particular sociopolitical character type. Chapter 2 explores the dynamics of character formation and the consequences of the various character types for modern societies and their politics. Of particular note, and the topic of Chapter 3, are the consequences that come with the exercise of freedom and responsibility, and the ways sociopolitical ideology distorts the understanding and relationship of these important functions. Chapter 4 examines the political structures that determine the prospects for preserving unarmored life with special regard to the difference between formal democracies, such as those currently prevailing in the West, and genuine work democracy, which is based on the social expression of individuals' core functions.

Part Two deals with present-day consequences resulting from the pathological social activity of armored humans. No understanding of the present politics and society in the West is possible without an in-depth understanding of the manifestations of individual and social armor and the shift from authoritarian to anti-authoritarian social structure that occurred in the last half of the twentieth century. This shift allowed the unprecedented release of distorted and destructive energies. Chapter 5 discusses the relationship between individual and social armor. Chapter 6 explores the transformation of society from authoritarian to anti-authoritarian. Chapter 7 examines some specific social manifestations that characterize the emotional plague. At a deeper level, the effects of individual armor are felt pervasively in disturbances of sexual and work relations, based on core functions, which are examined in Chapter 8. The final chapter, on the removal of social armor, provides measures that can be implemented to arrest the spread of the emotional plague, reverse the process of continued social disintegration, and improve social life.

This was not an easy book to write. The major difficulty has been my struggle to find a way to get through the perceptual and cognitive blocks (armoring) inherent in virtually all armored humans. These blocks prevent people from seeing and thinking about things as they really are. The difficulty is that armor produces perceptual distortions and biases in thinking that are manifestations of varying degrees of *contactlessness*;[12] that is, people are not sufficiently in touch with their inner *and* outer worlds, and that is the problem. Armoring prevents them from perceiving and thinking clearly and rationally. Unfortunately, those who are most out of touch with their own selves are also least aware of it. To make matters more difficult, how is it possible to effectively discuss the effects of armor on people's ability to perceive accurately when armor's existence and its consequences for human functioning are not even recognized, let alone acknowledged?

Historically, the contactless state of humankind is seen in the custom of Jesus speaking in parables to his disciples. Why did Jesus communicate in this way? Why did he not speak directly? It was not because he was incapable of conveying his ideas clearly or because he was some sort of mystical guru who wanted to mesmerize the public. It was simply because Jesus knew people could not understand the truth in any other way. He was fully aware of people's contactlessness and therefore spoke in a way that he hoped would allow him to get through people's perceptual blocks. In the following passage, Jesus describes the contactless state of the masses and explains why he speaks in parables:

---

12. The psychic defense mechanisms, such as repression, denial, displacement, and projection, are specific forms of contactlessness. However, the nonspecific manifestations of contactlessness in the general public are far more prevalent.

> The reason I speak in parables is that seeing, they do not perceive, and hearing, they do not listen, nor do they understand: with them indeed is fulfilled the prophecy of Isaiah that says: "You shall indeed hear but never understand, and you shall indeed see but never perceive. For this people's heart has grown dull, and their ears are heavy of hearing, and their eyes they have closed, lest they should perceive with their eyes, and hear with their ears, and understand with their heart, and turn for me to heal them." (Matthew 13:13–14)

Jesus illustrates this idea in the parable of the different ways that people *avoid* contact and *remain* contactless:

> Listen! A sower went out to sow. And as he sowed, some seeds fell on the path and the birds came and ate them up. Other seeds fell on rocky ground, where they did not have much soil, and they sprang up quickly, since they had no depth of soil. But when the sun rose, they were scorched; and since they had no root, they withered away. Other seeds fell among thorns, and the thorns grew up and choked them. Other seeds fell on good soil and brought forth grain, some a hundredfold, some sixty, some thirty. Let anyone with ears listen! (Matthew 13:3–8)

> Hear then the parable of the sower. When anyone hears the word of the kingdom and does not understand it, the evil one comes and snatches away what is sown in the heart; this is what was sown on the path. As for what was sown on rocky ground, this is the one who hears the word and immediately receives it with joy; yet such a person has no root, but endures only for a while, and when trouble or persecution arises on account of the word, that person immediately falls away. As for what was sown among thorns, this is the one who hears the word, but the cares of the world and the lure of wealth choke the word, and it yields nothing. But as for what was sown on good soil, this is the one who hears the word and understands it, who indeed bears fruit and yields, in one case a hundredfold, in another sixty, and in another thirty.
> (Matthew 13:18–23)

The same problem of the contactless state of the masses has existed throughout the ages and continues to be an insurmountable problem when any attempt is made to convey ideas related to the bioenergetic source of people's social problems. If enough people were capable of being in touch with knowing that the majority of their personal, emotional, and social problems had to do with their *own* armored condition and not with external sources, then they would be able to stop blaming others and start looking at themselves.

Freud came close to recognizing the source of the problem and the contactless state of armored humans when he identified the function of repressing feelings and ideas that are unacceptable to the individual. However, as we have seen, Freud lost his natural scientific orientation and instead became mired in the psychological concept of the unconscious. This error has had destructive consequences. If an individual's behavior is due to unconscious forces of which he or she is not aware, then it could be argued that he or she is not accountable for the actions that result from them. During the middle decades of the twentieth century, this idea rapidly crept into popular thinking and provided many people with a ready-made rationale to avoid individual responsibility and to excuse all kinds of destructive human behavior. When American society was transformed into an anti-authoritarian social order in the last decades of the last century, this view was already widely accepted. Today, another layer of psychic armor has been set in place with the formula that human destructiveness and irrationality are not a result of emotional illness but are due to genetic factors or to a biochemical imbalance. Little by little, the importance of personal responsibility and the reality of the contactless state of the armored masses have been systematically rejected. The stage has been set for the mechanization of psychiatry. No longer responsible for being emotionally sick, the source of humanity's emotional problems are neurotransmitter molecules residing in the brain. An expression of the emotional plague, this myth is universally accepted as gospel by psychiatrist and patient alike.

This also may not be an easy book to read. For one thing, it contains concepts with which most readers are unfamiliar, and familiar terms are used in unfamiliar ways. I provide a glossary, but terminology is often not the real source of difficulty. The stumbling block is that an entirely new way of thinking, *orgonomic functionalism*, is being applied to social phenomena. Because this form of thought is so different from the mechanistic and mystical thinking in current use, the conclusions derived from the new ideas will often be emotionally disturbing. When disturbed, people are likely to react defensively, but there is nothing wrong with being disturbed in this way. The disturbance results from being outside the framework of traditional thinking. If readers can stay with and tolerate these feelings, they will often arrive at new perspectives on important social topics. Additionally, to present this knowledge as accurately as possible, I have had to include scientific information that may not be familiar to the general public. The glossary will also help with understanding this material.

Social destructiveness arises from "the blocking of the functions of simple and natural life processes by social irrationality, which, produced in biopathic human animals, anchors itself in the human multitudes characterologically, i.e., biophysically, and thus gains social significance" (Reich 1953b, page xvi). An understanding of these bioemotional functions leads to accurate knowledge of social processes and to a genuinely scientific sociology. Before one can know why all past attempts at social improvement have met with failure or disaster, it is necessary to understand what happens when basic impulses of love or longing are blocked in their expression. Also, before one can recognize and address the numerous expressions of social anxiety and pathological behavior accompanying the breakdown of our formerly authoritarian social system, it is necessary to understand the various disguised manifestations of anxiety that armored humans experience unconciously when they are faced with the prospect of having to change. Most importantly, we must know the effects of armor on the perceptual function before we can recognize and appreciate the rampant contactlessness in today's society and its byproduct, *substitute contact*, which is often manifested as sociopolitical ideology.

The effect of armor on people's thinking is limited to only two kinds of irrational thought: it is either mechanistic or mystical. In the social realm, these forms correspond to political ideology on the left or the right. In Western society, those who think mechanistically and recognize the illusory nature of mysticism and the limitations of the political right line up on the left on the sociopolitical spectrum. Those who are mystical and recognize the shortcomings of the mechanistic scientific worldview generally side with social conservatism and find a place to the right on the sociopolitical spectrum. However, it is not sufficient to see the limitations of either the mechanistic-left or the mystical-right worldviews. One must both recognize the flaws of both the left and the right *and* understand that these flaws are components of a unified and mutually exclusive system of thinking characteristic of armored humans. It is called mechanistic-mysticism. This way of thinking is highly destructive when applied to natural-life processes.[13] The reader who steps outside the framework of mechanistic-mystical thought will enter into an entirely new system of thinking that provides an unparalleled view and understanding of the world and how the armored human functions. This understanding will provide a way out of humanity's trapped existence—a way to address and contain the transmission and spread of the emotional plague. The direction of this functional thought process is neither to the left nor to the right, but *straight ahead.*

---

13. These statements are not meant to imply that the solution to social problems is in the center between left and right. The center is a relative term that depends on the social climate of the time. Today's center, for example, is far to the left of what it was fifty or even thirty years ago.

CHAPTER 1

FUNCTIONAL THINKING AND THE BIOLOGICAL ORIGIN OF SOCIAL ORGANIZATION

This is not a philosophy . . . it is a tool of thinking
that one must learn to use if one wishes
to explore and deal with the living.
—Wilhelm Reich, *Ether, God and Devil*

Few people are aware of the way they think. In daily life this does not usually present a problem, but uncritical thinking on the part of natural scientists can have destructive consequences not only for scientific investigation but also for humanity. When the process of scientific thought does not correspond to the operation of natural functions, the effects on the individual and on society are necessarily ruinous. The toll that wrong thinking takes will be amply demonstrated throughout the course of this book.

One of the most important contributions to natural science is Wilhelm Reich's method of thought. It is significant in that, for the first time in history, there is now a method of thinking that corresponds to how nature functions. This method is therefore called *functional thinking.* Familiarity with functional thinking is absolutely essential to understanding social and other natural phenomena.

Development of Functions

Functional thinking corresponds to the development of natural processes. By convention, functional thinking can proceed in one of two directions: from comprehensive functions to specialized functions or variations, or vice versa. Figure 1.1 expresses this relationship linearly.

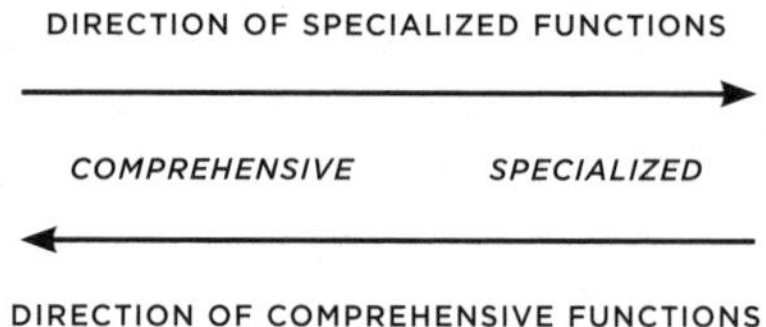

FIGURE 1.1

This relationship is expressed in the following orgonometric development equation written in abstract form (Fig. 1.2). The developmental equation simplifies the presentation of a functional process in that it conforms to the operation of natural functions.[14]

A3
A1
A4
A
→ etc.
A5
A2
A6

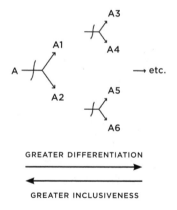

GREATER DIFFERENTIATION

GREATER INCLUSIVENESS

FIGURE 1.2

Examples of functional relationships in the social realm are provided throughout this book. Articles on applied orgonometry published in the *Journal of Orgonomy* deal with areas of natural science other than sociology.

---

14. For an introduction to functional thinking, see *Before the Beginning of Time* by Jacob Meyerowitz. Easton, PA: YRP Publishers, 1994.

A development equation can express any natural function that develops. Examples include the generation of daughter ameba from a single protozoan, the growth of the various cell lines of an embryo from the fertilized zygote, and the development of natural social organizations. In Figure 1.2, A represents the common functioning principle (CFP) of the variations to the right; A1, A2, A3, and so on represent the variations into which the common function A develops. Each vertical group of variations, (A1 A2), (A3 A4 A5 A6), and so on, belongs to a different domain of functions. The direction from left to right does not correspond to the direction of time, only to the structure of functional derivations. Functions from different, as well as from the same domain, occur simultaneously. Proceeding from the orgonometric left to the orgonometric right and vice versa shows the relation between the CFP and the functions derived from it. Note that "left" and "right" in the orgonometric nomenclature are not equivalent to or synonymous with the same generally used political terms.

Not surprisingly, the directional aspect of the orgonometric convention can have a neurophysiological basis. It corresponds to the direction of the eye movements that accompany cognitive functions. Since lateral eye movements are controlled by centers in the frontal lobe of the opposite side of the brain, cognitive activity occurring primarily in one hemisphere triggers eye movements to the opposite side. Thus, cognitive functions involving the left hemisphere, which is related to analytic and verbal activity, are accompanied by eye movements to the right. This corresponds to orgonometric equations representing specialized functions that develop from the CFP to its variations to the right. Cognitive functions involving the right hemisphere, which is related to synthetic activity, are accompanied by eye movements to the left. This direction corresponds to that from the orgonometric right to left representing comprehensive functions toward the underlying CFP.

Proceeding toward the orgonometric right, from comprehensive to specialized functions, leads to greater freedom of variations, specificity, and complexity of functions and of thinking. This direction corresponds to deductive reasoning. Conversely, moving toward the left leads to greater comprehensiveness and inclusiveness: There is greater lawfulness, depth, and simplicity of functions and of thinking. This direction corresponds to inductive reasoning.

If we begin with the current structure of society using such developmental representations of functions, we can move in the direction of development and see its effects on future generations. For example, if we begin with present-day authoritarian or anti-authoritarian upbringing of children as a CFP, we can proceed to an understanding and predict the type of destructive effects of both forms of childrearing on the individual and society. If, on the other hand, we consider our present-day social structure as a variation (or "consequence") of functions that developed in the past, we can proceed backward in the direction of the structuralized history of past society, toward the CFP. For example, our current social order can be viewed as a variation (or "consequence") of a particular kind of childrearing and the resultant character structure formation that took place in past generations.

In scientific investigation, the two directions of functional thinking do not exclude one another. However, when investigating any natural process, the researcher must clearly understand the direction in which he or she is proceeding. Functional thinking is flexible, and it is possible to change direction according to the needs of the investigative process. Mechanistic-mystical thinking works in these two directions but in a rigid, mutually exclusive fashion. Mechanistic thinking works exclusively in the direction of complexity and specialization. Mechanistic medicine, for example, develops toward ever-increasing specificity ("specialization") and moves away from the common functions on which life processes and disease are based. Hence, mechanistic medicine stresses the symptoms of diseases and ultimate, elemental, *material* particles (e.g., molecular biology and genetics) and not on their underlying energetic functions. Unable to understand the common functional energetic origin of most diseases, the mechanistic physician focuses exclusively on eliminating symptoms. The patient as a unique whole is ignored and often turns to the care of those outside the mechanistic establishment, the mystical "healers" and the "holistics." Conversely, mystical thinking moves exclusively in the direction of unification and universal concepts (e.g., God), *but without dealing with the concrete, physical functions that underlie health and disease processes.* Mysticism has little interest in comprehending actual physical relationships between natural functions, since it believes nature's presence (or

God, or "energy") is experienced through subjective "feeling" that cannot be objectively known. As an extreme example of mysticism, consider that in the highly mystical Islamic world, scientific spending accounts for just 0.2 percent of the combined gross national product. Its population of scientists is meager and its legal framework for innovation largely nonexistent.[15]

In the realm of sociology, mechanistic thinking proceeds exclusively in the direction of freedom and specialization (orgonometrically, to the right) in every aspect of human functioning. Examples include the human rights movement, freedom of thought, freedom to change human nature through genetic manipulation and stem cell research, and freedom from all forms of law regardless of the consequences. Change is valued over permanence. Society must be "redefined" or "reinvented." Taken to the extreme, this thinking leads to lawlessness, license, and breakdown of the current social order. For the arch-mechanistic communist, the concept of "historical development" unfolds inexorably, seemingly similar to the metamorphosis of a living organism. The goal is the utopian "end of the State." Free-thinking mechanistic social scientists idealistically favor international or global solutions to world problems. Because of this they are strong supporters of the United Nations. They oppose nationalism, since it elicits more practical solutions, deep feelings, a sense of unity with others and the cosmos, wholeness, and even divinity. These feelings, originating partly from the biological core, are alien and intolerable for the mechanistic individual. Mystical thinking, which operates to the orgonometric left, tends to favor lawfulness and permanence over freedom and change.

Regarding social problems, mechanism concentrates exclusively on extrinsic, environmental factors such as social, economic, and political forces as they impinge on humans and their psychological effects, a view that focuses entirely on the superficial layer of human existence. Symptomatic treatment is the rule. According to this view, the correct solution is to simply eliminate these immediate, external causes of social symptoms. To deal with the problem of school shootings, for example, mechanistic thinking leads people to advocate gun control. To deal with

---

15. See "Time to Unite Islam and Science," *Nature* 422: 69280, March 13, 2003.

the problem of narcotic addiction, the solution is to supply the addict with heroin or to prescribe methadone. To deal with the problem of teenage pregnancy, the solution is to advocate abstinence or abortion. The direction in this thinking corresponds to movement toward the orgonometric right in the development equation.

Mystical thinking, on the other hand, ignores or is blind to the source of the human condition and believes that it is God-given, the reasons unknowable. Humans must accept the status quo and, if necessary, suffer in life. Both mechanism and mysticism ignore the effects of human armor, the underlying biological basis of social pathology.

The Relationship of Functional Pairs

All functions of a CFP occur in pairs. The paired functions are either of the same kind (homogeneous) or of a different kind (heterogeneous). Most functions discussed in sociology are paired homogeneous variations. We will encounter one example of heterogeneous variations when we discuss the transformation of an authoritarian into an anti-authoritarian society.

Homogeneous paired variations can interact in one of four different ways. By attaching arrowheads to the basic operational symbol (ʃ) (Fig.1.3), we can abstract the manner of their interaction.

1. Simple variations—functions that are alike but nevertheless individually unique.

A1 ⨍ A2

FIGURE 1.3

In embryology, the orderly development of a particular tissue line constituting the various organs of the body (e.g., smooth muscle, skeletal muscle, thyroid gland) is an example. Each individual cell is related to any other individual cell of the same kind in exactly the same way, according to the common functions of that tissue.

2. Mutually attractive opposites—antithetical functions that attract each other and coexist (Fig. 1.4).

A1 →f← A2

FIGURE 1.4

Examples include male and female variations of any one species, the attraction between impulse and defense in the armored state, the relationship between the trophic hormones of the pituitary gland (adenohypophysis) and the receptors of the target endocrine glands, positive and negative electrically charged particles, the opposing poles of a magnet, and the relationship between the function of respiration (in animals) and that of photosynthesis (in plants) and so on.

3. Antagonistic opposites—antithetical functions that exclude each other (Fig. 1.5).

A1 ←f→ A2

FIGURE 1.5

Examples in nature include the antithetical relationship between sexuality and anxiety or between anger and fear, the reciprocal innervation of opposing skeletal muscle groups by the motor neurons of the central nervous system, and the antagonistic relation between the parasympathetic and sympathetic divisions of the autonomic nervous system. Some examples in armored life are sexuality as the antithesis of morals, thinking as the antithesis of feeling, and religion as the antithesis of science. In sociology, freedom and responsibility are two mutually exclusive directions of armored behavior. Liberal and conservative ideologies are expressions of two mutually exclusive directions of armored thought regarding social processes. Liberal ideology is based on thought processes exclusively in the direction of greater intellectual freedom (freedom of thought, freedom of speech), superficiality, and complexity of ideas. Conversely, conservative ideology is based on thought processes exclusively in the direction of greater restriction of ideas and simplicity of thinking.

4. Alternating opposites—antithetical functions that exclude each other but continually alternate (Fig. 1.6).

A1 ⇄ A2

FIGURE 1.6

The alternation between opposite paired functions is expressed as rhythmic (pulsating) motion in living organisms. Heart, lungs, intestines, and the bladder exhibit this functional relationship.

Because the number of relationships between paired functions is limited in this manner, it is possible to integrate the various branches of science into a unified picture of the world.

The Orgonometry of Social Organization

This discussion is intended as a brief introduction to a wide and varied field of study that remains to be investigated. To correctly understand the developmental process of any biological system including social organization, it is absolutely necessary to use the language of orgonometry, the language of functional thinking. Mechanistic science must keep the biological and social realms neatly separate, proceeding exclusively in the direction of increased specialization and segregation of natural phenomena. Clearly, this tendency to compartmentalize, an essential part of the defensive functioning of the mechanist's intellect, actually *prevents* a deeper, unified understanding of natural functioning. The mechanistic scientist does not see the whole forest for the trees, the trees for the leaves, the leaves for the cells, the cells for the organelles, the organelles for the molecules, the molecules for the atoms, the atoms for the subatomic particles, and so on because this is the direction of mechanistic thinking. This exclusive focus on the *structure* and not on the *function* of living things in every branch of natural science results in each of these realms being treated as a separate area of inquiry that remains separated from other branches. It prevents an understanding of the common functions underlying all realms of nature.

Writers with an intuitive understanding of the depth of human behavior, such as Aleksandr Solzhenitsyn and E.O. Wilson, have alluded to the similarities of the biological and social realms. In fact, the social behavior of animals and humans has a biological foundation, which in turn is ultimately rooted in cosmic mass-free energy functions. Careful observation reveals that identical energetic processes occur in *all* biological systems, from a single cell, to a collection of cells that compose a complex metazoan organism, to a collection of metazoan organisms that compose a society. The inescapable conclusion is that the biological and social realms are rooted in common energetic processes. They are variations that have roots in a deeper CFP.

The organization of biological systems is based on the development and differentiation of the energy functions that constitute it. The capacity of biological orgone energy to organize into ordered and self-regulating energetic systems from lower to higher energy states is a manifestation of the *orgonomic potential*, which is the CFP of social and individual organization. The orgonomic potential, which is the flow of energy from lower to higher energy levels, contradicts the universal application of the Second Law of Thermodynamics (which states that all systems in nature deteriorate into disorder, from higher to lower energy states). In point of fact, the exclusive application of the Second Law is valid only in mechanical systems, such as an automobile engine, and not in living systems (Fig 1.7).

Biological Organization from Lower to Higher Energy Levels (Orgonomic Potential)

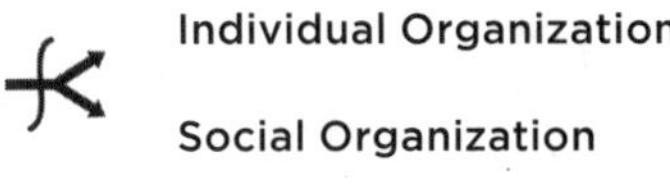

FIGURE 1.7

The disturbance in this developmental process, resulting from armor, is unique to humans and to human society. It leads to varying degrees of disorganization in the respective systems. In the case of an individual, the result is disease. In a social organization, the result is social pathology.

Just as the relationship among the several component organs of a biological organism is based on their biological function, so too is the relationship between the various social entities of a society (e.g., groups of workers, institutions) based on their biological work function. In the phylogenic development of living forms, a process of spontaneous organization occurs from lower to higher energy systems. For example, Reich found that bions, the orgone energy-containing vesicles that result from disintegrating living matter, can organize spontaneously into different kinds of protozoa.[16] These protozoa have the characteristics of a living biosystem: functional cooperation among various functional components (in this case, cellular organelles) that are necessary to maintain life, such as locomotion, ingestion, and excretion.

At a higher level of functional organization, the most primitive metazoan consists of a loose aggregate of individual cells. In this primitive biosystem, cellular differentiation first appears when specialized cells take over individual functions already present within the simple protozoan cell. An example is the development of simple contractile tissue in sponges. Later, sensory tissue, derived from the outer layer of cells, develops on the surface, in the neighborhood of and covering this contractile tissue. This arrangement is found in the tentacles surrounding the mouth of sea anemones. Development of functionally specialized tissue corresponds to the increased orgonotic charge and motility of progressively more developed biosystems. These functions take place locally since there is, as yet, no evidence of a central nervous system.

Specialized tissue function in an organism is identical to the specialized work function of individuals in a social system. From this perspective, we begin to appreciate the fundamental importance of the work function in all living systems. *Work* is a *biological function necessary for the survival and well-being of the organism and of society.*

From a functional energetic standpoint, life organizes on the basis of specialized tissues, that are themselves based on specific biological functions. Early in phylogenic development these functions remain local. As development proceeds with the formation of nervous tissue and greater integration, freedom of movement and specialization increase progressively. The component functions exist alongside the functions of the whole organism: Each organ system has a life of its own and is also at the service of the whole organism.

---

16. See Reich, Wilhelm, 1979. *The Bion Experiments.* New York: Octagon Books, Farrar Straus Giroux.

When functioning together as a group, higher metazoan organisms become a social system. The most primitive of these are insects. For the first time in phylogenic development, individual functions are assumed, not only by single cells and organs (to make up the whole organism), but also by functional members of a larger social system. Colonies of bees and ants are examples of individual work functions assumed by separate groups of organisms in a society. Distinct biological functions are expressed in the specialization of different organisms (castes) that together constitute the entire colony.

Societies of different phylogenic species are functionally different. In invertebrate societies, such as those of insects, individual organisms are structurally differentiated according to their specific function. In vertebrate societies, no such differentiation occurs, and the members of the social unit function as a whole, or herd. Because of the function of consciousness, this principle does not apply to human societies.

In insect societies, individual freedom and sexuality are subordinated to the functioning of the total insect colony (Wilson 1980, page 146). Two basic types of behavior are embodied in the sexually functioning organism and the reproductive neuter. In insect societies, these two types are functionally identical to the germinal and somatic tissue in vertebrate organisms. E.O. Wilson notes that the functional development of the neuter in insect societies removed the limit on the amount of possible caste differentiation among colony members. After this development, it became possible for specialized insect organisms to perform highly complicated tasks—functions—allowing the insect colony to match the feats of a single vertebrate organism. The specialized functions, or work, performed by groups of social insects in relation to the whole colony are identical to the functional differentiation of the various organs (tissue specialization) in relation to the individual organism.

The social organization and survival of higher vertebrates, such as a flock of birds or a herd of animals, depends on the entire group functioning in unison. The function of consciousness is unnecessary for this level of social organization. It would render the individual organism vulnerable and tend to fragment the social unit, actually endangering the survival of both. Humans, on the other hand, retain their sexual identity and capacity for individual freedom; individualism is often at the expense of efficiency on the part of the whole society. Human socialization is commensurate with the development of consciousness in the young child, particularly with the functions of orientation (the sense of self and of others) and the capacity to reason and communicate abstractly (as with speech).

With the development of consciousness, human society, as a whole, differentiates functionally in many different ways. One way is to differentiate into a center (private life) and periphery (public life). Private life involves the core functions of human life, which consist of genital sexuality and rational work. All humans require the undisturbed functioning of both for survival and to maintain biophysical health and emotional well-being. Public life involves the peripheral social functions, primarily rational political and economic activity.

The functions of consciousness, which sense both the self and the environment, must be fully developed in humans for social survival. When groups of humans behave like herd animals—mindlessly responding to the manipulations of a charismatic politician or religious leader, for example—their survival is often endangered. In schizophrenic psychosis, the afflicted individual's very existence can be jeopardized when the functions of consciousness are sufficiently disturbed. Here, the survival value of intact consciousness is immediately apparent. The political survival of any successful politician or entertainer is entirely based on a highly developed capacity to socialize effectively and to charm or entertain the public.

The distinction between invertebrate and vertebrate societies highlights the fact that identical bioenergetic functions (organization, specialization, work) are fundamental to both systems. The sum of the individual components is functionally identical to the total system.

A collection of cells forming an organism, a collection of insects forming a colony, or a society of individuals forming a nation constitute an orgonotic system, an orgone energy system, functioning simultaneously as a whole and in its several components. As the system develops, its various component functions become organized and specialized to operate with increasing specificity. It is not by accident that the concepts contained in the Constitution of the United States and the Bill of Rights derive their importance from these biological functions.

Any society of organisms can be understood in terms of its component energy functions. The organization of a number of individuals to form a society is based on the attraction function of biological orgone energy. In human democratic societies, the attraction function develops further to give rise to the paired variation *association* and *dissociation* (Fig. 1.8).

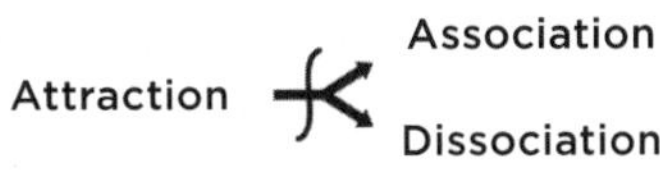

FIGURE 1.8

Association is evident in the bonding of individuals based on common work interests or needs. Dissociation arises primarily from two sources: Natural differences in the rank of each individual's specific work function and differences in character armor among the various members of society. The most salient example of the latter is the difference in sociopolitical character structure, which gives rise to irreconcilable differences of opinion on social issues. These differences spontaneously give rise to political parties. As I will later discuss at length, there is a central substantive dispute that is common to all political partisanship-based opinion. On any given issue, *one group will want to restrict public freedom, the other to extend it without limitation.* This dispute goes to the heart of the social problem regarding the relationship between freedom and responsibility.

Healthy biological and social systems function on the principle of self-regulation, not on unlimited freedom or restrictive regulation. In the biological realm, the same relationship exists between the components and the whole of any orgonotic system, whether it is a single cell (protozoan), a multicelled organism (metazoan), or a distinct group of metazoa (society). Simultaneously, the individual units function for themselves and in the service of the whole system. For example, the heart beats (functions) for itself *and* for the entire organism. The same can be said for every component organ system, organ, and organelle in the organism.

The American form of government is patterned closely after a core-periphery biological system. American society is highly diversified and is organized as a collection of autonomous cities and states that constitute the components of the whole nation.[17] Identical social, legal, governmental, and economic functions constitute both the individual cities and states and the whole of the American social system. The various governmental functions of the component states and the nation are identically separated into distinct branches: executive, legislative, and judicial. Every member of society is equal in the eyes of the law. Private and public life are separated (e.g., the separation of church and state).

The vitality of this social organization is partly determined by the degree to which the specific functions of the components and the whole are simultaneously carried out independently of one another. When the boundaries between the components and the whole are blurred, however, social functioning is disturbed. For example, the numerous independent regulatory agencies that have become a necessary part of the federal government, because of some people's inability to tolerate freedom (see chapter 5), have directly affected the freedom of *all* American citizens. These agencies combine executive, legislative, and judicial powers, and their decisions are therefore regarded not merely as administrative acts but take on the status of law. These centralized sources of power are a manifestation of armor in the social realm.

Social systems, like biological systems, can develop pathology. In pathological social systems such as socialist, communist, or fascist states, the previously attained specialization of social functions is lost. In communist states, for example, the people's work function becomes so restricted that it is reduced to the mechanical performance of simple tasks.[18] Centralized control, uniformity, and bureaucratic duplication in every walk of life are the prime reasons underlying the terrifying stagnation of socialist states.

---

17. The question of how the individual states were to be related to the central government was a major concern of the Founding Fathers. Were the states or the central government to be sovereign? This contradiction seemed to be an insoluble problem. Fortunately, the exigencies of reality forced a functional solution: the new society was to be *both* a nation *and* a federation of states.

18. Specialization of function must be distinguished from mechanical restriction, which can occur to a high degree in any type of armored society. What is being discussed here is functional specialization, which consists of the qualitative as well as the quantitative properties of the social function.

Because of America's shift to the political left, as a result of its transformation into an anti-authoritarian society, we are witnessing the same degenerative process in the direction of socialism. Consequently, in the analysis of American society that follows, I place greater emphasis on the pathology of the political left over that of the right because of the left's greater destructive behavior in today's anti-authoritarian society. Similarly, I emphasize the pathological behavior of the political right in my analysis of the past authoritarian society.

The development of any living system, whether biological or social, has two characteristics that are related as a functional pair: finiteness and unity on the orgonometric left are paired with infinity and its functional variations (specialization of function) on the orgonometric right (Fig. 1.9).

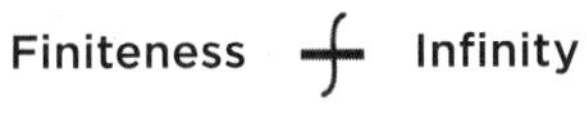

Finiteness ⨍ Infinity

FIGURE 1.9

Freedom (indeterminateness) to the right is paired with responsibility and natural law (determinateness) to the left.

In both biological and social systems, then, the individual and society alike originate from orgone energy functions. They are orgonotic[19] systems that develop and organize, reaching a certain *orgonotic* capacity level, following the orgonomic potential from lower to higher levels. After reaching and maintaining that peak for a certain time, they decline and die.

The human individual's orgonotic system is organized into a core (consisting of the autonomic nervous system), periphery, membrane, and energy field which interact with the environment. Biological impulses originate from the core and expand outward to the periphery, and from there to the environment. In a social system, the distinction between core and periphery is not immediately apparent. However, those aspects related to the individual's intrinsic right to privacy—functions relating to elimination, reproduction, including mating and giving birth, and all aspects of medical treatment (healing)—can be considered core functions of a society. In insect colonies, these activities occur in

19. See glossary.

the functional center of the system. These processes correspond to nuclear (central) activities in the biological realm. Similarly, in the realm of insects, adult members perform advanced social functions (food gathering) at the periphery of the system. Activities that are considered public in human societies (e.g., the complex social interaction between individuals) constitute peripheral or surface functions. Thus, education, commerce, the media, banking, and taxation are peripheral social functions. Both the individual and society, taken as a whole, are also organized functionally into different components. In the individual, functional differentiation is effected by tissue specialization. In society, separate groups of individuals form collectives, taking over separate social and work functions.

A basic natural function of the living is self-regulation or, expressed in social terms, self-government. Both biological and social systems involve a functional unit. In the individual organism, this unit is the cell. In contrast to the bion, which is the unit of life, the cell is the unit of the organism. In the human social realm, this unit is the family. What the cell is to the total organism, the unitary functioning family is to human society, the community, state, or nation. Component functions exist simultaneously with whole functions.

A system of laws derived from orgone energy functions (natural law) governs the entire system. Natural law is paired with freedom within the limits of the CFP of the social or biological system. The separate components interact harmoniously (free energy exchange) as they spontaneously organize in accordance with the functions of the whole system. Social organization, living and working together as the harmonious integration of individual members of a society into groups, is *functionally identical* to the spontaneous organization of the organs as component functions of the individual organism. The term *functional identity* refers to identical functions in different realms of nature. A naturally functioning biosystem is characterized by benignity, softness, and gentleness. It can turn harsh and violent when its life is threatened.

The Structure of Armored Humans

The Biological Core and the Secondary Layer

In both the individual and society, armor disrupts and impairs the organization and functioning of the system. In the individual, armor exists in two forms: psychic and somatic. Psychically, armor is identical to the character of the individual: His or her way of being is a whole, reacting function. Somatically, armor is identical to, and contained in, the component organs of the individual, primarily the skeletal musculature. An understanding of character armor is essential in psychiatry and sociology, and an understanding of muscular armor is critical in medical illness. The brain is involved either directly or indirectly with both forms. *Without an understanding of armor and its consequences for the biosocial functions of humanity, it will never be possible to distinguish what is healthy and requires protection from what is pathological and must be eliminated.* Without such an understanding, it will never be possible to initiate genuinely positive social change, change that is permanent and not merely cosmetic or palliative.

Armor determines not only how behavior is disturbed, but also what individuals do and do not see, hear, think, and feel. By its very presence, armor changes the natural quality of biological energy from its soft, gentle, pulsating benign form to one that is harsh, violent, and life-destructive. *The source of all human destructiveness comes about when free, motile biological orgone energy clashes with and turns violent in its attempts to break through the armor.*

Like an individual, society, too, can armor itself. The presence of ocular armor in humans is responsible for the same development in society. This is because the most important factor that determines the way that an individual relates to the world is the status of ocular functioning. Ocular armor consists in a contraction and immobilization of the greater part or all of the muscles in and around the eye, eyelids, forehead, and tear glands, as well as the muscles at the base of the occiput and the back of the skull. Holding back an enormous quantity of energy, it extends into and can selectively involve different parts of the brain itself and its vascularity. *Specific "verbotens" given to the young child, communicated either verbally or nonverbally, by attitude, manner, voice inflection, and so on, produce these chronic spasms of these muscles.* This results in an inhibited ability to look. When "looking" is inhibited, the ability to see things clearly suffers. Ocular functioning is involved with making sense of both the inner and the outer worlds in an immediate, undistorted fashion. Strabismus, the inability of one eye to sustain coordination and thus binocular vision with the other (because of an imbalance of the muscles of the eyeball), is just one of many ways in which an emotional disturbance produces a physical change in the visual system that then interferes with the ability to see things in full perspective, as they actually are. In the presence of ocular armor, perceptions and thoughts related to the internal and external worlds are distorted. This relationship is depicted as follows (Fig. 1.10):

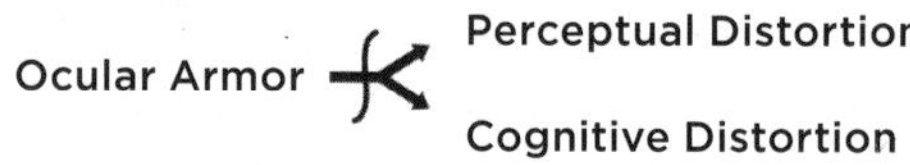

FIGURE 1.10

When ocular armor in the masses is extensive and severe, reality is misperceived to such an extent that lives are endangered and the destructive social consequences result in an outbreak of emotional plague. No longer controlled by social constraint, ocular armor permits serious and often dangerous cognitive distortions and misconceptions regarding social events that often lead to irrational behavior and conflict. Blaming others, scapegoating individuals or groups are a direct manifestation of ocular armor whereby individuals avoid seeing and facing painful emotions by projecting their conflicts externally.

Contactlessness, a kind of perceptual dullness, always exists where armor is present. The armored individual is out of touch with the self and the outer world in a variety of ways. There is a corresponding feeling of boredom, loneliness, or inner deadness and a reactive need for distraction and substitute gratification to relieve tension and boredom. Most people are somewhat familiar with the occurrence of contactlessness. The movies of Federico Fellini and Ingmar Bergman and the plays of Harold Pinter and Samuel Beckett focus on this state.

Contactlessness disturbs our ability to deal rationally and

constructively with situations in our personal and social lives. Contactlessness with the self and therefore with the environment is characterized by personal and social irresponsibility and ultimately results in a loss of freedom. Contactless persons are, to varying degrees, not in touch with their biological core and therefore cannot protect and satisfy their core needs of love and work. Because they cannot live according to these basic needs, their lives are governed by external social constraints and by the effects of their own internal armor. In general, those on the right of the sociopolitical spectrum are less contactless than those on the left and are therefore better able to safeguard our social survival in this troubled world.

Contactlessness prevents people from sensing and feeling fully and from reacting appropriately to stimuli that otherwise would be experienced as painful, unpleasant, or dangerous. It also prevents the full experience of the joy that accompanies being fully alive. The contactless state has two consequences. Responsiveness to inner and outer stimuli becomes diminished, and the individual strives to establish substitute contact in an attempt to overcome a sense of deadness or inner emptiness.

It is necessary to distinguish simple, direct, genuine social contact from its pathological counterpart, substitute contact. Once contact with the outer and inner worlds is interrupted and cannot be maintained directly, alternative functions develop that attempt to establish substitute contact. These efforts to establish substitute contact to connect with people must remain futile because of the presence of inner obstacles, armor.

Substitute contact can be recognized by its inappropriateness and artificiality. However, it was easier to recognize manifestations of substitute contact in the past. Today, thanks to ever-increasing sophistication, intellectualism, and impulsiveness, people have a more polished façade and are more able to hide their affectation, falseness, and hypocrisy. The present-day manifestations of substitute contact are more disguised and more pervasive. Examples include the endless chatter over trivial matters in social interactions and on television "talk" shows; interest in and vicarious excitement over the private lives of the rich and famous; excessive involvement in professional sports, television viewing and social causes; as well as false expressions of concern and caring by guilt-ridden liberals and self-serving politicians, and the willingness of the gullible masses to be taken in by such people.

To avoid experiencing painful emotions (e.g., loneliness, anxiety, fear) and to reestablish contact with the world, armored people often displace their personal conflicts onto the sociopolitical sphere and then act them out in the external world according to their character. For example, the impulse to backstab can be displaced socially and expressed in subversive action against the nation and its institutions. Alternatively, the energy blocked by armor may be excited by ideological rhetoric used to justify attacking groups of people (e.g., blacks, whites, Jews, Arabs) or those on the political left or right by blaming them for social problems. Displacement is a defensive function that protects a person from awareness of frightening emotions by shifting the energy attached to one object onto another, with the result that feelings for one object are exchanged for feelings for another.

One of the most dangerous social consequences of contactlessness in times of great social danger is that people remain unaware that they are in jeopardy. Many Americans, particularly the young, misperceived the very real world-wide Communist threat during the Vietnam War. In the 1930s, during Hitler's ascent to power, millions of European Jews did not recognize that their lives were in danger until it was too late. The same contactless state prevailed before the Japanese attack on Pearl Harbor. Prior to September 11, 2001, mass contactlessness existed in the face of a very real serious threat from Islamic fundamentalists. Contactlessness explains much of the lack of attentiveness to the menace they posed both before and after 9/11. Endless discussions of whether 9/11 could have been prevented serve to avoid recognizing the existence of mass contactlessness.

During *medical orgone therapy*, as destructive impulses contained in the armor are eliminated, patients lose their sadistic and violent tendencies. They become softer, contactful, more emotionally alive, and genuinely sociable. Children who are raised relatively free of armor and who can regulate themselves are not prone to self-destructive tantrums and other forms of destructive behavior. Sociological studies, such as those of Bronislaw Malinowski, reveal that children brought up with no interference in their sexual functioning, grow up to be relatively free of emotional problems. As late as the 1920s, the society of the Trobriand Islanders knew no sexual perversions, no violence, no neurosis. Their language had no words for "theft," "homosexuality," or "masturbation."

Natural morality is grounded in the undistorted perception of sensations of energy movement unimpeded by armor. Expressed from the biological core, natural morality preserves the core functions of life. However, when energy movement is blocked by armor, natural morality becomes distorted and turns harsh and rigid. This is the origin of the compulsive morality of armored humans. Historically, in the authoritarian society that existed until the second half of the twentieth century, power between the sexes was separated such that men typically assumed the role of authority and women typically were the bearers of compulsive morality. Just as natural morality serves to protect unarmored social existence, compulsive morality functions to protect armored forms of individual and social life.

From this we conclude there are two basically different kinds of human life, unarmored and armored. Unarmored life functions unimpeded in the areas of love, work, and the pursuit of knowledge. In the social realm, unarmored humans protect these basic life functions. In contrast, armored life fights to preserve its own deviant form of existence. The survival of political hacks, for example, depends on their gaining popularity and on being elected to public office. Groups of armored individuals form diverse social organizations (such as political parties and political action groups) based on similarities in their biophysical structure. They come into conflict when one group views the other as a threat to its existence.

Natural aggression originating from the biological core has to be distinguished from neurotic aggression originating from the secondary layer and contained in the armor, which is destructive to life. There is a profound difference in the *quality* of aggression of unarmored and armored organisms. In the unarmored, aggression is natural and appropriate to the circumstance, and it can lead to productive activity. In the armored, aggression is always harsh and obtrusive. It easily turns into destructive behavior. It follows that if any sense is to be made of human behavior, a distinction must be made between human expression emerging from the biological core and how these expressions change when core impulses meet armor and are thwarted. The former impulses, called "primary" drives, are natural expressions of biological orgone energy. The latter are "secondary" drives and, from the viewpoint of psychology, are identical to the Freudian unconscious. They make up the great secondary layer, which Reich identified as the Realm of the Devil,[20] and account for irrational and destructive elements in human behavior, both in individuals and in groups of people.

One cannot equate destructiveness per se with irrationalism. To destroy or immobilize those who destroy the biological life function is not an irrational act. *This distinction is critical if America is to wage an effective war on terrorism.*

The differentiation between the primary and secondary drives was first made by Reich in *The Mass Psychology of Fascism*. Without this crucial distinction, our understanding of the dynamics of the social functioning of armored humans cannot progress. The age-old problem of the antagonistic relationship between the individual and society is a case in point. This problem is typically stated in terms of the needs of individuals in opposition to those of society. Although those on the left and the right believe in individual rights, the conservative thinks that preservation of such rights serves the interests of society, whereas the liberal thinks that they exclusively serve the interest of the individual (Sowell 1987, page 185). What is overlooked is that human armor is responsible for the contradiction between the individual and society. The antithesis cannot be resolved unless the existence and function of armor is understood and the primary and secondary drives are distinguished and separated. In humans, the critical question is whether the particular needs of the individual arise from the biological core or from impulses that have become distorted while passing through the armor. The former are healthy, not destructive to the individual or to society, and are life-positive and capable of producing genuine satisfaction. The latter are destructive, life-negative and therefore require social constraint.

---

20. The idea of the "Devil" originates in the personal and interpersonal experience of the destructive secondary layer. This layer consists of a twisted and confused network of perverse impulses and inhibitions that constitute the "temptation" that separates the individual from nature and thwarts every human effort to escape from the trap of armored life. The identification of evil, the realm of the Devil, as existing in the biological armor of humanity is a major accomplishment of the functional method of thought.

The Orgonometry of Social Interactions

Any social interaction can be written as the simple attractive opposition of two individuals (A1 and A2), each operating alternatingly as excitant and percipient (Fig. 1.11).

A1 Excitant / Percipient — Percipient / Excitant A2

FIGURE 1.11

Human destructiveness must be recognized before it can be addressed. Therefore, it is necessary to specify *how* a destructive social act can be determined. A socially destructive act requires that at least one participant in the interaction, either the excitant or the percipient, behaves in an irrational (neurotic) manner. For the act to be destructive, both sides must fail to address the irrational behavior or idea appropriately (Fig. 1.12).

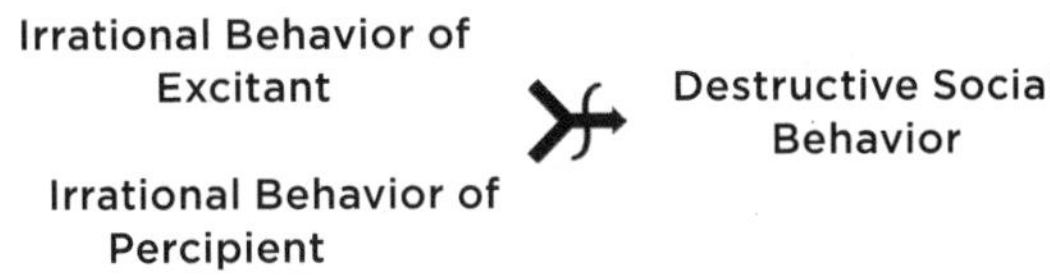

FIGURE 1.12

What constitutes irrational behavior and appropriate response is best determined by evaluating an act's effect or function. We must first ask: What are the consequences of a particular action on the core functions of individuals and of society? The social destructiveness of many actions goes unnoticed because this criterion is ignored. There is no other reliable way to identify socially destructive behavior than to consider the behavior's effect on society and whether it supports the core functions of life. With its mechanistic orientation, current sociological thinking cannot grasp the functional energetic basis of all human destructiveness: the inability to experience orgastic gratification and genuine satisfaction in work. It is this inability, the result of armor, that leads to the development of an endless number of secondary drives, with their sadistic and masochistic impulses. Armor gives rise to rigidity in social relationships and interactions.

The Orgonometry of Some Pathological Social Interactions

The following functional interactions, drawn from sociopolitics, are examples of some destructive manifestations of social armor (Fig. 1.13).

Mechanistic Medicine
Pharmaceutical Industry
Labor Unions
Management
Political Activism on the Left
Political Activism on the Right

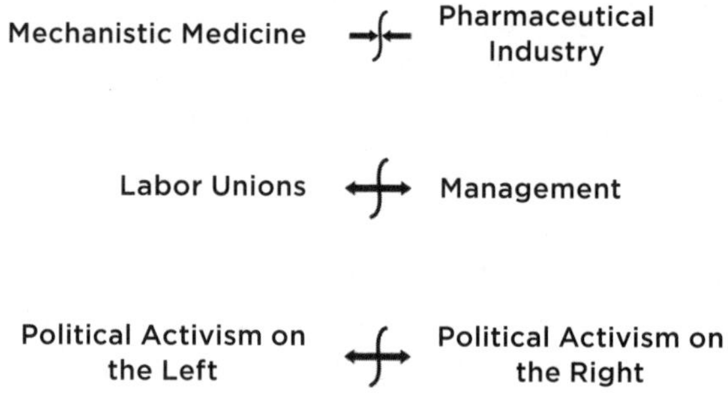

FIGURE 1.13

An example from European history are the social conditions leading up to the First and Second World Wars (Fig. 1.14):

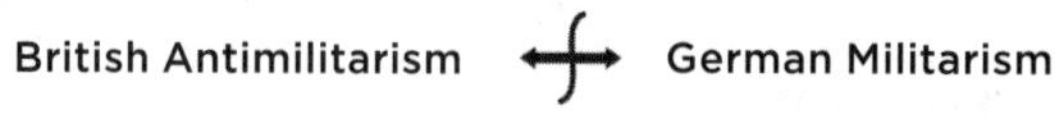

British Antimilitarism
German Militarism

FIGURE 1.14

An example from the extreme left (Fig. 1.15):

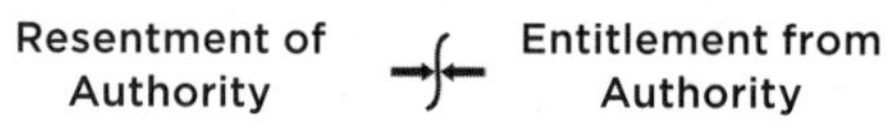

Resentment of Authority
Entitlement from Authority

FIGURE 1.15

An example from both political extremes (Fig. 1.16):

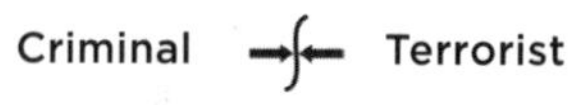

Criminal
Terrorist

FIGURE 1.16

With the exception of drug traffickers, criminals are psychopaths that operate within nations. Terrorists are psychopaths that operate internationally. Criminals and terrorists function as simple attractive opposite variations based on their common character structure, *psychopath*. This functional relationship explains why criminals world-wide are attracted to terrorist organizations and why terrorism is an international phenomenon.

Cruelty and sadistic behavior can arise in anyone when natural impulses from the biological core are thwarted by armor. Unfortunately, despite training in physical diagnosis, the mechanistically oriented physician simply does not recognize armor, its physical manifestations and its consequences, or its medical, psychiatric, and social significance in patients. A deadened expression in the eyes or a rigidly held chest during inspiration means nothing to the classically trained physician. Similarly, the sociologist may depict the horrendous manifestations of the secondary layer through the use of emotionally evocative words such as "barbarism," "genocide," "Holocaust," "massacre," "war crimes," and "crimes against humanity." However, this descriptive, intellectual approach is sterile and does not get to the heart of the problem, which is the source of human destructiveness. Without understanding the *bioenergetic* origin of human destructiveness, its elimination is impossible. To make matters worse, sociopolitical ideology largely prevents people from understanding the origin of these destructive impulses. Fascism, as it is commonly understood, is not restricted to any nationality, race, or group of individuals (Reich 1946). It can appear under certain social conditions in *anyone* where armor is present, and fascism is always excited by underlying genital frustration. For this reason, there are German fascists, Russian fascists, Jewish fascists, Arab fascists, American fascists, and so on. The difference in the manifestation of fascism depends only on which side of the sociopolitical spectrum, the left or the right, that the individual is on.

Even when not expressed as overt social destructiveness, under ordinary social conditions, armor is responsible for the rigid, stereotyped, and repetitive neurotic behavior that most humans exhibit. *The existence of the secondary destructive layer is why, despite the best intentions of well-meaning individuals on the left and the right, people's emotional lives never really improve.*

This is why the same social blunders are repeated generation after generation and why, despite the technological advances of civilization, people are as helpless as ever in dealing with the basic problems of life.

There has always been some awareness, among people of all eras, of the distinction between the core (often called "God" or "the Good") and the secondary layer ("the Devil," or "evil"). However, this understanding has been explored in literary and artistic traditions rather than in science. Some artists living in the late eighteenth and nineteenth centuries were fascinated by the destructive secondary layer and the problem of good and evil. The Faust legend depicts one man's struggle with the Devil. Writers like Dante, Goethe, and Dostoyevsky and composers like Liszt and Berlioz wrote extensively about this subject. Through one of his characters in *The Brothers Karamazov*, Dostoyevsky said prophetically: "If God is dead, then everything is permitted."[21] Since the relationship of God to the biological core was not understood, the only resolution to the problem of human destructiveness was through mysticism; that is, through appeals to God or to forces beyond human control. The preoccupation with the secondary layer that has predominated since the latter part of the twentieth century is based on man's inability to see any way out of his trapped existence, either mechanistically or mystically, *other than through social expression*—whether through political saviors, Prozac, gene manipulation, the second coming of Christ, or other ways. The mechanistic scientist is like the sorcerer's apprentice. Such a scientist can unleash enormous forces in nature but cannot handle them rationally.

Today, contact with the biological core, which is the source of all human achievement, is largely avoided. The subject matter of the cinema, the theater, and the daily news is often the endless variation of a single monotonous theme—the enormous capacity for destructiveness of armored humanity. Vulgarity, perversity, and ugliness, among other manifestations of the secondary layer, are permitted and portrayed as exciting, interesting, even admirable and something to be emulated. Often, the criminal deviant

---

21. Today, in the twenty-first century, with Islamic *jihad* on the rampage from the political right we can add: If God (Allah) exists, then everything, particularly the destruction of Western civilization, is permitted.

or social misfit is featured as the "hero." Consider how current movies depict criminals, drug addicts, and alcoholics as victims of capitalist society, as "good guys" who are portrayed sympathetically. Meanwhile, the police and other law enforcement agencies responsible for protecting the public are made to appear as the "bad guys." Art and literature touching the biological core are by far the exception.

Increasingly cut off from its biological core, humanity has become incapable of regulating itself. It needs and seeks the excitement of the secondary layer and the expression of its destructive and perverse sexual and violent impulses to feel something. Sociologists and sociopolitical groups are at a complete loss to understand and deal with phenomena related to the social degradation of armored humans. Caught between impotent solutions offered by opposing points of view into which we are polarized today—between the sociopolitics of the left and the sociopolitics of the right, between mechanism and mysticism—humanity is being helplessly and unknowingly led to its destruction. No one living in future generations will be able to understand what happened.

The Social Façade

Between the individual and society is a third, superficial layer through which armored humans interact—the social façade. Classical psychiatry penetrates only to the personality of the individual, but orgonomic biopsychiatry recognizes that the personality is identical with the social façade and resides in the superficial aspect of the bioemotional structure. The façade overlies "the great secondary layer," the province of armored life, which contains the person's character. The secondary layer is the energy source of the emotional plague. Beneath this layer lies the biological core, from which impulses arise that constitute the true nature of the individual. If the structure of armored humans consisted only of the biological core and the secondary layer, social strife would be constant, and social order would be impossible. Reich said, "In the superficial layer, the average individual is restrained, polite, compassionate, and conscientious. There would be no social tragedy of the animal, man, if this superficial layer were in immediate contact with his deep natural core. His tragedy is that such is not the case" (Reich 1946, page vii).

The social façade has two components: a genuine part in the service of expressing core impulses and a defensive part that holds back *or* expresses impulses from the secondary layer. It is through the social façade that the emotional plague is expressed. Without knowledge of the layering of the human bioemotional structure, an understanding of sociopolitical behavior is impossible because such behavior almost always contains elements from all three layers. For example, from the standpoint of the primary drives, the term *politics* refers simply to the science of political government—a rational core function dealing with the state's role in protecting social order and facilitating its operations. However, from the standpoint of the secondary drives, this term describes something entirely different—the use of intrigue, deception, or strategy to obtain and maintain positions of power or control. From the standpoint of the social façade, politics is identical to sociopolitical ideology.

The individual relates to others from the surface of the biosystem. In healthy social interactions, core impulses travel outward to the surface unimpeded by armor, and are expressed naturally and appropriately. Natural grace, charm, beauty, intelligence, and inquisitiveness are examples of these expansive interactions. Expressed simply and directly, these qualities are appealing and account for the attractiveness of healthy individuals. The healthy individual is naturally cautious or wary in the presence of armored people.

Armor prevents uninterrupted, spontaneous movement of energy and the expression of impulses from the core. If the armor inhibiting core impulses is complete, impulses never reach the periphery. If the block is partial, they become distorted by the individual's armor as they travel to the periphery, giving rise to destructive impulses and expressions that are stilted, harsh, and artificial. The biological surface of the organism must now take on a defensive function to contain these destructive elements.

The following diagram depicts the biophysical structure of unarmored and armored organisms (Fig. 1.17) (Reich 1949b, page 95).

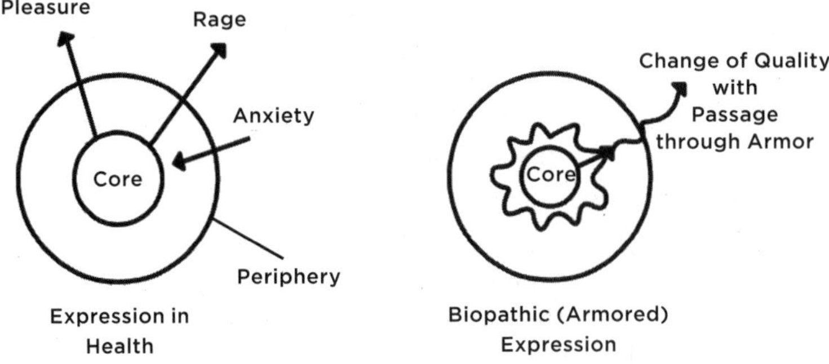

FIGURE 1.17

Armored expression is immediately sensed by unarmored individuals as being discomfiting, unnatural, unattractive, graceless, awkward, inappropriate, or in bad taste. An armored individual, in sufficient contact, also may have a sense of being insincere or false. In times past, destructive impulses and expression were better concealed by armor. Today, they are often perversely valued and emulated. Natural impulses that become distorted as they pass through the armor include intelligence, which becomes intellectualism; grace and charm, which become pretentiousness and affectation; beauty, which becomes narcissism; and natural aggression, which becomes pushiness.

The current restriction of emotional expression in armored individuals has resulted in a widespread degradation in our culture. In popular music, the expression contained in the extreme case of hard rock is restricted to the point of being harsh, mechanical, and offensive. With "New Age" music, one is left feeling vacuous. In fact, much of today's music has nothing to do with stirring emotions from within a person's depths. Rather, the music aims for impact, the bombarding of coarse, repetitive, jarring, and mechanical vibrations on organisms that are too deadened by armor to feel anything naturally. Emotional stirring arising naturally from within is replaced by external, mechanically produced sensations. The armor-inducing, harsh, mechanical ways in which infants are brought into the world and raised in early childhood largely account for the degeneration in the arts and in what has always been considered good taste and good manners.

The social façade contains the superficial layers of human character structure. In sociopolitics, the façade manifests as ideological defenses to suppress destructive impulses from the secondary layer. However, through the use of rationalization, these same defenses can be made to facilitate *expression* of destructive impulses. Therefore, the intellect, cut off from the biological core, is of no practical value in dealing with human destructiveness and the complex problems facing society. The rapidly accelerating breakdown of social structure since the end of the First World War and the global rise in social destructiveness today result from the emergence of the destructive secondary layer and the inadequacy of the social façade to contain it.

Although the defensive function of the superficial layer has always been present to some degree, the social façade has slowly gained prominence among segments of the population, particularly since the Age of Enlightenment. This rise was largely responsible for the polarization of society into the political left and right. Before this polarization, human armoring was confined primarily to the musculature. Therefore, most manifestations of social pathology involved overtly destructive behavior, typical of those on the right. Since the left, with its attendant hypertrophy of the intellect, had not yet become differentiated, undisguised expressions of cruelty and sadism were more common before the Enlightenment. As more and more members of the population developed the defensive use of the intellect, the left appeared as a sociopolitical entity. Intellectualism and rationalism in the form of sociopolitical ideology first appeared as social forces and social ideals—not as something real and practically attainable. Expressions from the secondary layer became disguised under a layer of highly destructive, specious reasoning.

There are two reasons, both defensive, for the rise in the social façade. In an increased effort to avoid contact with the biological core, which, in armored humans, is experienced with anxiety, people throughout the ages have fled in the *opposite* direction, into the brain, with all the distractions it can provide. Also, as already noted, in an attempt to deal with the recent social decline accompanying the emergence of the secondary destructive layer, humans have developed a more sophisticated façade. The rise of political correctness is a cogent example.

During periods of social decline, social activity from the superficial and secondary layers intensifies as core contact is weakened or completely lost. Correspondingly, confusion about how to deal with vital social issues, together with destructiveness resulting from the breakthrough of the secondary layer, lead to the resurgence of mysticism. The decline of the Roman Empire and the accompanying rise of Christian mysticism is a clear example. The success of early Christianity was partly based on its ability to effectively provide structure in the form of social armor amidst the disintegrating social order of the Roman Empire.

The following diagram depicts the functional relationship between the three layers of the armored human bioemotional structure (Fig. 1.18).

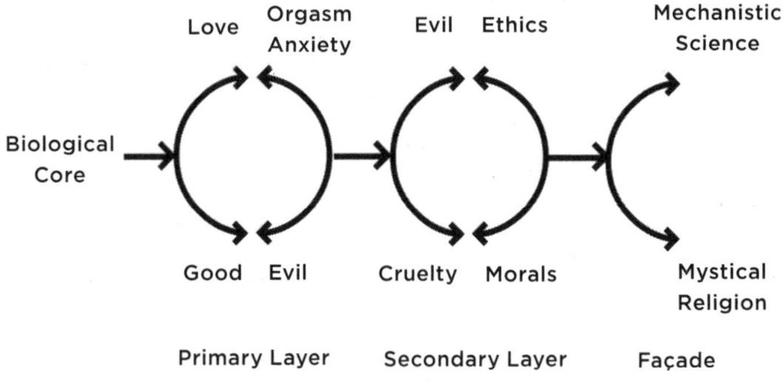

FIGURE 1.18

Energy originating in the biological core and its distortion by armor in the secondary layer appear as elements of what is commonly called "character." Orgonometry provides a functional tool for the study of both individual and social character. The understanding of character, in turn, provides a way to grasp past and contemporary social and political manifestations of the emotional plague, an understanding that can point toward their rational resolution. Chapter 2 deals precisely with such character development.

CHAPTER 2

CHARACTER FORMATION AND THE FUNCTIONAL IDENTITY OF INDIVIDUAL AND SOCIAL CHARACTER

This civilization forms the
mechanistic-mystical structures of men, and the
mechanistic-mystical character structures reproduce the
machine-mystical civilization.
—Wilhelm Reich, *The Mass Psychology of Fascism*

Without a working knowledge of characterology (the study of character formation), one cannot scientifically understand social phenomena or even begin to understand the destructiveness of the emotional plague. The events of the first few days and weeks of life are the most crucial in determining health. Character formation begins at birth and is essentially completed by the time of the first puberty, around the age of four or five. *Individual characterology* deals with how a person's character is determined by the way a child's environment affects the individual during the developmental years of life. *Sociopolitical characterology* deals with the adult's later attempt to control the environment, including society, so that it conforms to the irrational needs formed during individual character formation. Thus, the individual and society are in continual interaction and this is how armor is transmitted from generation to generation.

Neither conservatives nor liberals understand the *function* of character. For conservatives, the concept of character is permeated with strong moral overtones.[22] For liberals, character is a meaningless concept. Just as every individual develops a specific character type and employs that type in social interactions, every society and its component institutions also develop specific characters. Reich was the first natural scientist to understand the social function of character. He showed that armored society reproduces itself in the form of social institutions by securing itself in the character structure of the masses (Reich 1949a, page xxii). Armored society determines the formation of armored individuals and, in a vicious cycle, armored individuals determine the formation of an armored society.

If a child's emotional development were not hampered by parents and others in the environment, then the social functioning of humans would reflect rational interactions including disagreements and conflicts. Since emotional development almost never is allowed to progress naturally, emotional disturbances and irrational behavior are almost universal. These disturbances appear in the characteristic behavior of individuals and in the *social character* of every society.

Emotional Development of the Individual

Many factors determine the individual's development, as Reich and Baker pointed out (Baker 1967, page 37). However, the specific factors that produce character armor with its attendant cognitive and behavioral distortions are crucial to our discussion.

In the newborn, the various organ functions exist more or less independently. Except for suckling, the eyes, mouth, and limbs move in an uncoordinated and purposeless manner. During the first years of life the process of organismic coordination and integration occurs with the establishment of contact between bodily movements and the perception of these movements.

From the standpoint of emotional health, the coordination and functional integration of the erogenous zones are of central

22. The conservative attempts to deal with character problems by applying moral principles to human behavior. However, ideas related to right and wrong and value-related concepts such as value judgments become open to question when a distinction is not made between human activity originating from the core and the secondary layer.

importance (Baker 1967, page 16). There are four major erogenous zones: eyes, mouth, anus, and genital. These zones are paired at both ends of the organism, where contact with the environment has the potential to produce the most pleasure. During infancy and early childhood, integration proceeds in a lawful manner longitudinally from the upper to the lower regions of the body. Integration proceeds in a cephalocaudal (top-down) direction in terms of both neurological and psychosexual development. Each zone corresponds to a different stage of development. These are the ocular, oral, anal, phallic, and genital stages.

The integration of the erogenous zones begins with the eyes and mouth and ends with the genital. The developmental periods of the first three zones are known as *pregenital stages.* Healthy development proceeds without blocks—no armoring develops to prevent the progression of integration from the pregenital stages to genitality (genital primacy). In normal development, each stage fulfills its passing function, remains untraumatized, and, in future life, serves its role in giving pleasure.

A block, however, can form at any stage in a child's psychosexual development. When the child's normal development is interfered with, a conflict arises between the child's spontaneous expression of natural impulses and needs and the imposed limitations. The child *must* find ways to defend itself from the frustration and pain resulting from the conflict. The manner of protection, unique to each individual, is what Reich called "armor." Muscular armor forms perpendicular to the longitudinal axis of the body in any of its seven segments: ocular, oral, cervical, thoracic, diaphragmatic, abdominal, and pelvic.

Armor can be viewed as an internal prison that protects the individual from experiencing painful emotions and sensations. It also protects the individual and society from the destructive impulses contained in it by restricting destructive behavior.

The Ocular Stage

From the ocular zone, which includes the eyes, the continuation of the optic nerves into the brain, and all functionally related structures, the infant first establishes contact with the environment. In healthy newborns, the eyes are capable of focusing for brief moments immediately after birth. The ocular system continues to develop well into the second decade of life. Binocular vision, necessary to maintain optimal contact with the environment and to permit the development of full integration, hasn't been lost in healthy infants. Such vision provides a clear perspective of the world, places objects accurately in the environment, and allows an objective emotional attitude. Full visual contact, which includes the energetic-emotional component, is vital to all healthy future learning and development and is the cornerstone for rational social functioning.

Visual contact provides a sense of acceptance and well-being and encourages expansion and the ability to reach out to the world. When infants establish visual contact with their mothers, their eyes have an open expression and appear frank and inquisitive, with a serious but trusting quality. With continued development, the child becomes oriented, assumes a genuine sense of responsibility for itself and for its environment, and experiences pleasure from it. Through the eyes, the environment becomes an extension of the individual. Although the environment is experienced with the same acute awareness as the self, the self and the external world are never confused. The healthy child distinguishes between pleasurable and painful environmental stimuli with unfailing accuracy. Excitation from the eyes is often readily felt in the genital area as a pleasurable sensation.

Ocular disturbances, manifested as perceptual distortions of the inner and external worlds, can occur from the time prior to birth to the onset of adulthood. Ocular trauma occurs at birth if any medication is applied to the newborn's eyes, especially if it is irritating, or if the infant is greeted by adults with cold, frightening, or hateful expressions. Any traumatic experience at this critical time results in a temporary lack of contact. For example, an anxious mother or a cold, hostile nurse can cause a temporary contraction, resulting in withdrawal in the eyes and ocular armoring in the infant. If the situation continues, the armor becomes chronic, and the capacity for the infant to reach out through his eyes and function naturally becomes permanently impaired. Without loving contact, ocular development with binocular vision is inhibited or prevented. A mother who is not hostile but is excessively anxious, indifferent, or emotionally dead can also cause varying degrees of irreparable damage to the infant's ocular development. In extreme cases, the expression of the infant's eyes becomes chronically dull and lifeless, and binocular vision fails to develop adequately, if at all. *The prevalence of traumatization to the eyes at birth and during the developmental years is responsible for mankind's widespread contactlessness and its destructive social consequences.*

Development of muscular armor elsewhere (for example, a respiratory block) always produces some ocular armor because muscular armor in other parts of the body interferes with the integrating function of the brain. This further disturbs the individual's accurate sense of the world and, therefore, rational functioning. Ocular armor is the basis for the formation of psychological defenses—denial, projection, displacement, identification, rationalization, and so on—which occur in interpersonal relationships. A block in the development of ocular functioning thus results in psychic symptoms, as well as in all physical symptoms related to the ocular zone. And, as we will see, these defenses can also be activated when the individual attempts to control his or her environment via sociopolitical ideology.

A full range of psychosocial problems result from ocular armor. Because the individual is out of touch with the environment, there is a sense of alienation and a feeling that life is passing by without his or her full participation and pleasure in it. The quality of social and personal relationships is always disturbed in such persons. Examples include problems in parent-child, workplace, and marital relationships.

Without binocular vision, the individual must adjust to the world two-dimensionally, without full perspective. Widespread incidence of ocular blocking is *the* major reason for the omnipresence of confusion, social irrationalism, and the rise in destructive social activity. Ocular disturbances account for people's inaccurate comprehension of social phenomena and also for their social helplessness and withdrawal. This occurs in cases of schizophrenia, an illness in which ocular blocking is the primary source of pathology. From the widespread prevalence of social irrationalism, we must conclude that the majority of people cannot clearly see what is directly before their eyes.

There are fundamental differences in how armored humans perceive and view the world. For the first time, an understanding of cognitive distortions resulting from ocular armor provides a way to objectively characterize people in social terms. T*his is the foundation of sociopolitical characterology.*

Ideas are perceived in the brain but actually originate from bodily emotions and from sensations. To varying degrees, some neurotic people have retained the ability to perceive the world in a lively, emotionally contactful manner. Their ideas originate primarily from emotions and, to a lesser degree, from sensations. For them, the destructive *consequences* of human behavior are viewed as being more significant than their cause. These individuals fall to the right on the sociopolitical spectrum. In other neurotic individuals, armor more completely distorts the perceptual function. In them, the inner world is perceived in a superficial manner. Ideas originate primarily from their sensations and to a lesser degree from their emotions. Projected onto society, this way of perceiving produces an emphasis on and a need to solve social problems. The *cause* of destructive human behavior is viewed as being more significant than its consequences. Since behavior and ideas are believed to originate from and be governed by centers in the brain, the world in general and social processes in particular are perceived in a lifeless intellectual manner as being controlled from a central source—hence the desire for central planning and a centralized or world government. In today's world, these individuals generally fall to the left on the sociopolitical spectrum.[23]

Mysticism is also a manifestation of ocular armor. It arises from a distorted perception of core sensations, primarily repressed sexual excitation. Pleasurable sexual feelings are not immediately perceived as such but are experienced as if from afar. The following clinical vignette is illustrative.

> A twenty-six-year-old artist came from a household in which her parents were extremely mystical. She had a very strict religious upbringing. At one point in therapy, she realized that she perceived the external world and her inner sensations moralistically, as if everything she saw had to be judged good or bad. Expressing anger at this

23. The autonomic nervous system is the physiological basis of emotion. The central nervous system, which includes the brain, is the physiological basis of sensation. Hence, those in whom ideas originate from sensation are more likely to use their brain defensively.

> realization, she exclaimed, "I don't want to see moralistically!" She explained that "seeing moralistically" meant viewing the world in a dead, two-dimensional manner. She contrasted this view with seeing in an alive manner. As a child, her highly moralistic parents robbed her of her lively interest in the world by viewing her interests as if she were wrong for having them. Thus, to be lively and interested in things was forbidden. This realization of how she perceived the world enabled her to reach out with her eyes in a pleasurable manner and express this clarity in her artwork.

Widespread prevalence of ocular armor is the reason that ideological forces are so important in social life, including politics. Symptomatic of ocular armor, the inability to see accurately, especially to clearly see people in general and political leaders in particular, is responsible for the prevalent irrationality and gullibility of the masses at the hands of self-serving, dishonest politicians and religious leaders. This is why, time and again, mesmerizing politicians are able to charm the public while honest and decent, but less charismatic, candidates lose at the polls.

The Oral Stage

Maternal contact is critical for the developing newborn. An infant completely deprived of maternal contact would not long survive. The infant has been part of the mother for nine months and, at birth, all its needs must continue to be satisfied by her. During gestation, the two organisms are in constant contact, providing the excitation necessary for growth and development. After birth, the excitement reaches its peak during nursing. If the mother is in energetic contact with the child, her nipples are warm, erect, and alive. Such contact is vital for development and even for life itself. Where contact between mother and infant is strong, the infant occasionally experiences an oral orgastic convulsion.

The oral stage and later the genital stage are of particular importance because only the mouth and the genital can initiate the orgastic convulsion. These erogenous zones provide moist contact and fusion *(superimposition)* with another organism.

It is during the oral stage that integration occurs between the ocular and oral zones. This contact is enhanced by nursing and forms the basis for much of the individual's subsequent development. At a later stage, the movement of the hands becomes integrated with that of the eyes and mouth, a process that continues throughout the first year. By the end of this time, the lower extremities also become integrated with the movements of the entire organism, and the infant becomes a toddler. Accompanying this organismic integration is the appearance of consciousness.

If the mother meets the newborn's needs with contact and not in a mechanical way, the child soon becomes capable of self-regulation—that is, regulating according to his or her own needs. With developing maturity, the child must be taught only to avoid endangering itself and to distinguish and respect the rights of others. With oral satisfaction provided by contactful nursing, the child develops the capacity for clear and direct verbal expression of ideas and emotional needs.

However, because of a disturbance in their ability to make and sustain contact with the infant, mothers are often at a loss to know how to provide for the child's needs, and this leads to anxiety on the mother's part. There are two typical reactions of the mother in this situation: She aggressively and harshly clamps down on the infant and places restrictions on the child, or she goes overboard and anxiously tries to satisfy all of the child's needs. The first reaction results in an oral-repressed block. Repression at the oral level is produced largely through deprivation by the mother's cold, dead nipple; insufficient or poor-quality milk; and contactless nursing. The second reaction results in an oral-unsatisfied block. Here, the lack of satisfaction is usually produced by initial fulfillment followed by sudden deprivation, such as the mother abruptly discontinuing nursing regardless of the needs of the infant. This experience causes the individual to make up for oral satisfaction through substitute measures such as overeating, drinking, and excessive talking throughout life.

Early infantile experiences have far-reaching social consequences for later life. Where an oral-repressed block develops, the person will have difficulty expressing ideas and feelings clearly. Manifestations of an oral-unsatisfied block are recognized in the innumerable political speeches, publications, and debates that serve the function of drowning life's vital questions in verbiage.

The Anal Stage

The anal stage corresponds to the time of development, around two to three years of age, when the anal sphincter comes under voluntary control and is integrated with the organism's total functioning. *With voluntary control, toilet training occurs spontaneously.* This process is important in promoting satisfaction in elimination and natural, not neurotic or excessive, control. Satisfaction and pride in producing a bowel movement occur when the child is learning to separate from the mother and is gaining an independent identity. The more general development of pride and a sense of accomplishment and independence originate at this time.

If an overanxious, overly concerned mother interferes with this natural, self-regulating process, a vital stage of the child's development becomes disturbed. To please mother by attaining bowel control prematurely, before sphincter control has developed naturally, the child has to tighten all associated muscles, particularly those of the thighs, buttocks and pelvic floor, aided by retracting the pelvis and holding the breath. This attitude diminishes sensation and interferes with later genital stage development. Such regimentation also decreases spontaneity and renders the child compliant and dependent on outside instruction. At the same time, a deep stubbornness and stinginess—a holding back—develops, interfering with spontaneous giving. The social consequence of blocked development at the anal stage is that the individual turns into a human machine, as represented by petty bureaucrats in government and business corporations, as well as by compulsive, mechanistic, seemingly "natural" scientists. Such individuals often secretly derive sadistic satisfaction from controlling others' lives.

Premature toilet training, before control of the anal sphincter develops naturally, was often the rule in the past authoritarian era. Armor that developed during the anal stage contributed significantly to the formation of rigid authoritarian societies. Children grew up rigidly, depending on outside guidance and instruction for conducting their lives. Generations of mechanical humans were produced. Blindly subservient to authority, they craved leaders to tell them what to do. In Western societies, the response to this upbringing has shifted toward indulging the child and providing indiscriminate satisfaction of the child's every whim. Today's more permissive childrearing has contributed to the decline of authoritarianism and its replacement by the exact opposite, the current anti-authoritarian society. In part as a reaction to the chaotic state of childrearing, there has been a return to the custom of swaddling newborns and infants (see *The Happiest Baby on the Block* by Harvey Karp, M.D.). A symptom of the emotional plague, the effect of this cruel practice is to induce the formation of armor by curbing the young child's freedom of movement and expression. Swaddling produces a return to a generation of obedient, robot-like individuals ready to do the bidding of any self-proclaimed fuehrer who happens to come along. Nothing will have changed for the better.

The Phallic Stage

In healthy children, development passes rapidly through the phallic stage, the first phase of the genital stage, and the child attains genital primacy. In the phallic stage, sexual development is still undifferentiated. This is when the child first finds the genital and experiences the pride and pleasure that accompany this discovery. The context of the child's earliest sexual feelings is critically important in determining the individual's later psychosexual functioning.

A block occurs at this stage when the frustrating parent, usually in this case the parent of the opposite sex, cannot tolerate the child's proud genital exhibitionism and clamps down sharply. The effect is that the child develops a conflict with that parent, and the Oedipal conflict is activated.[24] Thus, an individual must have reached the phallic stage to form a neurotic character structure. Neurosis develops out of the Oedipal conflict when the next stage, the genital stage, is reached. *The Oedipal situation is created by the sexual repression of children in our culture and is not a natural conflict necessary for human maturation.* A frequently overlooked element that intensifies the Oedipal conflict occurs when a parent who lacks sexual fulfillment with his or her mate forms an overt or covert sexualized relationship with the child.

When a block occurs at the phallic stage and the Oedipal conflict is activated, this conflict is transferred to all significant

---

24. The Oedipus complex refers to the emotional-sexual relationship between the child and the parent of the opposite sex.

relationships the person develops in later life, giving rise to the phallic-narcissistic character. If development is arrested at this stage, genital activity functions in the service of revenge, not love. Aggressive movements change qualitatively and become harsh and forced. In sicker phallics, these movements are accompanied by sadistic impulses and fantasies. What would have been heterosexual love becomes instead revenge directed at the opposite sex. The degree to which revenge is overtly expressed in social relationships depends on the strength of the instinctual forces and the inhibiting forces opposing them. The sociological significance of this disturbance is that feelings of revenge originally directed at the child's parent are displaced onto society and drive much social and political activity, including the striving to attain power and control over others through ruthless business or political practices. These revenge-driven impulses are examples of substitute gratification that result from the inability to obtain genuine sexual satisfaction.

The same situation exists, in a general way, in social development. In the *authoritarian* society, repression of pregenital and genital impulses is the rule. As a result, the average individual develops a repressed character structure. Excess social structure restricts the individual's development. In contrast, in current Western *anti-authoritarian* society, impulses from all levels of psychosexual development are permitted indiscriminate expression. This attitude is commonly called "permissiveness." However, because of armor, there is at best only incomplete satisfaction with such limited release, and people are left chronically unsatisfied. This often produces a chronic sense of entitlement and, simultaneously, an endless yearning for satisfaction in one form or another. A lack of consistent social structure during childhood results in an arrest in human development. One manifestation seen today is the tremendous increase in impulsive and psychopathic behavior, including criminality in *all* segments of society, from computer operators to CEOs of giant corporations. Another is the extension of the adolescent period far into adult life. Occasionally, individuals never leave their adolescence. The frenzied and chaotic sexual activity commonly portrayed in today's cinema and television programming is an accurate reflection of armored people's distorted view of human sexuality.

In contrast to the anti-authoritarianism of Western societies, Arab countries in the Middle East have retained, until now, the traditions of an extreme authoritarian social order. These are currently in the process of breaking down.

The Genital Stage

A child who passes through the pregenital and genital stages without significant emotional trauma has the capacity for healthy genital function. There is complete sexual differentiation, and the child identifies with the same-sex parent. The genital functions to express love and pleasure in the genital embrace, and these feelings are felt most intensely in the sexual organ, which serves as an extension of the entire organism. The male and female genital serve strictly male and female sexual functions, with natural, soft characteristics. Aggressive movements are not forced and harsh, but gentle. They are accompanied by feelings of sweetness and tenderness.

A block at the genital stage results from a moralistic, sex-negative attitude on the part of the parent of the same sex. This gives rise to the hysterical character. Typically, the mother provides frightening information of her disillusioning experiences with the opposite sex to her daughter ("Men are all alike," "They are all after one thing," "Give them what they want if you want to keep them happy," etc.). This common attitude prevents a healthy resolution of the Oedipal conflict, which occurs when the child relinquishes her sexual feelings for her father and transfers them to males outside the family. When this does not happen, as a result of parental moralism, the child remains forever fixated at the Oedipal stage.

Character Formation and the Family

Final character formation begins as a definite form of resolution of the Oedipus complex (Reich 1949a, page 146). Social conditions leading to this particular form of the solution of conflicts are specific for character formation. Since social conditions in authoritarian and anti-authoritarian societies differ, individual character formation differs within these societies. The character structure of the average individual today is very different from that of one raised in the authoritarian era. At that time, resolution of the Oedipus complex occurred in three distinct stages:

1. The child identifies with the frustrating reality, the frustrating parent. This process gives the character its psychic content.

2. Aggression that was mobilized against the frustrating parent causes anxiety and is turned against the self. This, in turn, gives rise to the inhibiting aspect of the character.

3. Reactive attitudes toward sexual impulses are utilized to ward them off. This withdraws energy from the repressed impulses and reduces their ability to break through.

In the authoritarian family, repression is more effective. The father is both a rational authority figure and a supporter of the existing authoritarian, sex-negative social order. Standing beside the father and exerting both rational and frustrating influences on the child, the mother is the bearer of the authoritarian moral code.

The authoritarian social order gives rise to the Oedipus complex because parental prohibitions interfere with the child's natural sexual development at the various psychosexual stages. As a result, the child becomes emotionally tied, through identification, with the frustrating parent.

Character formation depends not merely on the fact that instinct and frustration create a conflict. It also depends on the nature of this conflict, the period at which the character-forming conflicts occur, and what impulses are involved. The following is a summary of these factors, which includes the *time* at which an impulse is frustrated; the extent and *intensity* of the frustration; *which impulse* the frustration is directed against; the *ratio between permission and frustration;* the sex of the main frustrating person; and the *contradictions* in the frustrations themselves (Reich 1949a, page 150).

Today's anti-authoritarian Western civilization results from the sharp rise in the number of anti-authoritarian families. These families, in a vicious cycle, reproduce an anti-authoritarian society. They include single-parent families in which the male authority is absent, as well as many two-parent families. In the latter households, the father has given up the role of authority. The father no longer supports the authoritarian values of the social order. Many fathers also have relinquished the role of *rational* authority in the home. Thus, the solution to the Oedipus complex in an anti-authoritarian family includes social castration of the father. The mother, typically dominant, has contempt and disrespect for the father's authority or, if a single parent, she may assume the role of authority in an attempt to stabilize the family unit.

In an anti-authoritarian family, frustration of the child's impulses results in emotional contactlessness between the parents and their children. The contactless state pervades every area of family life, including the resolution of the child's Oedipus complex and the formation of the child's character. This state of contactlessness can happen simply because of an absence of effective parenting. Since the father has been rendered powerless, the male child has no one to identify with or rebel against. The boy forms a weak sense of identity. Rebelliousness turns into impulsivity or hyperactivity. The girl, on the other hand, is left feeling alienated and lacking feminine identity. Along with the destructive effects of contactlessness with self and others, the child experiences a sense of alienation, emotional deadening, and a rise in anxiety, leading to increased hyperactivity and impulsive behavior. Aggression directed toward the parents produces anxiety and is not turned against the self but against the outer world. These children blame the world for their condition. Alternatively, the anxiety is shifted upward into the brain, giving rise to intellectualism, "smart-aleckness," and rationalizations to justify destructive behavior. Reactive attitudes such as brattiness and substitute measures (cult behavior, drug use, or sociopolitical activism) are used to release the undischarged sexual impulses.

Table 2.1 compares the factors that determine character formation in authoritarian and anti-authoritarian family structures. It shows the basis for the differences in character structure of the average individual in each social order. It also shows that the formation of individual and social armor is far greater in today's Western anti-authoritarian society than it was in the past authoritarian social order.

Factors Determining Character Formation	Authoritarian Family	Anti-Authoritarian Family
The stage of psycho–sexual development in which the impulse is frustrated	Variable	Variable
Extent and intensity of the frustration	Variable	Severe*
Impulse that is frustrated	Mostly secondary impulses, less so core impulses	Mostly core impulses, less so secondary impulses
Ratio between permissiveness and repression	Greater repression than permissiveness	Greater permissiveness than repression
Sex of the main frustrating person	Strong identification with the frustrating parent provides the psychic content of the ideology that supports the existing social order	Weak identification with the frustrating parent. Psychic content of the ideology that supports the existing social order is poorly defined because of severe contactlessness
Contradictions in the frustrations	Variable	Extreme

*Because of severe contactlessness.

Comparison of Factors Determining Character Formation in Authoritarian and Anti-Authoritarian Family Structures

TABLE 2.1

The Origins of Sociopolitical Character Armor and the Emotional Plague

The relationship between individual character and the existing social order is reciprocal. Armored society produces armored individuals through biosocial factors impinging on childhood development, and armored individuals produce an armored society. As stated earlier, knowledge of characterology is critical for understanding how people of different character types attempt to control their environment, including society, so that it conforms to the neurotic needs armoring has created in them. At the extremes of sociopolitical character, the destructive effects of armor in those on the left and the right spread the emotional plague. The emotional plague therefore manifests in the sociopolitical realm by liberal and conservative character types alike.

The overall character structure of a person has sociopolitical and individual components. However, assessing an individual's sociopolitical character type is different than making a psychiatric diagnosis. Psychiatric diagnosis requires examination of a patient by a physician with an understanding of medical orgone therapy. This includes an evaluation of the patient's chief complaint and past and present functioning. Identifying the sociopolitical character type, on the other hand, requires an accurate understanding of how the individual acts in public.

In addition to the neurotic individual's subjectively generated conflicts, there are typical social manifestations of character. For example, we know that the masochist suffers from a specific intolerance of expansion, with all of its characteristic sequelae. At the same time, these individuals provoke others to behave sadistically toward them in order to form a sadomasochistic relationship. People with sadistic tendencies would have fewer opportunities to express these impulses in their social interactions if individuals, including those with complementary masochistic tendencies, did not tolerate this behavior.

Other social relationships involve the symbiotic interaction of one individual's neurotic impulses with those of another. Those who control others or behave with neurotic aggression and narcissism can only do so if others passively accept or tolerate such behavior. The evangelistic minister cannot preach in a sanctimonious, self-righteous way without idolaters in his congregation to worship him. Such functional relationships apply to the social interactions of every character type.

Character forms and is first expressed within the social context of the child's relationship with the parents or parent surrogates. Later, character manifests in adult life. *Knowing the character structure of the individuals that constitute a social group makes it possible to predict the elements and patterns of behavior among the members' interactions.*

There are two periods of increased sexual activity in human development: the first puberty, around the age of four to five years, and the second puberty, which begins at about age twelve with the onset of adolescence.

The first puberty coincides with the Oedipal stage, and the formation of the superego follows. From a psychological standpoint, the superego is the component of armor that incorporates the parents' attitudes, values, and morals within the characterological and muscular armor of the young child. Biophysically, it composes part of the armor of the brain. The superego forms to bind the surge of sexual energy at first puberty. If the superego functions successfully in this period, it effectively contains the intensified energy charge and, from a Freudian psychological standpoint, represents a solution to the Oedipal conflict.

The second puberty is accompanied by hormone production, the intensification of the sexual drive, and the development of secondary sexual characteristics. It is therefore not surprising that interest in sociopolitical activity as a solution to the individual's sexual problems usually starts around late adolescence, following a period of intense sexual conflict and further armor formation.

The final formation of sociopolitical character armor is a consequence of the sexual push of the second puberty and the inability of the superego component of armor to bind this extra energy. The energy contained in the sexual conflict, having no place to go, can be displaced externally onto the sociopolitical arena. This fuels sociopolitical ideology. The neurotic, moral component of an individual's ideology originates from the previously instilled moral attitudes contained in the superego.

The Emotional Plague Character

Reich identified the first sociopolitical character type to be recognized orgonometrically, the emotional plague character. This character type is the vector of transmission of the emotional plague. Socially destructive behavior can be expressed by anyone who is armored, but these individuals, who typically have a high energy level and a strong pelvic block, function almost exclusively from the secondary layer. Sexual feelings are intolerable for them, and they do not have access to the usual defense mechanisms of ordinary neurotics, such as reaction formation, flight, and contactlessness. Instead, they handle their sexuality by attacking and attempting to destroy especially those elements in their environment they perceive as lively and exciting. Ordinary neurotics can control their excitation, especially sexual excitation, through internal mechanisms, but the emotional plague type controls feelings by influencing and controlling those around him.

For such individuals, natural, spontaneous expression of any kind excites intolerable longing, driving them to behave in a hateful, life-negative manner toward others—hence, Reich's use of the term "plague." However, because of their insurmountable pelvic block and intolerance of experiencing genital feelings, their social activity is directed against the expression of core sexual feeling in others. In authoritarian social systems, where armor in individuals and in society is more intact, plague individuals function by overtly opposing genital sexual expression, especially in children and adolescents. In today's anti-authoritarian Western society, they demean and destroy genitality by putting it on a par with any other nonemotional, physiological function and with all forms of pregenital sexual activity. The expression "different strokes for different folks" is an example of such an attitude, which equates oral, anal, sadomasochistic, and homosexual expression with loving, genital heterosexuality.

Natural sexuality is not the only form of expression that the emotional plague individual cannot tolerate and therefore hates: It is any of the innumerable vital expressions from the biological core that humans experience. All of these natural expressions have the quality of *involuntary, spontaneous movement* such as the movement of an unarmored newborn infant, the spontaneous social activity of a democracy, or the spontaneous movement of *living* cells as seen under the microscope. Ordinary neurotics suppress their terror and hatred of spontaneous movement and contain it within their armor. Emotional plague individuals are compelled to control and attempt to destroy what, to them, is emotionally intolerable. The method and virulence of the attack can range from petty gossip, slander, and defamation to cold-blooded murder, depending on the social conditions in which the attack occurs.

Since it is a function of their character, the destructive behavior of plague individuals is integrated and acceptable to their ego and strongly defended by rationalization. This identifies another essential trait of emotional plague characters: their destructive actions and the reasons given for them are never congruent. The real motive, intolerance and hatred, is always hidden behind a more socially acceptable and beneficial one, such as "for the common good." Babies are separated from mothers at birth and put in the newborn nursery "to avoid infection" or "so both can rest." Silver nitrate or antibiotic ointment must be placed in the newborn's eyes "to prevent infection." Male infants are circumcised "to prevent cancer or HIV infection." When the action is challenged or the underlying motive is exposed, anxiety and anger inevitably result.

Since the sexual function is identical with the life function, emotional plague characters and the groups they are associated with repress genital sexuality or confuse the distinction between genital and pregenital sexuality. Religious groups on the right and gay and lesbian groups on the left ostensibly seek the preservation of society as a whole or the "rights" of certain individuals, respectively. They are effective at character defamation, from which they derive sadistic sexual gratification. Perverse sexual behavior is almost always supported and is well rationalized, as when pregenital and pornographic sexual activities are promoted under the misplaced banner of "tolerance" or when religious groups mandate abstinence under the banner of morality. The attack on others' sexuality is most intensely directed against *natural* sexual expression, especially that of children and adolescents, not against pregenital sexual activity.

Just as emotional plague carriers hate natural sexuality, they are incapable of sustained work and often engage in nonproductive substitute activities, such as power politics, psychopathic activity or criminality, which do not require patient persistence and the biological development of the work function. These individuals nevertheless have a strong proclivity for effectively organizing political and nonpolitical social institutions and for infiltrating existing ones to carry out their destructive activities.

Consider this clinical example:

> A twenty-year-old, male, pre-law college student had problems establishing and sustaining relationships with women. The last few years had been marked by a series of disappointing encounters and difficulty tolerating the painful feelings that accompanied each separation. One day he came into a therapy session and announced he had given up his pursuit of a law career and was going into politics. No longer interested in facing his emotional problems, he wanted to devote his life to helping others less fortunate than he, for example, by opposing sweatshops manufacturing trendy sporting goods and becoming active in environmental causes. He was excited by the support and attention he received from his fellow students and by publicity he had gained from local newspapers. The recognition of others was a form of substitute gratification that filled his life with meaning and purpose. He is an example of an emotional plague character in the making. By externalizing his conflict, he no longer had to feel the depth of his misery.

Whenever an individual or group has a moralistic posture in relation to others, the emotional plague is usually in operation. Patterns of moral attitudes are as typical of those to the left on the sociopolitical spectrum as they are on the right. The rigid moralistic thinking of the right is easy to recognize. There is an inflexible demand for the maintenance of authority, social tradition (whether rational or irrational), and the status quo. The moralistic element of the emotional plague on the left is more pernicious, subtler, and more difficult to detect because it gives the appearance of flexibility and rationality, and it is precisely these surface qualities that conceal its malignancy. In today's Western societies, there is an inflexible demand that authority, social tradition, and the status quo give way to change in the pursuit of moral ends.

The left is also waging war on the free exchange of ideas. In America, political correctness as espoused by the left is as inflexible and inimical to life as is the moralistic attitudes on the right in its mechanical application of identical rules of social conduct to one and all. An example of this form of morality is illustrated by the media's emotional plague attack on a talk show host for expressing an opinion about homosexuality that was counter to one endorsed by the Gay and Lesbian Alliance Against Defamation (GLAAD). "If she can't be controlled, she must be stopped" was the response of the executive director of that organization. The media joined in to unleash a vitriolic attack on the perpetrator. She became an object of derision, was attacked by the press, denounced by two contenders for the 2000 Democratic presidential nomination, and was vilified on television talk shows. As a result, corporations were pressured into pulling their sponsorship and television stations that had picked up her show were picketed (Bruce 2001).

Irrational characterological attitudes of the armored masses throughout the world are fertile soil for the emotional plague. People in developing countries believe that the United States is out to control the world. This anti-American attitude is identical to the anti-authoritarian attitude of helpless neurotic adolescents who, because of *their* inability to be emotionally independent and self-reliant, accuse their parents or "the system" of trying to dominate them.[25] In Europe, as well, the emotional plague is directed against the United States by the emotionally helpless masses. The energy source of this hatred originates from the displacement of people's subversive attitudes toward authority figures. The United States is viewed as larger and more powerful than Europe, politically, economically and militarily. This greater strength is identified with the hated authority father figure, and feelings of resentment are displaced onto the strong one.

Because of their intolerance of any show of force and because of feelings of inferiority, including the idea that the United States is treating them as "satellites," European leftists respond with an attitude of *moral* contempt. America's approach to the war against terrorism is viewed as "simplistic, crude, war-mongering, and unhelpful." Any "civilized" individual would know that Amer-

---

25. Robert Harman, M.D., personal communication.

ica should develop "policies of engagement" (read "cowardice" and "appeasement") with countries such as North Korea, Iran, and Saddam Hussein's Iraq. Instead of being directed at the real enemies of the Free World, the hatred is directed toward America. This hatred is especially clear in the oppositional attitude against America's aggressive conduct of the war against terrorism. The European Union Charter of Fundamental Rights, currently being promulgated, forbids extradition of suspects to nations where they could be subject to capital punishment. European policy posited a moral equality between Yasser Arafat and Ariel Sharon, the former prime minister of Israel. Indeed, so long as the prime minister was a "hard-liner," European elites saw Israel as worse than the Palestinians. At the same time, the conditions at U.S. Camp X-Ray in Guantanamo Bay, Cuba, have sparked self-righteous indignation about the way the United States is fighting the war against terrorism and prompted calls from some for an international judicial system to deal with such matters. European elites are also convinced that the United States is trying to evade its environmental responsibilities by refusing to sign the Kyoto Treaty, a pact that places a heavy burden on the American economy, whereas the idea of a missile shield that could end the threat of nuclear ballistic missile blackmail alarms many powerful Europeans. (See "Our Friends in Europe," *Wall Street Journal*, March 8, 2002) These anti-American arguments barely conceal the European leftists' underlying hatred.

The source of the emotional plague from the Third World is a variation of that of European leftists. The United States is again perceived as an all-powerful nation, one that should be an all-giving father figure that should provide large sums of money to help impoverished Third World nations to raise their standard of living and reduce inequality, conditions which allegedly spawn terrorism. This use of the threat of terrorism to blackmail the United States into spending more money is simply another example of the emotional plague. The effect is not only to weaken the stronger economic nation in its fight against terrorism but, more importantly, to obfuscate the underlying problem by treating the masses in Third World countries like children, rendering them even more helpless and dependent emotionally, economically, and politically than they already are.

Emotional plague characters operate without consideration of laws that safeguard democratic institutions. By so doing, they interfere with harmonious, lawful, biosocial interactions at every level of social organization. In economics, they interfere with the free market. In politics, they interfere with rational administration of the state and with natural relationships among nations. Since plague characters are also opposed to international law, they do not recognize the nation as a natural social unit. They feel that they are morally above the law and therefore do not respect laws designed to protect individual freedom. *The doctrine of the inseparability of religion and state, a central tenet of Islamic fundamentalism, is an undisguised and highly destructive manifestation of the emotional plague.*

Sociopolitical Characterology

To accurately understand human social behavior, one must step outside the framework of current thinking. A functional energetic perspective and knowledge of sociopolitical characterology is essential.

Every person has his or her *individual character structure,* the result of how the individual's own life has been molded from birth by an environment unsupportive or hostile to natural expression and needs. He or she also has an identifiable *sociopolitical character structure,* the manner in which the individual attempts to mold the environment and society to fit his or her own irrational needs.

One of Elsworth F. Baker's major contributions to the understanding of sociopolitical character types was his identification of the pattern of an individual's armor in relation to sociopolitical character (Baker 1967, page 153). For the first time, the political left and right were defined in objective *biophysical* terms, *thus placing the origin of social pathology on a firm biological foundation.* From clinical observation, Baker found that armored humanity is roughly divided into two basic types. One type lives an intellectual, rather than a feeling, life. The other type maintains contact, whether genuine or distorted, with his or her basic emotions and is largely ruled by them. Baker called the types "liberal" and "conservative." Both are legitimate attitudes toward the world, and when socially represented in equal numbers, the opposing forces of left and right are in equilibrium (see Fig. 2.1).

Baker found that the distribution and degree of armoring below the ocular segment are generally the same in people on both sides of the political spectrum. Significantly, he found the degree of *ocular armor* is greater in those on the political left as compared to those on the right. This is manifested in the degree to which those on the left are unable to *clearly see* what is in front of them and by the use their intellect, their political ideology, to defend themselves from observing reality. They distort reality to fit their preconceived worldview. Their inability to see clearly is directly proportional to their idealistic thinking; that is, they see things as they think they should be, not as they are. In contrast, those on the right use character attitudes derived from *muscular armor*, not ocular armor, to mold their environment. Because they do not rely solely on intellect, they are better able to see things more realistically.

In the past authoritarian social order, the relationship between conservative and liberal character types was one of mutually attractive opposition (Fig. 2.1).

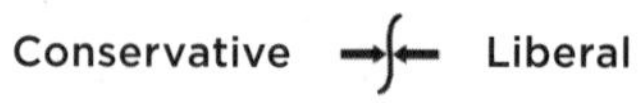

Conservative → ← Liberal

FIGURE 2.1

With the transformation of society during the 1950s and early 1960s, the relationship between conservative and liberal changed into one of antagonistic opposition, antithetical functions that exclude each other (Fig. 2.2).

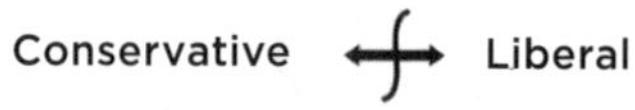

Conservative ← → Liberal

FIGURE 2.2

This change was accompanied by the polarization of society wherein virtually every social issue became politicized, a shift to the left of political center, and the rise of political activism. (See chapter 6)

A person's functioning on sociopolitical issues usually, but not always, defines the sociopolitical character type. To the extent that a person's energy is invested in sociopolitical ideology and activity, the individual functions as a sociopolitical character. Even when one is not politically inclined, it is possible to determine, in a general way, a person's sociopolitical character structure by evaluating his or her thinking, behavior, and distribution of armoring. The degree of core contact, the extent to which intellect or emotion governs the individual's life, and the capacity to function self-sufficiently and independently are all indications of sociopolitical character type. Baker writes:

> All of these characters are convinced of the moral superiority of their particular mode of expression. Politics, like sex and religion, is indeed a sacred cow. Furthermore, people are not accustomed to having their philosophies subjected to clinical appraisal. Therefore, insight is conspicuously lacking, and, unlike symptoms of their personal character structure, these symptoms are successfully rationalized; that is, they are not ego-alien. This is partly because the individual has the security of millions of others who share his views, and he does not have to stand alone. But even more important, they do not threaten or interfere with his personal life; rather they protect and support it. When he is isolated in therapy and rationalization is no longer effective, strong emotional reactions, panic, and pure venom often ensue. Thus in discussing the social character types, I expect to be accused of bias, stupidity, ignorance, and so forth, just as I am accused of such things by the individual patient when his defenses are exposed. (Baker 1967, page 157.)

Baker identified the sociopolitical character types according to the common and prevailing nomenclature. However, terms such as "conservative" and "liberal" are misleading, since in general usage they refer to the superficial sociopolitical aspects of human activity; that is, they refer to the expressed content of ideas.[26] This gives rise to a common misconception that medical orgonomists are "conservative" in the sociopolitical sense. This notion is

---

26. For example, regarding the issue of which entity has supremacy—the federal government or the individual states—liberals and conservatives in the nineteenth century held diametrically opposite views from those they hold today.

based on a mistaken understanding of the function of character. The "conservatism" of the orgonomist has to do solely with the focus on the protection and preservation of the unarmored life function in all its manifestations.

Baker's sociopolitical characterology encompasses something far more important than superficial, culturally based sociopolitical differences. For example, common usage of terms describing political ideas and attitudes in any society have been derived from their position relative to the accepted political center. Thus, terms such as liberal and conservative describe very different views in Europe, where the political center has shifted far to the left, and in Muslim countries, where the center lies on the right. As the center continues shifting further to the left in Western societies, attitudes and views that previously were considered to belong on the extreme left are becoming accepted as belonging to the liberal mainstream.

Baker discovered profound differences in the *configuration of armor,* and hence in the *functioning,* of "liberals" and "conservatives" living in America; that is, those on the left and the right of the sociopolitical spectrum's center. Manifesting most conspicuously by a fixed set of behavior and attitudes in the sociopolitical realm, the origins of these ideological differences are rooted in *biophysical* structure. They serve to protect and support the individual's way of life. As Baker used them, the terms are similar to the diagnostic nomenclature of the various nonpolitical individual character types. Despite their superficial descriptive aspects, these terms have assumed deep bioenergetic significance because of Reich's discovery of the function of character armor in determining human behavior. Similarly, the different sociopolitical character types describe profound differences in the behavior and attitudes of individuals whose expression is primarily, but not exclusively, in the sociopolitical realm. That the basis of these ideological distinctions is far deeper than the superficial sociopolitical realm is evidenced by the fact that they extend into major aspects of human functioning, such as thinking, work habits, and sexuality. These aspects will be discussed in Part II. Baker's identification of the "liberal" and "conservative" thus highlights the *biophysical basis* for the sociopolitical behavior of the left and the right, since one's sociopolitical character type, and not necessarily political party membership, determines one's political ideology. Baker's standardization of sociopolitical character types makes clear that the character structure of liberals and conservatives living in widely different cultures such as Western and Islamic societies are identical. (See chapter 8, The Democratization of Islam)

Baker arrives at these distinctions in sociopolitical character from his interactions with patients and from his biophysical observations of them during medical orgone therapy. Clinical experience reveals that the ocular armor of individuals on the political left, manifested by their defensive intellectualism, is more entrenched and more difficult to eliminate in therapy than such armor is in individuals on the political right. In conservatives, armor resides primarily in the musculature. With the discharge of rage from the muscles during the course of therapy, ocular armor manifested in the conservative's distorted political thinking is usually eliminated. However, persistent mystical tendencies, also an indication of ocular armoring, may render individuals on the political right more or less refractory to therapy.

Success in therapy depends on whether the patient's political ideology is relatively superficial (i.e., of recent environmental origin), or innate and structural. If superficial, the terms *environmental liberal* and *environmental conservative* apply. These people hold political views contrary to their true sociopolitical character structure because of environmental factors. Therefore, people's underlying sociopolitical structure must be distinguished from the political party to which they belong. Two factors determine an individual's affiliation with a given political party: basic sociopolitical character structure and the extent to which the environment alters this basic structure. In American politics, some Democrats are characterological conservatives and some Republicans are characterological liberals or pseudo-liberals. An example of the latter is present-day New York City Mayor Michael Bloomberg.

The following clinical vignette illustrates the origin and function of sociopolitical ideology.

> A forty-seven-year-old photographer came to therapy because of his inability to feel. His tendency to hold emotions in through stiffness and aloofness was greatly

> mitigated in the course of therapy, resulting in increased satisfaction in his personal and social life. At a certain point, the patient began to experience a return of his old symptoms of emotional deadness, indecisiveness, and dissatisfaction. Unable to overcome his frustrations, he began to argue with me about sociopolitical issues, complaining about the meanness and cruelty of President George Bush. Without confronting the patient on the level of an intellectual discussion, I encouraged him to express his dislike of President Bush on the couch. The patient responded by kicking, hitting, and screaming out progressively more vitriolic hatred toward his target. After this emotional discharge, his hatred of President Bush subsided, and he recognized that "Poor Bush didn't deserve all that hatred." In later sessions, he realized that, in reality, this hatred was really toward his own father, a self-righteous and cold individual. The patient became politically less polarized, and his hatred of President Bush has now almost disappeared.[27]

Sociopolitical Characters on the Left

The development of liberalism was an attempt to break away from the chains of repression and mysticism that held humanity in bondage for millennia. Seeking knowledge and reason as a solution to the human dilemma, people began to demand greater freedom from both their masters and their gods. Biophysically unprepared to accept and handle this freedom, they became anxious and guilt-ridden. This was a reaction to their inability to express their core feelings. Despite this biological impediment, liberalism has persistently appealed to armored humans. To further complicate matters, many Americans espouse liberal causes and ideas not because they are characterologically liberal, but because of the prevailing liberal sociopolitics in their environment. These individuals are designated *environmental liberals.* They grow up in a liberal environment but liberalism never becomes part of their structure, and their liberal ideas are given up spontaneously with therapy.

Liberal characters fall into three categories and are placed at different distances from healthy functioning according to their

27. Alberto Foglia, M.D., personal communication.

degree of disturbance (see Fig. 2.4 later in this chapter). From the standpoint of sociopolitical behavior and thinking, the true liberal is one step to the left of healthy functioning, the socialist is to the left of the true liberal, and the pseudo-liberal (or communist) is to the left of the socialist. At the farthest extreme, the pseudo-liberal is an emotional plague character par excellence.[28]

The True Liberal

The true liberal stands to the left side of a healthy attitude toward life. Although such persons express rational impulses and ideas, their intellect has assumed a defensive function against impulses from the destructive secondary layer. Historically, through an intellectual approach and activities, the liberal was able to produce greater emotional and social freedom than had existed in the past. Then, however, the intellect was called upon to defend armored humans from the consequences of this freedom.

Unable to tolerate bodily emotions and sensations, the liberal pulls energy up into the ocular segment, particularly into the brain, which then, through the defensive use of the intellect, deadens emotional expression from both the core and the secondary layer. Core contact is partially or completely lost. One direct social consequence of this is that liberals favor the absolute separation of church and state.

True liberals live in a world of words and ideas, which function as a defense against emotional expression. Words and ideas assume a reality of their own and, in a vicious cycle, this self-deception gives liberals the idea that that they are, in fact, realists, whereas they actually function essentially as idealists. They appear to be "up in their heads"—hence, the term "egghead." Their feelings often give the appearance of being deeply felt, but this is illusory since they are derived from the intellect, not from emotional contact. Hence, they are sentimentalists. Liberals cannot experience deep emotional and physical satisfaction since their lives are governed by intellectual, idealistic principles. They are typically nice people who sincerely believe that everyone, including convicted criminals and America's enemies, are capable of

---

28. Baker placed the socialist to the left of the "modern liberal" character. I do not believe this is correct. See the discussion of Figure 2.3.

changing and behaving as nicely and fairly as they themselves do. Attitudes and ideas that revolve around lofty *intentions*—"sincerity," "commitment," and "dedication to world peace"—are adopted and are central to their value system, but their ideas are not grounded in practical experience and therefore cannot bear fruit in genuine social improvement. Similarly, the liberal's patriotic feelings originate from the intellect and not from the biological core. As a result, loyalty to America and its fundamental principles is easily shaken and undermined by the confusing and destructive rhetoric of the pseudo-liberal.

Liberals have no sense of the central role of character in determining all human behavior. As a result, they are driven to find superficial, symptomatic remedies of all types for social problems. They therefore emphasize idealistic methods, rather than practical solutions that go to the heart of society's sickness. Thus, for example, government-funded educational programs become cure-alls. Little thought is given to the destructive consequences of programs undertaken in pursuit of these goals. Historical precedent and experience are ignored. Instead, liberals have a naïve belief in the perfectibility of all human beings and believe that even hardened criminals, through caring and economic and educational improvement, can be rescued. What typically happens, however, is that the very people who are supposed to be helped end up feeling contempt and hatred for the liberal's well-intentioned efforts.

A symptom of anxiety is a sense of urgency to bring about social improvement. Anxiety also leads to looking to society to provide a feeling of belonging and security that can extend even to irrational ideas of world-wide brotherhood. Liberals attempt to overcome their contactless state through substitute activities by associating with other intellectuals who support their way of thinking.

The erroneous belief that the body is controlled by the brain is projected outward and this is the reason liberals support measures advocating centralized control in every area of social life. This belief also promotes "politically correct" behavior, which comes from the need for external rules and regulations over people's lives. The view of political correctness is based (1) on a vision of a "classless society," a society not merely of equal opportunity but of equal conditions, and (2) on a single-factor, mechanistically causal explanation of history in which a certain group—defined by sex, race, and sexual orientation—has power over other groups. Political correctness is the pseudo-liberals' application of the mechanistic economic thinking of Marx to social behavior. It is a form of moralistic thinking that aims to bring about a society of radical egalitarianism, enforced by the power of the state (Lind 1999).[29] In actual fact, political correctness is an expression of masked racism in which certain preferred minority groups (blacks, Hispanics, feminists, homosexuals, and some others) are believed a priori to be virtuous, while other classes of people are believed to be evil, without regard to the actual behavior of individuals. It does not recognize individual differences between people such as nonfeminist women or conservative blacks and conservative homosexuals. Political correctness functions through expropriation, penalizing some groups and granting privileges to others, as is done through policies of affirmative action. The method of analysis called deconstruction "proves" the correctness of the ideology. People conform to the pseudo-liberal's rules of politically correct behavior out of their own feelings of anxiety and guilt. If it becomes the rule, the end result will be the transformation of American society into a socialist state.

The orgonometric relationship between the true liberal and the pseudo-liberal is one of attractive opposition. Pseudo-liberal politicians and the intelligentsia in charge of the media seize upon the anxiety and confusion that they themselves help to generate and present the public with socialistic, politically correct nostrums and government programs they deem necessary for the public good. The confused, liberal-indoctrinated masses passively accede to these programs because to oppose them is to open oneself up to accusations of bigotry. This tactic of the emotional plague plays on the guilt of virtually every armored person. It not only creates sympathy for the "victim" and the "downtrodden," the chosen minority who suffer because of "oppression" by the "evil upper class," but also transfers political power to them, further undermining the authoritarian order of society.

In reality, the liberal's mandate for greater freedom has been practically accomplished in only one area of social life, in the

29. This is not true for libertarians. They see freedom and economic progress as the solution to society's problems.

technological advances made by mechanistic science and medicine. People now have washing machines, television and artificial heart valves, but the origin and treatment of human bioemotional problems remain as poorly understood and ignored today as in the past. (See chapter 9)

True liberals adhere to social justice as an ideal. They are not blinded by ideology and are potentially open to reason and facts that contradict their preconceptions. Unlike those further to the left, they honestly believe in the importance of fair play and the laws that apply to one and all.

The liberal's defensive use of the intellect is a manifestation of ocular armor. However, the liberal's intellect can only ward off his or her *own* destructive impulses. He or she cannot use it to respond rationally to or prevent the expression of the destructive secondary layer of others. The liberal is an idealist believing that all human problems are amenable to negotiated solutions and that all people, no matter how socially destructive, deep down share a universal spirit of goodwill and brotherhood. For the liberal, evil does not exist. The war on terrorism is a figment of right-wing imagination. If only America would stop its aggressive policies throughout the world and leave the Islamic people alone, so the reasoning goes, there would be peace. This is a defensive attitude, a denial of the mortal danger that America and the Western world face from the Islamic fanatics. It originates from the liberal's need to remain stuck in the superficial layer of his armor and serves to oppose experiencing aggressive impulses from his own destructive secondary layer. The liberal may even believe in the reality of the emotional plague, but only as an idea. He or she has difficulty recognizing individuals actually afflicted with it.

Because the liberal fears aggressive impulses from the biological core, he or she abhors the use of force. The necessity of using force is an admission of the limitation of the liberal's power of reason and a threat to the defensive intellectualization which is directed against his own destructive impulses. For the same reason, liberal ideology precludes acknowledging the existence of intractable hatred, or intransigent political will.[30]

---

30. This trait of English liberals was a major factor in starting the First World War. It was well known at the time that every Englishman, including the prime minister, his colleagues, advisors, and English people throughout the world, hated the idea of war and would have done—and in fact did—everything possible to avert it. The German military, sensing this reluctance, believed that they could pursue their expansionist policies. They tragically misjudged the situation (Oliver 1916).

Incapable of sustaining the use of force, liberals favor faint-hearted diplomacy, ineffectual economic sanctions, and ideological rhetoric (crusading against human rights violations) to oppose governments that encourage violence. History has repeatedly shown that this method of containing the emotional plague does not work. In fact, it is viewed by the aggressor individual or nation as appeasement and is invariably exploited, met with contempt, or viewed as an open invitation for more hostility. Ultimately, the liberal's method of curbing destructive activity proves to be more socially destructive in the long run than the threat or direct use of force.

The reason for the liberal's incapacity to counteract destructive activity in others is that, because contact with the biological core is weak, aggressive impulses from the core also are weak. Fascist rulers on the left and right who seek world domination always have had an intuitive sense of and contempt for the liberals' incapacity to be forceful and to resolutely oppose their expansionism. Think of Khrushchev's arrogance toward the liberal John F. Kennedy during the Cuban Missile Crisis or Hitler's disdain of Franklin D. Roosevelt prior to the Second World War. The same interaction is occurring today between the liberal leaders of Western democracies and the Arab fundamentalists (Black Fascists) and North Korean Communists (Red Fascists). Because they fear aggression, liberals are much more likely than sociopolitical characters on the right to be intimidated by and succumb to emotional and political blackmail. Liberals are blind to the reality that the Free World is in a life-and-death struggle with an enemy that despises Western values and considers them the epitome of decadence and weakness. This blindness is an example of *contactlessness.*

The usefulness of liberalism as a social philosophy came to an end when the masses first became in charge of their own destiny; that is, when monarchies were overthrown and formal democracies were first established in America and across Europe. Liberal philosophy has never been able to go beyond that and be able to handle the enormous social problems that have resulted from people having to take care of themselves.

Why today's liberalism cannot contain human destructiveness and why *it is itself a destructive social force* can be understood by its historical origins. Liberalism arose as a healthy reaction to the rampant mysticism of the Middle Ages. However, limitations of knowledge at that time made it impossible to distinguish between the destructive elements of mysticism, which legitimately required opposition, and the constructive core impulses embedded in it. *As a result, liberalism eventually changed from being a rational response against mysticism, and thus from being a life-positive force, into a defense against both mysticism and genuine religious feelings and ideas originating from the biological core.* Paradoxically, liberalism today has become more tolerant of unhealthy expression originating from the destructive secondary layer than of any natural expression of healthy core impulses (i.e., more accepting of licentiousness than of genuine freedom). This is because secondary layer impulses, the revenge component anchored in armored humanity's sociopolitical attitudes, are closer to the surface and more easily accessible to the liberal's character structure than the deeper biological core impulses.

The defensive use of the intellect causes liberals to be out of touch with destructive impulses from their own and others' secondary layer by denying their existence, and helpless in dealing with social problems involving destructive aggression in others. For example, the liberal cannot protect the crime victim, not out of any personal antipathy, but because the liberal is biophysically unable to rise to preventive action. (This limitation is felt as guilt.) Such action calls into question the deepest convictions of liberals and shakes their character structure to its core. As a result, the liberal's intellectual façade necessarily supports expression of the secondary layer of others. One sees this daily in their inability to use the criminal justice system to effectively implement law enforcement, and in their intolerance of the aggressive manner in which America and Israel are conducting the war against Islamic terrorists. Through fear of aggression, which is rationalized as a desire for peace, the liberal identifies with the emotional plague in others and masochistically submits to them. (See chapter 8)

The Socialist

The aim of socialism is to transfer the means of production from private ownership to the ownership of organized society, the state. Cut off from the core, the socialist, like the true liberal, lives in a world of words and ideas. But the socialist takes the liberal's defensive intellectualism and idealism even further. Socialists are blinded by their longing for the realization of their sociopolitical dreams. They have constructed a complex thought system designed to solve every one of the world's problems. They are collectivists and therefore oppose private property and support its confiscation by the state. Personal responsibility is replaced by collective, state responsibility. The wealthy few are seen as guilty of and responsible for the deprivation and misery of the poor masses. Socialists believe that only the state can, with justice, direct and protect the interests of everyone and provide economic security. Valued above personal freedom, economic security is considered the right of all and the cure of the world's ills. Socialists stress what are supposed to be the evils of capitalism. For the socialist, capitalism has failed and must lead to imperialism and totalitarianism. Socialists deny the natural differences in individuals and long for a classless society through confiscation of private property and taxation of the wealthy, whereby riches and material possessions are equally dispersed. Egalitarian to an extreme, the socialist believes that unequally distributed wealth is *the primary cause* of social problems and that only its redistribution will bring peace and harmony to the world. The transfer of wealth is implemented primarily through tax legislation whereby those with a higher work capacity, and hence greater income, must provide for those with a lesser work capacity.

The socialist state is like a zoo, wherein all of its inhabitants are cared for but individuals are not free to rely on their own initiative to survive or to reach maximal functioning. The movement toward socialism in our society is both a consequence and a perpetuator of human armor. Punishing productivity and rewarding lack of initiative destroy the individual's ability to work and reduces society to the lowest level of social functioning.

The Pseudo-liberal or Neo-communist (Red Fascist)

Communists and socialists aim to socialize the means of production. Only sociopolitical tactics differentiate communism from socialism. Socialists are overt whereas communists are covert in their attempt to achieve their goal. We have stated earlier that the ideological content of a person's thinking may not be a true indication of character structure. During the post-Revolutionary War period in America, for example, the ideological content of the pseudo-liberal or neo-communist character was different from what it is now. Then, these individuals espoused many of the ideas advocated by conservatives today. What characterizes the pseudo-liberal character of all ages is a narrow-minded, rigid idealism in defiance of all realistic considerations. The character structure of the pseudo-liberal is deceptively similar to that of the true liberal and the socialist, but his beliefs and attitudes are even more extreme. More often than not, the pseudo-liberal is the pathogenic agent of the emotional plague while the liberal under his influence is the carrier that spreads the pestilence.[31] Whereas the pseudo-liberal's façade serves the expression of the secondary layer, the liberal's façade defends against it.

Characterologically, the motives and actions of pseudo-liberals exactly oppose those of true liberals. Pseudo-liberals are actually communists who live in a noncommunist, free society. Since it is not fashionable in this day and age to openly espouse communist principles, the pseudo-liberal must escape social detection by publicly appearing to identify with the true liberal. Before pseudo-liberals can act out their social destructiveness, they must first establish their credibility by masquerading as loyal Americans. Pretending to defend against the destructive middle layer is one of the cardinal traits of the communist and is evidence that the two character types are identical. The pseudo-liberal's unstated agenda—to socialize American society and subjugate America to the authority of the United Nations—is identical to the bygone Soviet Union's stated goal of world-wide socialism. The only difference is that with the demise of the Soviet Union, it has been replaced by the United Nations as the center of power. *Liberals are typically blind to the true identity and intentions of the pseudo-liberal, and they therefore automatically support the pseudo-liberal's ideological agenda as their own.* Both the communist and the pseudo-liberal function as political plague characters to the extreme left on the sociopolitical spectrum. They have the same

31. Baker called the pseudo-liberal the "modern liberal" character type. However, this term is misleading. These individuals are not truly liberal, nor is their appearance a recent phenomenon. It is more accurate to use the designation "neo-communist."

avowed goal: to destroy democracy in America, centralize power and politically control society.[32]

The pseudo-liberal is a political radical, and he carries himself with a solemn social façade that conveys an air of moral superiority, all the while expressing destructive secondary impulses through well-thought-out rationalizations. A covert hatred of America is thinly veiled by an affectation of being a "citizen of the world." Pseudo-liberals feel that any difference between *what* Americans and Europeans believe is a sign that Americans are simplistic and need to "listen" to the more sophisticated and learned Europeans. When their defenses are threatened, pseudo-liberals become openly contemptuous, derisive, and respond with verbal formulas and sarcasm. Pseudo-liberals have an unshakable conviction in their own infallibility and intellectual and moral superiority. Attempts to disturb their defensive ideology shakes them to the very core of their defenses and stirs up hatred. The pseudo-liberal righteously holds onto his or her ideology for dear life. I have seen these individuals in social situations lash out with hatred even when they were not being threatened.

The ideologies of the true liberal and the pseudo-liberal are deceptively similar. However, pseudo-liberals expound theirs not for its own sake, but *because it bestows a sense of righteousness and purposefulness leading to sociopolitical action.* Like the communist, the pseudo-liberal's concern for the downtrodden shows itself to be mere pretense if, by chance, such a person, as a political leader, gains governmental control. Witness the behavior of Stalin and Castro before and after assuming power. The pseudo-liberal's ideology justifies his hatred for those in society whom he wishes to tear down. As a substitute for genital potency, the pseudo-liberal acts and lives entirely in the intellect, in this respect resembling the phallic-narcissistic individual who uses his erect penis to pierce his environment in order to feel superior. Pseudo-liberals use their intellect and hauteur as a weapon to pierce anyone who threatens their belief system. Phallic contempt is replaced by intellectual contempt, arrogance, and clever verbal castration. The pseudo-liberal's wit is barbed, amusing, and

32. Thomas Sowell refers to these types as "the anointed ones." Those who accept their vision are deemed to be not merely factually correct but on a higher moral plane (Sowell 1995, page 3).

almost always at the expense of others. Coupled with the defensive use of the intellect, the pseudo-liberal subscribes to a brand of anti-intellectual populism, political correctness.

Pseudo-liberals lack genuine kindness, but their display of concern for the downtrodden in their various causes stops all argument. Anyone who "feels so deeply" about social injustice must surely be above reproach, they rationalize. Anyone opposed to present-day reparations for American blacks for the past events of slavery is accused of being insensitive at best or racist at worst. A recent campus demonstration in response to an ad in a student newspaper entitled "Ten Reasons Why Reparations for Slavery Are a Bad Idea and Racist, Too" produced comments such as "It hurts so much" from one protester and "Indescribably hurtful" from another. Another person's reaction was "Disrespectful to the minority population . . . it was completely opposed to what I've been taught" (Leo 2001).

Through the ideology of political correctness, the pseudo-liberal divides the world into "oppressors" and "the oppressed," with only those they have chosen as being oppressed having the right to free speech. Pseudo-liberals, for example, make much of their compassion for the less fortunate, their concern for the environment, and their antiwar sentiments—as if these attitudes distinguish them from people with opposite views on social issues. Through intellectualization and reaction formation, the pseudo-liberal places himself on higher moral ground. He has withdrawn energy from the pelvis up to the brain and uses intellectualization as a primary defense against feeling emotion, especially guilt and anxiety. These feelings color and pervade all of his attitudes. Free-floating anxiety makes it seem imperative to pseudo-liberals that social programs be initiated immediately. Because of this ever-present sense of urgency, they favor revolutionary rather than evolutionary tactics,[33] and advocate governmental social planning at the federal rather than the local level.

Thomas Sowell outlines the following steps leading to political activism:

---

33. The pseudo-liberal Hillary Clinton gave a commencement speech at the University of Texas in April of 1993. The *New York Times* Sunday Magazine reported that because she wrote this speech so soon after the death of her father, she used it to pour out her innermost feelings. The central point of this speech was to "redefine who we are as human beings in this post-modern age," something that requires "remolding society" and "reinventing our institutions." And, of course, the engine of all this change is government.

1. Assertions of a great danger to the whole society, a danger to which the masses of people are oblivious;
2. An urgent need for action to avert impending catastrophe;
3. A need for government to drastically curtail the dangerous behavior of the many in response to the prescient conclusions of the few; and
4. A disdainful dismissal of arguments to the contrary as uninformed, irresponsible, or motivated by unworthy purposes. (Sowell 1995, page 5)

Through sociopolitical activity, the pseudo-liberal acts out unconscious personal conflicts in daily life. Behind these is the unresolved Oedipal conflict with the authoritarian father, against whom the pseudo-liberal is in secret rebellion. Because of an Oedipal fear of open competition, however, the pseudo-liberal hates both competition and the father. Thus, the pseudo-liberal identifies with the underdog, the loser, and the indolent. Subversively defiant, the pseudo-liberal is incapable of openly showing aggression. Aggression is covertly expressed through ideological activism and anti-authoritarian causes. In these ideological crusades, they express their hatred of the father through revenge on society. Favoring international solutions whenever possible, the pseudo-liberal identifies America with the hated father and holds both in contempt. They also associate tradition and traditionalism with the father and go to great lengths to undermine social custom and convention. This is why pseudo-liberals disdain learning from history and will distort and rewrite historical events to suit their cherished beliefs. Pseudo-liberals will even redefine words to suit their sociopolitical agenda, such as “harassment,” “discrimination,” “homophobia,” “violence,” and so on.

The pseudo-liberal’s pretended egalitarianism is a direct consequence of his intellectualism, guilt, fear, and hatred of the father. Feeling guilty for the success or advantages they enjoy, pseudo-liberals are opposed to differences in social status. This guilt is relieved if the pseudo-liberal can feel that all people are the same. No one (the father) is better, no one (the criminal, drug addict, even the terrorist) is worse than them (Baker 1967). Because of their guilt, pseudo-liberals tolerate every form of pathological behavior, including criminal and psychopathic behavior. This is because they unconsciously identify with sociopaths, vicariously deriving pleasure from their aggressive, guilt-free behavior. Indulging the criminal is rationalized as an enlightened, modern attitude of *understanding* the criminal. Pseudo-liberals cannot effectively oppose criminal activity because punishing the criminal activates guilt and interferes with their ability to suppress their own criminal impulses. Additionally, except for giving lip service to the contrary, the pseudo-liberal opposes whatever represents greatness in human life and supports everything that drags society down to the lowest level of existence. Like the socialist, the pseudo-liberal expects the government to remove all differences among people.

The pseudo-liberal views the military and police with fear and contempt because (1) the purpose of these groups is to protect and preserve society, not to destroy it; (2) these are not intellectual careers but active, aggressive ones; and (3) persons involved in these careers represent authority figures. Pseudo-liberals deride what they cannot accept. That the military and police provide for their personal safety at great peril to their own lives, evokes no feeling of admiration or gratitude.

The Infestation of the Political Left by the Emotional Plague

The pseudo-liberal succeeds in his destructive activity by masquerading as a true liberal. On the other hand, the true liberal unwittingly follows the pseudo-liberal's sociopolitical agenda. Confounding these two character types has had numerous disastrous social consequences, not the least of which has been the change in the relationship of the true liberal and the true conservative from attractive to antagonistic opposition. As a result, the conservative attacks *all* liberals, true and pseudo-, as if they were one and the same, resulting in endless political battles on practically every social issue including, in particular, questions of national security. It is therefore vitally necessary to make a clear distinction between them. Knowledge of sociopolitical characterology allows one to tell these different sociopolitical character types apart. The following are some of their distinguishing features:

True Liberal	Pseudo-Liberal
Intellectual defense against secondary layer	Pretense at intellectual defense against secondary layer
Pro-American	Anti-American, Internationalist
Authoritarian (respects authority)	Anti-authoritarian (resents authority)
Egalitarian	Falsely egalitarian
Supports democratic ideals	Supports socialist ideals
Political idealist	Political activist

Comparing the salient traits of the true liberal shown above with those of the conservative reveals that both are, essentially, very similar. Their social and political beliefs differ only in degree. *Yet, today the true liberal functions ideologically like the pseudo-liberal because of the operation of the emotional plague.* The true liberal has become the host infected with the plague by the pseudo-liberal who is the carrier or vector.

How did the liberal become infected? Many liberals unconsciously began shifting to the left and supporting communism when the evilness of Black Fascism first came to light during the Second World War. During that war, the U.S. government was infested with Soviet agents. However, the infection did not really take hold of the American liberal populace until the McCarthy era. With the fall of Senator McCarthy, the pseudo-liberal's entrance into the liberal mainstream was ensured. The clear-cut distinction that had always existed between the communist/pseudo-liberal and the true liberal became totally and permanently obfuscated. By blurring the differences between them, the pseudo-liberal succeeded in passing himself off as a true liberal and henceforth increasingly became the dominant voice of the political left. It must be remembered, however, that until the middle half of the twentieth century in America, the ideologies of the true liberal and the conservative were fundamentally alike.[34] Once the infec-

34. The conservative movement in America developed strength in the 1950s and the early 1960s as a reaction to this development. However, there have been characterologically conservative individuals throughout history. Many of them identified themselves as liberals in prior times.

tion took hold, the true liberal and the communist/pseudo-liberal character functioned sociopolitically as one and the same. The left's infestation with the plague in large part contributed to the transformation of society from authoritarian to anti-authoritarian. Among the many destructive consequences of this transformation was the ideological polarization of the left and the right, and the intensification of irreconcilable political differences over vital social issues that we see today in America. As noted, from then on, the relationship between the left and the right changed from attractive opposition to antagonistic opposition. (See figures 2.1, 2.2 and chapter 6)

As part of their unstated goal to wreak havoc on American society as it currently exists, pseudo-liberals attempt to subvert and destroy virtually every important legitimate function of government. They energetically support governmental activities that are not in its jurisdiction, such as assuming responsibility for taking care of the public, and oppose activities that are basic functions, such as protecting America from its enemies. Consider, as an example, the left's opposition to America's effort to establish democracy in Iraq and the Middle East. The liberal plays into the hands of the pseudo-liberal plague individual because he, the liberal, is also not comfortable with aggression. Liberals were easily intimidated by Saddam Hussein's Stalin-like benevolent persona. Blind to the pseudo-liberal's malevolent intent, the liberal cooperates with his political agenda.

The left's fear of direct confrontation and open aggression is demonstrated by their inability to tell the difference between its healthy and destructive manifestations. Seen from the deepest bioenergetic standpoint, the pseudo-liberal's fear of aggression is rooted in a *terror of biophysical collapse*. They project this fear onto the external world as a dread of violence, biological or chemical warfare, and atomic disaster. This fear also gives rise to a compensatory need to "belong" in the form of social dependency.

Pseudo-liberals confuse all forms of dictatorship on the right with fascism, while turning a blind eye to revolutionary regimes on the left or somehow equating them with democracy. To avoid confusion, therefore, we must distinguish between dictatorships on the right, such as Franco's Spain or Pinochet's Chile, and a true fascist state. Dictatorships are formed in a last-ditch attempt to maintain the authoritarian social order and to retain whatever level of freedom the armored masses can tolerate. In contrast, fascist states on the left and right permit no personal or economic freedom at all.

The following case illustrates the therapy of a pseudo-liberal character.

> A twenty-four-year-old, highly talented artist came for therapy. After having read some of Wilhelm Reich's books, he was especially impressed by the concept of genitality and his stated reason for seeking therapy was to become a genital character.
>
> From early adolescence he had been attracted to leftist ideas. He felt himself to be a believer in communism and espoused its doctrines, often provocatively, knowing that they would upset most listeners. He was highly intelligent and spoke in an intellectual, "heady" manner. He was openly contemptuous and envious of artists he considered better than himself. He showed undisguised contempt for people with conservative political attitudes. His therapy took place during a time in which the Soviet Union was intact, and he spoke with admiration of the achievements of communism, extolling the accomplishments of the people whom he considered exemplary products of the Soviet system.
>
> The most prominent aspect of his physical appearance was the size of his head, which was disproportionately large. His eyes appeared in good contact but at times expressed wariness and fear. His biophysical examination was remarkable for the absence of significant armor in the lower segments, except for pelvic armor.
>
> His initial experiences with his previous medical orgone therapist had been positive. There had been an improvement in his emotional well-being and his positive response to therapy had bolstered his preconceptions as to the benefits of medical orgone therapy. He saw no conflict between his leftist ideology and Reich's ideas and, in fact, was under the false impression that Reich's social ideas were in harmony with his own. This mistaken assumption was due to the fact that his previous therapy had not addressed his character defenses. As a result, that therapy quickly reached an impasse. The patient was then referred to me.

> Once work on his character began in earnest, and once his covert hatred of authority and contempt for people was pointed out, his seemingly positive transference to me suddenly disappeared. He became contemptuous and derisive of me and disillusioned with therapy. He terminated treatment. He developed an interest in behaviorism, claiming that this form of therapy was objective and therefore superior to the clinical approach of medical orgone therapy. His disappointment turned into bitter hatred and he vowed to write an exposé of the shortcomings of medical orgone therapy but never did. His intense defensive reaction was a clear indication that he had been confronted with aspects of his character that he could not face.

It is not possible to eliminate the pseudo-liberal's ideological defenses in the course of medical orgone therapy. Baker posited a qualitative difference in the protoplasm of the pseudo-liberal character to account for the therapeutic difficulty. This difference is likely the result of a severe disturbance in the capacity for true emotional contact, especially an inability to accurately perceive strong emotional charge from the core and the secondary layer. The energy contained in emotions, which originate from the vegetative centers of the abdominal and pelvic segments, has been shifted upward from the core and becomes concentrated in the brain, serving a defensive function. This understanding helps explain why the pseudo-liberal cannot experience deep emotions, and cannot recognize and respond appropriately to the expression of core emotions or to the destructive behavior of others.[35]

35. For an understanding of the biosocial determinants of sociopolitical thinking, see Konia, C. 2001. The Biophysical Basis of Sociopolitical Thought. *Journal of Orgonomy* 35(1).

The Pseudo-liberal in American History

Whether the pseudo-liberal character is a recent development in the history of armored humans is unknown. We can hypothesize that a tendency for the pseudo-liberal type, as distinguished from the true liberal, has always existed but that they did not appear in great numbers until relatively recent times when people had to assume political and social responsibility for their survival. From historical accounts, we can surmise that before the Enlightenment people were not as well defended against the direct expression of emotion from the secondary layer. This stage of social development coincided with a formidable and defensive development of the intellect. Prior to the Age of Reason, overt expression from the destructive secondary layer was socially tolerated, if not fully accepted. Around the late eighteenth and the early nineteenth century, energy contained in the secondary layer and held in the voluntary musculature (where it manifests in overt sadism, hatred, etc.) shifted upward to the brain. The French Revolution and the period that followed is a classic example. Intellectual development at this time had fostered a belief in natural law, universal order, and confidence in human reason. The period of the Enlightenment most probably gave rise in the public arena to large numbers of individuals with a liberal or pseudo-liberal character structure. This was the time when responsibility for the care of the members of society was shifted and placed squarely in the hands of the people themselves.

Today, the pestilent pseudo-liberal character pervades every circle of social influence. Consequentially, the emotional plague has spread through all areas of social life, both nationally and internationally. Baker first identified this character type in the early 1960s, when Western society was transforming from an authoritarian to an anti-authoritarian form. Although Baker had a clearer picture than Reich of the deadly nature of this sociopolitical type, the true significance of the pseudo-liberal character had not yet been fully revealed. Baker therefore placed the pseudo-liberal to the right of the socialist in his schema and referred to this sociopolitical character as a "collectivist." Social events since then have made it abundantly clear that *the pseudo-liberal is a far greater threat than the socialist*, and that this character type is not substantively different from the communist. Consider that many revolutionaries in the forefront of the leftist movements of the 1960s and 1970s in America are today placed in the highest positions of social influence in education, politics, and the media. These well-heeled revolutionaries are the intelligentsia directly responsible for molding public opinion according to their leftist ideology. As pollsters, in turn, gather public opinion data, the predominant results of which reflect leftist views, the political center continues to shift further and further to the left. The pseudo-liberals' destructive effect on America as a society and an independent nation has reached crisis proportions.

Illusions as to the pseudo-liberal's agenda are no longer possible. Their agenda is to destroy the authoritarian social order in Western democracies by causing chaos, and to replace it with anti-authoritarianism. If successful, this will necessarily lead to some form of centralized government of the communist type. The intentions of pseudo-liberals today in America are exactly the same as those of the Bolsheviks prior to the downfall of the czarist government of Russia in 1917—to destroy the existing social fabric of society.

Examination of United States history reveals that, in conjunction with accommodating liberals, the pseudo-liberal has been wreaking havoc on American life since its founding, at times bringing this nation to the brink of disaster. For example, an evaluation of historical materials relating to Thomas Jefferson indicates that he was a pseudo-liberal character. Although Jefferson is revered and remembered as the author of the Declaration of Independence, his many disastrous political blunders as secretary of state in George Washington's cabinet and later as president of the United States have been ignored. Chief among them were his attempts to undermine the formation of a strong union of states after the War of Independence (see Oliver 1928, page 270). His efforts rendered the infant nation vulnerable to attack by hostile governments. Also, he maintained that states' rights had precedence over those of the Union, and this emboldened the states of the Deep South to believe that they could successfully secede through force of arms. Had the Union been stronger from its inception, with the individual states functioning as integrated components within the whole as Washington and Hamilton had wanted, the issue of the abolition of slavery would likely have been settled peacefully and the catastrophe of the Civil War avoided.

Likewise, in the Citizen Genêt affair, Jefferson's pseudo-liberal egalitarianism almost caused a disastrous war between America and Great Britain. Shortly after the French Revolution, France declared war on Great Britain and Holland. In 1793, after the French Revolution, France sent a minister, Citizen Genêt, to ask the United States to declare war against the English. When Genêt arrived in America, Jefferson embraced him with open arms and supported the French plan. Genêt appealed to the people for support, knowing that many were sympathetic to France. He also engaged American privateers to prey on British shipping and provided armaments. Everywhere Genêt went, he spoke enthusiastically of the alliance between the two republics as though it already existed.

In response, Hamilton wrote a series of newspaper essays that began to turn the tide of public opinion and, at Washington's request, he drafted effective legal rules to enforce American neutrality. Hamilton later drafted letters to Genêt and the American ambassador in Paris demanding Genêt's recall. Jefferson, the secretary of state, was obliged to append his signature to them. Jefferson's doctrine, that "French ships and privateers may come and go freely, English ships may not," was emphatically repudiated.

Other historical examples abound. When war erupted in Europe in 1914, President Wilson, who also was a pseudo-liberal, proclaimed neutrality and urged the United States to be "impartial in thought as well as action . . . neutral in fact as well as in name." Wilson identified strongly with Jesus Christ and saw himself as a great statesman whose mission was to resolve the European conflict and bring about world peace (see Freud and Bullitt 1967). Wilson was also an idealist with an extraordinary ability to ignore facts and an enormous belief in the reality of words. He had a repressed phallic character structure (a "minister" type), and behind this façade there was an intolerance of aggression. It was this that caused his fear of direct, forceful confrontation and the need to avoid open conflict.

Despite Wilson's pledge of strict neutrality, his actions belied his words. Openly violating his own promise of neutrality, he allowed massive economic and military support in the form of cargoes shipped primarily to Britain and its allies. Profits for American businessmen soared. These supplies simply fanned the flames of this protracted conflict, and also alienated Germany. Had Wilson more clearly assessed the situation, he would have acted in accordance with his own policy of neutrality and restricted commerce to both sides. The European conflict might well have burned itself out and been contained to the Continent. People were already war-weary and would have stopped fighting if the prospect of America entering the conflict had not been imminent.

To make matters worse, in 1916, Wilson meddled in the conflict as a "peacemaker," inflaming the Germans' arrogant hostility with his confused and vacillating manner. He did nothing to soften the absurd demands of the Allies and drew the United States inexorably and helplessly into the war. The consequences for the world were disastrous. After the armistice, Wilson, who had devoted much of his life to developing eloquence in public speech, mesmerized Europe with his idealistic vision of peace, but then proved himself incapable of marshaling enough personal aggression to even oppose the harsh and punitive Versailles Treaty. The effect was to cause irrational social longing throughout the world. When this longing was not fulfilled, it increased mass social anxiety. These events contributed to the destruction of the fabric of German society, destabilized the entire continent of Europe, and started Germany's slide into political extremism on the left (the rise of German Communism) and the reaction to it on the right (Nazism). Thus, Wilson's "war to end all wars . . . to make the world safe for democracy," led directly to the tragedy of the Second World War and the subsequent rise of world communism. Wilson spent the remainder of his public life pursuing yet another hopelessly idealistic project, his flawed plan to achieve permanent world peace through the League of Nations.

The relationship between Roosevelt, a true liberal, and Stalin, a communist, during the Second World War illustrates the affinity between the liberal and the emotional plague character.[36] FDR was a superb political tactician, a master of public relations, and

36. The relationship between British Prime Minister Neville Chamberlain and Hitler is another example of the affinity of the true liberal character for the emotional plague character.

a patrician. He was also extremely naïve and often ignorant about global political strategy. Like most liberals, he took the Soviet Union at face value—as a self-described, peace-loving "people's democracy" with a genuine desire to improve the working conditions of people all over the world. Despite the many who warned Roosevelt about Stalin's true nature, including Winston Churchill, FDR naively trusted the opinion of pseudo-liberals and the liberal press who said that Stalin—later found to be the murderer of thirty million of his own people—had honest motives and was a benevolent democrat. FDR trusted *New York Times* Moscow bureau reporters Harold Denny and Walter Duranty, who both knowingly presented a severely distorted, positive and misleading picture of the Soviet Union. One of Duranty's favorite sayings was: "I put my money on Stalin" (quoted in Johnson 1997, page 790). FDR's trusting approach to dealing with Stalin and the Soviet Union was reinforced by his liberal, characterologically rooted belief that all anti-communists were paranoid reactionaries of the worst sort. He included in this category many of his State Department advisors and Churchill himself.

To circumvent the influence of those who opposed his views, FDR began dealing with Stalin directly. This was disastrous. In March 1942, he wrote Churchill: "I know you will not mind my being brutally frank when I tell you that I think I can personally handle Stalin better than either of your foreign office or my state department. Stalin hates the guts of all of your top people. He thinks he likes me better, and, I hope he will continue to do so." At another time he said of Stalin: "I think that if I give him everything I possibly can and ask nothing of him in return, *noblesse oblige*, he won't try to annex anything and will work with me for world democracy and peace." But what FDR gave to Stalin, over Churchill's protest, was not his to give—the lives and freedom of millions of people. In handing over to Stalin practically everything he asked for, Roosevelt committed a catastrophic blunder, thus making possible the immense empire of communist totalitarian states in Eastern Europe that lasted until just before the fall of Soviet Communism at the end of the 1980s. Harry Truman, another liberal president, said of Stalin: "I like old Joe. Joe is a decent fellow."[37]

37. *New York Times*, "Obituary: Stalin rose from czarist oppression to transform Russia into mighty socialist state," March 6, 1953.

One more example of the extent of liberal illusions, so easily played upon by communists, is provided by the well-known conductor-composer Leonard Bernstein, a member of the "radical chic" of the 1960s and 1970s. In his commencement address to the Johns Hopkins graduating class of 1980, the following excerpts of which were gleaned from the June 10 *New York Times* Op-Ed page under the title, "Just Suppose We Disarmed," he said:

> Let's pretend that any one of us has become president of the United States, a very imaginative president, who has suddenly taken a very firm decision to disarm, completely and unilaterally. . . . The hypothetical enemy has been magically whisked away, and replaced by two hundred-odd million smiling, strong, peaceful Americans. . . . The Russian people certainly don't want war; they have suffered far too much; and it is more likely that they would displace their warlike leaders, and transform their Union of Socialist Republics into a truly democratic union . . .

These lofty sentiments which were delivered *after* Russia invaded Afghanistan and *while* the American left was becoming radicalized is an example of the severity of the liberal's characteristic blindness to the emotional plague. (See chapter 6, The Radicalization of the Left . . .)

There is no better example of the destructive social consequences of the liberals' blindness and destructive behavior than the conduct of the war in Vietnam during Lyndon B. Johnson's presidency. Johnson was a liberal and his administration was dominated by people with a pseudo-liberal character structure, most notably Secretary of Defense Robert McNamara. Despite the overwhelming military superiority of the American forces, political interference in the military's war effort and a vociferous liberal press combined to make an effective, aggressive war campaign impossible.

Because the pseudo-liberal hides behind a façade of being a loyal American, people in America could not fully recognize the deadliness of the communist threat. With the help of American pseudo-liberals, the communists were prepared to fight an all-out war against America and, since human life is an expendable commodity to them, they were willing to sacrifice unlimited numbers to achieve their ends. On the other side, the American leaders had the idealistic belief that a limited war could be successful. The cost of this tragic miscalculation was the loss of 58,220 American lives and untold numbers of casualties. On the home front, a seemingly endless military conflict increased social anxiety, particularly among the young. They were vulnerable to the demoralizing, agitating, ideologically based propaganda originating abroad from the Soviet Union, North Vietnam, etc. and effectively promulgated by the radical left and liberals here in the United States. This anxiety was more than they could tolerate and led to antiwar protests and student riots. Any one doubting the importance of events on the American "home front" to the success of the North Vietnamese war effort should read the *New York Times* article of May 1, 1985, describing Ted Koppel's *Nightline* debate between Le Duc Tho, a senior member of the Vietnamese Communist Party Politburo and their chief negotiator at the Paris peace talks, and Henry Kissinger, the former American Secretary of State. During this debate, on the tenth anniversary of the North Vietnamese victory, Le Duc Tho "offered thanks to the American people 'for their support and contributions to our present victory.'" Nothing has changed. The same ideological battle is currently raging in America over how to defeat the Islamic terrorists. Should U.S. foreign policy be to confront and overcome the terrorists or should they be mollified and appeased?

These examples illustrate the socially malignant synergy between the liberal and the pseudo-liberal. They also show that an understanding of how sociopolitical characters spread the emotional plague is indispensable to a full, accurate comprehension of historical and contemporary social events.

Sociopolitical Characters on the Right

The conservative side of the sociopolitical spectrum is a product and perpetuator of the patriarchal, authoritarian system that until recently dominated social life. The conservative movement became politically organized in reaction to the marked shift to the sociopolitical left that occurred in American society around 1960. The range of sociopolitical behavior on the right is as wide as that on the left. In today's anti-authoritarian society and as a reaction to it, the social behavior of conservatives comes closest to health of any group. In their personal lives, however, conservatives maintain a sex-negative attitude via a claim to authority over the life of the family. Therefore, the conservative also has been and continues to be a carrier of the emotional plague.

Until the 1960s, the authoritarian structure of the family unit was identical to that of society as a whole. In their extreme forms on the right, the reactionary and the fascist have been responsible for many social horrors. They have persecuted or murdered nearly every great man who tried to improve society, from Jesus to Freud and Reich. Today, the Black Fascist, the fascist on the right, has appeared on the social scene in the form of the Islamic fanatic. Indeed, the conservative can be as destructive as the liberal. However, instead of the left's rationalization that it stands "for the benefit of social progress," the conservative's destructiveness is "for the preservation of the existing social order."

Conservatives tend to maintain tradition in social and political life. Slow to promote innovation, they prefer gradual development to the liberals' push for rapid change. Conservatives favor a feeling attitude toward life, a mystical explanation of natural phenomena, and a discriminative attitude toward social living. They stress traditional views, which are opposed to new, untried solutions to social problems. Conservatives may have an exaggerated sense of personal responsibility. Their mysticism emphasizes the deterministic aspects of nature and a return to religion ("God"), while a selective attitude toward social life underscores the conservative's strong independence based on greater core contact. Individuals further to the right on the sociopolitical spectrum have muscular armor that is more rigid and inflexible, and for this reason the individual's insistence on asserting independence becomes extreme. They tend toward violence, political isolationism, and other extreme forms of neurotic social behavior.

A major difference between those on the near left and those on the near right is that core contact, whether genuine or distorted, is always greater in the conservative. Conservatives are thus aware of themselves as independent beings. Their sense of self-confidence is stronger and they are more concerned about the freedom to live life as they choose than about personal security. Conservatives plan their lives responsibly and feel that others should be expected to do the same, sensing correctly that individual freedom is an illusion if one depends on the state for economic survival. They believe that relying on the state will inexorably turn even an industrious, self-reliant person into one who is weak and dependant.

Because of their greater core contact, conservatives show concern for people quite differently than liberals. Sensing the finiteness of his own resources and those of others, the conservative is selective in choosing to help only people he feels truly can be helped: those who can be responsible. The liberal, believing that *everyone* has equal potential for improvement, has no sense of his own limitations or those of others. The conservative rejects the idea that all people have equal potential and is opposed to the leveling attitude of the liberal, which penalizes industry and ability and encourages inefficiency.

True conservatives react emotionally to the environment from the biological core, rather than through the intellect, as the conservative's defenses are in muscular armor rather than in the brain. Conservatives are more prone to keep their word since they are less likely to make unrealistic promises they cannot keep. While liberals identify with the underdog and are covertly against authority (the father), conservatives identify with the father, even when they are not particularly satisfied with him. They often strive to do better than the father and compete openly with him. In the more neurotic conservative, this tendency leads to extreme competitiveness in life and ruthlessness in business practices.

To the degree that his core contact is distorted, the conservative has the potential for mysticism. With religion to handle personal guilt feelings, conservatives do not have to atone with their social behavior. The conservative also has a moralistic attitude regarding sex and believes its expression should be reserved for marriage. On the surface, the conservative male may emphasize the importance of chastity and being faithful, but in practice he often employs a double standard.

As a representative of the authoritarian social system, the conservative is inclined to exaggerate differences between the sexes and treats females as inferior. On the other hand, because of an egalitarian attitude, the liberal tends to minimize or eliminate differences between the sexes. *Both conservative and liberal attitudes represent different ways to negate genital heterosexuality.*

The conservative is strongly opposed to sexual expression from the superficial or secondary layers (pornography and perversion), while the liberal makes little distinction between sexual expression from the different layers.

Until rather recently, Americans kept their personal neurotic problems out of the sociopolitical arena. They either confined them to themselves and their personal relationships or worked them out through religion. Therefore, they did not impose their political ideologies on others in the form of "social solutions." However, largely as a reaction to ever-increasing pressure for social change exerted by pseudo-liberals, and in an attempt to preserve social order, many conservatives have become socially and politically mobilized, mainly by opposing pseudo-liberal programs. A prime example is the formation of the conservative movement in the 1950s and '60s. Reaction from the right is the inevitable consequence of the pseudo-liberal obsession for continual and reckless social change. It happened after the French Revolution with the rise of Napoleon, it happened after the First World War in Germany with Nazi opposition to communist foment, and it is happening now in the United States in the form of a resurgence of the numerous religious movements on the political right. It is also evident in the reaction of many Muslim immigrants in the West to the breakdown of the authoritarian social order.

The Extreme Conservative, the Reactionary, and the Black Fascist

As we proceed to the right of the conservative on the sociopolitical spectrum, we meet first the extreme conservative, then the reactionary, and finally the Black Fascist. The differences between these distinct character types appear both as increasing degrees of rigidity in thinking and muscular armor and as an increasing propensity for irrationality, including mysticism, violence, and emotional plague behavior. Correspondingly, core contact becomes increasingly distorted and, in the case of the Black Fascist, is finally lost entirely. With distorted core contact, mystical feelings become progressively more important in determining the individual's daily actions. Because mysticism also provides a way to express restricted core feelings, religious feeling and practice become more devout. Such people may develop a façade of piety, a reaction formation, to counteract and conceal the increased pressure of hate contained in their rigid armor. All the traits of the conservative become progressively exaggerated in individuals whose character traits tend further to the right in the direction of the Black Fascist. Sexuality becomes more moralistic, which fuels sadism. Finally, sexual desire is considered animalistic, even brutal, as they feel justified in expressing their hatred in the sexual act. The Black Fascist expresses mysticism through his particular reactionary ideology. Ocular armor can give rise to paranoid ideation.

The zealous fascist with his reactionary belief system represents the ultimate form of destructive rebelliousness. Like the pseudo-liberal or communist (Red Fascist) on the left, the Black Fascist is an emotional plague character and stands for absolute authoritarianism. This type lives almost entirely in the brutal secondary layer. Race ideology, top-sergeant mentality, mysticism, and robot-like allegiance to the leader are all biopathic symptoms stemming from the Black Fascist's orgastic impotence.

Both the communist and the Black Fascist have an insuperable pelvic block. Both strive for absolute power over the masses. But while communists seek power through the leveling ideologies of egalitarianism and internationalism, Black Fascists rationalize their craving for power with a greater mystical passion, through religion, to maintain the purity of their nation or race. In the case of the Islamic fundamentalists, the Islamo-Fascist mullahs will stop at nothing to eliminate anyone who they believe threatens the purity of those who see themselves as the people chosen by God. Both groups employ random violence for its own sake and righteously suppress and attempt to control every natural, living function, all the while blaming their victim as the cause of the problem. Since both groups have identical biophysical structures, they can adapt to each other, understanding and empathizing with each other quite well. (See chapter 8, the section on the Islamo-Fascist)

Figure 2.3 (on page 125) illustrates the functioning of the sociopolitical character types from the three layers of the armored bioemotional structure. The diagram has been modified from the one found in Baker's *Man in the Trap;* the major change is that the pseudo-liberal is now placed to the left of the socialist, next to the communist. *In terms of social functioning, the pseudo-liberal is identical to the communist.* The only real difference is where the individual lives—in a democracy or in a fascist society. As one proceeds from the center to the extremes on the right or left, secondary layer expression increases and core contact decreases.

Ideological extremism exposes the flaws in all the various ideologies and can cause some members of extremist groups on the left and the right to become disillusioned and form splinter groups. The disastrous social consequences of the pseudo-liberal's leftist extremism have spawned a political counter-reaction, with members from both sides of the sociopolitical spectrum shifting to the right. Rejecting accommodation with attitudes toward the Soviet Union as dangerously utopian and naïve, a group of anti-Stalinist American liberals shifted their political thinking to the right and became "neoconservatives." These individuals are defined as environmental liberals in Baker's sense. The clearing up of their ocular armor allows such persons to shift their political thinking from the left to the right of center. The neoconservative platform was one of containing communist expansion abroad and continued social reform at home. The same shift, in a direction farther to the right, is now affecting the political right itself. The Christian Coalition, America's largest group of religious conservatives, with 1.5 million present members and representing some 31,000 churches nationwide, recently proposed a ten-point political program including such diverse issues as school prayer, criminalization of abortion, transfer of federal education funds to local governments, and financial restitution by criminals to their crime victims. Its appeal for a return to "traditional family values" and religion is vague, misleading, and ultimately destructive. If successful, it will bring about a return to the mystical and sex-negative family attitudes that helped give rise to the liberal movement in the first place. The result will be a slow erosion of the necessary attractive opposition embodied in the separation of church and state and, with it, the bulwark of a formal democratic society.

As we have noted, the degree of ocular, including brain, armoring is the most salient factor in determining an individual's sociopolitical character type. The manifestations of ocular

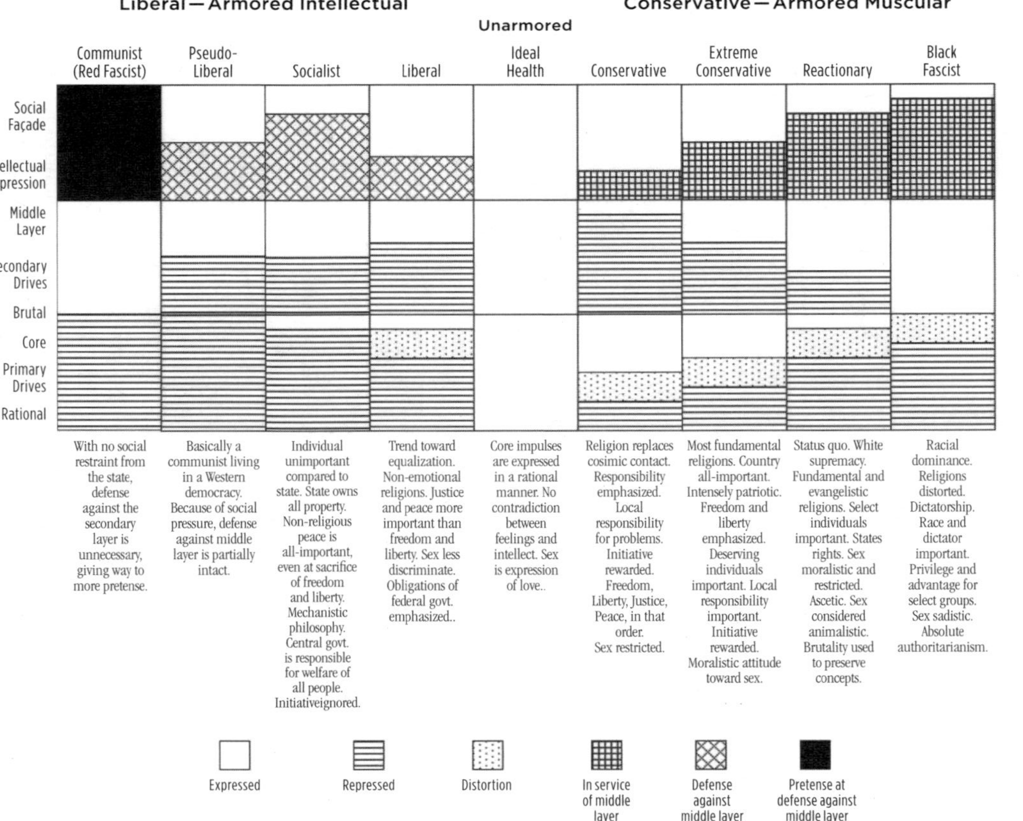
Liberal—Armored Intellectual
Unarmored
Conservative—Armored Muscular
Communist (Red Fascist)
Pseudo-Liberal
Socialist
Liberal
Ideal Health
Conservative
Extreme Conservative
Reactionary
Black Fascist
Social Façade
Intellectual Expression
Middle Layer
Secondary Drives
Brutal
Core
Primary Drives
Rational
With no social restraint from the state, defense against the secondary layer is unnecessary, giving way to more pretense.
Basically a communist living in a Western democracy. Because of social pressure, defense against middle layer is partially intact.
Individual unimportant compared to state. State owns all property. Non-religious peace is all-important, even at sacrifice of freedom and liberty. Mechanistic philosophy. Central govt. is responsible for welfare of all people. Initiativeignored.
Trend toward equalization. Non-emotional religions. Justice and peace more important than freedom and liberty. Sex less discriminate. Obligations of federal govt. emphasized..
Core impulses are expressed in a rational manner. No contradiction between feelings and intellect. Sex is expression of love..
Religion replaces cosimic contact. Responsibility emphasized. Local responsibility for problems. Initiative rewarded. Freedom, Liberty, Justice, Peace, in that order. Sex restricted.
Most fundamental religions. Country all-important. Intensely patriotic. Freedom and liberty emphasized. Deserving individuals important. Local responsibility important. Initiative rewarded. Moralistic attitude toward sex.
Status quo. White supremacy. Fundamental and evangelistic religions. Select individuals important. States rights. Sex moralistic and restricted. Ascetic. Sex considered animalistic. Brutality used to preserve concepts.
Racial dominance. Religions distorted. Dictatorship. Race and dictator important. Privilege and advantage for select groups. Sex sadistic. Absolute authoritarianism.
Expressed
Repressed
Distortion
In service of middle layer
Defense against middle layer
Pretense at defense against middle layer
Modified from Baker (4)

Sociopolitical Characterology

FIGURE 2.3

armoring are most pronounced in those at the extremes of the sociopolitical spectrum, leading them to the lawless behavior and fanaticism characteristic of emotional plague characters. Tragically, the masses are not able to recognize the criminal nature of this behavior because these individuals successfully masquerade as political and religious leaders (Fig. 2.4).[38]

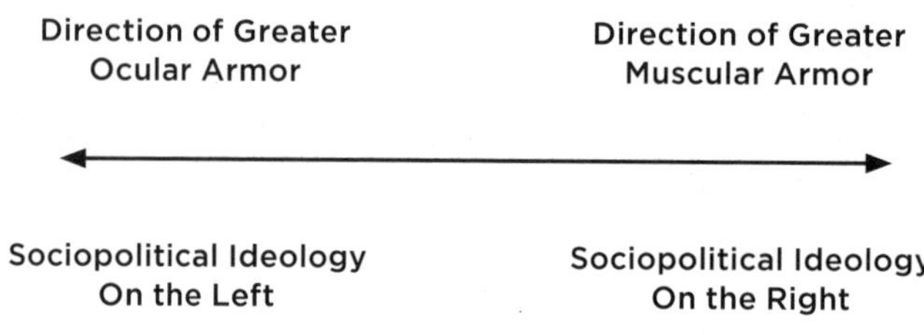

FIGURE 2.4

At the extremes of this spectrum, where ocular armor reaches its greatest degree of severity, left and right worldviews merge and assume the ideological aspects of totalitarianism. This phenomenon explains why, after the Second World War, many who had belonged to Hitler's Nazi Party (Black Fascism) switched allegiance and became communists (Red Fascism). Paul Mathews writes:

> Rightist terrorists are basically structured like leftist ones. The difference is in their façades, which tend to be nationalistic and racist rather than internationalistic and leveling like those of their leftist counterparts. Both groups are elitist in assuming that they know what is best for the masses. As the old adage goes, the Nazis kill you for their own good and the Communists kill you for your own good. Both groups are motivated by random violence for its own sake and by the need to suppress and control all natural, living functions. Therefore, they are adaptable to each other, and understand and empathize with each other quite well. The defeated Nazi cadres, for exam-

38. This classification does not apply to sociopathic politicians who, in response to public opinion, simply change their political convictions for the purpose of maintaining political power.

ple, readily adjusted themselves to the Communist regime in East Germany, and no 'War Crimes Trials' were held there. These cadres merely exchanged their Nazi armbands for Soviet symbols. They behaved as righteously in the interest of the Soviet international Communist "brotherhood," as they had for Hitler's *ubermensch* ideology, and still do.[39] With the breakdown of social structure, the incidence of individuals having mixed character types has increased significantly. A recent clinical example is the individual who simultaneously expresses a blend of mechanistic and mystical attitudes and ideas as espoused in various "New Age" movements. This admixture intensifies the pre-existing state of contactlessness.

39. On Terrorism. *Journal of Orgonomy* 16 (2): 238, 1982.

The Functional Identity and Attractive Opposition of Individual and Social Character Armor

Just as every individual has a specific character structure, so too does every society and its institutions. Martin Goldberg has shown that the character of individuals and the character of groups function similarly (Goldberg 1989, pages 190–209). Social character, the particular character of society at any given epoch, originates from the specific manner in which individuals' characterological disturbances manifest socially when their neuroses are displaced onto and expressed in the social realm.

The function of social armor is identical to that of individual armor. Both consist of equilibrium between two opposing forces. In the case of individual armor the equilibrium is between the forces of impulse and defense. In the case of social armor the equilibrium is between the social forces of people on the political left and the right, each side believing in the correctness of its approach. Both individual and social armor are expressions of the structuring of the genital disturbance in the masses. Both utilize the same psychological defense mechanisms (denial, displacement, projection, reaction formation, and so on). When successful, the opposing forces are in a relationship of attractive opposition. In both cases, the equal and opposite forces of armor prevent the emergence of anxiety and also of impulses from the destructive secondary layer. When the forces are unequal there is either increased anxiety and social breakdown or excessive repression and social rigidity. In Western societies, where the forces of the left predominate over those of the right, social chaos and degradation are on the rise. In Islamic societies, social rigidity and changelessness prevail. (See chapters 6 and 8)

Individuals spread the emotional plague, and plague-infected social institutions, neurotic families in particular, produce more and more such individuals. The rise, in recent decades, in overt pregenital activity and other forms of neurotic and destructive behavior in Western societies, together with the increased incidence of criminal behavior, have resulted in social decline necessitating greater social armor. This functional identity between individual and social character armor is illustrated in Fig. 2.5.

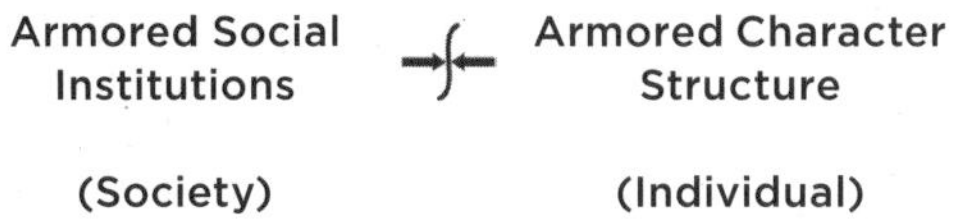

Armored Social Institutions	→⟨←	Armored Character Structure
(Society)		(Individual)

FIGURE 2.5

Reich showed that armored society, in the form of armored social institutions, perpetuates by anchoring itself in the character structure of the masses; that is, in individuals (Reich 1946). This relationship between the individual and society also applies to the healthy components of each.

As we will see, the foundation for an armored society in post-colonial America started when Jefferson and other pseudo-liberal individuals tried to subvert the efforts of the federalists to form a strong union. This subversive behavior was a typical manifestation of the socially destructive behavior of the pseudo-liberal's sociopolitical character. These individuals formed a party opposed to the federalists allegedly because they were against the idea that a strong federal government was important and necessary to preserve and protect the safety and the lives of existing and future generations of Americans from tyranny. Instead, they chose to protect their short-term personal interests, which in the South included preserving the institution of slavery.

Thus the destructive sociopolitical consequences of a two-party system in the United States originate from the common functioning principle *social armor*, which took the form of ideological forces on the left and the right in opposition. At the same time, the opposing forces of the two-party system were essential for the formation and survival of armored American society. The opposing attractive forces contained in the social structure of a formal democracy correspond in every detail to the opposing forces contained in the structure of the armored neurotic individual.

Armored social institutions consist of all life-inimical influences on the developing infant and child—not only the parents, the family, and the educational organizations that the child comes into contact with, but also, to an ever-increasing degree because of its own enormous influence, the media. Under these influences, childrearing negates the child's primary sexual drives and represses the resulting secondary drives. In the average person, this creates a sense of helplessness, a dependency, and a need to be led.

The relationship of the child to the main frustrating parent or parent substitute is one of the critical factors in the formation of the neurotic character (Reich 1949a, page 150). The individual's displacement of original parent-child conflict onto the social realm usually happens around the time of adolescence when the sexual drive is strongest. It can take two forms: authoritarian or anti-authoritarian. In an authoritarian society, children defend themselves by identifying with and internalizing the threatening impulses of the frustrating parent. This happens when they are not permitted to stay in emotional contact with and express the fear and anger they feel when damaging parental attitudes frustrate and threaten their core impulses of love and natural aggression. In its authoritarian form, individual character armor consists of a child's hostile, neurotic identification with the parent and assumption of the same threatening characteristics. This outcome is distinguished from healthy identification, which is based on love, not hatred or fear. As Reich wrote:

> Suppression of the natural sexuality in the child, particularly of its genital sexuality, makes the child apprehensive, shy, obedient, afraid of authority, good and adjusted in the authoritarian sense; it paralyzes the rebellious forces because any rebellion is laden with anxiety; it produces, by inhibiting sexual curiosity and sexual thinking in the child, a general inhibition of thinking and of critical faculties. In brief, the goal of sexual suppression is that of producing an individual who is adjusted to the authoritarian order and who will submit to it in spite of all misery and degradation. At first, the child has to submit to the structure of the authoritarian miniature state, the family; this makes it capable of later subordination to the general authoritarian system. The formation of the authoritarian structure takes place through the anchoring of sexual inhibition and sexual anxiety.
>
> (Reich 1946, page 24)

Thus there arises a vicious cycle: Having submitted to existing authoritarian social structures as a child, parents reproduce that submission and the distortions of core impulses in raising their own offspring.

In the same way, anti-authoritarian society reproduces and perpetuates itself in the anti-authoritarian character formation of the masses. If the family structure is not overtly sex-negative but is instead out of touch with the child in a chronically permissive way, the child will also lack rational, constructive parental guidance based on a loving relationship. In the anti-authoritarian society, the father or authority figure has been divested of influence and, in effect, has been castrated. He is typically stereotyped by the liberal entertainment media (e.g., in sitcoms) as a "buddy" in relation to family members—ineffective, bumbling, the butt of jokes. It seems that everyone, including his children, is wiser and more mature than Dad. In real life, however, things are not at all funny. What actually happens, in fact, is that the child lacking parental guidance develops intense anxiety which is masked by an anti-authoritarian character attitude. The result is an individual who is not rationally obedient and appropriately well-behaved, but one who is disrespectful, bratty, willful, unruly, and chronically out of touch with him or herself and with others. Feeling anxious and emotionally out of touch with his own core and environment, the child is without inner motivation. In an effort to make contact with the core, he is likely to seek substitute gratification through drugs, alcohol, and pregenital sexual activity or to form relationships with others that substitute for the family structure missing in childhood.

The role of women in past authoritarian society included being responsible for maintaining sexual (genital) repression in themselves and their children, especially in their daughters, and transmitting moral values to the next generation.[40] In today's anti-authoritarian society, women have been "emancipated" from the burden of having to preserve the authoritarian family. If their moral function is displaced onto the social arena, political activism and politically correct attitudes serve to advocate leftist causes and candidates that support the centralized, anti-authoritarian state.

In a healthy family, the child identifies with and incorporates the positive traits of both parents. Genuine love is based on the

---

40. The social function of women in an authoritarian society is clearly expressed in the lyrics of this once-popular American song: "*Love and marriage go together like a horse and carriage. Dad was told by mother, you can't have one without the other.*"

parents' protection and appropriate gratification of the child's emotional needs, consisting not simply of tolerance toward genital sexuality but a *genuine* positive attitude toward it. This is the contactful attitude of parents toward the child's emotional freedom of expression. Since such circumstances do not involve Oedipal ties to the parents, children are free to develop and direct their lives according to their natural disposition. In addition to allowing the child the freedom of self-expression, genuine love also requires that the child be taught not to interfere with the lives of others. This enables the individual to become self-regulating and an independent member of the family and society. A child raised in this way has a natural respect for and trust in the parents' guidance as well as for rational social authority. *Since such children trust rational authority, they do not need to be rebellious.* Genuine gratification of the child's biological needs leads to emotional independence, which is a prerequisite for social independence and rational social functioning.

Because individual and social (societal) character is functionally identical, the contradiction between natural sexual expression and sexual moralism is present in both the attitudes of armored society as a whole and in each of its individual members. In the authoritarian social system of the past, the individual developed fear of authority, coupled with a need to be led by a strong leader. This relationship was based on the suppression of natural aggression and sexuality, with a strong moralistic component. The same contradiction exists in today's anti-authoritarian, emotionally unsatisfied, amoral society, but in a more covert and destructive manner. In today's society, which is seemingly permissive but no less genitally repressive and unsatisfied, the child or adolescent develops intense anxiety. This occurs because of insufficient muscular armor to bind energy and an absence of rational parental guidance: the child or adolescent is left feeling bewildered and adrift. The unsatisfied behaviors to which this situation gives rise, including pregenital sexual activity, aimless rebelliousness, and drug abuse, are unsuccessful attempts to overcome anxiety. An example of increased pregenital sexuality is that casual fellatio has become the preferred form of male-female sexual contact for millions of adolescents. Neither the conservative nor the liberal recognizes the toll that this practice has on the emotional life of the adolescent. Emotionally crippled and left directionless, these adolescents must lean on their peers for support and settle for illusory mystical and substitute, rather than real and durable, gratification of their biological and emotional needs.

In armored societies world-wide with a few rare exceptions, the authoritarian family structure and the rebellion against it have been the basis for the conservative-liberal antithesis. The biblical story of Cain and Abel is an example. The conservative individual, Abel, identifies with the authority of the father and openly competes with him. The pseudo-liberal, Cain, rejects the father and covertly rebels against him. He displaces his anti-authoritarian rebellious behavior onto the social scene (Baker 1967, page 172). As we have seen, the psychosocial differences in these two types of individuals are a manifestation of profoundly contrasting *biophysical* states based on differences in patterns of armor.

Social Armor, Character Armor, and Behavior

Social armor in the form of correct moral behavior once effectively curbed destructive manifestations of aggression and maintained sexual repression of secondary and primary core drives. This was due in large measure to the generally intact structure of the authoritarian family. However, social structure has gradually broken down since the end of the First World War, and this erosion markedly accelerated in the 1960s. (See chapter 6) Prior to this time, Western society was relatively stable because the opposing forces well-anchored in tradition and social institutions from the left and the right were equal. This equilibrium in various parts of the West was occasionally disturbed by sporadic outbreaks of social destructiveness in the form of self-limited wars. These conflicts had meager social consequences and did not alter the basic armored structure of society. However, the social unrest that led to the great wars of the twentieth century was different. These wars were followed by the breakthrough of enormous amounts of energy from the destructive secondary layer.[41] This was a major contributor to the breakdown of the authoritarian social order and was accompanied by the same process in the individual. (See chapter 6)

41. Energy breaking through the armor *must* turn into social destructiveness. This is because it is not available for orgastic discharge, the only effective safeguard against social destructiveness.

It was the dismantling of the authoritarian family that enabled all forms of pregenital activity and antisocial behavior to emerge. The increased incidence and acceptance of criminality and psychopathic behavior that we are witnessing today is a direct result, as well as a cause, of this social breakdown. Consider as a typical example how former United States President Bill Clinton's mendacity, display of pregenital sexuality, and contempt for the public he served was viewed not with outrage but with *indifference and apathy* by a large segment of the population, including the media, and actually condoned outright by millions.

It is not surprising that the world-wide eruption of terrorism has come about with this transformation of society from authoritarian to anti-authoritarian. The forces that suppressed emotional plague activity in the past authoritarian era had to be overcome by well-constructed rationalizations promoting licentious and irresponsible behavior that the public at large readily accepted. With the transformation of society into anti-authoritarianism, these suppressive forces are no longer operative. The floodgates have opened. Destructiveness and brutality held in the secondary layer are now directly expressed as undisguised acts of terrorism and sadism. With dulled sensibilities and without the ability to feel outrage, the public tolerates these violent, brutal breakthroughs from the secondary layer with hardly a whisper.

In the authoritarian society of the past, armor imposed personal and social responsibility by means of repression. This was at the expense of individual freedom. Today's permissive, anti-authoritarian society has released destructive impulses in the form of irresponsible behavior often bordering on criminality. This has been encouraged by the political left under the guise of "freedom of expression." In sharp contrast to this liberal approach, healthy individuals and societies are capable of self-regulation—capable of freedom and liberty without license and of responsibility without repression.

CHAPTER 3

FREEDOM, RESPONSIBILITY, AND SOCIOPOLITICAL IDEOLOGY

The finding of facts does not ask whether the facts are welcome or not, but only whether they are correct or not. For this reason, it always comes into sharp conflict with politics which does not ask whether a fact is correct or not, but only whether or not it serves this or that political purpose.
—Wilhelm Reich, *The Mass Psychology of Fascism*

Freedom and responsibility belong to the social realm but are derived from deeper, more inclusive biological functions. Originating from the biological core, individual freedom and social responsibility are present in every area of social life. When both coexist, the conditions allow the individual to function in a rationally authoritative manner.

In health, the perceptual and excitatory functions of biological orgone energy give rise to contact with the self, the environment, and the cosmos, and the individual is capable of self-regulation. For example, in the healthy adult, sexual freedom and sexual responsibility go hand in hand. This relationship also holds true for the work function.[42] However, people trapped as they are in

42. Healthy individuals are responsible and tend to be self-sufficient. Since they are capable of taking care of themselves, they do not require assistance from the government. They are not only the mainstay of society but also relieve the masses of a great tax burden.

their armor cannot experience real freedom or the responsibility that accompanies it. Clinical experience shows that the restrictions of armor are unlikely to be shed unless the patient first tries to achieve greater social independence and personal responsibility. The presence of armor distorts the reciprocal relationship of freedom and responsibility, resulting in lopsided thinking that appears as sociopolitical ideology on both the left and the right. Armor gives rise to ideological thinking and, conversely, ideological thinking maintains armor. As a result, advocates of freedom without responsibility or of responsibility without freedom have drowned out the voices of those who know that only the presence of *both* can produce healthy individuals and a healthy society. Freedom without responsibility leads to chaos and anti-authoritarianism. Responsibility without freedom leads to authoritarianism.

Rights versus Responsibility: The Orgonomic View

The orgonometric development equation in Figure 3.1 can be used to define the functions of freedom and responsibility.

A1 → A3, A4

A → A1, A2 → etc.

A2 → A5, A6

Freedom
Individualism →

← Determinism
Responsibility
Cooperation

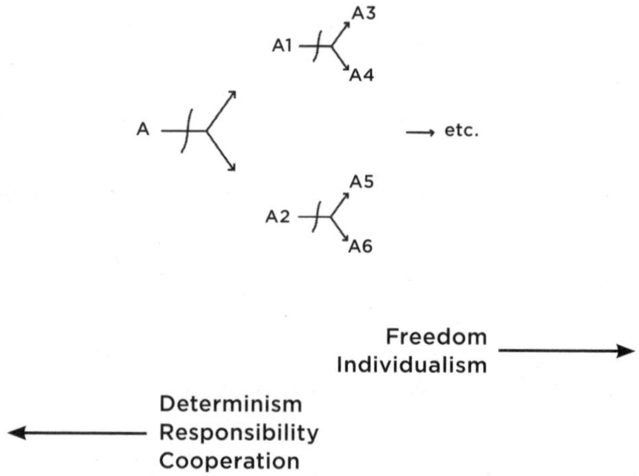

FIGURE 3.1

The qualities of freedom and responsibility are derived from the two directions of the equation. The direction of developmental variations to the right is identical with greater freedom; the direction toward the left, the common functioning principle, is identical with greater determinism, which in the social realm translates into cooperation and responsibility. In humans, functions that are farthest to the orgonometric right assume the features of "free will." In healthy people, freedom and responsibility function harmoniously. Freedom to develop does not interfere with responsibility and, conversely, responsibility does not interfere with freedom. The common functioning principle depends on the particular function (e.g., childrearing, work relationships, and so on).

In health, freedom is defined functionally as an individual's capacity to move and to develop unhampered by external constraints or the internal constraints of armor. Complete freedom to develop is based on full contact with oneself. Responsibility is defined as an individual's capacity to respond with full contact with one's environment. The following orgonometric relationship shows that freedom coexists with responsibility (Fig. 3.2).

The Functional Relationship of Freedom and Responsibility

FIGURE 3.2

An increase in freedom requires greater responsibility, and a decrease in freedom results in a decrease in responsibility. For example, granting the freedom or "right" to perform a certain function, e.g., driving a motor vehicle, carries with it the obligation that it is done responsibly. If the individual cannot responsibly perform a function, he or she should not have that freedom. Conversely, if the individual is not freely able to perform a function because of constraints, he or she cannot function responsibly. For example, increased restrictions on physicians in the form of rules imposed by the federal government reduce the physician's ability to be responsible to the patient. Such regulations, in effect, lower the standard of health care by shifting responsibility onto others. The responsibility to be free occurs simultaneously with the freedom to be responsible. An understanding of these principles is essential in the function of childrearing.

The extent to which the equation depicted in Figure 3.1 develops to the orgonometric right—that is, the degree of freedom—depends on the particular function. Freedom to worship as one pleases, or to not worship, varies more than the freedom to assemble and petition the government. These principles involving freedom and responsibility apply to every domain of human functioning, from the deepest (on the orgonometric left) to the most superficial (on the orgonometric right).

With the development of the larynx and bipedal locomotion, early hominids became free to vocalize and to fashion tools of varying degrees of specialization. These abilities led to an increase in the size and structural complexity of the brain, as well as the development of consciousness in humans. Unlike other species, humans can function in nearly limitless ways, the particular manner depending on how the individual is integrated. At different times, an individual can play a musical instrument, perform a medical procedure, drive a car, fly an airplane, or perform innumerable other highly complicated tasks, depending on the kind of integration of the component functions of that person's organism. Similarly, in social life, an individual can function as a spouse, as a parent, in cooperation with others as a co-worker, or independently, and so on, depending on the social context. The responsible exercise of most rights requires the development of multiple functions.

Consider the most important human core social function, the raising of healthy children. The capacity to procreate is necessary but not a sufficient determinant. In our armored society, the health care professions and society itself pay little if any attention to a woman's capacity to *responsibly* raise an emotionally healthy child.

From an orgonometric viewpoint (see Fig. 3.1), responsible childrearing defines the whole function A. To the right of the development equation are the component functions that constitute the whole function responsible childrearing. Most important among these are the biological and emotional maturity of the woman. Farther to the right is the woman's desire to have a child; the healthiness of her relationship with her mate; her capacity to provide for the child's future material needs, adequate prenatal medical care, preparation for delivery, and postnatal care;

and her ability and willingness to provide for the child's physical and emotional needs in early life. Women who do not have these capacities and functional relationships are not capable of fully exercising the responsibility necessary for raising a healthy child. To make matters worse, the functions to the right of the development equation, such as the biophysical readiness to have children and the nature of adequate prenatal and postnatal care, are poorly understood. It is not enough to take vitamins regularly or to know that breast milk is better for the baby than formula.

Consider a different example farther to the orgonometric right, the Second Amendment right to bear or possess firearms. Learning to use firearms responsibly—for sport or for self-protection—defines the whole function A. To the orgonometric right of the equation are the various basic components of the function of responsible gun ownership. Among these are: chronological maturity, neurological integration, the capacity to maintain full consciousness, and so on. Further to the orgonometric right are those functions that the individual is required to master, such as understanding firearm safety, storing and properly maintaining firearms, and discharging them accurately and safely. People who do not have these functions, for whatever reason, cannot use firearms responsibly, and their irresponsible use leads many to question the right to possess firearms at all. Those ideologically opposed to that right, however, ignore the fact that most people are law-abiding and, with proper training, fully capable of handling firearms responsibly, and therefore have the right to possess them.

Obviously, an individual with a physical or emotional disability, such as epilepsy, blindness, or criminality, cannot be a responsible gun owner and therefore cannot responsibly exercise the right to bear arms. Most people find it easy to see the rationality of the functional relationship between the freedom to bear arms and the necessity to do so responsibly. This is because the steps between A (the responsible gun owner) and the variations A1, A2, A3, and so on, which constitute the prerequisite requirements and skills in discharging a firearm, *are limited to a small number of domains.*

On the other hand, the social skills involving the functions necessary to support the right to hold office responsibly are highly developed and specialized. These functions involve a more inclusive domain to the orgonometric left and therefore extend far to the right of our development equation. They include an in-depth understanding of human nature, extensive experience, and the highest characterological qualifications, such as the capacity for accurate judgment. The functional relationship between those qualified to exercise these specialized skills and the whole function, that is, the individual politician's capacity to responsibly hold office, *is too far-reaching for most armored individuals to comprehend*, especially those with serious ocular armoring. Unfortunately, people with serious ocular armor include most eligible voters. They simply are not capable of recognizing the importance of the functional relationship between the responsibility to perform the required task and the legitimate authority (personal qualifications) to hold public office. These considerations are taken for granted or are ignored, and this helps to bring about the political success of inept, corrupt politicians and despots.

Armor's Disturbance of the Capacity for Personal Freedom and Social Responsibility

Disturbances in the capacity for freedom and responsibility are a primary social manifestation of human armoring. This occurs because armor reduces or eliminates the individual's core contact. As a result, personal freedom and a sense of social responsibility are not fully experienced. Self-regulation is thus also disturbed in the direction of either too little freedom and too much responsibility or too little responsibility and too much freedom. In both cases, the capacity for simultaneously exercising freedom and being responsible is impaired. Individual and social development is blocked by the rigid, unalterable structure of armor. In the social sphere, one set of functions becomes predominant and acts in a defensive manner over the other. As a result, self-regulation is either replaced by the principle of moral regulation or is lost altogether, with varying degrees of moral relativism, impulsivity, and license. The importance of freedom and responsibility in directing social life have been with us since armored humans first became responsible for their own lives. Ideologies arose because armored people were unable to think functionally about the relationship between freedom and responsibility.[43]

We are living in the age of the glorification of the individual, with everywhere a demand for individual rights. On the political left, pseudo-liberals, socialists, and psychopathic politicians use ideological issues of freedom defensively ("freedom peddling") against individual or personal responsibility, encouraging social and political license. These individuals espouse a socialistic premise based on a neurotic attitude of entitlement: People have a right to say and do whatever they please without any thought to the possible destructive *consequences* of their words and behavior, either for themselves or for society.[44] Litigiousness is endemic in today's American society. As Phillip Howard has put it, "Individual rights have become an epidemic, spreading from their original role as protectors of freedom to the nooks of our daily choices . . . Modern rights seem limitless. For the price of a lawyer, anyone can transform his sense of entitlement into a legal claim. This has changed the way we live, infecting our choices with legal fear. Our playgrounds are being stripped of seesaws. Paranoid doctors order unnecessary tests." As a result, "America, so proud of its rule of law, no longer provides legal rulings to defend reasonable conduct. We no longer have a sense of what we can and can't do."[45] The socially destructive consequences of this distorted view of individual rights are self-evident.

In the healthy person, the freedom to write a book or newspaper article and the freedom to speak occur simultaneously with the responsibility to do so in a truthful and factually honest way. However, *the capacity to be truthful in word or deed depends on the person's character structure;* that is, *the degree to which his or*

43. Von Mises gives an excellent description of the irrationality of ideologies. He states that ideologies "are mostly an eclectic juxtaposition of ideas utterly incompatible with one another. They cannot stand a logical examination of their content. Their inconstancies are irreparable and defy any attempt to combine their various parts into a system of ideas compatible with one another." (Von Mises 1949, page 184)

44. Alexis de Tocqueville anticipated the degeneration of American democracy, thinking that it would occur either in a tyranny of the majority based on claims for "the right and the ability to do everything" or in a sort of democratic despotism (De Tocqueville 2000, page 600).

45. Phillip K. Howard, "Too Many Rights Make a Wrong, *Wall Street Journal*, April 26, 2001.

her armor distorts perceptual functions, thinking and behavior. In sociopolitical ideology, the truth is distorted in direct proportion to the extent to which armor increases as an individual shifts further to either the sociopolitical left or the right. Armor is the reason why people rigidly hold onto their ideologies for dear life. This is the protective function of armor.

Pseudo-liberals use their powers of rationalization to minimize and excuse the criminal's responsibility for antisocial behavior, especially those individuals belonging to preferred minority groups. They insist, for example, that criminals are "too sick" to behave differently, that they can be rehabilitated, or that their behavior results from a "bad social environment," clearly implying that criminals should therefore be excused for their behavior. This is both a masochistic attitude and, by unconscious identification with the criminals antisocial behavior, an example of emotional plague. In effect, this attitude discourages and undermines the capacity for personal responsibility in everyone and sanctions further criminal behavior and licentiousness by the individual. Ignoring the trapped energy—rage—hidden in the destructive secondary layer of the criminal causes an insidious deterioration in that individual and also in society. This is regularly accompanied by increased individual and social anxiety.

Those on the right stress the importance of personal responsibility in a moralistically defensive fashion, either overtly or covertly, depending on how far they have shifted to the right. Liberals also stress responsibility in a distorted way. However, their emphasis is not on personal responsibility but on the *collective* responsibility of society, a responsibility that is imposed on the individual moralistically through the ideology of political correctness. Although more aware of the social consequences of their belief system than the liberal, conservatives also expect others to behave as they do. Since this does not make a distinction between core and secondary layer functions, genuine freedom is undermined with greater regimentation. Sex and work become a duty or obligation—compulsive marriage and duty-bound work—and not something to be enjoyed. The biological origin of work and sexual disturbances eludes them as well.[46] Again, since the existence and function of armor is not recognized, nothing is done to deal with the energy trapped in it. Social conditions continue in a downward spiral.

The idea that individuals *have to* do or *have to* be this or that is essentially a conservative notion. Patients with a conservative structure sometimes express pessimism about ever experiencing much pleasure by saying that they have no chance to enjoy themselves because they *have to* do this and do that. If liberal patients say that they *have to* do some necessary but unpleasant task, they mean only that they are aware that negative consequences will result if they *choose* not to perform the action in question. When one suggests to conservative patients that they may have a *choice*, it provokes discomfort. Liberals, on the other hand, become acutely uncomfortable if they hear that they or others *have to* behave in a certain way. The conservative senses personal responsibility as the governing principle of an individual's life, whereas the liberal senses freedom as the governing principle. In both cases, freedom is separated from responsibility.[47]

In childrearing, liberals typically allow their children unrestricted freedom and the right to do whatever they please before the children develop the capacity for responsibly handling their lives. Without guidance, these youngsters are left adrift and out of touch with themselves, with *less* capacity to tolerate freedom. Such children feel chronically anxious and directionless, exhibit delinquent behavior, use drugs, or engage in body piercing to alleviate tension and increase sensation. On the other hand, conservative parents expect their children to behave responsibly long before they have the ability to do so, and this restricts their freedom to develop. Too often, their children are expected to remain celibate before marriage, even when they demonstrate a capacity to exercise sexual responsibility. At each stage of development, children are expected to "behave themselves," to "grow up" and "act like adults." In extreme cases, they are not allowed to have

---

46. Until recently, conservatives have not promoted social programs designed to "improve" the human condition. They simply resisted liberal "solutions." This has left them vulnerable to liberal attacks of doing nothing. In reaction, conservatives have become mobilized socially and have begun recommending programs of their own. Society is becoming increasingly polarized.

47. Robert Harman, M.D., personal communication.

childhoods. Many of these children, especially those with high energy, react to such upbringing by becoming rebellious, socially irresponsible, and caught up in leftist causes. Their shift to the left is a protest against their authoritarian upbringing.

In both conservative and liberal ideologies and lifestyles, genuine freedom is compromised and the capacity of the individual to self-regulate is disturbed. However, in our "enlightened" age of indiscriminate permissiveness, social decline, and increasing anxiety, it is liberalism—because it espouses "freedom" at the expense of responsibility—that is the more dangerous alternative. It directly accounts for the decline in standards in every area of social life.

Longing to be free from the restrictions of armor, without assuming appropriate responsibility, takes many irrational forms, as seen in clinical practice. Examples are those patients who expect the therapist to "cure" them without any real effort on their part, or those with the expectation that they will be cured by a "magical pill." They tend to blame a spouse for his or her own contribution to marital problems or to blame "society" for their own personal problems.

Disturbances in social functioning due to armor, with their corresponding restrictions on the capacity for functioning freely and responsibility, have necessitated ever-increasing governmental intervention into social life. There are two kinds of government activity: rational and irrational. Rational government is based on three types of responsibility. The first is to protect the core functions of life and to protect individuals and society from physical harm. The second is to facilitate commerce and to establish an effective administrative system of government. The third is to protect people because of their armored condition—that is, to safeguard humans because of their neurotic helplessness, their inability to make rational decisions, and their inability to be responsible for their own lives. This is the rational basis of certain welfare programs.

Irrational governmental activity results from makeshift, symptomatic programs that encourage dependency on the federal bureaucracy. A much larger segment of the population is capable of securing or maintaining self-sufficiency *if the government did not interfere with people's inner healthy resources for survival.* This was shown by the sharp drop in welfare payments after passage of federal legislation in 1999 that was designed to actively encourage welfare recipients to work.

Of all the reasons people gave for the Great Depression of the 1930s, few recognized the role played by the inability of armored humans to regulate their lives, both before its occurrence (as manifested in the work disturbance–based greed to amass quick fortunes in the stock market) and afterward (as seen in work disturbance–based helplessness in the face of having to find work and earn a living). Public welfare programs were originally intended solely for the care of the indigent. Following the Great Depression and Roosevelt's New Deal of the 1930s, politicians justified the government's increased involvement in public welfare and other assistance programs as a "solution" to the social manifestations of human dependency and helplessness. Unfortunately, politicians knew nothing about the *biological* cause of helplessness and irresponsibility. Instead of seeing these symptoms of human armor correctly, as a major contributor to social irrationalism throughout society, they saw it as an opportunity to exploit, further contributing to that irrationalism by providing makeshift solutions.

We know that human helplessness and irresponsibility empower politicians and power-hungry "saviors of humanity" of all denominations in their quest to gain dominion and political control. This occurs in two ways: Either the helpless masses passively seek to be taken care of by politicians, or people organize politically into special-interest groups and demand special treatment from their politicians, whose main interest is to get reelected. In either case, the stage is set for political corruption and mismanagement. This relationship is expressed in the following manner (Fig. 3.3):

Ambitious, Power-Hungry Leaders Willing to Lead the Masses

Social Helplessness, Greed, and Irresponsibility of the Masses

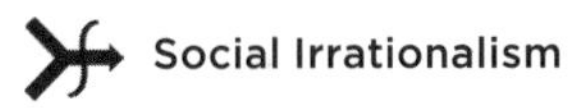

The Interaction Between the Armored Masses and Their Leaders

FIGURE 3.3

Only when enough people are sufficiently healthy from a *bio-physical/bioemotional* standpoint can they expect individuals, who can responsibly and rationally represent them, to run for office—and for the public to elect them. Instead, at best, people elect politicians whose policies provide only symptomatic relief, neglecting the underlying problem. Misguided efforts to increase government responsibility for individual lives, such as "affirmative action" programs, have fostered a sense of entitlement,[48] rendering the helpless masses even more helpless, irresponsible, and dependent. This has drained productive segments of society and, most tragically, ignores the cause of social problems altogether.

The Bill of Rights was originally intended to protect individuals from government intrusion and oppression. It was conceived and written at a time when the importance of individual responsibility in personal and social life was not questioned. Today, this document is commonly used not to safeguard and protect individuals from state tyranny (a core function), but to permit expression of the secondary layer by socially irresponsible politicians, criminals, and others. "Free speech" as a First Amendment right is so protected that any private individual, self-righteous politician, or member of the press can say virtually anything he or she pleases with impunity, regardless of the destructive social consequences. The social effect of this behavior is not just tolerated by liberals, but championed by them, as they believe it is the price of a free society. Although conservatives generally recognize the destructiveness of such license, they respond only moralistically, an ineffective solution in our permissive culture.

The political left responds to the pervasive social evidence of human helplessness and destructiveness by blindly minimizing or ignoring the importance of personal responsibility. Mindlessly, the left emphasizes individual "rights" and the responsibility of the government in procuring others' "rights." Liberals encourage the "right" to say and do whatever one pleases in every area of social life.[49] Quality of life is minimized in favor of quantitative factors—more and more freedom. However, freedom peddling

48. Some government programs are, in fact, formally referred to as "entitlement programs."

49. The one notable exception is the right to bear arms. This is because the liberal abhors the use of force.

stirs in the masses a longing for a better life that, because of their biophysical limitations, can never be fulfilled. The consequence of freedom peddling is a vicious cycle that furthers the dependency of the already helpless on others. By increasing the authority of the state, such peddling expands governmental responsibility and bureaucracy and its social service workforce. For example, protecting the "right" of welfare recipients to bear children irresponsibly while they continue to receive public benefits supports their helplessness and reinforces their sense of entitlement. This can only negate the importance of personal responsibility in the decision to have, care for, and raise healthy children.

By minimizing the importance of personal responsibility, the liberal politician's position fits hand-in-glove with that of the mechanistically oriented geneticist. If the homeless, schizophrenic, or manic-depressive is incapacitated because of a flaw in his genetic makeup, then his condition, behavior, and social problems cannot possibly be his fault. In the United States, homosexual activists have climbed on the bandwagon and embraced the homosexual brain/homosexual gene explanation for their "natural" sexual preference, stating that new "scientific" evidence supports their contention that those who oppose their lifestyle choices (and political agenda) and consider them dangerous to others, especially the young, are biased homophobes.

Conservative arguments and programs are also inadequate to cope with the enormity of the disturbance of humanity's capacity for freedom and responsibility. This is true as well for the libertarian approach to protecting individual freedom, which emphasizes personal responsibility and opposes socialistic government, with its attendant centralization and bureaucratization. Both the conservative and the libertarian are incapable in any way of addressing human destructive impulses because they lack knowledge of the existence of and necessity for human armoring. Consequently, they have no basis to understand its destructive social effects: social helplessness and dependency on the one hand, and the striving of politicians for power on the other.

An understanding of the social manifestations of the destructive secondary layer (evil) is accessible only to those social scientists who have a *functional energetic* understanding of social problems and who can step outside the crippling miasma of ideology. Only through functional thinking can one grasp the fact that the decline of the authoritarian social order has simultaneously broken down the social façade and led to a corresponding increase in destructive social behavior. The attendant social irresponsibility now *necessitates* repressive social action in the form of more and more laws, with all their drawbacks, more police, judges, prisons, and so on. Still, without these laws, and the will to enforce them, and these other measures, further social chaos is inevitable.

Social armor leads to only two possible outcomes: (1) issues involving freedom are used defensively, that is, moralistically, against assuming personal responsibility, as with the ideology of liberals; or (2) issues involving responsibility are used moralistically to repress personal freedom, as with the ideology of conservatives. Either way, the capacity for *genuine* freedom and responsibility is diminished. In the case of liberal ideology, sexual "freedom" turns into promiscuity, pornography, and perversion. With conservative ideology, sexual "responsibility" turns into antisexual moralism, or the individual remains love-starved in a marriage out of a sense of duty to the spouse. Whether liberal or conservative, ideology distorts freedom and responsibility and severs their mutual relationship.

Cognitive Distortions Inherent in Ideology

Ideologies are sociopolitically related ideas originating from and symptomatic of brain armor, which includes ocular armor. Ideologies function as a powerful social force—people live and die for them. Since those on the left defend themselves predominantly by their intellect, the ideology of the political left is a more powerful social force in today's anti-authoritarian society than the ideology of the right.

Armored thinking consists of a rigid application of the two fundamental directions of thinking. In general, liberals and others on the left think primarily in the direction of freedom, specialization, and complexity; conservatives and others on the right think in the direction of personal responsibility, determinism, and unifying principles. Thus, the belief systems of conservatives and liberals are derived from these two basic directions of thought. (See chapter 1, Figure 1.1)

The belief system of those on the political right centers on the "truth" as absolute, a concept related to whole functions. Mystics of all denominations believe in their own interpretations of the truth (the word of God), disregarding factual information that contradicts their preconceptions. An example is creationism, the Judeo-Christian version of the origin of the universe, our world and its inhabitants: God willed everything into existence.

The belief system of those on the sociopolitical left focuses mechanistically, with the same absolute certainty, on "the facts," concepts related to specialized functions in nature. With the mechanistic thinking of the left, it is not possible to relate the innumerable facts of science to each other to form a coherent picture of the real world. Furthermore, mechanistic laws apply to machines but not to nature and they are incapable of providing a unified and accurate worldview: Mechanists cannot see unifying principles (the truth), for their seeking in ever greater detail the "facts" that, upon discovery, add to the highly complicated body of scientific knowledge. Their theories are often based on conjecture, not on accurate observation, as, for example, when they declare that nature behaves like a machine or that all energy flows downhill. In this mechanistic-mystical system of thought, ideas related to the truth (theories) and ideas related to the facts function as antagonistic opposite variations (Fig. 3.4):

Theory ←∫→ Facts

FIGURE 3.4

Contrast this relationship to functional science, wherein theory and facts function as attractive opposite variations: theories about nature and factually based observations about nature support each other (Fig. 3.5):

Theory →∫← Facts

FIGURE 3.5

In our declining anti-authoritarian society, the conservative's thinking in the direction of whole functions (unifying principles) preserves society and provides a clearer perspective of actual social interrelationships than does the liberal's thinking. In rigid authoritarian societies, the thought processes of liberals in the direction of freedom and specialized functions provided a closer approximation of reality than the conservative viewpoint. Since political attitudes and thinking stem from and remain mired in the secondary layer, views can only shift between the limits of the left and the right on the sociopolitical spectrum. This is why the thinking of armored people forever shifts between left and right and why they never develop and move forward.

Any sociopolitical ideology has three components (Fig. 3.6).

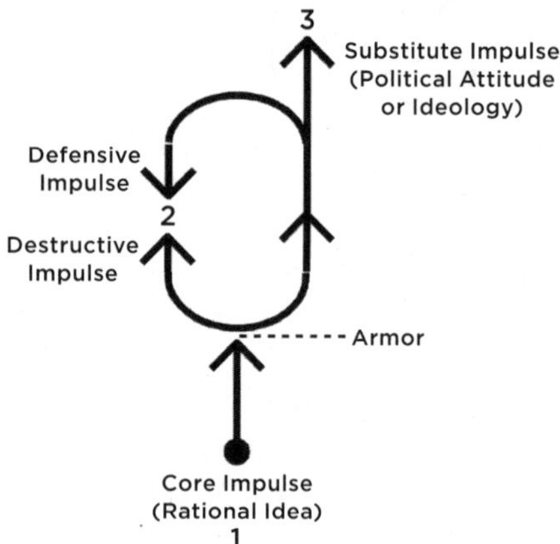

FIGURE 3.6

The first is the rational component, which attempts to deal with social issues at hand and is derived from the biological core, although its expression is necessarily distorted because of intervening layers of armor. This "core of truth" is the rational element contained in all social causes and includes ideals (such as justice, liberty, freedom, and responsibility), as well as truths (such as the rational element in "prejudice"). The second component, irrational and destructive, originates from blocked emotions contained in the armor. This serves as the rationale for expressing the irrational ideas, the ideology. Armor always consists of the destructive secondary impulse and the defense against it. The defensive function protects the individual from experiencing the displaced painful sensations and emotions related to his own conflicts. When a primary emotion (1 in Fig. 3.6) passes through the armor, it loses its rational biological quality and becomes irrational, harsh, and destructive. This is the source of the sex-negative elements of the ideology (2 in Fig. 3.6). Finally, there is the third component, the political ideology or attitude itself, which is a substitute impulse that has its origin in the personal conflicts of the individual expressed in sociopolitics (3 in Fig. 3.6).

Distortions of sociopolitical thought are somewhat clearer when the relationship between freedom and responsibility is examined. Thomas Sowell explains that concepts such as freedom and responsibility mean entirely different things to liberals and conservatives[50] because they hold different visions or views of reality (Sowell 1987, page 18). Sowell has demonstrated that people perceive the world differently, that the cognitive functions of liberals and conservatives are totally dissimilar. He refers to this difference as "constrained" versus "unconstrained" vision. In general, the constrained vision corresponds to the conservative's view as defined by Baker and the unconstrained vision corresponds to the liberal's view. From an orgonomic perspective, it can be added that these two visions, or worldviews, are based on ideological differences originating in the *character structure of the individual*, on specific distortions that result from the person's armored ocular functioning. Sowell alludes to this disturbance when he states that visions have a logic and momentum of their own that tend to generate conclusions that are the logical consequence of their assumptions.

Each vision deals in a one-sided way with different functional relationships, such as that between the individual and society, freedom and responsibility, and so on. Regarding individual rights, for example, the constrained vision allows society to restrict certain freedoms in order to protect its interests over those of the individual. In the unconstrained vision, individual freedom is more or less unchecked and bears no relationship to society's interests. Furthermore, in this vision freedom is defined only in terms of whether the individual is free to move about in society—not in terms of his ability to act responsibly unhampered

50. Here, the terms "liberal" and "conservative" are used as they apply in Western democracies.

by armor. The liberal defines freedom simply as the absence of externally imposed impediments and circumstantial limitations that reduce the range of individual choice. Freedom is supposed to be achieved by removing these external restrictions, if necessary (and for the liberal it is always necessary), through sociopolitical action. The pseudo-liberal maintains that, if one lacks the external means of achieving one's goals, then there is no freedom *in the result*, even if there is freedom *in the social process*. This assumption gives rise to freedom peddling, as often occurs in affirmative action programs or in the crusade for free speech—freedom in the service of defense against responsibility. In fact, placing rights of preferred minorities over the rest of the society serves the same defensive function in leftist ideology that racism does in the ideology of the right.

Like the liberal, the conservative also fails to comprehend the biological basis of freedom. Unaware of the role played by armor, conservatives also define freedom in strictly social terms. Whereas conservatives emphasize social processes that transcend the individual and the responsibility of people to abide by these processes, liberals stress words and concepts that revolve around individual *intention*. For example, "sincerity," "commitment," and "dedication" are central to how liberals think about freedom. On the other hand, the conservative's economic doctrine of laissez-faire assumes that intention has no relationship to effect—that capitalism's benefits are not part of a capitalist's intentions. This lack of correspondence between intention and effect is the reason that liberals often portray the capitalist system as cold and insensitive to the needs of "the people." To the pseudo-liberal, the imagined malevolent intentions and decadent personal life of capitalist businesspeople are more important than the fact that they create and provide countless jobs.

The conservative describes social processes not in terms of intention or even ultimate goals, but in terms of the characteristics inherent in the social system deemed necessary to contribute to these goals (Sowell 1987, page 91). For the liberal it is important whether individual rewards are merited or merely reflect privilege and luck. The liberal does not care if the "poor" merit reward. They should be rewarded regardless, *because as the underdog*, they have been wronged by society. To the conservative, social processes, not individual action, are more important in extracting the maximum social benefit from human potential.

The conservative view of equality comes closer to genuine work democracy than the liberal view. Again, equality exists as a process for conservatives and as a result for liberals. For conservatives, all people have equal rights but not equal material goods. For them, equal treatment has nothing to do with whether such general rules applied to specific situations lead to results that are more favorable to one individual or group than to others. For liberals, equality of opportunity means equalized probabilities of achieving given results, whether in education, employment, health care, or amassing material possessions (Ibid., page 123). These equalized probabilities are seen as necessary. and if necessary, externally imposed on society and controlled by the state through legislation.

In fact, however, the presence of an operative work democracy *within* American society *to the degree that it exists* provides the conditions for everyone, including minorities, to achieve success in work and, in many cases, to reach the top of their profession. As a result, equality is not achieved at the lowest level of social life, the goal of liberalism, but at a higher level of human functioning.

Similarly, for liberals, "security" refers to *social* security, a guarantee that the state will care for people. For conservatives, "security" refers to securing the social conditions under which people are free to live according to their wishes.

Conservatives also have a better intuitive grasp of armor, the existence of evil, and the inherent limitations of human beings. To ameliorate human suffering and promote progress, conservatives preserve existing traditions and social institutions. They emphasize personal responsibility by supporting "tried and true" social processes, such as moral tradition, the marketplace, and family values. Conservatives are wary of people who stand for unproven social programs and they strongly support adequate checks and balances in government. Unfortunately, neither the liberal nor the conservative recognizes that the biological capacity of humans to be free depends on the emotional health of the individual.

The view of freedom peculiar to liberals originates from their defensive use of intellect. They use their intellect in their struggle to free themselves from the restraints of armor located predominantly in the brain. Liberals use their intelligence to defend against the emergence of destructive impulses, and they do this in an attempt to free themselves of the limitations imposed by armor. This is the bioenergetic origin of their unconstrained vision. Through volition and intellect, liberals believe that they can become free from *any* constraint and perfect themselves by overcoming their defectiveness; and by extension, they think that they can eradicate all social iniquities through education. Hence, liberals think that the good intention to benefit others, largely a product of the intellect, is *the* supreme social virtue and the road to human happiness. Emotional plague characters who are in political power easily exploit this liberal ideology for their own nefarious purposes.

As noted, in today's anti-authoritarian society, the conservative's view of freedom is more grounded in reality. Conservatives are in better contact with the movement of energy within their organism than are liberals, and they have a clearer sense and appreciation of the evil contained in the secondary layer. They are unlikely to take the freedom of living in America for granted and recognize the need to protect their freedom by favoring strong police and military forces.

Regarding responsibility, the conservative's constrained vision emphasizes the importance of individual responsibility, while the liberal's unconstrained vision shifts responsibility onto external agents and institutions. Both views of responsibility are a manifestation of armored thinking, since they rigidly view the interests of society and the individual as antagonistically opposite. The unifying principle of a harmonious society as a natural biological system lies outside the framework of armored thought. For liberals, responsibility for social decisions resides in a surrogate individual or collective decision-maker—in other words, in a central locus. Once again, their idea of responsibility reflects the central role of the brain in the biophysical structure of the liberal character. In the mechanistic liberal worldview, the brain controls, directs, and is responsible for the activities of the body, just as the social center, or government, controls and directs social functions. By placing greater responsibility with the central government, liberalism undermines individual responsibility. In the conservative worldview, responsibility resides within each individual. Authorities exist, but their role is to preserve a social framework within which individuals are free to exercise discretion and have the opportunity for self-regulation.

Sowell extensively documents disturbed ocular functioning in the masses—both liberal and conservative—and how, from a cognitive standpoint, these disturbances form the basis for the left and the right segments of the sociopolitical spectrum. Although Sowell even-handedly presents the cases for both visions, it is clear that he is partial to those who agree with the constrained vision. Sowell's inability to justify this preference results from his unfamiliarity with Reich's and Baker's elucidation of the function of human armor. Such knowledge would enable him to understand what he intuits: Ocular armor prevents mankind from achieving the goals of freedom and happiness as understood by the unconstrained vision. The rigidity of sociopolitical ideology of both the left and the right lies in the fact that neither group is capable of seeing what is right about the point of view of the other. *Only by seeing the whole, undistorted picture is it possible to behave in a socially constructive manner.*

From a clinical standpoint, ideologies and behaviors of the left and the right are simply two different ways for people to focus externally on social issues and avoid looking inward to find the source of their personal problems. In so doing, both act in ways that are individually and socially destructive. Rival sociopolitical ideologies give rise to different and often conflicting social attitudes and policies. When this happens the pent-up rage contained in the ideology is discharged as irrational ideas and behaviors. Such conflicts are responsible for all degrees of destructive social activity, from relatively unimportant disagreements between different groups (civil strife, local warfare) to global warfare. For example, this exact situation was responsible for bringing about the tragedy of both World Wars. The German Kaiser would never have been emboldened to pursue the aggressive militaristic policy that culminated in the First World War had he not been confident that the British government, controlled at that time by the Liberal Party, would step aside and not oppose the aggression of Germany. The British foreign secretary, Sir Edward Grey, was a liberal character who clearly misjudged the forces that were opposing him. Many people in nineteenth-century England had come to believe that war was a thing of the past (Oliver 1916, page 72). The same situation happened at the start of the Second World War. Today, there are those who believe that a global nuclear war can never happen. Such wishful thinking is the result of an ignorance of the dynamics of sociopolitical characterology.

The real function of sociopolitical ideology is the exact opposite of its stated purpose: It actually blocks humanity's awareness of the origin of its plight. At the same time it maintains the illusion that external factors, rather than powerful, inner biological forces, govern human life. This dangerous notion gives rise to the destructive idea that people are not responsible for their own predicament. Those on the left blame environmental circumstances, such as poverty and unequal distribution of wealth, while those on the right seek answers to humanity's wretched existence in cosmic factors such as original sin, the flawed nature of humans, and God's will. Those on the left search for political solutions, while those on the right, fatalistically clinging to religion or mysticism, have (until very recently) remained politically indifferent.

Freud came close to supplying the correct answer to the predicament of humanity by discovering the destructive forces of unconscious life. However, and of great importance, because it was restricted exclusively to the superficial psychological realm, psychoanalysis lacked the necessary scientific, *biological* foundation to provide a complete solution to the problem of human destructiveness. As a result, Freud had to *mystify* biological functions by resorting to a "death instinct" theory to explain the source of human destructiveness.

Attributing human problems to external sources relieves mankind of the pain and responsibility of honestly experiencing their own lives and prevents them from feeling gratitude for the freedoms that come with living in America. Others—the government, union bosses, God, or whomever—are responsible, and the individual is the victim of external forces. Reich's discovery of armor solved the riddle of the origin of human destructiveness. By disclosing the existence and function of armor, orgonomic biopsychiatry has provided humanity with a door out of its trapped existence. But this can happen only at a price: People must stop evading themselves by looking for political and social solutions. This means that they must experience the painful feelings, the "truth" they are avoiding, trapped within their armored structure. As painful as it is, this restorative process has the power to increase contact with the self and provide a greater sense of responsibility and a capacity for freedom in one's own life.

CHAPTER 4

DEMOCRACY IN ARMORED SOCIETY: FORMAL DEMOCRACY VERSUS WORK DEMOCRACY

Natural work democracy exists and is in constant operation, no matter whether this or that political party or ideological group knows about its existence or not.
—Wilhelm Reich, *The Mass Psychology of Fascism*

The effect of ideological thinking is to fragment society. The left fragments social groups with a view that reduces everyone to the same socioeconomic level, while the right selects certain groups over others. Reacting to the tendency of armored humans to splinter society, mystics use religion in an attempt to unify humanity on the basis of *ideas and principles* that have no basis in reality. They are therefore of no practical value. The common *biological* functions uniting people of different races, cultures, and nations into a single society remain unknown or are consistently overlooked.

It is remarked that we are living in the age of the Common Man. However, there is no objective standard for measuring the functioning of this representative human. Because of distortions that armor produces on thought processes, the Common Man is unfortunately too often petty, mean-spirited, and small-minded in his personal and social life. With the current breakdown of social structure and a rise in sociopolitical activity, the secondary layer has become manifest with increasing prominence. It would be more accurate to say that we appear to be living increasingly in the age of the Little Man (Reich 1948b). In the following passage written in the 1830s, Alexis de Tocqueville describes a major aspect of the Little Man in nineteenth-century America:

> The first thing that strikes one in the United States is the innumerable multitude of those who seek to get out of their original condition; and the second is the small number of great ambitions that make themselves noticed in the midst of this universal movement of ambition. There are no Americans who do not show that they are devoured by the desire to rise, but one sees almost none of them who appear to nourish vast hopes or to aim very high. All want constantly to acquire goods, reputation, power; few envision all these things on a grand scale. And this is surprising at first sight, since one does not perceive anything, either in the mores or in the laws of America that would limit desires and prevent them from soaring in all directions. (Tocqueville 2000, page 599)

This description could have been written today.

Race hatred, a manifestation of the emotional pestilence, is one characteristic of the behavior of the Little Man and it is popularly believed that prejudice is morally wrong and therefore should be eliminated. However, this idealistic attitude, combined with simple suppression or denial of the existence of prejudice, won't eradicate it because there is always some rational aspect to prejudice and this must first be acknowledged. For example, some, *but not all*, whites, blacks, Jews, Protestants, Catholics, Arabs and so on behave in a petty, socially stereotypical, objectionable or destructive manner. This must first be acknowledged —only then can the deeper, irrational aspect as an expression of the plague be effectively addressed. The origin of irrational, prejudicial ideas and attitudes is rooted in self-contempt which is projected onto others. This occurs because of people's underlying intolerance and viscerally felt hatred of their *own*, particularly genital, sensations. Therefore, prejudicial ideas and racism are permanently eliminated only when the armor that contains their energy source is removed. It is no accident that the objects of blame, contempt, and opprobrium are often directed at ethnic groups that are similar enough to the aggressor to the point of being indistinguishable (e.g., non-Jewish Germans and Jewish Germans in Nazi Germany, Jews and Arabs, in the current Middle East conflict, and so on).

Reich compared the thinking of healthy and armored humans in social affairs. Rational thinking based on accurate perceptions of reality is productive. When a core impulse that gives rise to a rational idea passes through the armor to the surface, it changes qualitatively and becomes distorted. It loses its fluidity and becomes rigid, unproductive and destructive, reflecting the qualities of the armored organism from which it originated. Reich showed that behind the petty, circumscribed, and confused ideas of armored humans, there were originally simple, great thoughts. He described this relationship as the *Little Man parallel* (Reich 1953a).

Table 4.1 on the next page gives some examples of great thoughts originating in the biological core that have been distorted by armored people into the Little Man parallel.

Creative Thought	Little Man Parallel
Equal opportunity for men and women	"Women's lib," feminism
Protection of private property	Greed, plunder
Striving for self-betterment	Resentment, envy, covetousness
Independent social thinking and behavior	Spiteful, resentful thinking and behavior
Productive natural science	Mechanistic–mystical technician
Tolerance of homosexuals	Persecution of homosexuals
Homosexuality is a sexual disturbance	"Gay rights" activism
Prevention of armor in children	"Childrens' rights"
Protection of the environment	Environmental radicalism
Systematic breakdown of armor by a qualified medical orgonomist	"Alternative" therapies, medication treatment
Rational political activity, civic responsibility	Sociopolitical activism
News reporting	Yellow journalism, editorializing news, news as entertainment
Privacy in sexual matters	Secrecy in sexual matters
Sexual revolution	Sexual license, pornography, perversions
Natural need for love	Lasciviousness and sexual gossip
Knowledge	Information explosion
America is a melting pot	America is a multicultural society
Governmental administration	Bureaucracy
Government secures the conditions under which freedom can flourish	Government is the "provider" of freedom
Finding the biological root of social problems	Liberal "solutions" to social problems
Every armored person is a potential carrier of the emotional plague	Original sin
Natural morality	Compulsive morality (on the right), Moral relativism (on the left)
Functional thinking in the natural sciences	Mechanistic thinking in the natural sciences
Rational authority	Authoritarianism, anti-authoritarianism

TABLE 4.1

We will show that conservative and liberal thinking are not absolute, as is commonly believed, but derive significance from their relationship to existing political and economic conditions. Furthermore, a social attitude is life-positive to the extent it preserves the conditions supportive of unarmored life.

Formal Democracy and Work Democracy

What political structures preserve unarmored life? Any discussion of democratic processes must distinguish between a formal democracy, which is nothing more than a *utopian social ideal* originating from the superficial layer of armored humans and democracy based on *actual work relationships*. Work function originates from the biological core and constitutes the greater part of all genuine social activity. This distinction between formal and work democracy was one of Reich's major contributions to sociology. It originated from Reich's discovery of character armor and how this interferes with social functioning. Democracy is essentially a philosophy which insists on the right and capacity of a people, acting either directly or through representatives, to control their institutions for their own purposes. Reich found that character armor actually prevents people from being able to rationally direct the activities of the state. Therefore, all attempts on the part of armored humans to form a truly democratic society must become distorted and turn into formal democracy.

Reich understood that work, like sex, is a basic biological activity vital not only for survival but also for emotional well-being. Thus, orgonomic functionalism places the origin of work performed by all living systems, including humans, in the biological realm, an activity that is determined by the movement of biological orgone energy. Because orgone energy governs all living functions, and work is critical to regulating the energy economy of the individual, the self-regulating function of work is central to the economic activity and well-being of society.

Defining work as a bioenergetic function allows us to recognize its manifestations even in primitive life forms. Certain highly specialized behaviors of social insects are a manifestation of the work function. Here, the work performed is linked to, and is inseparable from, the physical structure of the insect. The tools used by insects to perform work are part of their morphology. These insects perform only a single, specialized task. The biological work function of higher vertebrates is more fluid and is not determined exclusively by the structure of the organism. Humans fashion complex tools to serve particular work functions. They can fashion tools to make other tools endlessly. Because this allows adaptation to the widest range of environmental conditions, the work capacity of humans is potentially limitless.

It appears that the work activity of adults originates in the exploring and creative play of children, occurring around five years of age, at the genital stage of psychosexual development. This is when the integration of pleasurable organ sensations and motor activity becomes somewhat organized. According to Curtis Barnes, "Work originates with bioenergetic tension, which the organism perceives as feelings of longing, desire or discomfort; physical work activity follows, and, finally, contact is established with the work product, which produces a relaxation of tension felt as pleasurable gratification" (Barnes 1979, page 127).

Each individual has certain unique abilities or talents, each with quantitative properties affecting work capacity and qualitative properties affecting the type of work for which the individual is suited. Parents and teachers are responsible for recognizing these innate abilities in children and providing them with opportunities to develop their innate talents. However, the middle biopsychic layer, the armor, interferes with the realization of these abilities in characteristic ways that differ for each individual.

The capacity to acquire the knowledge and to learn the skills necessary for work is an expansive function and is developed from the periphery of the bioemotional apparatus. In healthy individuals, the capacity to learn and to develop proficiency is based on contact with the environment as well as with the core. In all armored individuals, the contact between core-related work impulses and the capacity to learn is disturbed.

Work-related frustration is like sexual frustration in that undischarged biological energy in both leads to frustration and fuels ideological thinking and irrational social and political behavior. Western ideologues on the left, who displace their personal neurotic conflicts onto the social sphere by striving for greater freedom and social equality, do so with no regard for the consequences of their actions. In reaction, people on the right justly oppose this irrational social behavior, however, with their own ideological thinking. Conflicts arising from political polarization serve only to discharge pent-up emotional energy through irrational sociopolitical activity, ultimately making matters worse. This unfortunate situation, seen world-wide, is the inevitable consequence of a biological impulse striking the armor, becoming distorted, and then expressed destructively in the social realm. *Armor deflects an originally rational impulse and turns it into an irrational, socially destructive force.* When, for whatever reason, political opposition between the left and the right is temporarily suspended, the aggressive forces continue to press for release and become internally directed. This gives rise to political in-fighting—another example of the destructive nature of the political activity of armored humans.

Under natural conditions, work, like sexuality, is pleasurable and goal-directed. However, if the natural development of the work function is impeded for any reason, destructive consequences are inevitable. People with intact work function feel intense frustration when their work process is disturbed. In contrast, most armored individuals experience work as a burden, since it is cut off from the core and produces little or no gratification. They often feel relief when they are not burdened with work.

Reich (1949a, page 261) described the biological work function of the healthy person, the neurotic character, and the emotional plague character in terms of each type's work capacity. Healthy people have retained their capacity to work and their ability to derive satisfaction from working. To the extent that work gives them pleasure, they approach it spontaneously and with pleasurable anticipation. Interest is directed toward the work process, which spontaneously results in a product. The healthy person guides the work achievement of others by example, not by dictating the process or product.

To some extent, most neurotics have retained their ability to work but do so compulsively and without pleasure. This group includes those engaged in mechanical, repetitious (e.g., assembly line) work that, by its nature, leads to limited contact with the overall process and hence results in little satisfaction. Such persons focus exclusively on the product. Depending on their degree of responsibility, these individuals require varying degrees of external restraints or internal compulsions provided by their armor. In extreme cases, their compulsive work habits turn them into "workaholics" and they work to the exclusion of other activities. They are responsible and have retained their ability to work, but they do so without gratification. Some workaholics appear to "love" their work. On close inspection, however, it is clear that work is their way to avoid anxiety.

The ability to assume and exercise responsibility provides an additional means of evaluating work capacity. Those in whom the work function has deteriorated such that they are no longer responsible for the work process are severely impaired. Responsibility for their work has shifted to someone else, seen as a boss, union official, or subordinate. An example is the mechanical worker who limits his or her responsibility to the drone-like completion of an assigned task. At this level of disturbance and dependency, the work function approaches the level of slave labor.

This classification of the disturbances in people's work function does not necessarily indicate a person's functioning in other areas. Psychopaths and certain politicians have a very high energy level and can be considered "successful," yet they have no capacity whatsoever for productive work. In these individuals, the resultant energy stasis is diverted to fuel destructive social activities. Also relevant are ideological leftists and their political agendas which stress personal freedom while ignoring the importance of individual responsibility in social life. The popularity of this leftist attitude has had a destructive influence on work function, as many who once retained some responsibility for their work now tend to give it up; while others who could once work only under someone else's authority have now become unable to work at all and instead rely on the state's welfare system for their survival. People afflicted with the emotional plague derive no satisfaction from work, nor are they able to work productively. They strive to get themselves into a position of authority so that they can then tell others how to work. (See chapter 7, the section on Work)

In a formal democracy, power resides in (1) armored individuals and institutions and (2) the core functions of society. No distinction is made between these two sources of power. As a result, there is widespread confusion between these two sources. In a work democracy, power resides in the work process itself, which originates from the biological core. It is the organizing force of a *truly* democratic society. Formal democracies are based on the rule of universal suffrage in a multiparty system in which there are competitive elections. Additionally, the following minimal constraints are required: (1) The legislature cannot be dismissed by any body or person other than itself. (2) The courts are independent of the legislative and executive branches. (3) The executive cannot appoint judges without approval of the legislative branch. (4) Only the legislature can pass laws.

Formal democracies came into existence during the Age of Enlightenment around the seventeenth and eighteenth centuries. This form of government became possible because there was a dramatic increase in people's *specialized* work functions. This development gave rise to the prominence of merchants, lawyers, physicians, and professional experts and corresponding guilds of all kinds. This specialization in economic life was accompanied by the establishment of the rule of law and of formal democracies across Europe. *In these cases, the development into formal democracy occurred from within the armored social system.*

The appearance of formal democracies occurred as a result of a combination of healthy, primary and neurotic, secondary drives. It is the inevitable result of the way armored humans function. Their distorted form of democracy is one that is fully in accord with their armored way of thinking. The operation of a formal democracy is modeled according to the erroneous tenets of mechanistic science and mystical religion. As a result, democracy is partially divested of its organizing principles, which are derived from fundamental biosocial core functions, thereby giving rise to its rigidly formal, idealistic features. (See section on Functional Economics in this chapter) For example, a common idealistic belief is that it is possible to simply declare a democracy in a country by writing a constitution, passing laws legalizing political parties, and ensuring universal suffrage. The illusory nature of this way of thinking has been amply demonstrated in the case of South American countries and now in Russia and Iraq. In fact, the exact opposite is closer to the truth: Democracies cannot be imposed. People will function democratically *only if they can regulate themselves to begin with;* that is, if their work and sexual functions are already sufficiently in order. Another example: it is believed that simply by providing job opportunities people will want to work. This is a mechanistic and idealistic view that does not consider the fact that the work function originates from within, from *internally generated, pleasurable impulses.* Work function cannot be imposed on people. The opportunity to work is necessary but hardly enough to ensure the individual's capacity to work.

As we have seen, what is true for individuals is true for societies. Neither democracy nor fulfilling economic activity can be forced from outside the social system by mechanically applied measures. The economic cornerstone of a free economy is a free market, but as the recent catastrophic developments in Russia have also shown, a viable free-market work democracy cannot be externally imposed on armored society any more than the capacity to work can be dictated to an armored individual.

We know from clinical experience that when armor is suddenly removed from an individual who has not been prepared for it, chaos ensues. With inadequate preparation after the Cold War, the Russian people were too sick to function democratically under conditions of economic freedom. Once social armor provided by Communism was removed, every manifestation of social pathology from the secondary layer, including uncontrolled criminal activity, emerged. Armored conditions, with authoritarian, governmental control of society, needed to be imposed to bring about a semblance of order in Russian society. This is why the legislative branch, the Parliament, was dissolved by presidential decree in October 1993, and why the Russian courts are completely subordinate to the executive. One by one the freedoms that the Russian people were given with the demise of the Soviet Union are being taken from them by their leaders. The breakup of the old Soviet regime is being replaced by a new monolithic structure. The obvious question is, *"How much will it resemble the old one?"* No one ever asks, *"Why has this degradation of freedom happened?"* Without a more than superficial answer to this important question, which only orgonomic sociology can provide, there can never be any possibility for enduring social improvement.

The breakthrough of the destructive secondary layer is now

also rampant in the Middle East and the restoration of armored conditions in the form of authoritarianism is mandatory to prevent social chaos there as well.

In an earlier article it was shown that from a functional point of view, the Communist Soviet Union had the same relationship to Western democratic governments that the disease cancer has to the whole organism. That country's survival depended on sapping the vitality of other nations, because the social system of communism is functionally identical to the carcinomatous shrinking biopathy[51] in the individual organism (Konia 1986a, 1986b). The Soviet Union could only have survived if it had maintained a tightly controlled economy and was allowed to continually expand its territory and sphere of influence to include the entire world. Short of this, its social, political, economic and military collapse was just a matter of time. Indeed, a strict policy of containment combined with the strongly anti-communist Reagan administration accelerated the decline, and the collapse of the Soviet Union as an international power occurred within the next decade. This practice is exactly analagous to the current method of medical or surgical containment used in the treatment of the cancerous process in the individual.

The same relationship between the social disease of communism and cancer existed not only between the Soviet Union and Western democracies, but also inside the Soviet Union itself. The same process that occurs within the individual biosystem of a cancer sufferer occurred in the social realm with the demise of the Soviet Union. That is, the whole Soviet system collapsed, with the loss of the Eastern-European satellite countries and former Soviet republics accompanying the socioeconomic collapse of the system's internal fascistic structure.

With the fall of the Soviet Union, prominent Westerners, from presidents to journalists to economists and investors, remained optimistic in predicting that economic reform and the democratization of Russian society was at hand. The West continued to invest heavily in the Russian economy, closing its eyes to what was really happening. Since the defeat of Germany and Japan following the Second World War resulted in their dramatic postwar recovery into two of the strongest economic powers in the

51. Cancer.

world, economists and others expected that the fall of the Soviet Union and the end of the Cold War would somehow, in like fashion, lead to a dramatic recovery in Russia's economy. Despite the West's continued heavy investment in Russia, functional thinking allows us to understand why this did not happen.

Following the fall of the Soviet Communist empire, Western governments and economists attempted to impose a free market system upon the defunct, emotional plague-ridden Communist economies of the Soviet Union and Eastern Europe. These Western governments failed to comprehend the enormous obstacles to the attainment of this goal because they knew nothing of *biological armor* and how it interferes with establishing such a free market system. To make matters worse, the Soviet reign had crippled what remained of the natural, self-motivating work function of the Soviet peoples that existed prior to 1917. The obstacles to reestablishing a free market economy after it has been destroyed were far greater than the effort it took to destroy it.

Under Lenin and Stalin, the most productive segments of the population were systematically wiped out. A preliminary accounting of emotional plague manifestations of Soviet Communists shows the following:

- The execution of tens of thousands of hostages and prisoners without trial, and the murder of hundreds of thousands of rebellious workers and peasants from 1918 to 1922.
- The famine of 1922, directly caused by ruinous government depletion of seed stock, caused the death of over five million people.
- The deportation and extermination of the Don Cossacks in 1920.
- The murder of tens of thousands in concentration camps from 1918 to 1930.
- The liquidation of almost 690,000 people in the Great Purge of 1937–38.
- The deportation of two million kulaks (and alleged "kulaks") from 1930 to 1932.

- The death by starvation of at least four million Ukrainians and two million others through a man-made, systematically enforced famine in 1932–33.
- The deportation of hundreds of thousands of Poles, Ukrainians, Balts, Moldovans, and Bessarabians from 1939 to 1941, and again in 1944–45.
- The deportation of the Volga Germans in 1941.
- The wholesale deportation of the Crimean Tartars in 1943.
- The wholesale deportation of the Chechens in 1944.
- The wholesale deportation of the Ingush in 1944. (Courtois 1999, page 9)

Those who were not murdered were indoctrinated for decades to believe that capitalism is corrupt, immoral, and exploitative. The moralistic rationalization based on this outlook, and shared by many Western liberals and Islamic fundamentalists, is that anyone successful in business must be an evil profiteer. This is yet another aspect of the emotional plague—generating confusion as to what are the constituents of the primary and secondary layers of human functioning. This example relates to the work function: Some, but not everyone who is successful in business, are corrupt.

Under socialism, the Russian people were looked after by a low-quality but comprehensive welfare state. After the collapse of the Soviet Union, the Russian people had to trade security for the unproven freedom promised by capitalism. The situation is identical to suddenly stripping away the crippling armor in a severely disturbed patient and expecting the patient to function in a healthy manner. It is also identical to expecting someone recovering from a broken leg to start walking normally immediately following removal of the cast. The character structure of those who had their ability to work broken under Communism had become deeply ingrained with the fear of taking risks, of competition, of change, of something new.

For a short while, the lifting of socioeconomic repression provided unparalleled economic opportunities for the Russian people. Yet, for people used to a constitutionally guaranteed job, these same transformations greatly increased the level of anxiety. Managers of new private companies had great difficulty in finding workers not afflicted by the lackadaisical work ethic fostered by the Communist system. Unemployment resulted not only from the unavailability of work, but also from the unavailability of individuals *capable* of work. The suicide rate and the rate of per capita alcohol consumption, both signs of anxiety, have risen dramatically. Over the past decade, the population of Russia has been shrinking due to a plummeting birth rate and a rising number of deaths from violence and the consequences of alcoholism. Predictions are astonishingly grave: The country could lose a third of its population by mid-century.

The reason Russian society failed in its expected recovery from seventy years of Communist oppression is obfuscated by the fixed, idealistic belief that democracy can simply be imposed on a nation regardless of whether the masses are sufficiently healthy and free of armor, and therefore capable of working independently and functioning democratically. The same illusory premise was behind the Russian Revolution in 1917 and is behind attempts to establish democracies in the Arab nations of the Middle East. The capability to function democratically is dependent on the emotional health of the average citizen.

It soon became apparent that except for a small minority, the Russian people were not able to adapt to the enormous social changes required to establish a viable democracy: They could not simply relinquish socialism and begin to function as a free people in a free market economy. Their poor state of emotional health was evident as the Russian people sat around helplessly watching their economy, government, and military succumb to wholesale criminality, greed, embezzlement, bribery, and cronyism, all done with an astonishingly sophisticated manipulation of global monetary mechanisms.

Following the Great Depression of the 1930s, a similar situation of social helplessness occurred in the United States with a free market economy. At that time President Roosevelt first instituted centralized, governmental, regulatory programs to deal with the problems of mass unemployment. These programs had to be introduced because the American workers could not regulate themselves by adapting to the change in economic conditions, necessitating external social regulation.

Because of this emotionally based helplessness, it is the rare individual who can change his work function when external circumstances necessitate. This is the underlying reason why unions continue to exist and why the government intervenes: Both institutions function to protect and care for the emotionally crippled worker population. For example, farm subsidies become necessary when farmers cannot adapt to a change in social conditions that require a change in farm production. Similarly, factories must shut down when their product cannot compete in the marketplace because factory owners and workers cannot shift to more economical manufacturing or to the production of a product that is in greater demand. This inability to self-regulate is temporarily overcome during wartime conditions, when demand for production increases.

The rational basis for governmental control of society is the necessity for regulation of those who cannot regulate themselves because of disturbed functioning. The external collapse of the Soviet Union as a world power and the abrupt removal of the social armor of socialism, all within a few short years, were immediately followed by the internal collapse of Russian society. Vladimir Putin's policies of inducing contraction of the state by increasing the power of the central government, curbing certain kinds of lawlessness and abuses of freedom, thus make sense from the standpoint that these measures protect society by providing much-needed social armor. The effect of this intervention was to arrest the process of social disintegration. As a form of social armor, increasing governmental control of society restricts freedom necessary for healthy social life, but it also prevents further disintegration. Just as with individuals who are dysfunctional because of insufficient armor, Russian society *first has to re-armor and return to a more contracted, less chaotic state* before the process of armor removal can hope to bring about a formal democracy. Only time will tell if these measures will be successful.

Despite the widespread corruption and the restriction of freedom currently imposed on Russian society from above, there are some signs of improving economic well-being. Although far from attaining the status of a formal democracy, the Russian government's greater fiscal responsibility and weaning the country from reliance on outside financial aid has led to socioeconomic improvement. By early 2000, Russia had roughly stabilized the ruble. The Kremlin took hold of the budget and has even been running a surplus. Russia has paid off $10 billion of some $18 billion owed to the IMF and has refused fresh IMF assistance. In 2001, the Russian economy expanded by about 5.5 percent. With personal income taxes cut to a flat rate of 13 percent from 30 percent, and income tax revenues increasing by more than 50 percent, it remains to be seen whether the positive trend in the Russian economy will continue.[52]

Democracy is meaningful only when *people's capacity to tolerate freedom* and to *responsibly perform vital work* determines their social relationships. This necessarily imposes an order of rank upon individuals in a society. The inclusion of rank has two aspects to it, one quantitative and the other qualitative. *Quantitatively,* a greater work capacity for a particular work function confers a more prominent social rank, with greater responsibility and greater freedom to develop. This is the basis of *rational* authority. Correspondingly, those with higher order of rank, as determined by work capacity and experience, necessarily have greater social and economic influence and therefore greater power. This form of authority is natural and is a core function: it is not irrational or authoritarian. The degree to which this rational relationship exists between the individual and society determines the degree to which any social organization functions in a work-democratic manner. *Qualitatively,* the *work function* of individuals is also different, and hence this too differentiates rank. In a work-democratic relationship, the quantitative and qualitative aspects of work function correspond to the person's social status in a *biologically* rational manner. For example, consider a research laboratory in which qualitatively different functions are performed by persons of different rank: the research scientist, the technical assistants to the scientist, the maintenance people who preserve the working conditions of the laboratory, and so on.

By including the social rank of an individual's work function, we avoid the pitfalls of egalitarianism on the one hand or of

---

52. See *Wall Street Journal* editorial, "A Russian Revival," November 12, 2001.

expecting too much from the worker on the other. These errors, common to today's mechanistic view of work, lead to confusion as to an individual's capacity for *quality* work and therefore constitute a major source of work-related problems.

Human irrationality, the result of armor, interferes with this highly ordered, natural social organization. In formal democracies, irrational behaviors (such as striving for social power, envying or undermining people in authority either overtly or covertly, trying to please the boss, avoiding work, bureaucratization, and so on) are part and parcel of the sick environment in the armored workplace. Individuals deal with these problems every day, sometimes successfully, sometimes unsuccessfully, but always having to contend with a drag on morale and a drain on energy.

In the socialist and the pseudo-liberal character, resentment and envy of rational authority and of private wealth based on individual merit, coupled with the desire to reduce everyone to the same level regardless of ability and desire to work, undermines and eventually destroys people's work function. Power and authority shift from qualified working individuals to inept corporate and government bureaucrats. Under socialism, society is governed rigidly by the mindless, mechanical rule that all are equal—except, of course, the governing elite. Little value is placed on individual capabilities.

The relationship of democratic idealism to armored society is identical to the relationship of the ego ideal to the armored individual. Both social and individual ideals are mechanistic-mystical attempts on the part of armored systems to attain certain desired goals or plans in life. In a formal democracy, everyone's opinion is given equal value *as an ideal to be achieved*, especially in human affairs, regardless of the person's abilities, character structure or level of independent functioning, training and experience—with disastrous social consequences. For example, in their affirmative action programs, government bureaucrats with no vital role or expertise in the work process have the power to dictate who is allowed and is not allowed to work, regardless of the level of the individual's work function. This reduces the quality of work and the morale of the entire workforce, including, and *especially*, those minority individuals with higher work abilities. Unless biologically driven work is recognized and valued, any naturally existing work-democratic relationship deteriorates. This results in a merely formal democracy and the ongoing and ever-increasing polarization and fragmentation of society into political parties and contending groups. Then, in the face of overt disruptions and to maintain order, certain individuals will succeed in attaining political power and control over the emotionally crippled masses. This debasement, from formal democracy to an authoritarian social order, can occur either to the political left or the right. It is the inevitable consequence of humanity's armored social existence.

The rational component of political thought is not absolute but is dependant on social conditions. It is rational in the case of formal democracies to adhere to liberal attitudes during periods of social growth and ascendancy and to conservative views during periods of social decline. Similarly, in the case of Islamic fundamentalist or communist totalitarian states, since conservatism maintains social repression, liberalism, which always seeks to change or destroy the existing social order, is more rational, although it cannot provide definitive social solutions. The formal-democratic movements of nineteenth-century Europe, the resistance movement against the Nazis during the Second World War, and Prime Minister Gorbachev's undermining of Soviet Communism are all examples. However, in a declining formal-democratic society such as the one in America today, conservatism is rational because it preserves whatever degree of freedom currently exists. In a declining society, by randomly seeking ever-increasing degrees of "freedom" and change, liberalism accelerates the destruction of the democratic social order, since it induces divergence and polarization and, in reaction, social repression, the very opposite of its intended goal.[53]

Ignoring these factors and rigidly adhering to preconceived ideas regardless of current social conditions can have disastrous consequences. For example, partly because of the Nazi Holocaust and partly because of the outsider's tendency to identify with the

53. The pseudo-liberal is predisposed to act. Pseudo-liberals give the appearance, especially to the politically naïve masses, of being "for" the betterment of humanity. In reality, they are interested only in promoting their own welfare and exercising political control over people. In contrast, those on the right are essentially reactive in general, and reactive to leftist programs in particular. Unfortunately, the gullible masses perceive those on the right as being "against" social improvement. This perversely distorted view of both the left and the right is promoted by the liberal-dominated media.

underdog, many American Jews, even though they are characterologically conservative, identify with leftist movements and oppose conservative political policies, as if the form of democracy in contemporary America is no different from that of German society in the 1930s. This myopic view is an example of the social destructiveness of ocular armor. Many Jews traditionally side with leftist organizations because throughout recorded history they were alienated. As a result, many have a deep-seated fear and suspicion of any form of externally imposed authority. No longer justified in today's America, this suspicion is irrational and a symptom of the social mistrust, even paranoia, that ocular armor can cause. In their dogmatic, mistaken support of liberalism, these American Jews are actually helping to bring about what they fear most: regression to a centralization of political power and to an increase in anti-Semitism.

These developments are already happening. The critical task of preserving unarmored life requires that the crucial distinction is made between the primary core and the armored secondary layer of the human bioemotional structure. An important characteristic inherent in functional sociological thinking is its focus on the *effect* of a given social activity or policy, not its *apparent value*. Thus, conservatives can think functionally when they perceive the destructive effect of liberal social programs. However, their thinking is rigid and one-sided when they ignore pressing social issues. On the other hand, liberals recognize the existence of social problems but cannot act rationally because they cannot make contact with the biological depths from which these problems originate. Both characters are armored, and both think rigidly and moralistically. For example, liberals vehemently oppose dictatorships on the right but are blind to those on the left, while conservatives generally are blind in the opposite direction. During the 1930s, many on the left were apologists for Stalin, while many on the right did not recognize the threat of Hitler. Neither form of thought can illuminate the social processes giving rise to dictatorships in the first place.

Armor, Ideology, and the State

Armored humanity cannot deal rationally and constructively with the structure, organization, and administration of the state. The destructive effects of armoring result mostly from disturbed ocular function, with its attendant perceptual and cognitive distortions. Individuals of similar character structure view the world alike and spontaneously group together, organize socially, and form political factions.[54] This phenomenon, first noticed by Reich, was vividly demonstrated in Germany in the 1930s when the conflict between left and right became polarized into a battle between Red Fascism (Communism) and Black Fascism (Nazism). He states: "*The class struggle took place between members of the same class.* When I spoke with friends from the youth organizations about that, they understood my question: 'How does it come about that these workers, office employees, small business men, housewives, domestics split up in such a way in spite of their common economic pattern, so that contradictory political opinions developed?'"(Reich 1953b, page 112; italics in original).[55] The formation of political factions that leads to the development of a social system precludes the possibility of arriving at rational solutions to social problems. Now the irrationality of sociopolitics enters the scene. As political solutions to the problems of humanity begin to fail, as they inevitably must, political activity becomes progressively more irrational, desperate, and destructive. The history of partisan politics in the United States perfectly illustrates this process. The following is an account of how partisan politics first came about in America.

Emerging Political Partisanship in the United States

The creation of the American republic in 1776 was a first in the history of the human race. It was an event of monumental proportions. Following the American War of Independence, a group of prominent individuals, some with exceptional abilities, worked

---

54. In contrast, most sociologists think that political organizations are based on economic or other "realistic" factors. Reich showed that such rational factors are not determinants in the sociopolitical realm (Reich 1946). Any successful psychopathic politician, such as Hitler, intuitively knows this and uses it to his advantage.

55. This question has been answered with the discovery of sociopolitical character types by E.F. Baker, M.D.

together to organize a form of government that was unique in the entire history of civilization. For men like Washington and Hamilton, the Revolutionary War was necessary to achieve greater personal and social *independence*. Functionally speaking, then, it was not a revolution, but a war of independence. In varying degrees, people in the thirteen colonies had their fill of British rule and wanted to govern themselves. Because of their greater degree of independence, which was amply demonstrated by their prodigious accomplishments, their chances of being successful in being able to regulate themselves were fairly good. In sharp contrast, later revolutions inspired by the American War of Independence, such as the French and Russian revolutions, originated from leftist *ideas about freedom*; that is, from the intellect of the revolutionaries, not from their biological core needs. The sociopolitical character structure of the French and Russian revolutionaries were entirely different from that of the Americans. Stoked by the utter contempt and lack of contact that these monarchies had for their subjects' lives, these conflicts started as true revolts against the authority of the state and later turned into bloody pandemics of the emotional plague.

Before the United States of America could become a nation, it first had to win the War of Independence. After this victory, however, the Founding Fathers had much work ahead of them in uniting thirteen separate states with widely different interests. *How this organization occurred was critical to the future development of the country*. During this period, Alexander Hamilton was the driving force. Irrational social behavior and thought, particularly ideological thinking about social issues, was a primary source of difficulty in this organizing process but *political parties were never originally* a *part of America's founding*. Cognizant of the flaws in human character, the Founding Fathers—having no better understanding of characterology or of ways to address the tendency of humans to behave destructively—spoke of a need for "virtuous citizens" and "disinterested leaders." They created the Constitution which was designed to embody and protect the fundamental principles on which the newly formed republic was founded, and they took practical measures to prevent concentration and abuse of power by establishing three separate branches of government. For the first time, therefore, the conditions were set in place, in principle, for an independent work-democratic society. These conditions were and are based on the capacity of people to function independently and responsibly. Following the War of Independence, the first presidential election involved no partisanship. George Washington's election was undisputed. Nevertheless, Washington was well aware of the destructive effects of the irrational political activity rampant in the American colonial period and in his own administration. In his Farewell Address, he issued grave warnings against "the baneful effects of the spirit of Party" and hoped that ideological thinking, the inevitable consequence of partisanship, would not undermine the operation of the new government. Political parties, nevertheless, had already imposed themselves by the end of the eighteenth century under Washington's own administration.

Using the best knowledge available to them, the Framers of the Constitution produced a document to ensure the nation's survival and well-being. However, the primary obstacle to implementing financial, commercial, foreign, and other social policies was the emotional health of the people, something no document could address. This impediment prevented people from fully living and working together harmoniously. The bioemotional factors determining human behavior that we know today were unknown at the time. Despite the decline in people's functioning, the government continues to survive. Unfortunately, the decline cannot continue for much longer before it becomes irreversible.

Fixed political parties result from basic differences in the sociopolitical character structure of armored people, differences that themselves result from fixed ways of viewing the world and controlling the environment. Irrational political power arises from the need to control the environment in ways specific to armored character structure. Political power is neither good nor evil. Its value depends on its *function*, on whether it serves to protect the core life functions of the individual and the nation.

To accurately picture the history of a particular era, we must know not only the historical facts concerning significant social events but, just as importantly, the sociopolitical character structure of the individuals participating in them. Historical events have traditionally been the province of the historian, not the psychiatrist trained in character analysis, and so the determining role of the underlying sociopolitical characterological factors has not been previously recognized.

Even as early in our history as the period surrounding the War of Independence, we can look back and identify individual characterological differences that would later lead, inevitably, to trouble. The difficulties resulted from major differences in sociopolitical thinking, attitudes and behavior that were not unlike what we are currently experiencing. For example, people like John Adams, who viewed the conflict between the colonies and England as a *war of independence,* later showed themselves to be characterologically conservative, and though they favored becoming an independent nation, they identified socially with the British, their forefathers. In orgonometric terms, their relationship to the British was one of attractive opposition (Fig. 4.1).

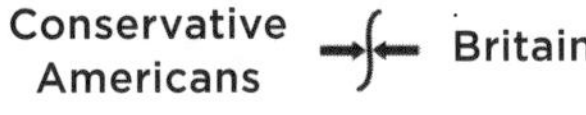

FIGURE 4.1

On the other hand, those who viewed the conflict as a *revolutionary war* for "greater freedom" later showed themselves to be true liberals or pseudo-liberals. They saw themselves as antagonistic to Britain and many were sympathetic to the revolutionaries in France. In late 1792, after the French monarchy was overthrown and the republic proclaimed, these Americans, giddy with freedom, gave themselves up to the most extraordinary series of celebrations in honor of the achievements of another country which in no way directly concerned them. In orgonometric terms, their relation to the British was one of antagonistic opposition (Fig. 4.2).

FIGURE 4.2

Since both groups of Americans shared a common goal—victory over England—their differences in sociopolitical character structure did not surface and become a social problem until that goal was achieved.

After the American colonists won their independence, the

major question was whether the thirteen colonies should organize into a strong union to protect the interests of the component states, or whether the states should retain autonomy in a federal government. The Federalists under Washington favored a strong central government, encouraging industries and independence from the influence of foreign governments. During his administration, the nation's young economy prospered with a sound fiscal policy, while the governmental structure was expanded and an honest, efficient administrative system was developed. Opposing the practical achievements of the Federalists, Jefferson, who was politically antifederalist and characterologically pseudo-liberal, formed the Democratic-Republican Party in 1791, while still Secretary of State in Washington's cabinet. The antifederalists opposed a strong federal government, supported a broad distribution of wealth, and were suspicious of urban commercial interests. These ideals, which came to be known as Jeffersonian democracy, were based on faith in the virtue and goodness of the common man. Through much political maneuvering, Jefferson convinced Madison and others, who hated and feared the tyranny of the union, to cooperate with those who were sympathetic to the ideals of the French Revolution.

Jefferson's political manipulation effected a strange alliance between the party of states' rights and the party of the rights of man.[56] The Democratic-Republican Party was named, planned, organized, and inspired by Jefferson. A sentimentalist and a shrewd politician, he was responsible for attempting to undermine the principles of the Federalists. The party, which originated from democratic ideas in vogue around the time of the Enlightenment, embodied all the idealistic principles of a formal democracy. At every turn, the Democratic-Republicans attempted to pare down the powers and whittle away the sovereignty of the Federal union. At this time, however, the real danger was not the survival of the states but the possible extinction of the federal government, which was in its infancy and struggling for its very life.

The following passage reveals the full extent of Jefferson's leftist leanings and sympathies. Upon hearing of the massacres

56. The same obsession with revolution, "freedom," and the utopian hope for a better society that swept up Americans with a leftist character structure at the end of the eighteenth century also occurred in the twentieth century with the Russian Revolution. Nothing was learned from the past.

in Paris between September 3 and September 7, 1793, in which 1,400 men, women, and boys were murdered or executed, the third President of the United States wrote:

> In the struggle which was necessary, many guilty persons fell without the forms of trial, and with them some innocent. These I deplore as much as anybody, and shall deplore some of them to the day of my death. But I deplore them as I should have done had they fallen in battle. *It was necessary to use the arm of the people,* a machine not quite so blind as balls and bombs, but blind to a certain degree. A few of their cordial friends met at their hands the fate of enemies. But time and truth will rescue and embalm their memories, while their posterity will be enjoying that very liberty for which they would never have hesitated to offer up their lives. The liberty of the whole earth was depending on the issue of the contest, and was ever such a prize won with so little innocent blood? My own affections have been deeply wounded by some of the martyrs to this cause, but rather than it should have failed I would seen half of the earth desolated; were there but an Adam and an Eve left in every country, and left free, it would be better than as it now is. I have expressed to you my sentiments because they are really those of ninety-nine in a hundred of our citizens.
>
> (Oliver 1928, page 326; italics in the original)[57]

With minor changes, these ideas could have been expressed by Lenin, Stalin, or Hitler.

The Federalists were in no position to put an end to Jefferson's subversive sociopolitical activity. Not only was he a clever political tactician, but no one understood how to effectively deal with the *characterological* basis of his irrational ideas and behavior. This was a biopsychiatric problem for which there was no knowledge at that time. All the Federalists could do was address, point by point, each of his disastrous sociopolitical policies. However, this strategy could work only as long as the Federalists retained political control of the government.

With the defeat of the Federalists in 1800, Jefferson became

---

57. This book not only provides an accurate account of the early years of America's history but also clearly illuminates the character structure of the individuals who participated in it.

president. From this point onward, the history of American politics can be best understood in terms of the interaction of two opposing ideological forces, left and right, forever entangled in the sociopolitical process of a two party system. Part and parcel of a formal democracy, the party system brought out ideological forces that were deeply rooted in human character structure. Throughout his administration, for example, Jefferson resorted to sociopolitical activity that was consistent with his pseudo-liberal character structure. The embargo of 1808 is one example (Adams 1889, pages 32, 1115–1126).

The Constitution of the United States is a necessary but insufficient means to ensure that the government conducts itself according to the intent of the Founding Fathers, which is to protect the core functions of life. It is insufficient because of two reasons: First, although intuitively grasped, the core functions were then poorly understood, and second, the fact remains that despite the changelessness of these core functions, the Constitution's continuing interpretation depends on the ever-changing cast of interpreters—the justices of the Supreme Court, each with their own individual and sociopolitical character structure. Consider the following example.

As articulated in the Declaration of Independence, the concepts of "life, liberty, and the pursuit of happiness" are idealistic terms, fraught with ambiguity that lead to widespread confusion with destructive social consequences. Since the origin of life is a complete mystery to those with a mechanistic-mystical view of the world, it is not surprising that ideology-based opinions as to when life begins are also polarized. This uncertainty fuels controversy and arguments on both sides of the abortion issue. Similarly, the concept of liberty, which is usually defined as freedom from arbitrary or external control, gives rise to conflicting views because the function of freedom itself is poorly understood. (See chapter 3, Cognitive Distortions Inherent in Ideology) Happiness is another vague and ambiguous concept, and its meaning varies with different ideologies. Finally, one of the Constitution's purposes, "To . . . promote the general welfare," has been interpreted to justify socialistic legislation, although the concept of welfare refers not only to receiving financial aid from the government but also, and primarily, to an individual's state of good fortune, well-being, and prosperity. Conservatives attempt to rectify these ambiguities by attempting to return to the original sense of the Framers, but this does not address the source of the problem.

The American War of Independence occurred partly because the colonists wanted greater independence from British rule. However, the extent to which it was a true war of independence in which individual colonists attained personal, political and economic freedom was actually determined by each colonist's biophysical capacity to *tolerate* being free and behaving responsibly in daily life, particularly in the emotional sphere. In this respect, subsequent historical events have shown that the war was only partly successful. Armor restricts emotional freedom, and thus the war was no more than a revolt against British rule and the replacement of one formal democracy with another.

Because individual work and genital satisfaction was not the exclusive foundation upon which the democratic principles of America were based, these principles could only exist as a formality.[58] This crucial limitation inevitably gave rise to democratic idealism, that is, *democracy as a social ideal, not something attainable in practice*. Because people behaved as if *ideas* about democracy, rather than genuine freedom and responsibility based on healthy functioning, were the determinants of human relationships, sociopolitics became more and more an irrational force in government. Social issues, real or otherwise, could not be dealt with objectively and scientifically, but only in "political"—that is, ideological—terms. This shift away from reality was already well underway by the end of the eighteenth century during Washington's first administration, and as early as 1791, Jefferson and Madison secretly began to undermine the Federalists' efforts to form a stronger union. Since the two men dared not attack Washington openly, they focused on other Federalists, particularly Hamilton, who was the Secretary of the Treasury.

When Alexis de Tocqueville visited the United States in the 1830s, he recognized that "*a new political science is needed for a world entirely new*" (italics added). Of European democracy, he declared:

58. "Democratic" is used here to define a form of social organization in which people have the right *and the capacity* to govern themselves. Strictly speaking, until recently, the United States has been a federal republic.

> Never have the heads of state thought at all to prepare for it in advance; it is made despite them or without them knowing it. The most powerful, most intelligent, and most moral classes of the nation have not sought to take hold of it so as to direct it. Democracy has therefore been abandoned to its savage instincts; it has grown up like those children who, deprived of paternal care, rear themselves in the streets of our towns and know only society's vices and miseries. One still seemed ignorant of its existence when it unexpectedly took power. Each then submitted with servility to its least desires; it was adored as the image of force; when afterward it was weakened by its own excesses, legislators conceived the imprudent project of destroying it instead of seeking to instruct and correct it; and since they did not want to teach it to govern, they thought only of driving it from government.
>
> As a result, the democratic revolution has taken place in the material of society without making the change in laws, ideas, habits, and mores that would have been necessary to make this revolution useful. Thus we [Europeans] have democracy without anything to attenuate its vices and make its natural advantages emerge; and while we already see the evils it brings, we are still ignorant of the goods it can bestow. (De Tocqueville 2000, page 7)

De Tocqueville believed that American democracy was different, although still at risk for the "vices" of democracy.

The presence of irrational political considerations in social interactions complicates any attempt at remedial action. Therefore, to be successful, any action must be preceded by a distinct separation of rational social needs and related goals from the irrational, destructive component. The latter will only give rise to ideologically based political partisanship. Without such a distinction, efforts to bring about social improvement will fail.

Political opportunists on the left and the right thrive on the confusion that comes about from the failure to differentiate between impulses originating from the core and impulses originating from the destructive secondary layer. This obfuscation allows them free expression of their own destructive social attitudes and behavior. The conflicting ideological attitudes that result from their political mischief have become part and parcel of the rigid fabric of armored humans and of formal democracies. They arise from not identifying the *biological* origin of work and sexual functioning, and the importance of their role in biological health and in determining social processes.

Functional Economics

Work is a basic function of biological orgone energy. To understand the extent to which a particular social structure best preserves the conditions for unarmored life, one must consider the functional role played by economics. Economic activity originates within the social realm, which derives from the biological work function. Such activity is pleasurable and necessary for the survival of the members of society and for society itself. A healthy economy has a life of its own. Unfortunately, armored people with their disturbed work function view this natural process with anxiety and therefore attempt to manipulate and control it. All past efforts to determine the vitality of an economic system have been sterile because they relied heavily on mechanistic determinants that emphasize *external* forces impinging on the system. Focusing exclusively on quantitative factors and using lifeless mathematical and statistical techniques to understand and address economic problems, economists have evaded and ignored the crucial importance of subjective factors—the pleasure function in work and the individual's natural capacity to work. Neglect of these all-important qualitative individual factors has resulted in the corruption of the free market system with the appearance of secondary layer activity, such as striving for power and criminal behavior, which distorts and cripples economic life. (See section on Work and Armor, page 193)[59]

In the development of an unrestricted (work-democratic) society, a given function (psychologically: "need," economically: "demand") spontaneously results in the creation of a pair of variations, that of *provider or supplier of the need* and that of the *supplied individual* (see Konia 1986a, page 62). For example, people's need ("demand") for shoes results in the manufacture ("supply")

59. The term "plunder" is used by classical economists such as Mill and Bastiat to describe the violent appropriation of work products.

of shoes. From this functional relationship, society spontaneously organizes on a local level. As another example, the commerce of a city naturally becomes organized according to special areas (districts). Beyond the barter economy level of social development, "need" creates another function, a medium of exchange (money) that facilitates the interaction between the supplier and the supplied. The deeper biological function determines the socioeconomic relationship between the two (Fig. 4.3).

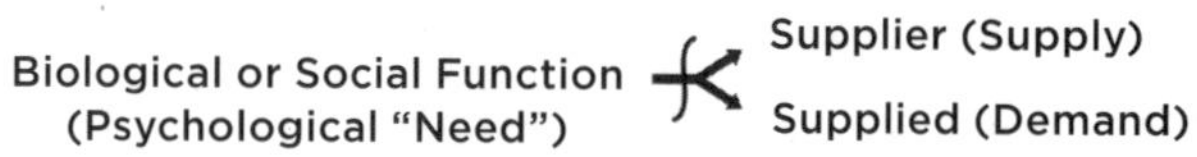

Biological or Social Function (Psychological "Need") → **Supplier (Supply)** / **Supplied (Demand)**

FIGURE 4.3

This equation shows that a biological or social function (psychological "need") is the common functioning principle of the variations the supplier of the need and the supplied. The need and the corresponding work activity can arise from any layer of the biopsychic apparatus—the core, secondary layer, or façade.

In this development, the relationship between the supplier and the supplied is close and is based on mutual satisfaction and their pleasurable give-and-take interaction. The worker receives pleasure in creating the work product and the buyer derives pleasure from receiving the product. The supplier acquires money, and the supplied acquires the product or service. This *socioeconomic energetic* interaction resulting in charge and discharge is functionally identical to that which occurs in all biological systems. The very complicated economic realm of modern society originates in the very basic physical activity of give-and-take that arises from the deeper *biological* function of charge and discharge.

Through work, the provider gives ("discharges") a product or service to the buyer. In return, the provider receives ("charges") monetary compensation. The buyer pays money ("discharges") and receives goods or services (the "charge" of the provider) in return. The similarity of this interaction with the pulsatory function in the biological realm is unmistakable. In striated muscle, for example, the functions of charge and discharge occur simultaneously in opposing muscle groups to effect motor activity. *The identical process in the social realm effects economic activity.*

The reciprocal interaction of provider and receiver is expressed in the following functional relationship (Fig. 4.4).

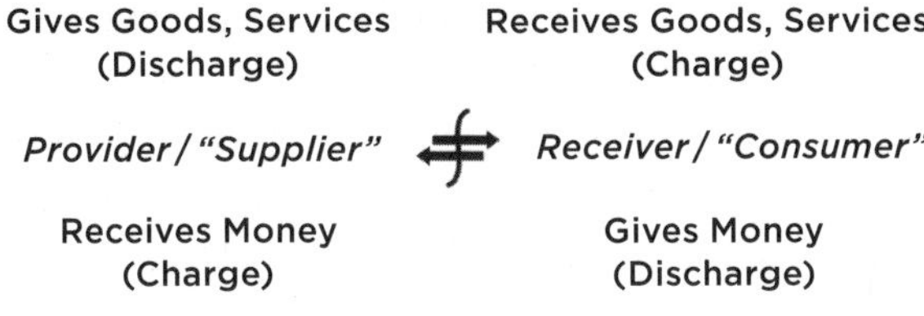

FIGURE 4.4

Mutual profit is the consequence of this voluntary exchange and pleasure is the motivating force, without which there can be no life-positive work. Both provider and receiver are both satisfied in the psychological or emotional sense, as well as in their energy economy.

The totality of these functional interactions between the supplier and the supplied forms the "market." In a healthy, unarmored society, the market is self-regulating and free to regulate itself. A truly free market can only exist, however, to the extent that armor does not interfere with people's work function. Armor disturbs the biological process, giving rise to destructive economic practices that interfere with the capacity of the market to be self-regulating.

The relationship between the provider and the receiver is determined and driven by the specific function (need) that is to be exchanged. For example, the relationship between a doctor and a patient is different than that between a salesperson and a customer. All needs, though, are specific to individuals and therefore can be most effectively and efficiently satisfied in the private sector, not the government. *Since the state can derive no satisfaction, it is neither desirable nor rational for it to assume the role of provider except for very special functions*, such as providing military security or justice in the criminal justice system. Even for the military, the basic need is to protect the life, liberty, and property of individuals. A general rule is that as corporate and governmental structures increase in size they became more complicated and dysfunctional because of increasing rigidity (armor) of the economic system.

Large private corporations or the state should not interfere in basic biological economic processes. The *smaller* the supplier, the more direct and immediate is the gratification on both sides. Corporate or government intrusion in the economic life of society is a result of the destructive socioeconomic practices of armored humans. For example, when medical insurance companies and the government interfere with the relationship between the supplier (physician) and the receiver (patient), the quality of medical care deteriorates.

Socialists and others on the political left cannot grasp the essential nature of a free market economy for several reasons, all related to limitations secondary to their biophysical structure. Since their armor is largely in the brain, they cannot have a "gut reaction" to sense what to do. They are therefore less tolerant of freedom and less able to regulate themselves than conservatives. Their view of the marketplace is distorted. They see the situation between the supplier and the supplied as a competitive win–lose relationship: If one party wins (e.g., the supplier), then the other (the supplied) must lose. We have shown, however, that in a healthy situation this relationship is actually a cooperative one in which both parties stand to benefit from their economic interaction. Curtis Barnes points out:

> Confounding profit with its antithesis, plunder, makes it all but impossible to protect pleasure-based work functions. To say that profit is a matter of one person taking advantage of another would be like assuming that all sexual intercourse is a matter of a man taking advantage of a woman, or vice versa. If no distinction were made between rape and the loving genital embrace, there could be no way to protect the genital health of members of a society save by rigid moralistic or mechanical rules governing relationships between men and women. If those who have a healthy, productive work function cannot engage in mutually productive exchanges, cannot defend such positive acts against those who would destroy that pleasure, there is no hope of achieving a life-positive social order. (Barnes 1979, page 132)

Any work function, such as the skill, ability, or work capacity of an individual, can be viewed as human capital. The source of *all* capital originates from human endeavor (the biological work function) and is therefore private. Capital concentrated in the private sector and capitalist activities go hand in hand with the development of democracy.[60] The transfer of capital to the state can be accomplished lawfully through tax legislation, as in democratic societies, or illegally by usurpation, as in a fascist state. In the latter, any possibility of gratifying work or generating capital is lost.

The same relationship between charge and discharge exists in the contractual arrangement between borrower and lender. Functionally, assuming debt ("charging") presumes a certain work capacity of the debtor to be able to pay off ("discharge") the debt. Without a capacity to work or its monetary equivalent, debt cannot be discharged. Therefore, work capacity is an economic measure of the individual's orgonomic charge.

If charge and discharge are paired variations, they must have a common functioning principle operating in a deeper domain. What is this CFP? We know that in the biological realm the CFP of charge and discharge is metabolism. This relationship is stated in the following orgonometric equation (Fig. 4.5):

FIGURE 4.5

In the biological realm, charge and discharge accompany bioenergetic regulation of the organism. If charge and discharge are manifestations of the biological work function in the economic realm, we are also justified to use metabolism as the CFP of charge and discharge in the economic realm (Fig. 4.6):

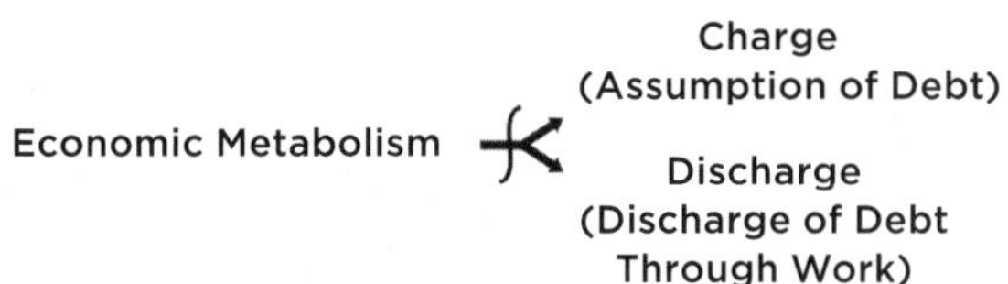

FIGURE 4.6

60. Private capital is an essential feature of a free market economy. The term *capitalist system* is a misnomer.

The function economic metabolism is the energy of economic activity. A very large part of social life, economic activity is derived from the biological realm. Accordingly, the vitality of an economic system can be measured by the unimpeded activity of the paired functions of charge and discharge. By identifying common energy functions in different realms of nature, functional thinking can unify the different branches of science in a practical manner.

Charge and discharge operate as alternating opposites and give rise to economic self-regulation (Figs. 4.7, 4.8):

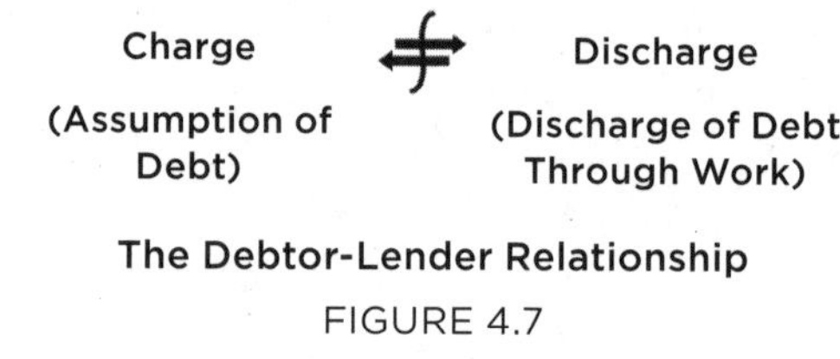

The Debtor-Lender Relationship

FIGURE 4.7

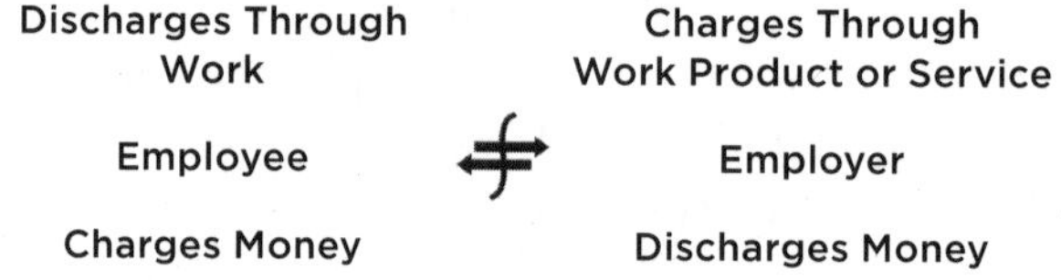

The Employer-Employee Relationship

FIGURE 4.8

Any disturbance in this energetic interaction will result in pathology in the economic system.

In most economic relationships, currency functions as a medium of exchange for goods and services, enabling the system to reach a high level of efficiency and mobility. However, in the hands of armored people, money often fulfills the widest variety of destructive secondary drives that undermine social functions at all levels of organization, from individual families to giant corporations. The various secondary drives interfere with both individual self-regulation and society's ability to be self-regulating. In a socialist state, economic self-regulation is not possible.

Work and Armor

If allowed to develop without blocks, the biological work function is inherently rational and lawful. The pleasurable discharge of work has an organizing effect on individuals and society. Armoring interferes with this spontaneous social interaction, disrupting and immobilizing the work process to varying degrees. Natural satisfaction in work and its results—"a job well done"—are reduced or eliminated. If humans were not armored, their work function would not be impeded by armor, and the market would function without interference—as a free, self-regulating energy system. In the presence of armored individuals, however, market activity must be regulated, and the reality of a free market turns into an ideal, with conservatives extolling its virtues and liberals faulting its abuses, and neither group understanding what is actually happening. In fascist or socialist states, where society is totally armored, the government is in total control of the market.

Just as armoring limits pleasure in the work process of individuals, so too do the socially destructive, armored leaders of the fascist or socialist state prohibit pleasure in the socioeconomic life of society and its citizens. In the socialist state, total appropriation of work products by its agencies reaches an apex, all self-regulated work and work-product relationships are prohibited. According to the Austrian economist Ludwig Von Mises, "The Fascist economy retains the appearance of ordinary markets, price, wage, and interest rates." But, he says, "Market exchange is merely a sham.[61] Such wages, price and interest rates are fixed by the government; they are merely quantitative terms in the government's orders determining each citizen's job, income, consumption and standard of living. The government directs all production activities." (Von Mises 1949, page 718) One is reminded of the old communist joke: "They pretend to pay us, we pretend to work." In a socialist economy, taxation seriously undermines the incentive to work. In Denmark, where the tax rate is as high as 60 percent on an individual's income, a physician earns as much money after taxes as the average payment to a welfare recipient.

61. The sham of the Soviet Union's economy, for example, was dramatically revealed with the fall of Communism, and the return of the free market economy resulted in the collapse of the ruble. This was in large part due to the liberation of the work function of the producing sector which far outpaced the work function of the average consumer.

In effect, the rational concept of fair remuneration for one's work and the incentive to improve one's living standards through work are undermined.

In unarmored individuals, biological energy oscillates between work and sexual activity. These functions do not oppose each other, as in neurotics, but *alternate*. Work does not serve to suppress the sexual urge, nor are there sexual fantasies to interfere with work. Work and sexuality support each other and there is a sense of genuine self-confidence based on the individual's ability to live and work unimpeded by internal or external constraints. Interest is concentrated fully, without conflict, either in work or in sexual activity. The observation of individuals with intact work function suggests that each person possesses *specific* abilities based largely on innate constitutional endowment. The most apparent examples are those with special musical, artistic, linguistic, intellectual or athletic abilities. If people were allowed to develop freely through childhood and adolescence, their natural abilities would give rise to their specific, individualized work functions. The social conditions in America come closest to making this possible.

As stated, armor gives rise to various disturbances in work function. In fact, few people in any society have an unimpaired work capacity. Their disturbance is directly related to armoring particularly of the ocular segment, especially affecting perception and cognition. However, there are exceptional individuals who have relatively intact work function despite their armor. Partly because of their special abilities and partly because of a fortunate environment, these individuals have not lost their uniquely creative abilities and are capable of highly productive work. Such persons are said to have a "hole" in their armor through which their work function is expressed, more or less undistorted, from the biological core. Examples are the great scientists and people who create great works of art and music despite their armor.

An understanding of the work function is obscured by many common misconceptions. One is that in the relationship between worker and manager or owner, the worker is the only one doing "real" work, the role of the manager actually being considered subordinate to that of the worker. In reality, worker and manager are mutually involved in the work process. It is more accurate to use the terms "managed worker" and "worker's manager." Each has a specific, equally important function in the work process. Their relation is one of attractive opposition (Fig. 4.9).

Managed Worker →∫← **Worker's Manager**

FIGURE 4.9

Another misconception is that workers have no power unless they are organized. Actually, from a functional energetic viewpoint, the opposite is true. Workers most need union representation when they are emotionally crippled, when their work functioning is impaired, or when their particular work is not in demand. People who are independent and whose work function is intact are flexible and able to adapt to a changing marketplace. For example, many professional people, uprooted from their lives in their home countries, who flee to America for a better life are able to surmount their difficulties when they must find lesser skilled work than what they had been accustomed to doing in their native land.

The basic Marxist theory of the contradiction between the owners of the means of production and the workers has been refuted in America. Workers often own the means of production, either through personal ownership of stock or through collective efforts to accumulate sufficient capital and credit. The Marxist idea that workers must violently seize the means of production is self-defeating and unnecessary, and an expression of contempt for the unique work function of the entrepreneur who creates the very possibility for others to work.

When the biological origin of work is ignored it leads to an impasse in understanding and dealing with other work-related social problems. It gives rise to the mistaken belief that most work-related problems, such as chronic unemployment, can be addressed by manipulating the work environment. For example, providing financial incentives to welfare recipients so that they keep some of their benefits when they get jobs does little to improve their work functioning. This same narrow and symptomatic approach serves to obscure people's underlying work disturbance. For example, the lack of understanding of the vital importance of work allows people to overlook the destructive effects of strikes not only on management and society, but more importantly on the *striking workers themselves*. There is nothing more demoralizing than the sight of people whose work has been stopped idly standing around.[62] The same state of demoralization and alienation must be experienced by the striking worker himself. Too emotionally crippled to find work, the inability of armored workers to seek other employment when they are not satisfied in their present work or when their jobs are terminated immediately reveals the underlying biological source of the problem.

The working conditions in the nineteenth century that originally led to the formation of labor unions and union bosses were a rational reason to establish these organizations but, by and large, they do not exist in this day and age. With the weakening of labor unions, political saviors in government have taken advantage of the situation by stepping in to become the modern caretakers of people through the enactment of job training and health care legislation.

Without in-depth understanding of the biological origin of work problems, there cannot be any chance for improvement. Individuals with special biopsychiatric skills are becoming available to deal in a more constructive manner with conflicts in the work place. Knowledge of the orgonometry of social relationships is essential to deal with social problems such as those between management and labor or work-related character problems. (See chapter 7, the section on Work) Social scientists with the necessary orgonomic qualifications will soon be able to prevent discord from degenerating into a situation in which unionization and governmental intervention become the only apparent alternatives.[63]

With regard to human sexual and work functioning, Reich was the first to distinguish between the neurotic armored individual who functions according to duty and compulsive moral regulation and the healthy individual who functions in a self-regulatory manner (Reich 1948a, page 130). As is the case in their sexual

62. Work stoppages in our present-day economic climate produce little lasting benefit. The reaction to strike in the realm of work is functionally identical to individual spite reactions in the emotional realm. In both cases people's energy system is immobilized.

63. The training program in social orgonomy of the American College of Orgonomy is designed to address these and other social problems.

life, neurotics work more or less mechanically, deriving little pleasure from it. This occurs because work impulses passing through the armor become forced and joyless and are not experienced as vital to emotional health. This kind of work often serves to deaden the sexual urge and conflicts with it. Sexual fantasies interfere with the work process, resulting in neurotic mechanisms that restrict work capacity. Reich described this graphically in Figure 4.10 (Ibid., page 137):

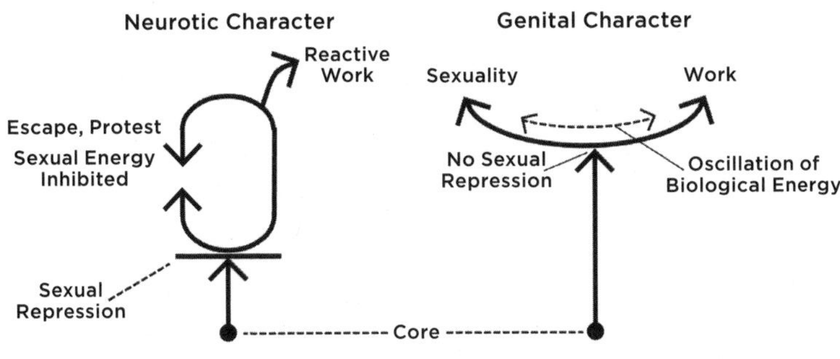

Reactive (Neurotic) and Healthy Ways of Working
FIGURE 4.10

The functional equivalent of work, earning money, can also become a neurotic or substitute activity. To avoid feelings of emotional insecurity, people often turn to wealth accumulation to provide a sense of security, social status, and power, all forms of substitute gratification. These individuals also feel little or no pleasure in the process of working. Making money (financial security) becomes a substitute for happiness (emotional security), and an end in itself. Since the capacity to enjoy work is lost, there can never be enough money to be made. In such instances, the making of money, no matter how much, never brings a sense of satisfaction. Pleasure in work is often replaced by a feeling of monotony or boredom.

Until the early 1960s, the average American's work function, though restricted, was fairly stable because muscular armor was intact and ocular functioning was usually not significantly compromised. Impulses from the biological core passed through the muscular armor and work was often compulsive and devoid of pleasure, but individuals nevertheless maintained a steady work function.

However, accompanying the transformation of society (see chapter 6), the pattern of armor in individuals shifted from the musculature to the ocular segment, resulting in a qualitative change in work. This shift effected an increase in ocular armor, a resultant expansion of intellectually based work and a decline in the ability or interest to perform physical work. Intellectual work relies primarily on computers that are mechanical representations of reality. As a result, there is now a mechanistically oriented service economy increasingly based on unrewarding and emotionally deadening "McJobs" that are often performed by robot-like humans. As mechanization becomes perfected, these intellectually driven jobs will be increasingly taken over by computers. No one considers the destructive effect of this shift in the work function on people's emotional health.

Neither do people understand the relationship between work and sexuality, the two basic biological core functions. On the left, socialist writers proclaim that the task of socialistic regimes should be "to make work, which today is a burden, into a pleasure, so that people will enjoy working and the workers go joyfully to work." On the right, conservatives believe any joy of work is merely an indirect one provided by the satisfaction of earning a living and the self-respect that accompanies it.[64] Those on the political left do not recognize the biological origin of work and its profound relationship with human sexuality. Neither do they understand the difference between the work function in health and that same function in the presence of significant armoring. Conservatives have an intuitive sense of the importance of work and the worker's responsibility for the work process. However, they see a work disorder as a moral failing. The conservative stresses the lack of moral cultural values and attitudes in our society as the root cause of poverty, citing the rapid upward mobility of Asian immigrants compared with immigrants from Mexico and Central America. This view ignores the fact that cultural values are themselves a reflection of deeper biological functions: the sexual and work

---

64. See Von Mises, L. 1981. *Socialism*. Indianapolis: Liberty Classics, page149.

functions. Differences in the pattern of body armor determine the differences in cultural values and these differences influence the work function. The conservative view also does not explain how exceptional individuals who progress socioeconomically continue to come out of poverty-ridden cultures. They do so because armor has not destroyed their work function.

Alternatively, socialists who obsessively long for increased social freedom view most work as capitalistic exploitation of the masses of workers. The pseudo-liberal has an even poorer sense of the importance of work in the energy economy of humans. Issues revolving around freedom but derived from the intellect (e.g., the "right to strike") only serve to obfuscate the biological origin and necessity of work for all people.

America is truly the land of opportunity. *Given sufficient health*, people in America can achieve almost any kind of satisfying work skill that they desire. Neither the left nor the right recognize the biologically based fact that *economic poverty in America primarily results from disturbances in the work function of armored humans.* All other currently stated reasons are unessential. The biological process of armoring disrupts work function through immobilization, and this impairs the individual's ability to develop and find satisfying work and to earn an adequate wage. This process takes place at the individual level leading to individual poverty, or at the national level leading to national poverty.

PART II

TOWARD ERADICATION OF THE EMOTIONAL PLAGUE

CHAPTER 5

THE DIAGNOSIS OF SOCIAL ARMOR

Whoever realizes that our civilization . . . is disintegrating will not hesitate to agree that no ideology of guilt or morals will ever solve the tragic contradiction in man's existence.
—Wilhelm Reich, *Ether, God and Devil*

Wilhelm Reich often asked why orgone energy was not discovered earlier in the history of civilization. The answer is: *Because of the presence of individual and social armoring.* Armor not only prevents painful and frightening ideas from reaching consciousness, but it also prevents the undistorted perception of emotions and sensations from which knowledge of the world is derived. We may, therefore, conclude that it is both individual and social armor that prevents undistorted contact with, and knowledge about, nature within and outside of oneself. This contact, when present, leads directly to a sense of a unifying energy principle in nature, which Reich discovered and named orgone. He showed that the properties of orgone energy are quite different from known forms of energy.[65] Many scientists and philosophers have tried to apply energy concepts in attempts to make comprehensible the essence of *living* functioning. Berg-

65. For a discussion of the physical properties of orgone energy see Reich 1949b, page 111.

son's *élan vital* and Dreisch's *entelechy* are examples of a vital energy principle pertaining to and governing living matter. As these forces were not tangible and objectively demonstrable, they inevitably led to a dead end. This failure facilitated the triumph of mechanistic thinking in natural science. In contrast, orgone energy is a *physical* energy that can be readily substantiated and worked with to the benefit of mankind. Its operation successfully accounts for all biological and other natural functions.

Social systems are integrated energetic systems with many characteristics of the living. In a healthy living organism or in a biosocial system such as a working organization or nation-state, energy pulsates out from the center to the periphery and back causing expansion and contraction, and it is this function that governs the system as a whole. In the contracted state, defensive functions predominate. In the individual, these consist of excitation of the sympathetic division of the autonomic nervous system, respiratory inhibition, and contraction of the skeletal muscles. This is accompanied by the emotions of fear and rage and this, in turn, determines how the individual functions and shapes his environment.

Such a reaction is a rational response when an external threat endangers either system's integrity, as occurs in a social system's state of emergency during war or following a financial crisis or a natural disaster. During these times, people naturally coalesce and work together for their collective safety. In the expanded state, excitation of the parasympathetic division of the autonomic nervous system is accompanied by and accompanies pleasurable experiences in the individual (biophysical expansion) and by harmonious social and economic activity, including expansive work relations. The rational forces contained in the core functions of love and work sustain individual and social processes.

Health is characterized by the capacity to pulsate fully and the ability to tolerate biophysical expansion (pleasure) *and* contraction (fear). In health, expansion predominates over contraction. In contrast, armored organisms cannot tolerate wide energetic swings. Their lives are constricted and they remain fixed in a state of chronic contraction. This is experienced as anxiety (chronic worrying). Others experience a reactive expansion to counter the underlying contraction. The chronically contracted cannot tolerate expansion. Conversely, those who are chronically expanded cannot tolerate the feelings accompanying contraction, such as responsibly attending to one's life.

It is relatively easy to recognize the manifestations of neurosis in the chronically contracted, anxious and worried person. Evidence of neurosis is less obvious in the chronically expanded. Such people can often be lively and energetic, and they may appear quite healthy to an untrained observer. A fairly recent phenomenon of growing prevalence in society, this state comes about as an attempt to overcome underlying feelings, especially anxiety and guilt, by people who cannot tolerate these painful emotions. Some social manifestations of this biophysical over-expansion include hyperactivity in children and impulsivity in adults. It is characterized by irresponsible behavior such as an endless craving for distractions, diversions and external stimulation, a need to "get high" with alcohol and drugs, and intemperance, financial and otherwise. A prominent symptom of Western society, this incapacity to tolerate anxiety or other unpleasant feelings renders one unable to face and overcome the adversities and challenges of everyday life.

Armor always disturbs natural energy pulsation and with it the energy economy of individuals and social systems.[66] It gives rise to immobilization and to socially destructive impulses. As a protective function, armor guards against painful feelings and against the expression of destructive impulses arising from the secondary layer. Unfortunately, given the reality and function of armor, the capacity for self-regulation is diminished or lost entirely and greater externally imposed moral or legal authoritarian regulation becomes necessary.

As noted, the armored individual is stuck in either a state of chronic contraction or chronic expansion which serves to block an underlying contraction. With chronic expansion, which is the current state of Western society and on the increase world-wide, personal and social irresponsibility leads to destruction of the individual and the social system. To deal with the chronic expan-

---

66. Much human activity is biosocial. This is true of the developing fetus in the maternal organism, the parent-child relationship, and the sexual union itself. It is essential that the distinction between natural biosocial functions and irrational social activity be understood and maintained.

sion in individuals and society, and to prevent further deterioration, it is necessary to induce a contraction. For Western society, this is accomplished by instituting social armor in the form of authoritarian measures. In sharp contrast, most Islamic societies are in a state of chronic contraction.

In individuals and social systems, armoring is maintained through the interaction of opposing forces, the instinctual forces from the biological core striving for expression and the defensive forces arrayed against them. Armor is the common functioning principle (CFP) of the instinctual forces and defensive forces. When the opposing forces are equal, equilibrium exists (Figs. 5.1, 5.2).

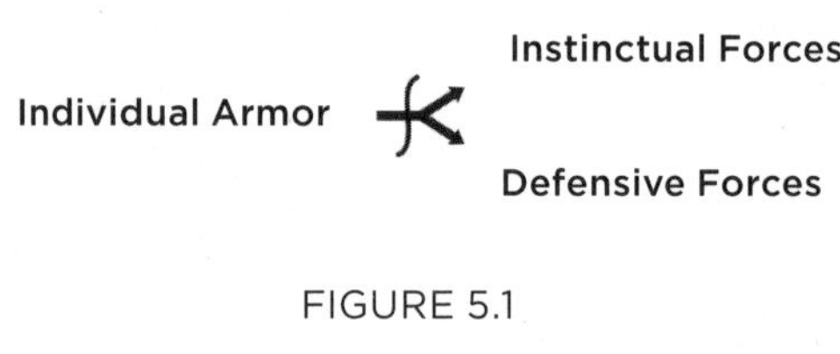

FIGURE 5.1

Instinctual Forces →|← Defensive Forces

FIGURE 5.2

Instinctual and defensive forces function according to the principle of simple attractive opposition. Armoring and the immobilization resulting from it reduce energy levels of the individual, checking anxiety and destructive behavior. Feelings of inner deadness or contactlessness, however, is the very high price of this equilibrium.

If we understand armor and its function, as the work of Reich and Baker permit, we can begin to recognize how armor can be overcome, first in individuals and then in society. The crucial first step toward a healthier society with less armor is to reverse man's state of contactlessness with himself and the environment. (See chapter 9) A disturbance in contact caused by armor blocks rational thinking and the *very recognition* that there is the problem of contactlessness. This disturbance in perception is universal and provides the basis for mechanistic-mystical thinking. Improved perception in society will come about with improved contact between mother and child in the early days and weeks of life. However, inroads can be made to reverse the effects of armoring, individually and socially, through an understanding of the destructive effects of mechanistic-mystical thinking about the living. This will go far toward restoring man's contact with his biological core.

Social Armor

Social armor is the CFP of its variations mechanistic and mystical thinking (Fig. 5.3).

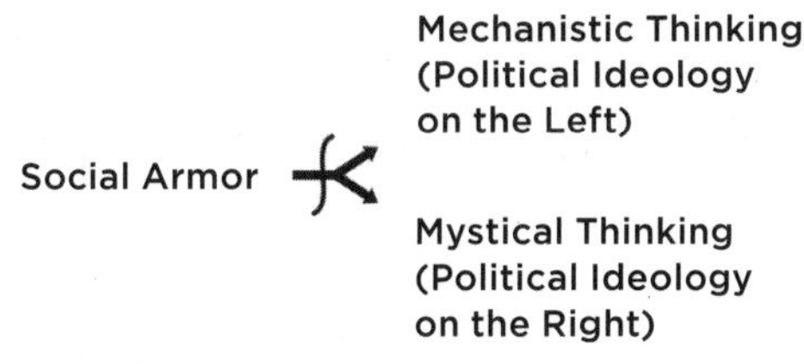

FIGURE 5.3

In an *authoritarian* society, the ideological forces on the left and the right are related to each other as mutually attractive opposites (Fig. 5.4). These ideologies supply the energy that maintains social immobilization through the opposing forces of mechanistic and mystical thinking. The strength of these forces depends on the rigidity of the social armor.

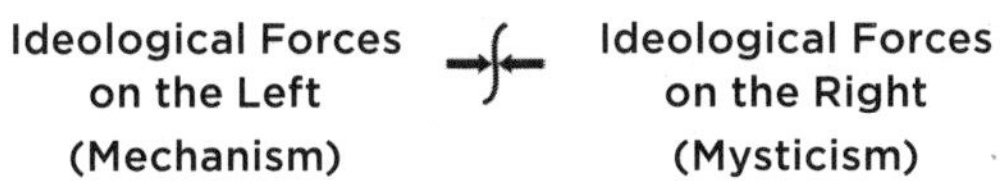

FIGURE 5.4

Although different social institutions and organizations appear to be predominantly mechanistic or mystical, the character of *any* armored society, as a functional whole, is *both* mechanical and mystical, that is, mechanistic-mystical. When mechanistic or mystical thinking is shared by a group, it assumes the characteristics of ideology. Table 5.1 shows the relationship of mechanistic and mystical thinking to the political ideology of the left and the right as well as to their CFP social armor. This table illustrates the similarities between *liberal ideology and the mechanistic world outlook* and between *conservative ideology and mystical thought.*

Social armor is the CFP of mechanistic and mystical ideology and is maintained and perpetuated by the dynamic interaction of these two opposing forces. During any given epoch, depending on the social situation, each social force can function either as an instinctual impulse from the core (by containing an element of the "truth") or as a defense against it (the "counter truth").[67] Thus, those who oppose abortion are concerned with the life of the fetus ("the truth"), but ignore the life of the mother (the "counter truth"). Those who favor abortion have the opposite perspective. If a free market in an armored society leads to greed and corruption ("the truth"), then the government must control the economy ("the counter truth"). Thus, mechanistic-mystical thinking functions as a *unified and internally consistent thought system and mode of behavior* in which both components mutually interact to maintain social armor. Each form of thought supports the other or keeps it in check. When a mechanistic interpretation inadequately explains a natural phenomenon, mysticism (an "in order to," a teleological explanation or goal) is invoked. Conversely, when a mystical interpretation fails, a mechanism ("cause") is supplied. In either case, this thought system leads to and expresses ideological thinking, which serves to impair full perception of reality and clear thinking.

67. The concepts of truth and counter truth are the products of functional thought processes that describe mechanistic-mystical reasoning. Functional thinking considers antithetical functions (including thought processes) simultaneously, whereas ideological thinking is one-sided and is a defensive function.

Liberal Ideology	Corresponding Mechanistic Thought
Humanity is able to be rational and its capacity to change is limitless.	Nature can be understood entirely according to mechanistic laws.
Humanity is perfectible.	Nature is machine-like and behaves in a perfectly lawful manner.
Through reason, humans can attain unlimited knowledge and control their behavior.	By applying mechanical models ("thought experiments"), it is possible to understand and control nature, at least in theory.
Equalization of material conditions is socially desirable.	Nature functions according to the Second Law of Thermodynamics ("all energy systems flow downhill").
Social progress through change is inevitable.	Mechanical events in nature are "inevitable."

Conservative Ideology	Corresponding Mystical Thought
Humanity is limited in its ability to understand nature.	God is unknowable, and therefore nature is unknowable.
Humanity is naturally capable of destructive acts that must be restrained.	Humanity is innately morally corrupt (original sin) and must be redeemed through God.
Knowledge comes from personal experience and tradition.	Knowledge about God comes through personal experience (divine revelation).
Society must not change. Social customs and traditions must be preserved.	God's work is eternal and cannot be changed.

Similarity Between Liberal Ideology and the Mechanistic World Outlook in the Natural Sciences and Between Conservative Ideology and Mystical Thought

TABLE 5.1

Since mechanistic and mystical thinking are paired homogeneous variations, they are related in one of four ways: simple variations, simple attractive opposites (the principle of synergy), antagonistic opposites, or alternating opposites. (See chapter 1, The Relationship of Functional Pairs) As an example of the mutual attraction of the opposing forces of mechanistic and mystical ideologies, consider the attitudes regarding the preservation of human life in the medical profession on the one hand and the Catholic Church on the other. Mechanistic medicine and religion support each other in saving human life, regardless of social circumstances or social consequences. No expense is spared in the medical treatment of a lifelong criminal, drug addict, or a hospitalized, profoundly demented geriatric patient. Mechanistic medicine functions ethically and like a machine, independent of real-life considerations. Mystical religion supports this position on moral grounds (abortions are never to be performed and life support is never to be withdrawn). Mechanistic ethics and mystical morals are mutually attractive opposites.

Consider as another example the relationship between the medical profession and the public. The thinking of physicians fits well in the mechanistic treatment paradigm and they view every medical condition as an aberration of the human machine. Patients, on the other hand, mystically expect that the physician's medication will relieve all their physical symptoms and emotional suffering. The mechanistic physician and the mystical patient are in a relationship of attractive opposition.

Different social conditions at different times give rise to a variety of functional relationships between mechanistic and mystical social institutions. These are listed below and graphically illustrated in Fig. 5.5 (numbers in parentheses refer to Fig. 5.5).

- The antithetical attraction of mechanism and mysticism (1, 2)
- The parallel existence of mechanism and mysticism (3, 4)
- The antithetical opposition of mechanism and mysticism (5, 6)
- The identity of mechanism and mysticism in the structure of the armored masses (7, 8)
- The biological core before the effects of armor (9)

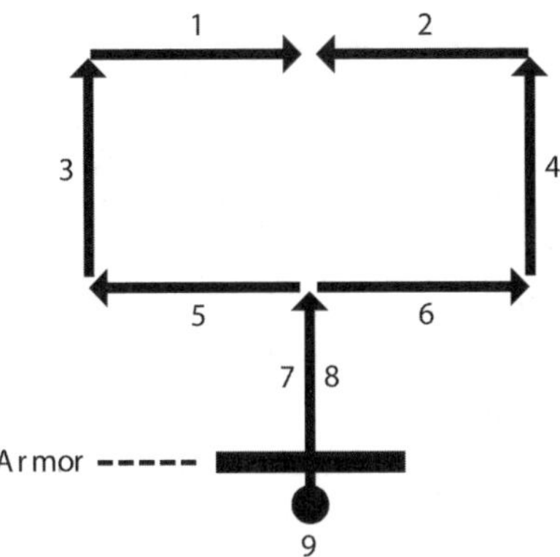

FIGURE 5.5

All of these functional relationships can be identified in the example of the relationship between the Catholic Church in Cuba (mysticism) and Communist Cuba (mechanism). In 1998, Pope John Paul II was welcomed to Cuba by the Communist leader, Commandant Fidel Castro. Cubans were urged to take to the streets and greet the Pope. This event illustrates the antithetical function of mysticism and mechanism attracting each other (1, 2 in Fig. 5.5). Both sides acknowledge and accept that the Communist leader has secular authority over the masses, while the mystical leader has spiritual authority. From around 1961 to 1991, the time of the fall of the Soviet Union, Communism and Catholicism in Cuba led separate but parallel existences (3, 4). From around 1959 until 1961, Communism and the Catholic Church functioned as antithetical opposites. Mechanism (communism) and mysticism (the Catholic Church) were unalterably opposed to each other (5, 6). The Communist Cuban government took over Catholic schools and expelled foreign priests, accusing the Church of being reactionary and dedicated to the interests of the rich. These actions, together with restrictions on religious expression outside Church walls, severed the Church from much of society. Prior to 1959, before the rise of communism in Cuba, the mechanistic-mystical structure of the masses already existed and was the foundation of *both* Christian mysticism *and* communist mechanistic materialism (7, 8). At the deepest level, deeper than the mechanistic-mystical structure of the masses, is the biological core of humanity, which existed before armor and which, unfortunately, is inaccessible to most individuals (9).

Armored human thought cannot delve deeper than the antithetical relationship between communism (mechanism) and the church (mysticism) (5, 6). The contradiction between the attraction (1,2) and the opposition (5,6) of these antithetical social forces is ignored, while their identity (7,8) and their common origin in the biological core (9) cannot be understood.

Since the primary function of social armor is to preserve armored society's existence, mechanistic-mystical thinking *cannot* provide rational guidelines for protecting unarmored human life. Armored thought cannot be used to escape the trap of armor. Nowhere is this clearer than in the realm of moral values. Because the mechanistic approach to natural science strives to completely eliminate the subjective impressions of the observer, the mechanistic scientist is largely excluded from true scientific investigation. By default, valuation or judgment falls to the mystic, philosopher, or priest, those who deal mainly with the subjective, qualitative aspects of human life. The mystic judges and evaluates without considering real-life events in the physical world. Lacking a physical, objective basis for valuing life, the mystic can only operate *idealistically* in a moral, other-worldly fashion. Good and evil are absolute, and antithetical to each other.

The rigid, mechanical way of valuing reality is the necessary consequence of the morally based regulation that is so characteristic of armored humans. Their thinking, distorted by armoring, gives rise to black-and-white valuations that are rigidly opposed to each other. Thus, if discrimination is evil, then the lack of a discriminatory faculty and the consequent reduction of the standards of social behavior to the lowest possible level (leveling) is desirable. If the oppressor is evil, then the victim (the oppressed) must be virtuous. If greed is evil, then poverty must be good. If teenage pregnancy is bad, then celibacy until marriage must be good. If child abuse and ignoring the child is bad, then coddling and indulging the child's every wish must be good. If nationalism is bad, then internationalism must be good. If authoritarianism is bad, then anti-authoritarianism must be good. Moralistic thinking even views itself morally. If moralism is bad, then immorality must be good, or vice versa. *These examples illustrate the rigid quality of mechanistic-mystical thinking, a direct result of the immobilizing effect of armor on thought.* Humans have lost the capacity for binocular vision, which is essential to having an accurate perspective on social issues, to see with clarity what is happening in front of their eyes. More and more, they are developing a machine-like "cause and effect" or moralistic "good/bad" way of seeing and thinking. The ultimate consequence of such armored thought is to put a stop to all social development.

Functional thinking distinguishes *natural morality*, which is in the service of preserving core life functions, from *compulsive morality*, which preserves armored life. Those on the right often confuse natural and compulsive morality; those on the left typically replace conventional morality with political correctness, an entirely new form of morality.

Today, we are confronted with the breakdown of old, authoritarian social structures and the rise of an anti-authoritarian society. This trend began with a weakening of the authoritarian family and social order and was accompanied by a loosening of muscular armor in the masses and a corresponding increase in ocular armor. The consequences have been:

- A decrease in strength of the ideological forces on the right
- A shift to the left-of-center in the sociopolitical thought of the masses, with pervasive pseudo-liberal ideological and political activity
- A corresponding reaction from the right

Because muscular armor has weakened and ocular armor has intensified, the destructive secondary layer is able to break through the social façade with the help of rationalizations of all kinds. This is expressed socially with an increase in pregenital sexual activity and irrational and destructive social behavior, including increased criminality. Social anxiety has increased along with efforts to overcome it through increased contactless substitute activity. Other compensatory expansive behaviors have appeared, particularly the following:

- A rise in mysticism
- An increase in religious fanaticism
- Mass political action
- Increased legislation to curb secondary layer behavior.

The loss of contact with the biological core has given rise to personal and social alienation, disillusionment, and gradual disintegration in every area of social life. These have been accompanied by increasing political reaction from the right.

Table 5.2 summarizes the salient characteristics of the two opposing functional variations of social armor, mechanism and mysticism.

Mechanism	Mysticism
Understanding nature according to the laws of mechanistic materialism	Belief that God (nature) is unknowable (spiritualism)
Distorted reasoning	Distorted belief
Cultural relativism	Cultural absolutism
Collective solutions to human problems; "one world"	Individual solutions to human problems; "isolationism"
Freedom valued over responsibility	Responsibility valued over freedom
Objective valued over subjective ("science")	Subjective valued over objective ("religion")
Quantity valued over quality	Quality valued over quantity
Sociopolitical forces (ideology) on the left	Sociopolitical forces (ideology) on the right

Social Armor: Mechanism Versus Mysticism

TABLE 5.2

The Stratification of Social Armor

The structure of armored society is similar to that of the armored individual. In both cases armor is layered or stratified from superficial to deep. Each layer of society is distinct and is composed of like-minded individuals who spontaneously organize and settle into their social level. Within this layer, each institution maintains its functional separateness from other groups through a common belief system (ideology). Institutions belonging to the superficial layers of society such as those involved with the media, the entertainment industry, and education consist of people with a liberal character structure. Because of their well-developed façade, these people function well, albeit neurotically, on the social surface. Individuals functioning primarily from the secondary layer (criminals and other psychopaths) also organize and settle into a distinct social layer ("the underworld"). Individuals functioning from the still deeper social layer (the core) consist of those with a conservative structure. Until recently, that is, before the anti-authoritarian era, medical and religious organizations and leaders were respected examples. They functioned to maintain the authoritarian social order. Most importantly, there has never been an institution that functioned exclusively from and through the biological core.

Seen in every area of social life, this process of stratification is responsible for the durability of ideologically based social institutions, especially those involving social, political, religious and scientific thought. Individuals within each group share a common bond of a preconceived belief system. Thus, mechanistic scientists, religious mystics, liberal journalists, pseudo-liberal politicians on the left, conservative reformers on the right and so on spontaneously organize either officially or unofficially to find their own strata in armored society. Within each layer, there can be many finer degrees of stratification as, for example, when religious mystics segregate into various denominations. When these organizations and institutions become nonproductive and stagnant, they often turn into a breeding ground of the organized emotional plague.

Today, human society is at the same exact point in confronting the problem of social pathology and the emotional plague that existed around the beginning of the nineteenth century when it first began to understand the origin and epidemiology of infectious disease. As in the case of these medical diseases, without an objectively based diagnostic classification of social disease processes, there can be no effective treatment approach to social pathology. This principle is axiomatic in the medical sciences and holds true as well in the social sciences. Therefore, to address the ills of society, we must first identify, then diagnose and understand social processes from the functional energetic viewpoint. Focusing on the functional dynamics of social interactions, the chapters that follow will help to clarify current social conditions. Ways of effectively dealing with social pathology emerge from this understanding.

Reich's sociological investigations provide a basis for a functional dynamic understanding of social processes. He first introduced the idea of diagnosis to social pathology when he identified the emotional plague. He also showed that this specific form of social pathology is determined by particular behavior in individuals so predisposed by their armored character structure. Baker extended our understanding of social pathology with his identification of different sociopolitical character types based on differences in the pattern of armoring. He found that these differences generally correspond to the political thinking of the left and the right on the sociopolitical spectrum. This was a giant step forward because it placed the characterological diagnosis of social pathology on a firm, scientifically objective basis. This advance has made possible a true "therapy" of social pathology, one that reaches to the energy source of social disease processes.

CHAPTER 6

THE TRANSFORMATION OF SOCIAL ARMOR AND THE RISE OF ANTI-AUTHORITARIAN SOCIETY

In order to describe a functional realm, it is not sufficient to know the present state of the functions; we must know their functions of transformation if we want to comprehend the whole as a process.

—Wilhelm Reich, *Orgonometric Equations: I. General Form*

Much of the history of the past several hundred years can be viewed as an account of how armored humans have attempted to cope with the destructive social consequences resulting ultimately from their sexual and work disturbances. Such attempts have largely consisted of people turning to leaders in authority for answers. It slowly began to dawn on people that these authorities were not only unable to be of help but were making matters worse. When this happened, the masses increasingly became disillusioned with their leaders and many lost confidence in all authority. As a result, the structure of authoritarian society that once had been effective in containing the destructive impulses of armored humans became transformed into its antithesis, *anti-authoritarian society*. This transformation and its nightmarish consequences are what we in the Western world are currently witnessing and living through.

Healthy individuals and societies are rare but they nevertheless do exist and have been studied. From these studies the true nature of the relationship between individual and state authority can be learned. Such knowledge is derived from understanding the cumulative personal experiences and traditions of relatively unarmored individuals and their social institutions, past and present.[68]

In a healthy society, authority is in the service of protecting and developing core functions of its members, such as raising healthy children, guiding their development, safeguarding healthy sexuality of adolescents, and so on. This kind of authority is not opposed to the interests of society or to *genuine* individual or social progress. Orgonometrically, the authority of the individual in the healthy family unit and the authority of that individual functioning as a citizen in the unarmored State interact as simple variations—variations that are alike but nevertheless unique (Fig. 6.1).[69]

The Authority of the Individual in the Family ⨍ **The Authority of the Individual in the State**

FIGURE 6.1

There is no contradiction between the individual's instinctual needs and the social conditions that are necessary to allow these needs to be satisfied.

When society armored, the regulatory function of sexuality became disturbed. As a result, rational social authority became distorted and authoritarian. In past formal democratic societies, authority still originated from and served to protect core impulses (with the notable exception of the sexual function). Additionally, it also served to curb secondary destructive impulses so as to preserve armored society. Containing a mix of rational and irrational elements, authoritarianism allowed partial expression from the core and also held in check destructive impulses originating

68. See the works of Bronislaw Malinowski, in particular his book *The Sexual Life of Savages*.

69. The ideology of Black Fascism, that is, fascism on the right, gives the *illusion* of this relationship since it reproduces by means of the authoritarian family.

from the secondary layer. To the extent that authority became opposed to impulses from both the core and the secondary layer, authority became increasingly irrational and extreme.

In the past authoritarian society, individual authority and family and state authority were related to each other as attractive opposite functions. People were loyal to their families, to the principles of their country, and united under God. Individual and state authority functioned to attract each other and coexist (Fig. 6.2).

Individual Authority → ← **State Authority**

FIGURE 6.2

The rigidity of an authoritarian society depends on the extent to which authority originates from the secondary layer and not from the core.

The transformation of Western society to anti-authoritarian has necessarily altered the relationship between family and state authority. *In today's anti-authoritarian society, the authority of the family, to the extent that it still exists, has shifted to the state.* The relationship between the individual and the state is becoming one of antagonistic opposition. In this situation, the interests of the individual and the state as well as individual and state authority *necessarily* exclude and oppose each other. The authority of the state functions mainly to control the lives of its citizens and constrain impulses from their destructive secondary layer. It is no longer concerned with protecting the individual's core functions. At the same time, the individual's freedom must stand opposed to the controlling requirements and dependency on the state. This is, in fact, the relationship between the individual and society in a socialist state (see Figure 6.3).

Individual Authority ← → **State Authority**

FIGURE 6.3

The antagonistic relationship between the individual and society is the necessary consequence of the leveling effect of anti-authoritarian ideology on the masses. The end result is the idealized state government (socialism) on a national scale and the centralized world government ("One World," global socialism controlled by the United Nations) on an international scale.

The authoritarian family was once the foundation of authoritarian society. Social order and stability was maintained by the authoritarian family's active suppression of the sexual impulse in each succeeding generation. Sexual suppression was necessary because it was the basis for containing the destructive secondary layer impulses (neurotic rebelliousness) and maintaining the authoritarian social order. Armor also partially distorted core impulses rendering their expression artificial and forced but left other impulses intact. Today, armor deadens core impulses almost completely in virtually all individuals; inappropriate social behavior ("bad manners") and crudeness are seen everywhere. People no longer are capable of showing genuine respect for, and gratitude and loyalty to, *rational* authority. As a result, what remains of the authoritarian social order is no longer able to keep destructive impulses in check. A pervasive attitude of distrust, disrespect, and hostility directed toward all forms of traditional authority, rational and irrational, is being instilled in the younger generation.

The middle of the twentieth century was a major turning point in Western civilization. The traditional form of social organization, represented by the authoritarian system of the past, was gradually replaced by an anti-authoritarian social order—one that allowed increasing free rein to human destructive impulses. Those who lived before the second half of the twentieth century never fully experienced the horrific consequences that were about to occur throughout the world as a result of this nightmarish event. Those born after experienced nothing of the old authoritarian order and, as a result, remain unaware that an ongoing disintegrative process is taking place. Those who have lived in both periods have the opportunity of witnessing the convulsions of a violent and momentous sociological upheaval of monumental proportions.

Although many have written astutely about this social transformation,[70] its true nature and underlying factors remain a mystery to those without a functional perspective. Most sociologists, trained in the traditional mechanistic-materialist schools of social thought, are not capable of knowing what to make of the fact that society is disintegrating right before their eyes. Others, who are more intellectual, believe that *any* social change away from the authoritarian social order, no matter how destructive it may be, is desirable. Only functional thinking can provide an accurate perspective of the significance of this transformation.

The Transformation of Social Armor

In his investigation into the neurosis, Reich found that the authoritarian social order, with its patriarchal family structure and mystical-moral underpinning, serves to perpetuate armoring from one generation to the next. When he made this remarkable discovery, the antithetical component of authoritarian social armor, anti-authoritarianism, was hidden below the social façade and had not yet manifest. But Reich had anticipated a key factor that would be responsible for the world-wide breakdown of the authoritarian social order:

> The anchoring of a social order which frustrates the gratification of needs to a considerable extent goes with the development of psychic factors which tend to undermine this characterological anchoring. Gradually, with the development of the social process, there develops an ever-increasing discrepancy between enforced renunciation and increased libidinal tension: this discrepancy undermines 'tradition' and forms the psychological core of attitudes which threaten the anchoring.
>
> (Reich 1949a, page xxiii)

Thus, manifestations of social armor are not static and unalterable, but develop and can be understood according to principles revealed by functional thinking.

Delegating authority to duly elected or appointed officials was the organizing principle of the American Republic. During the

70. See, for example, Bork (1996), Hitchens (1999), and C. Murray, "Prole Models," *Wall Street Journal*, February 6, 2001.

past authoritarian era, people lived in a relatively well-ordered society. The family was intact with generally accepted forms of social behavior. Social life was primarily organized around the family. Men and women in their twenties were expected to marry and raise children. Sexual repression was the rule. Sexual matters were never publicly discussed and, according to established tradition, sexual activity was confined to marriage. Men worked five or six days a week, usually from nine to five, and women took care of the household. Sunday was a day of rest when work stopped, all businesses were closed, and people went to church. There was a general consensus as to what was right and wrong. The secondary layer was held in check by individual and social armor, by accepted codes of behavior and by statutory laws. Social anxiety was at low levels but, because of sexual repression, the underlying forces behind the sexual misery and sexual longing of the masses were intensifying.

Then suddenly, in the span of a few short years during the early 1960s, destructive impulses from the secondary layer broke through individual and social armor in full force, traditions were undermined, and American society as a whole transformed from an authoritarian to an anti-authoritarian system. This was a discontinuous event of monumental proportions. With the eruption of the secondary layer, almost every kind of socially destructive behavior came to be tolerated, if not accepted outright, because people were completely unprepared to deal with it. The accompanying loss of contact with the core functions of life touched off the start of the decline of American society. Although the transformation occurred abruptly, the events leading up to the rejection of authoritarianism was gradual and took many decades.

The historical events leading up to the transformation can be traced to the total socioeconomic collapse of Germany following its unconditional and humiliating defeat in the First World War.[71] This devastation of a great world power destabilized the continent and led to a sharp rise in social anxiety manifested by an increase in sociopolitical activity and social restlessness that spread rapidly from Europe to America. The breakdown of social

71. The part played by U.S. President Woodrow Wilson in the First World War was presented earlier. Wilson was an idealistic liberal who functioned as a pseudo-liberal character. See the previously discussed relationship between the social behavior of the pseudo-liberal character and the emotional plague.

and economic order in Germany set the stage for a sharp increase in the popularity of German Communism and, as a reaction to it, Nazism, which was partially a desperate and reckless attempt to regain social stability.[72]

It was hoped that Hitler's defeat would finally put an end to fascism, but it only revealed an even more malignant evil hidden behind the social façade of communism. Following the Second World War, the threat of communism became an additional source of heightened social anxiety and it was during this time that the social transformation occurred.

With the crumbling of the Soviet empire and with the support of American liberals, *pseudo-liberalism has become the most potent destructive social force in the world.* A clear expression of the plague, this ideology functions to set free impulses from the destructive secondary layer and, at the same time, to undermine all natural core functions in Western society. It has contributed to the very confusion it seeks to remedy by subverting America's military resolve against the Islamic fanatics and by *promoting international brotherhood under the banner of the United Nations,* which it offers as the ultimate solution to achieve world peace. By disguising himself as a true liberal, the pseudo-liberal is now a dominant social and political force and *the* critical factor that has roiled society and hastened its anti-authoritarian transformation. This ideology is directly responsible for the intensification of destructive secondary layer sociopolitical activity expressed as the emotional plague throughout the world. It has left America particularly vulnerable in dealing with the plague of Islamic Fascism. Having helped to bring about the emasculation of authority and the dismantling of the authoritarian social order and, with it, the chaos and confusion that has followed, the only possible solution will be the reorganization of America into some form of socialist state. When this happens, the ultimate goal of pseudo-liberalism, to render America subservient to the authority of the United Nations, will be a relatively simple matter. Significantly, this goal was identical to that of world communism advocated by the Red Fascist plague during the Soviet Communist era. It is therefore vitally important that the

---

72. Significantly, Reich's social hygiene movement in Germany was taking place during this time.

Free World in general and the true liberal in particular recognize the deadliness of the pseudo-liberal plague individual. True liberalism must be kept separate from the pseudo-liberal plague.

When the ever-present fascist tendencies contained within armored people on the political left and the right intensify, society becomes polarized and the risk of social disintegration and international conflict dramatically increase. (See Reich quote below) This development, currently taking place in certain South American countries and to a lesser extent in America, was predicted as a central problem by Reich in 1944, shortly before the defeat of German Fascism:

> Even after the military victory over German Fascism, *the Fascist human structure will continue to exist in Germany, Russia, America and everywhere else.* It will continue to grow subterraneously, will seek new forms of political organization and will inevitably lead to a new catastrophe, unless the responsible people all over the world will rally to protect and utter truth as today only the political lie is protected and uttered. This can be predicted with absolute certainty. (Reich 1953b, page 17; italics added)

During the 1920s and 30s in America, many social forces acted together with pseudo-liberalism to weaken the existing authoritarian system (Allen 1931). Freud's misconstrued influence on America was one important factor. His popularized theories were misunderstood and distorted in the minds of armored people and they had a powerful but, unfortunately, destructive effect on the American people. One message, distorted by freethinking liberals that became imbedded in the popular mind, was that the most important requirement for mental health is an uninhibited sex life. Another erroneous and equally destructive concept was that, because there is an unconscious mind, people are not accountable for their destructive behavior. A third destructive effect was that of psychoanalytic technique itself, which relied heavily on the individual's analytical faculties. Attempting to achieve self-understanding, intelligent people in all walks of American life became caught up in "analyzing" and questioning themselves. They became "stuck in their heads," asking themselves "why" they thought or behaved as they did. This practice most often only served to intensify the intellect and, from then on, understanding itself came to be widely used as a defense by deadening emotion. A new and more sophisticated layer of psychic armor was incorporated as an entirely new lexicon emerged: technical psychiatric terms such as *paranoia, Oedipus complex, inferiority complex, sadism, masochism, and obsessive-compulsive* became popularized and were bandied about by lay people with little genuine understanding of their meaning. Lastly, a related factor that served to aggravate the use of the intellect as defense was that psychoanalysis had little to say about the importance of the function of emotions and their role in health. It will be shown that these mistaken views and limitations of Freudian ideas were also largely responsible for the decline in the quality of psychiatric practice that we are seeing today.

The growing independence of women was another key factor that brought about the transformation. In 1920, women won the right to vote, and their position as man's equal moved toward consolidation. It was also about this time that women started to become emancipated from routine household chores. The manufacture of labor-saving machinery, such as the washing machine and the vacuum cleaner, provided women with more freedom, sometimes more than they could tolerate. New work opportunities became available and with them came greater economic independence and emotional freedom. The divorce rate began to climb. For every 100 marriages, there were 8.8 divorces in 1910, 13.4 divorces in 1920, and 16.5 divorces in 1928. In later decades the social disgrace associated with divorce also declined correspondingly. This served to weaken the authoritarian family.

The Second World War accelerated the process of women's economic emancipation. The need for factory labor to replace the men who were fighting the war forced women out of the home and into the job force. This gave them economic independence but also served to further disrupt the structure of the authoritarian family. It was the children of the broken families of the war generation, the "baby boomers," who became the rebellious adolescents and young adults of the 1960s, caught up in the aborted, so-called "sexual revolution." Many of these young people were left without the sorely needed influence of parental authority and rational guidance. This absence led first to feelings of anxiety and rage directed at their father then to hatred for all forms of authority.

In the authoritarian social order, women were the bearers of morality. Their function, based on the requirement of celibacy prior to marriage, was as necessary to preserve the existing social system as the function of men in their authoritarian role. This arrangement corresponded to the structure of the average individual. Most males were phallic narcissistic characters and readily assumed the authoritarian role and most females were hysteric characters and easily functioned as the bearers of morality. The dissociation of authority and morality into male and female roles, respectively, had given rise to the "double standard" of sexual behavior, but with the breakdown of the social order, women were no longer held to this standard.

A third factor was the effect of two World Wars on America. It exposed millions of American soldiers to the horrors of war and near annihilation, forever changing these generations of men. This further led to a widespread breakdown of traditional restraints and taboos. Upon returning to the humdrum routine of daily life, men were expected to settle down as if nothing had happened. Many of the older generation, who had not experienced the immediate effects of the wars, also found themselves restless and disoriented, questioning much that had once seemed true and worthy. After each World War, disillusionment weakened confidence in the authoritarian social order and fueled sentiments for greater freedom from the traditional restraints of social life.

A fourth factor was America's awakening to racism. In 1954, the Supreme Court in Brown v. Board of Education overturned laws and court rulings supporting segregation in education and set off a psychological chain reaction across America, forcing people to examine their time-honored beliefs regarding the difference between blacks and whites. Speaking for the unanimous Court decision, Chief Justice Earl Warren said: "The doctrine 'separate but equal' has no place. Separate educational facilities are inherently unequal." There was a crisis of confidence in the authority of the law. Americans had been taught to trust judges to mete out justice. Brown exposed generations of judges who uniformly had been unjust regarding issues of race. Most of the rest of America had also tolerated segregation and second-class status for blacks.

After desegregation, Americans began to question themselves and their legal system. It took nearly a century for the rift formed by the Civil War to heal sufficiently before the racial issue could be addressed in a somewhat rational manner. (See chapter 8, Black/ White Relations in the United States)

Lastly and most importantly, the transformation of society from authoritarian to anti-authoritarian resulted from the abysmal failure of mechanistic science and mystical religion to lead the way to a natural scientific, *not mechanistic,* understanding of biological and social processes on the one hand and to knowledge of the functions underlying man's relationship to nature on the other. These shortcomings created a vacuum leaving the masses without rational guidance in these two critical areas. Despite this failure, armored humans continue to cling to their destructive ways of thinking partly because they have nothing else to replace it with and partly because they are terrified of any forward motion. Their underlying terror of moving forward is why they are always shifting from the political right to the political left, and back again. This terror has given every freedom- and salvation-peddling politician and religious demagogue the chance to wreak havoc on society. What follows is an account of the social components of this transformation.

The Breakdown of the Authoritarian Family

In no small part, the two World Wars brought about a dramatic decline of the family unit as a force of social stability. The family is a social unit and, at the same time, the unit of the whole society. The characteristics of society originate and are replicated from the structure of the family unit. *It is necessary to distinguish between the authoritarian family, characterized by its sex-negative organization, and the family structure organized according to the principle of sex-affirmation.* In the *sex-affirmative* family, the biological needs, including sexual needs, of infants, children, and adolescents find appropriate satisfaction. Since such a family structure leads to neither deprivation nor overindulgence, the child develops without forming repressed or unsatisfied blocks and is, therefore, capable of self-regulation. These children have a very strong sense of independence and responsibility and stand out because of their natural healthy characteristics. They grow up to be independent, responsible adults.

The disintegration of the authoritarian family was accompanied by an increase in centralized government power. The protective and moral functions of the authoritarian family were transferred from individual members of society to the state. This transfer of power from individuals to the state is the origin of socialism. The compulsive moralistic attitude of the past turned into a new kind of morality, political correctness, and the authority of individuals was replaced by the collective authority of "Big Brother," the caretaker state.

The social policies advanced by the Kennedy and Johnson administrations illustrate the deleterious effects of the shift toward a collective state authority. Both presidents were true liberal characters who came to be influenced by the pseudo-liberal rhetoric that began to infiltrate the political mainstream at that time. Kennedy began to transform social welfare programs into forces of social progress. They were no longer targeted exclusively toward the sick, the aged, and the disabled. Now, more than in the past, the government actively assumed responsibility for people's helplessness (Murray 1984, page 14). From 1950 to 1980, using constant dollars for comparison, federal social welfare expenditures for health, public assistance, education, social insurance, and housing rose between 600 and 12,900 percent, depending on the program. However, programs transferring wealth from the "haves" to the "have-nots" left the "have-nots" even more helpless and dependent than they were before they received governmental assistance. Charles Murray states:

> In only three years, from 1964 to the end of 1967, social policy went from the dream of ending the dole to the institution of permanent income transfers that embraced not only the recipients of the dole but large new segments of the American population. It went from the ideal of a colorblind society to the reinstallation of legalized discrimination. They were polar changes that were barely recognized as such while they were happening. (Ibid., page 24)

Typically, two different but equally destructive attitudes toward the institution of the family predominate. To the degree that individuals are armored, those on the right support the principle of "family life," regardless of its life-negative effects. Their stress on "the importance of the family" and "family values" evades the very real, central need for individual sexual happiness. In contrast, the left fails to appreciate the importance of an intact family as the basis for healthy social organization.[73] Ignoring the importance of emotional functions, they stress only socio-economic factors.

The authoritarian family structure was maintained by repression, especially sexual repression. As a result, most members of society were repressed characters, primarily repressed hysteric characters (females) and repressed phallic characters (males). People who could not conform to the prevailing authoritarian social order, such as criminals and chronic schizophrenics, were institutionalized or lived on the fringes of a fairly well-ordered society. The weakening of authoritarian family structure led to social chaos in varying degrees. Societal breakdown brought about partly by the disintegrating authoritarian family was followed, of necessity, by increased centralization of governmental power over people as authority was being transferred from the family unit to the government.

Permitting and indulging the child's every wish combined with a lack of parental guidance have replaced authoritarian repression. This has led to aimlessness in children, an inability of the individual to take charge of his or her life, and anxious, chaotic behavior. Parental repression *and* indulgence of the child's impulses causes impulsive or sociopathic behavior. All three forms of childrearing—authoritarian, anti-authoritarian, and a contradictory mix of the two—if left uncorrected, inevitably lead to society's further breakdown. Symptomatic of this breakdown is the prevalent lack of emotional connection between parents and their children. This is widely recognized and is commonly referred to as the "generation gap."

---

73. The failure to distinguish between health and sickness is a hallmark of neurosis. As a result of armor, the neurotic homogenizes the world and accurate, sustained perception of the world with *rational* discrimination is not possible. People are finding it increasingly difficult to distinguish between friend and foe.

In a vicious cycle, the weakening of the authoritarian family and the resulting permissiveness, sexual and otherwise, have contributed to the deterioration of social and individual functioning. This has occurred, in no small part, because of the increased ocular armor that necessarily accompanies a decrease of pelvic armor. With respect to the individual's ability to function, less pelvic armor in the presence of armor in the upper segments, primarily in the ocular and oral segments, does not translate into a capacity for healthier functioning and greater sexual satisfaction. To the contrary, the premature mobilization of sexual impulses from the pelvis, a direct result of the breakdown of the authoritarian family structure, has brought about sexual activity for which the masses today are totally unprepared, and which can only result in less satisfaction, increased anxiety, and confusion.

The Vietnam War period presented mass psychological evidence of the intensification of ocular armor. The existence of a Communist threat to the West was increasingly misperceived, not seen, especially among the young. The social turmoil that resulted led to political interference and to confusion in the management of the war effort with, as we have seen, catastrophic consequences. A clear perception of who the enemy was, the Soviet Union, was lacking. Today, there is the same widespread misperception of the continued threat of pseudo-liberalism and the global threat of Islamic fundamentalism.

Census bureau data indicate an alarming breakdown in family structure in the decades since 1970. During this time, of all households, married couples with children declined from 40 percent to 25 percent. During the same period, the percentage of single-parent families in all American households more than doubled, from 6 percent to 13 percent (Fig. 6.4).

From 1960 to 1997, out-of-wedlock births increased more than 500 percent. During the same period, the marriage rate dropped 25 percent and the divorce rate more than doubled (Bennett 1999). These social phenomena are testimony to and a direct result of the breakdown of the authoritarian family.

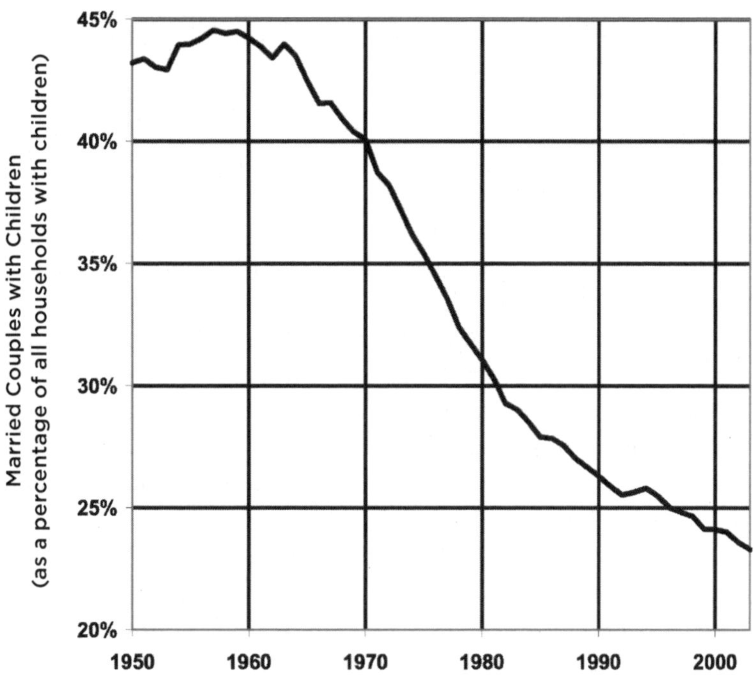

The Decline of Married Couple Households with Children
FIGURE 6.4

Accompanying this breakdown, the fabric of social structure has become fragmented at every level, including the relationship between parent and child, doctor and patient, teacher and student, experienced worker and apprentice, and so on. The age-old concept that one can learn from others who have greater experience or benefit from knowledge handed down from past generations has also been denigrated. In this age of glorification of youth and the individual, "having fun" and "doing one's own thing" are considered to be politically correct and of prime importance.[74]

74. The emergence of the syndrome of hyperactivity, attention disturbance, and impulsivity, the hallmarks of attention deficit hyperactivity disorder (ADHD), is a direct result of the transformation of the family from authoritarian to anti-authoritarian. Without structure and necessary discipline, the child cannot develop the ability to integrate into a stable, self-regulating individual.

The Weakening of the Authoritarian Social Order

The failure of mechanistic science, humanism, or mystical religion to provide satisfactory answers as to the nature of humanity and its problems, or its true relationship to the universe, have been major factors in the breakdown of the authoritarian social order. This failure has directly affected all established social institutions. As a result, the authority of mechanistic science and of organized religion has been challenged. This has led to anti-authoritarianism in the form of alternatives to science and religion. In the past, physicians were highly respected members of society. Rightly or wrongly, their authority was rarely questioned. Today, the general public fancy themselves as knowledgeable on any medical question by virtue of their "education" gained through the media—television, magazines, newspapers, or the Internet. Brief accounts of the latest medical study have made everyone an expert. Except for highly specialized branches of science, "authorities" are everywhere. This attitude conveys the general belief that there are no genuine authorities.

During earlier periods of social change, authoritarian social order, although weakened, was intact enough to absorb these changes. However, the social upheaval that began during the early 1960s was more than the existing social structure could withstand. Indeed, shortly after Reich's death in 1957, the authoritarian structure of American society began to crumble, and the antithetical function emerged full force (Fig. 6.5).

FIGURE 6.5

This transformation occurred simultaneously in every part of the world that was under the influence of the West. For example, with the collapse of the British Empire in the 1960s, colonialism was replaced by anti-colonialism with all of its destructive consequences.

The Sociopolitical Red-shift

The transformation of society was directly responsible for and the result of the precipitous shift of the political center to the left on the sociopolitical spectrum. This meant the ideology of the left became accepted as the norm while every idea to the right became marginalized and identified with right-wing extremism. This shift began as early as the 1950s during the McCarthy era, when American pseudo-liberals (communists) succeeded politically in labeling anyone who favored investigation of communist infiltration of the federal government as paranoid, as a right-wing extremist—a favored tactic, by the way, of the Soviet Union's propaganda machine.

The red-shift resulted in a qualitative change in the culture of Western society. The transformation into an anti-authoritarian order was responsible for the reduction in the quality of every aspect of social life. (See chapter 8) More than ever, Americans have lost touch with the importance of the biological functions of love and work that formerly sustained the integrity of social relationships. As a substitute for these core values, people have become involved with distractions of every kind. Examples include instant gratification and materialistic preoccupations, such as compulsive shopping and addiction to television, video games, computers, the Internet, and electronic gadgets. On the mystical side there are an endless variety of New Age movements, preoccupation with herbal remedies and health foods, physical fitness gurus, and even psychics—all ways of avoiding genuine emotional contact.[75] In the past authoritarian social order, contact with inner core emotions and sensations, however partial it may have been, gave people a sense of value to their lives. This

75. Television and its counterparts (e.g., computers, movies) serve two non-functional purposes in our society: as a *distraction* (to fill time or to entertain) and as a *substitute for genuine contact*. Here, the emotional excitement in life is limited to that experienced in watching television. As a distraction, it is fairly benign. As substitute contact, it is far more destructive. In this role, the violence, unhealthy sexuality, and extreme distortions of reality become readily confused with true emotional contact. Those with empty lives and with no real emotional excitation turn to such forms of substitute contact. As a distraction, the amount needed for satisfying the individual defines whether it is "just entertainment" or has become a symptom of contactlessness. When used as a substitute for contact, it is no longer entertainment—it becomes reality. In fact, the media exploits this need for substitute contact by popularizing "reality" shows.

sense has gradually disappeared, and there is no turning back to the old ways.[76]

The transformation into anti-authoritarian society has been accompanied by a change in the relationship between the political left and the right into one of antagonistic opposition. (See next section) This change has disrupted and polarized legitimate governmental and individual functions at every level. One such primary governmental function is the protective role of the police and military. Because the left and the right have opposing views about the need for aggressive action against terrorists, for example, America's ability to defend itself against its enemies is being seriously compromised. The old idea of a unified and consistent bipartisan foreign policy in time of war, such as that associated with the Japanese attack on Pearl Harbor, has been thrown to the wind because there is no consensus that there is a war in the first place.

The anti-authoritarian social policies promoted relentlessly by pseudo-liberals have proven to be far more inimical to life and a greater distortion of reality than its authoritarian counterpart.[77] The authoritarianism formerly expressed in the structure of the family unit has been replaced by a paternalistic authoritarianism of the state.

Accompanying this transformation has been a change in the interrelationship between the individual and society. With authoritarianism, individual freedom was restricted to varying degrees, but a sense of independence and responsibility for one's personal life was nevertheless retained. Also maintained was a sense of the importance of the family and the protection of the nation and the authoritarian social order. Rebelliousness was a common reaction to authority among people with high energy levels whose armor was insufficient to bind their energy,

---

76. This process of transformation was temporarily slowed after the attack on America and the destruction of the World Trade Center on September 11, 2001. For a while, people's contact with themselves and the contractive functions of society reversed the chronic overexpansion. People spent more time at home with their families, were less distractible, and so on.

77. It is currently in vogue to refer to today's society as being permissive. Using the term *anti-authoritarian* captures something more than the permissive element. Just as the authoritarian society of the past involved undiscerning loyalty, respect, and obedience to all forms of authority, rational as well as irrational, there is currently blind opposition to, and disrespect for, those in authority and all they stand for.

but its attendant destructiveness was relatively minimal. In contrast, with anti-authoritarianism, freedom has been more or less replaced by licentiousness, an attitude of entitlement, and contempt for authority. There is little sense of personal responsibility or of the importance of protecting the family, the nation, or social order. This is so because in leftist ideology, responsibility for one's personal life is secondary and is replaced by responsibility to social causes that are deemed morally meaningful and socially necessary. The rebellious tendencies in people have been more and more left without much to rebel against because, in people's minds, authorities no longer exist. As a result, rebelliousness has been replaced by indifference and impulsiveness.

The Polarization of Society

The shift to anti-authoritarianism in Western societies was accompanied by deterioration in the quality of every component function of society and is evident in all social institutions: education, medicine, the sciences, the legal system, and, most importantly, the raising of children. As we will see, we must pay particular attention to the latter function if we are to reverse the social consequences of armor and restore people's capacity for greater contact with their biological core.

As a result of the weakening of authoritarian society and the ensuing social chaos, the opposing sociopolitical forces of the left and right could no longer function according to the principle of attractive opposition. They became polarized into two ideologically irreconcilable groups that can function only as antagonistic opposites (Fig. 6.6).[78]

Ideological Forces on the Left (Mechanism)

Ideological Forces on the Right (Mysticism)

FIGURE 6.6

No corrective action can take place unless we understand what is happening from this functional standpoint. The social changes occurring with this transformation are qualitatively and

78. The historian Arnold Toynbee described this feature accompanying social disintegration. To recognize a disintegrating society, Toynbee wrote, look for a "riven society." See the chapter entitled "Schism in the Soul" (Toynbee 1946).

quantitatively unlike anything that has happened before. Several features of this transformation deserve special mention:

- Although the process was gradual, the transformation itself was a discontinuous event. It occurred suddenly, in a relatively few years, yet the authoritarian-moralistic underpinning of society was irreversibly altered.
- The position of the sociopolitical center shifted to the left, and disorder and chaos replaced the orderly development of society.
- There was a dramatic rise in sociopolitical activism, such as the civil rights movement, the women's rights movement, student unrest, and so on.
- The relationship between the left and the right changed from attractive opposition to antagonistic opposition.
- There was a qualitative change in the relationship between individual members of society, such as parent and child, physician and patient, parent and teacher, teacher and student, and employer and employee.

All of these changes occurred in front of everyone and without anyone being aware of the full social significance of what was happening.

The Degradation of the Rule of Law

The rule of law is one of the indispensable institutions of Western democracies without which there can be no social stability and continuity. The rational function of law is to protect and secure the core functions of both the individual and society. When observed and rationally applied, the rule of law safeguards social processes that guarantee social survival. It must be used as a bulwark against the emotional plague. In the current anti-authoritarian society, the rule of law has been flagrantly subverted by the public and this has been reflected by judicial activists on the political left. As a result, the secondary layer has been increasingly protected at the expense of the biological core.

The United States Supreme Court under Chief Justice Earl Warren was the most politically motivated in American history, politicizing every area of law it touched. A characterological liberal, Warren once confessed, "I never heard a jury bring in a verdict of guilty but that I felt sick at the pit of my stomach."[79] Activism is in the service of promulgating any desired social result deemed positive in the eyes of the Court. Unfortunately, even if it were possible, *judges do not have the necessary training or experience to understand and deal with biologically rooted social problems of today, the result of the breakthrough of the destructive secondary layer of armored humanity into social life.*

The Bill of Rights was amended to the United States Constitution in order to guarantee individual liberties. The interpretation of this document must consider the proper historical context of such liberties. It was written when authoritarian society was highly ordered. *The words and phrases meant something entirely different to people living 200 years ago than they do to people today.* Unfortunately, liberals interpret them as if they were written by people in today's anti-authoritarian society. To them, the original sense is entirely lost. The First Amendment, in particular, has been a source of intense controversy because it deals with the issues of freedom and responsibility and the relationship between the individual and society. It states: "Congress shall make no law respective an establishment of religion, or prohibiting the free exercise thereof; or abridging the freedom of speech, or of the press, or the right of people peaceably to assembly, and to petition the Government for redress of grievances."(1)[80]

Neither the Constitution nor the Bill of Rights was intended to deal with the explosive social problems that have erupted with the breakdown of the authoritarian social order and the breakthrough of the destructive secondary layer. This is why attempts to deal with social issues involving individual rights through judicial measures cannot succeed. Using legal means can only result

---

79. *The Almanac of American History*, Arthur M. Schlesinger Jr. General Editor, page 569, 1993. Feeling guilt in response to an aggressive act is typical of the liberal character.

80. For the following few pages, references to legal decisions are supplied in the form of numbered endnotes.

in increasing social armor by restricting the freedoms enjoyed by the majority, as greater "rights" are bestowed on the minority groups demanding redress. The following clauses of the First Amendment are provided as examples.

The Speech Clause

The Supreme Court had no occasion to consider First Amendment speech claims until the second decade of the twentieth century (2). In the case of *Abrams v. United States* (1919), the defendants were convicted for circulating pamphlets construed as harmful to the war effort. In a dissenting opinion, Oliver Wendell Holmes wrote: "But when men have realized that time has upset many fighting faiths, they may come to believe even more than they believe the very foundations of their own conduct that the ultimate good desired is better reached by free trade in ideas—that the best test of truth is the power of the thought to get itself accepted in the competition of the market, and that truth is the only ground upon which their wishes safely can be carried out."(3)

The assumption is that given enough time, human beings are capable of thinking rationally. This opinion set in motion a destructive precedent in the Court. *Somehow,* this line of thought asserts, *rationality in thinking and behavior will prevail over irrationalism and destructiveness. In fact, the exact opposite happened.* Originally, the core function of the First Amendment speech clause was to serve as a protection of speech that informs and guides rational social and political processes essential to a democratic government, processes that protect the biological core functions of society.

The free speech clause deteriorated in a line of cases culminating in *Brandenburg v. Ohio,* which laid down the rule that the speech clause does "not permit a state to forbid or proscribe advocacy of the use of force or of law violation except where such advocacy is directed to inciting or producing imminent lawless action and is likely to incite or produce such action."(4) That ruling allows demagoguery to bring its audiences to a fever pitch of excitement and permits state intervention only when the incitement is likely to result in immediate action. This degradation of the speech clause rapidly escalated to an alteration of the law regarding lewd or obscene expression. In 1973, when a five-justice majority narrowly upheld minor restraints on pornography in *Miller v. California* (5), there was a sharp outcry from the political left about censorship. In *Cohen v. California*, the Court gave First Amendment protection to a man who came into the courtroom wearing a jacket with obscene writing on it that directed the reader to perform a sexual act with the Selective Service System (6).

The floodgates were now open. In *Rosenfeld v. New Jersey*, Rosenfeld addressed a school board meeting of about one hundred fifty people, including about forty children, and on four occasions used the adjective "mother-f---ing" to describe the teachers, the school board, the town, and the United States. In *Lewis v. New Orleans* (7), Lewis shouted the same epithet at police officers who were arresting her son. In *Brown v. Oklahoma* (8), Brown used the same language in a meeting in a university chapel. None of the convictions—for disorderly conduct, breach of the peace, and the use of obscene language in a public place—were allowed to stand.

The failure of society to maintain minimal acceptable standards of social behavior indicated a major change in the structure of society. In the *United States v. Playboy Entertainment Group, Inc.* (9), the Supreme Court held unconstitutional a congressional statute that required cable television channels "primarily oriented to sexually-oriented programming" to limit their transmission to hours when children are unlikely to be viewing. The Court majority found that the law restricted the content of speech in a way that was not justified because there appeared to be other, less restrictive ways of protecting children. Confusing the graphic depiction of sexual acts with freedom of speech, the Court ruled that "basic principles are at stake in this case."(10) Confusing the depiction of all kinds of sexual activity with free speech the Court, in effect, defended pornography and other perverse and unnatural secondary layer behavior over core functions. In a dissenting opinion, Justice Scalia wrote: "Where the design benefit of a content-based speech restriction is to shield the sensibilities of the listeners, the general rule is that the right of expression prevails. We are expected to protect our own sensibilities 'simply by averting our eyes.'"(11) The Court's "avert-your-eyes" solution is a way of saying that people must not look in order to protect their sensibilities. The majority of people are required to form yet another layer of ocular armor by *not looking* in order to protect the secondary layer behavior "right" of a few pestilent individuals. Pornography, obscenity, and calls for violence and law-breaking are now better protected than life-sustaining core impulses. The Court has become, in effect, an agent in the service of encouraging and protecting the destructive secondary layer as it is promulgated by the anti-authoritarian establishment. In front of everyone's eyes, the Court has been turned into a destructive force responsible for promoting a relationship of antagonistic opposition between society and its members.

The Establishment Clause

The Supreme Court's decisions with regard to the establishment of religion clause show the same partiality to radical individual autonomy as do the speech cases. Colleges and universities are permitted to indoctrinate students with any form of leftist socio-political ideology, yet the mere mention of the word God in public schools is forbidden. In actual fact, the words, "Congress shall make no law respecting an establishment of religion" was simply meant to preclude government recognition of an official state religion, or to prohibit discriminatory aid to one organized religion over another. From an orgonometric perspective, the ruling was meant to maintain the separation of church and state so that the relationship between them remains one of attractive opposition.

The Court became interested in the establishment clause of the First Amendment when it first began to consider the speech clause, around the second half of the twentieth century. In the early history of America, no barrier to any interaction between government and religion existed. Not only did the Continental Congress employ a chaplain, but so did both houses of the First Congress. The same Congress also provided chaplains for the Army and the Navy. From the beginning of the Republic, Congress called upon presidents to issue Thanksgiving Day proclamations in the name of God. All the presidents complied, with the sole exception of Jefferson, who thought such proclamations to be at odds with the establishment clause (12).

Today, the liberal and pseudo-liberal influence on the Court has led to hostility toward organized religion in public life. In *Lee v. Weisman*, a six-justice majority held that a short, nonsectarian prayer at a public school commencement amounted to an establishment of religion (13). In *Santa Fe Independent School Dist. v. Doe*, the school district arranged student elections to determine whether invocations should be delivered before high school games and, if so, to select students to deliver them (14). The Court majority held that "School sponsorship of a religious message is impermissible because it sends the ancillary message to members of the audience who are nonadherents that they are outsiders, not full members of the political community, and an accompanying message to adherents that they are insiders, favored members of the political community."(15)

Because contact with his biological core is weak, the liberal jurist on the Supreme Court cannot distinguish between what is a natural core function in religion (and what therefore can be allowed expression) and what is pathological. He or she can only render opinions and judgments intellectually. The Court has attempted and to date succeeded in bringing organized religion and the masses of people in the community into a relationship of antagonistic opposition. In doing so, it further weakens whatever remains of core contact in people in, among other things, their love of country. All aspects of emotional life related to core contact, such as respect for others, pride in one's self and for one's country, loyalty to country, and gratitude for one's good fortune to be living in a free country, are summarily dismissed.

The primary function of government as framed by the Founding Fathers was to protect the core functions of human life from the destructive secondary layer functions. However, since these core functions were ill-defined and since the existence and operations of the emotional plague were not then recognized, the protections that were instituted to safeguard social life were vulnerable to the emotional plague. This made it inevitable that the principles underlying American government would one day come under attack.

Today, the emotional plague is active primarily in the form of pseudo-liberal ideology. The attack is directed exactly at the point where the protective role of American jurisprudence is most vulnerable—where there is a lack of clarity regarding the core functions of life which, in the social realm, deal with the concept of freedom. Recognizing that freedom is highly vulnerable to attack, the Founding Fathers made a special effort to enumerate those areas that required protection. The Bill of Rights was the document that culminated from this effort, and the First Amendment is the one most vulnerable to attack because it deals with the principles of life that are least understood.

Unfortunately, knowledge crucial to an understanding of social life was not available to the Founding Fathers. Not only was the concept of *freedom* unclear, but the existence of the emotional plague was only vaguely recognized and its mode of operation would not be understood for another century and a half. Furthermore, crucial knowledge regarding the means of survival of both individuals and society, such as the existence and function of armor and the effect of armor on thinking and behavior, were also not yet known.

A century and a half later, Wilhelm Reich developed this knowledge. His discoveries revealed that today's social issues—such as abortion, homosexuality, feminism, for example—are symptomatic of the emotional disturbances of armored people. They can only be addressed by those with a thorough understanding of emotional functions. They cannot be addressed politically or legalistically and therefore are outside the province of the Courts. The safeguards that were placed in the Bill of Rights in order to protect the core functions of life could not withstand the onslaught of attacks against its substance that have been perpetrated by sick humans some two hundred years later. Only a clear knowledge of the existence and operation of the emotional plague and of the function of armor can contain these irrational human behaviors, much as other infectious diseases were eliminated once the pathogenic agent was medically identified and the mode of transmission understood.

What distinguishes liberal from conservative jurists is that the former practice "judicial activism" while the latter respond by opposing these activist decisions. Referring to themselves as "Originalists," conservative jurists practice law according to the *original* intent of the Constitution by discerning from the relevant materials the principles the ratifiers understood themselves to be enacting.[81] This distinction may be true from a formal standpoint but, functionally, conservatives are judicial "reactionaries," people reacting to the activism of liberal jurists.

The relationship between liberal and conservative jurists is one of attractive opposition. Both are a necessary part of the judicial system. When they become entangled in social issues that are not properly in the sphere of the courts, they become negligent in carrying out their work function. *Jurists and legislators cannot rightly address the current problems resulting from the breakdown of authoritarian social armor without first making the crucial distinction between the core functions and the destructive secondary layer of human life. The former must be protected, and the latter must be suppressed.*

The following case illustrates the destructive social consequences that arise when the emotional plague is not recognized and dealt with.

> Bono, the famous rock-music performer, speaking on the television broadcast of the Golden Globe Movie Awards to millions of people, described one of the winners as "F---ing brilliant." This incident sparked everyone in the television industry to petition the Federal Communications Commission to affirm that Bono had a right—protected by the United States Constitution and the needs of the "artistic community"—to say "F---ing" on prime time television.
>
> The long list of petitioners included the ACLU, the Directors' Guild, Actors' Guild, Writers' Guild, Viacom, and the Recording Industry Association. The petition stated: "The commission's aggressive crackdown on coarse speech has sent shock waves through the industry."[82] At the heart of the petitioner's claim is the belief that they will suffer great economic loss if their performers are not free to express themselves using vulgar and objectionable language.

---

81. By opposing judicial activism, conservative jurists, in effect, express the opinion that issues involved with all sociopolitical activism are outside the province of the courts.

82. See "F-word Fight Isn't Over Fei, Fi, Fo or Fum" by Daniel Henninger, *Wall Street Journal*, April 23, 2004.

The First Amendment of the Bill of Rights states in part: "Congress shall make no law . . . prohibiting the free exercise . . . to petition the government for redress of grievances."

The destructiveness of the petitioner's claim, and what identifies it as emotional plague, is that the well-being, emotional and otherwise, of a minority of individuals (the entertainment industry), is placed over the good of society. It is destructive because it normalizes and further sanctions vulgarity and obscenity at the expense of the sensibilities of the already armored public. Such behavior only causes people to become perceptually more armored than they already are and more insensitive to the world around them. By altering people's capacity to accurately and sensitively perceive and to feel, the entertainment industry has successfully created for itself an audience that is increasingly susceptible to the harsh and ugly images and deafening sounds that are passed off as art. The masses, their senses dulled, must now demand more and more degraded stimuli from the anti-establishment to excite them.

Without distinguishing between the three layers of human structure—the façade, the destructive secondary layer, and the biological core—one cannot arrive at a satisfactory understanding and solution to this and other similar social problems.

The underlying sociological basis for this particular problem is that the entertainment industry is almost exclusively populated by people from the political left. Having little or no core contact, and functioning mostly from the superficial layer, such persons can reach only into the depth of their destructive secondary layer in their lives and work. Through this layer they express their vengeful hatred on members of society they perceive as authority figures. By doing so, they confuse vulgarity and obscenity with genuine art.

The alleged reason given in the petition to the FCC ("economic loss") is not the real reason, which is the need to obtain satisfaction (relief of tension) by expressing and promoting their secondary layer drives in social life, and calling it "art." Since such expressions can provide only partial and temporary relief, the emotional intensity behind them continues to build and requires ever more violent and vulgar forms of expression.

In our armored society the superficial and secondary layers are represented socially, but, unfortunately, the biological core is not. The social problem shown by this case is a result of the secondary layer of armored humans. It must therefore be seen for what it is: a manifestation of the emotional plague. This plague reaction, the petition to the FCC, was activated when the work function, which originated in the secondary layer, was threatened.

Work originating from the superficial and secondary layers does not strengthen social life. It is not capable of productive growth and does not need governmental protection. In contrast, work originating from the biological core is life-affirmative and demands some form of governmental protection, when necessary.

The wide swings of sociopolitical activity between left and right always leads to polarization and social fragmentation. For example, successful pressure from pseudo-liberals for increased governmental involvement and regulation provokes a reaction from those on the political right who feel forced to engage in political activity to preserve a way of life they feel is being threatened.

Another example of polarization is the response of many Jews to Hitler's anti-Semitism during the Second World War. In a defensive reaction to the persecution of Jews by the Nazis, many prominent Jews became intensely pro-Semitic. Men like Freud and Bergson, for example, who previously had always been culturally and politically assimilated into European society and had identified themselves as Germans and Frenchmen, were two such individuals. This life-positive reaction strengthened the Zionist movement and was largely responsible for the birth of the State of Israel. The political turmoil in the Middle East that has followed it is a tragic consequence.

The tendency toward political extremism is generally less pronounced in those on the right than in those on the left. This is because character attitudes based on muscular armor (more developed in those on the right) are more stable than those originating from the brain (more prominent in those on the left). Because of this instability, leftists are more easily radicalized. This can occur suddenly, in a matter of weeks or months, or more gradually, as has occurred in American society since the early 1960s. Ironically, pseudo-liberals are fond of congratulating themselves, believing that they are responsible for the positive aspects of social change—women's rights and the civil rights movements—that have occurred.[83] In reality, these developments were already far along prior to the leftist movements of the 1960s and would have continued to develop even without leftist sociopolitical activism. What the left actually does deserve credit for is the polarized state of modern society and the continual political agitation that has driven the masses to levels of excitation (sexual and otherwise) far beyond their limit of tolerance. This has resulted in the disastrous consequences we are witnessing today.

This process of radicalization and extremism that is so apparent today is a direct result of the weakening of the authoritarian form of individual and social armor. Authoritarian social armor is difficult to recognize when intact but its absence is more easily detected in a process of social breakdown. When successful, authoritarianism obscures its actual existence.

It is instructive to compare what is happening to people in today's society with what happens to an individual undergoing medical orgone therapy. In the case of the individual, the freedom resulting from armor removal first brings with it increased levels of energy and anxiety.[84] Central to the therapeutic process is the therapist's role in helping the patient to gradually stand the intensity of his feelings. This is done by having the individual experience the underlying emotions that had been held in the armor. At the same time, the patient gradually tolerates increased levels of functioning and the freedom this brings. However, when armor is haphazardly and aggressively removed by unqualified therapists, the individual's functioning breaks down and this state is accompanied by disorientation, contactlessness and often by a phenomenon called "freedom giddiness." This is exactly the situation that is currently being experienced by many people living

---

83. One is reminded of the proverbial metaphor of the fly on the elephant's back: Whenever the elephant moves, the fly believes that he is responsible for the movement.

84. The intensification of anxiety and the release of destructiveness from the secondary layer that results from liberal and socialist freedom peddling is no different from what happens to individuals whose armor is disturbed by unqualified and, therefore, irresponsible therapists (e.g., "Reichians" and the wide range of "body therapists" practicing world-wide). The clinical picture is often acute distress, contactless, destructive and self-destructive behavior, and social alienation, the result of an unsystematic and haphazard breakdown of armor. The effects of responsible and systematic restructuring performed by a qualified medical orgonomist, on the other hand, produce a *greater* capacity to tolerate freedom and responsible behavior, a stronger sense of integration within oneself and with the healthy aspects of society, and a greater ability to protect oneself from society's unhealthy, destructive aspects.

in Western society as a result of the social transformation into anti-authoritarianism.

The symptom of freedom giddiness was also prominent in American society following the War of Independence when the people suddenly gained freedom from British rule. At that time, many Americans became enamored of the French Revolution and were more excited by what was happening in France than they were about enjoying their newly won independence. From the very beginning of their history, Americans have had more freedom than they have known what to do with. Yet, irresponsible politicians continue to market freedom to the public in the form of socialist programs.

Reich prophetically anticipated today's process of social deterioration in *Ether, God and Devil:*

> The incapacity of the armored biosystem to cope at all with strong bioenergy, the great amount of forthcoming energy due to lifelong stasis, and the quite different nature of deep biophysical functioning as compared with the superficial everyday living of the armored individual, constitute the danger. Thus, the armor has a very important function to fulfill, as pathological as this function actually is. It renders protection against a situation which, though natural to the unarmored human, (i.e. freedom) amounts to nothing less than disorientation in the chronically armored human. What we call "freedom giddiness" is due to this inability of the armored organism to function naturally. We see "freedom giddiness" in children as well as in adults who are too suddenly transplanted from an environment functioning entirely in line with the principles of self-regulation. *If today or tomorrow the authoritarian state organization were suddenly abolished so that people could do as they pleased, not freedom but chaos would result. Years of utter disorientation would have to pass before the human race would learn to live according to the principles of natural self-regulation.* (Reich 1949b, page 107; italics added)

Chaos (lawlessness) and disorientation is exactly what we are experiencing in this anti-authoritarian era.

Social Anxiety on the Rise

As Western social institutions such as the authoritarian family, organized religion, and other traditional organizations that supported social structure have eroded, energy from the secondary layer, once contained by authoritarian social armor, has now broken through in force.[85] Authoritarian social armor was maintained in the mass individual's musculature. When authoritarian social armor weakened, people's armor shifted upward from the body's musculature to the ocular segment. *This change was significant because it resulted in more armor in the brain.* Furthermore, with the decrease in armor of other segments and its protective function, a rise in both individual and social anxiety occurred (see Glossary). This manifested in ominous symptoms such as increased confusion, disorientation (see Reich quote, preceding page), sociopolitical activism, deterioration of the work ethic—in sum, a progressive decline in individual and social functioning.

Political activism in American government first started in the executive branch with President Franklin D. Roosevelt's welfare programs during the Great Depression of the 1930s. This extended into the legislative and judicial branches in the 1960s. Both were times of heightened social insecurity and anxiety. Political activism in public life began on the political left during the nineteenth century and is now a prominent feature in almost all segments of society including the political right. Today, political activism on the right is pursued in various conservative programs by, for example, demanding greater social restraint, a return to traditional moral values, and by undermining the traditional separation between religion and the state.

Social anxiety provides fertile ground for the eruption of the emotional plague through sociopolitical activity. An example is the groundswell of international sociopolitical irrationalism from the political left, particularly in Western democracies, directed against America and its allies in their efforts to democratize Islamic countries. American leftists among others have been quick to organize politically in order to undermine the U.S. war effort in Iraq. These symptoms of the emotional plague have come about largely as a result of heightened social anxiety triggered, in part, by social ten-

85. Another cause for the rise in social anxiety was the decline in the effectiveness of the protective function of the police and military forces.

sions in the Middle East. An increase in anxiety induces individuals who are inclined to emotional plague behavior to displace their tension-producing inner conflicts onto the sociopolitical arena. These conflicts are then expressed as political ideology, beliefs, and in acting out behavior such as political demonstrations.

The weakening of authoritarian social armor and the resultant increase in ocular (brain) armor brought about greater rigidity in (ideological) thinking and a greater restriction of rational, contactful social activity. This process began locally and sporadically, but with increased social disintegration, society as a whole became caught up in it and social anxiety now permeates every area of life. A specific example is provided by leftist policy makers in government and advocates of the theory of global warming, who politically exploit social anxiety about human-induced climate change to their own advantage. Their fear-mongering raises public demands for action—do something, anything—which in a vicious cycle, feeds more anxiety and alarm.

As people are becoming increasingly more anxious and irrational there is a corresponding rise in mass confusion and a sense of helplessness. Pleas for federal and state government assistance by a crippled public increase regulatory legislation (control) of social and economic life. Alternately, rising social anxiety culminates in various forms of behavioral pathology such as civil unrest, public agitation (including riots), increased craving for authority, and increased impulsive behavior and criminality.

Social anxiety is functionally identical with individual anxiety experienced when armor fails to bind energy, giving rise to distress, clinging and increased dependency, depression, and even psychosis. Rising anxiety can also bring about regression to primitive forms of social organization, such as tribalism, cultism, and gang activity. Simultaneously, it results in greater rigidity in social functioning, as seen, for example, in automatic or stereotyped, "politically correct" behavior in certain individuals.

Anxiety also leads to a decline in personal responsibility accompanied by a sense of entitlement. This attitude is always a symptom of emotional helplessness and neurotic dependency on others. *A manifestation of humanity's sickness, it is the primary cause of the movement toward socialism and, helped by the emotional plague, it leads to the widest variety of socialist mea-*

sures through increased governmental involvement in everyone's life. Almost every segment of society has come to feel that the government owes it a special privilege or favor. Big business feels that the government should protect it from the rigors of market competition. Manufacturers feel that the government owes them protective tariffs or subsidies for their products. Farmers feel that the government owes them crop subsidies. Unions feel that the government should keep members' jobs protected from nonunion competition. Residents of coastal areas feel that the government should give them funds to maintain rivers and harbors and to provide flood insurance. Scientists feel that the government should fund their research. Religious groups feel that the government should fund their schools. The unemployed and unemployable feel that the government owes them a subsidized living. These demands are all a symptom of individual anxiety displaced onto the social scene. *They are attempts of bioemotionally sick humans to alleviate anxiety by obtaining security from the government.*

Another consequence of the increased mass anxiety is a dramatic rise in mystical tendencies in those on the left and the right, and the regression in people's thinking to all kinds of New Age movements and to religion.[86] Reacting to the breakdown of the authoritarian order and to the failure of the "sexual revolution" of the 1960s and 1970s, people have been left feeling increasingly helpless and adrift. To overcome their fearfulness, many turn to religion and to mystical leaders to tell them how to live and to give meaning to their lives.

The increase in mysticism has encroached on all educational levels. Traditionally, United States universities have hired religious studies professors regardless of whether they practiced or admired the faiths they taught. Now, some universities are bending to the views of generous donors and state legislators by hiring

86. See Konia, C. 2005, Applied Orgonometry IV: Mysticism. *Journal of Orgonomy* 39 (2). Mysticism often appears in scientists who have come to feel uncomfortable carrying on research in a mechanistic fashion. They may turn to preexisting mystical alternatives to mechanistic science or form their own brand of mystical system. Words and phrases such as "heightened consciousness" and "moving the energy" are telltale indications of a tendency to mysticism or outright mystical thinking. Mystical tendencies in patients lay behind the expectation that the therapist will cure them and are identical to the attitude of people who hope for religious or political salvation. These are defensive reactions familiar to all medical orgonomists. Patients who cannot tolerate medical orgone therapy may turn to other therapies or join religious organizations to satisfy their mystical longings and expectations.

the faithful. Privately funded professorships in specific religions are being established. These university chairs include faiths ranging from Islam to Sikhism. They are usually underwritten by donors of the same religion. The barrier between religion and the state, which has been a cornerstone of American society, is breaking down as people are becoming more and more dependant on both institutions. It is to be expected that with the current, widespread dissatisfaction in the mechanistic approach to the life sciences that the propensity for mysticism will increase.

The growth of religious fundamentalism and occultism since the 1970s is demonstrated by the following graph comparing the percentage of adults in 1976 and 1998 who stated that they believe in various mystical ideas (Fig. 6.7).[87]

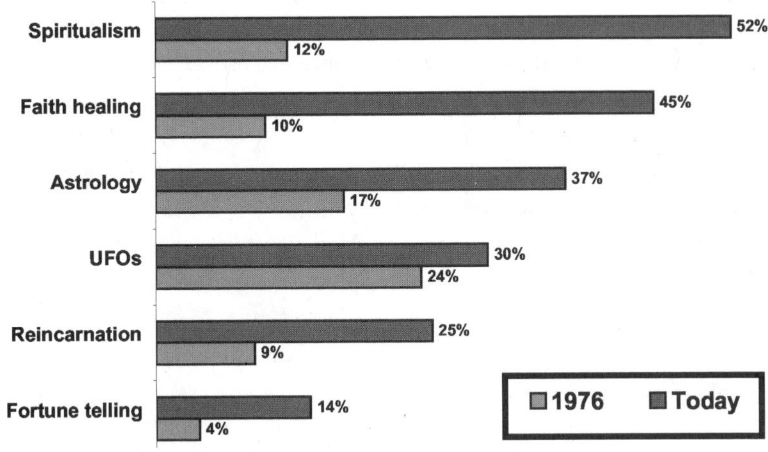

FIGURE 6.7

Conservatives easily shift toward fundamentalist religions because their preexisting tendency toward mysticism becomes exaggerated. Liberals become mystical when they become dissatisfied and disillusioned with mechanistic materialism. An example can be shown in the mechanistic scientist who in his later years becomes preoccupied with religious or other mystical pursuits. Through spiritualism, individuals maintain partial, albeit distorted, contact with the nature within them and in the surrounding world.

87. *USA Today*, April 20 1998.

The growth of mysticism has been accompanied by a wide-scale breakdown of traditional religious beliefs. An article in the *Wall Street Journal* entitled "Redefining God" states: "Dissatisfied with conventional images of an authoritarian or paternalistic deity, people are embracing quirky, individualistic conceptions of God to suit their own spiritual needs. Although a steady 90 percent of Americans continue to say they believe in God, the number of those who say no standard definition 'comes close' to their notion of the deity has more than doubled in the past twenty years."[88]

It was believed in the past that mysticism is primarily a product and characteristic of people on the political right. However, with the transformation of social armor from authoritarian to anti-authoritarian, resulting in the breakdown of social structure, and with the resultant increase in social anxiety and the dehumanizing effect mechanization has had on people, it has become evident that mysticism is no longer confined to the political right, but has crept into the lives of people on the political left. Mysticism provides people with a sense of belonging, albeit a distorted one, in an uncertain and increasingly dangerous world.

The rise of mysticism parallels the rise in ideological thinking, since both serve the same function. Derived from mysticism, the ideologies of the left and the right interfere with seeing the world as it really is. The blindness of mysticism is not usually an immediate threat to social life except during times of national emergency. At those times, any ideology can serve to avoid recognizing that the nation is in mortal danger. When it originates from the political right, this shortsightedness is manifested in a rigid, defensive adherence to certain traditional attitudes and beliefs that override and invalidate all other considerations. The ideological opposition to abortion is an example. When it originates from the political left, the blindness is masked by a façade of naïve idealism.

The following are some of the characteristics of the left's mysticism:

- All people are capable of improvement and achieving happiness through mystical practices, alternative therapies, Scientology, Christian Science, and so on.

88. *Wall Street Journal*, April 21, 2000.

- All people, even one's enemies, are capable of redemption through social intervention, humanitarian efforts, and so on.
- "Higher" knowledge can be attained by anyone through mystical experiences and practices without observing the real world.
- The gaps in knowledge left by mechanistic science can be filled through mystical experiences.
- Truth and law are relative to the individual's particular world view. Hence, there are many truths.

From the standpoint of America's national security, the combined effect of the mystical, ideological thinking of the left and the right is deadly.

The mystical longing for achieving a perfect life in this or the next world corresponds to the materialistic longing for quick riches, which will supposedly bring true happiness in this one. Both are examples of magical thinking, efforts to overcome underlying anxiety with a false sense of hope and expansion. While mystics long for salvation through divine providence ("the hand of God"), gamblers and greedy financial speculators look to chance ("Lady Luck") for their good fortune. It is no accident that most chronic gamblers are found among the so-called "poor," those who can least afford to gamble and whose work function is most disturbed. Neither group is in touch with the underlying anxiety that drives them to pursue their destructive substitute activities. From financially risky, get-rich-quick schemes to playing the lottery and casino gambling, gamblers and financial speculators seek momentary substitute gratification and look for an easy path to alleviate their insecurity and anxiety.

Employment in the gambling industry is an example of work originating from the destructive secondary layer. The rise of gambling in America is documented by the fact that ten years ago, gambling was legal in only two states. Today, it is legal in forty-seven. Gambling for money and imprudent financial speculation are symptomatic of underlying anxiety.

Another indication of the increase and intolerance of anxiety is the extensive, indiscriminate use of anti-anxiety and antidepressant medications such as Prozac, Zoloft, and Valium. Taking prescription medication or self-medicating with illicit drugs, as well as the excessive use of alcohol, is widespread in all socioeconomic classes. By doing away with the perception of anxiety, these drugs also reduce or eliminate the perception of other painful emotions, such as fear. However, fear is essential to mobilize defensive reactions that are necessary for survival in daily life and especially in times of crisis. Eliminating this vital reaction with medication causes individuals to lose touch with themselves and their environment. Seen in this light, the potential for the destructive consequences of widespread use of psychoactive drugs is very great. Supported and encouraged by the medical profession, the indiscriminate practice of prescribing these agents generates an anxiety-free, false sense of well-being in people. The administration of psychoactive medication for the symptoms of depression and anxiety by the mechanistically oriented physician is much like putting a bandage on an infected wound. Furthermore, the long-term effects of these drugs on individuals and their offspring through succeeding generations have yet to be determined.[89]

Another symptom of greater levels of anxiety is overeating and the resultant increased incidence of obesity in the general population. The failed, so-called "sexual revolution" of the 1960s led directly to increased levels of anxiety in the younger generation and, over the following decades, contributed to overeating in an effort to quell these feelings. Fat binds energy and is a form of armor.[90] Like drugs, overeating is yet another means of reducing anxiety. Seen in this light it is understandable that attempts to eliminate the symptom of obesity by reducing caloric intake without addressing the underlying *source* of the problem can, at best, produce only temporary, transient results.

---

89. The medical orgonomist has no objection to this form of therapy when such treatment is appropriate. The responsible psychiatrist is required to distinguish those individuals for whom the treatment of choice is medication from those who are capable of tolerating the therapeutic process of armor dissolution.

90. Fat contains nine calories per gram compared to four calories per gram for protein and carbohydrate.

Intolerance of Freedom

> If "freedom" means, first of all, the responsibility of every individual for the rational determination of his own personal, professional, and social existence, then there is no greater fear than that of the establishment of general freedom. (Reich 1946, page 273)

The most important, but certainly the least noticed, manifestation of mass anxiety that has resulted from the transformation of society is people's increased intolerance of freedom. Accompanied by a decline in personal responsibility and the increased sense of entitlement, this intolerance is especially striking with respect to the core functions of work and sexuality. Anxiety restricts the individual's capacity to be free.

The symptoms that result from this intolerance, which is *biophysical* in nature, can be recognized in many contemporary social phenomena. They are seen most frequently in Western society in general and in the United States in particular where, paradoxically, the opportunity for personal freedom is the greatest. Intolerance of freedom appears as an increasing preoccupation and fascination with distracting pastimes, events, trivia, and vicarious interest in famous personalities, all at the expense of attending to the essential, vital needs of one's personal and social life in a responsible fashion. In some instances fear of freedom brings out doom-and-gloom prophets on the social scene, a phenomenon akin to the depressive reaction that functions to decrease anxiety in the case of certain individuals.

Intolerance of freedom also fosters disorderliness, social unrest, and social disturbances. In order to relieve their inner tension, irresponsible political activists demand social change and urgently press for immediate solutions to social problems regardless of the consequences, cost, or even the likelihood that change or remediation is possible. Some current issues seen as justifying action are the campaign for and advocacy of minority "rights," which rationalize discriminatory government programs including quotas and affirmative action (the "politics of victimization"), and the defense of sociopaths and criminals, including terrorists, both nationally and internationally, This political activism is socially destructive and leads to further social fragmentation. Activism increases lawlessness, the disintegration of social institutions, and brings about less freedom for everyone. This licentious social behavior is rationalized as a claim for the justness of group rights and for greater personal "freedom." Paradoxically, moralistically determined political activism, rationalized as "social responsibility," is valued over individual freedom. These attitudes are symptomatic of an underlying *biophysical incapacity for and intolerance of genuine individual freedom and natural self-regulation.* In health, personal freedom and social responsibility are in harmony.

Alternatively, the attempt to overcome anxiety can lead to a pathological reactive expansion accompanied by a false sense of well-being. This may take many forms, including compulsive materialism ("flight into wealth"), financial intemperance, and defensive socialization such as that which occurs with involvement in support groups and other similar group activities. Increased ocular armor that results from marijuana use also produces a false sense of expansion. Some related social attitudes arising from armor of the ocular segment include bad manners, inappropriate and blasé behavior, glibness, "laid-back" indifference, self-complacency, and mystical involvement in New Age groups and activities. Finally, blurring boundaries between private and public life can lead to cultism, allowing the individual to act out past family conflicts in his or her current social relationships.[91]

The Decline in Genuine Expansion

With the reactive overexpansion and intolerance of freedom that occurs in anti-authoritarian society there is a decline in *natural* expansive functions. This appears as decreased *genuine* social contact, such as dating and courtship which provide an extended, unhurried opportunity to get acquainted with a person of the opposite sex. This decline in genuine contact also accounts for what is commonly recognized as the cultural degradation that is currently taking place in Western society. It is manifested in the lowering of the standards of acceptable social behavior, in the nonobservance and disregard of appropriate social manners and social form, in the degradation in artistic creation, and, most importantly, in the deterioration in the value of the core functions of life: love, work, and knowledge.

---

91. Anti-American sentiment world-wide and a return to fundamentalist forms of religion in America and elsewhere are two opposing reactions to chronic overexpansion.

Another indication is the erosion in the bond between Americans and their country, the bond of pride and emotional warmth, both expansive functions. During the Vietnam War era, this bond was more or less permanently destroyed. For the first time in history, America was viewed by the younger generation with suspicion, resentment, and even hatred.

Because learning and creative expression are also expansive functions, the decline of natural expansion contributes to the reduction of educational and artistic standards in every sphere. The decline in standards of excellence and the corresponding rise in mediocrity inevitably lead to egalitarianism. This is one of the most troubling symptoms of our time and an undisguised attack on authoritarian society. Equality for all without regard to ability or the absence of the perseverance necessary to succeed has given rise to political ideologies championing preferred minority groups, affirmative action programs, inflation of student grades to raise "self-esteem," racial quotas, and so on. The politically correct concept that every individual has equal abilities also results in the relentless debunking of heroes and heroism and the appearance of the anti-hero on the social scene. Call-in talk radio shows and instant polls enforce the belief that, for the price of a telephone call, every person has a right to an opinion on *any* subject and that one person's views are as valid as that of anyone else.

The younger generation's increasing fascination with and acceptance of perverse or unattractive behavior originating from the secondary layer, especially in the form of crudeness, violence and pregenital sexuality, is in no small part a symptom of anxiety-induced intolerance of genuine freedom. Words, in the past related to human vice, such as "decadent," "evil," "bad," "wicked," "sinful," and "ugly," are redefined and given a positive twist. Disregarding the fact that criminals disdain law and order and destroy the lives of honest, decent people, the entertainment industry, taking advantage of a money-making opportunity, panders to the public's titillation by and fascination with the destructive secondary layer, producing all manner of crime-related films and TV programs romanticizing and glorifying criminals.

Natural sexual expression is soft and gentle. It is never found in the sexually promiscuous. Farther away than ever from having any contact with their biological core, today's armored humans ignore natural sexuality altogether or respond to it either pornographically or moralistically. We hear in music not tenderness, sweetness or the emotions of longing, sadness, and joy but rather music that is frenzied, agitated, and harsh—*all expressions from the secondary layer.* Rapid-succession bombardment with harsh stimuli, such as violent scenes in cinema, on television, and in the print media, as well as the harsh, mechanically amplified sounds that pass for music, distract and desensitize people to all that is natural. Many people today have to immerse themselves in their secondary layer to feel anything at all. They are for the most part completely out of touch with their core.

Today's ever-increasing widespread acceptance and tolerance of virtually every kind of secondary layer behavior is accompanied by an increased *intolerance* of natural human activity that is avoided in moralistic or politically correct attitudes and behaviors. There are now increasing numbers of people who would deny others their pleasure in eating meat, wearing perfume or fur, drinking coffee, or simply eating extra-large portions of food. In these situations, telling others how they should think and behave is a manifestation of the emotional plague.

Most importantly, anxiety-induced intolerance of freedom appears in the blurring of the distinction between healthy sexuality and other forms of sexual activity. Examples include the general acceptance of homosexuality as "just another life style" and an increased emphasis on pregenital sexuality, asserting that all sexual behaviors are equal and therefore interchangeable.

As anxiety rises, armored individuals become even less able to tolerate freedom which, in turn, leads to greater anxiety. This vicious cycle occurs because, with increased anxiety, expansion is inhibited and people are less able to tolerate the natural build-up of bioenergetic charge than in the past. It is only through energy charge and discharge that pleasure in daily life is experienced and productive work is accomplished. Therefore, anxiety brings about the deterioration of both sexual and work functions. It also results in impatience and the need for instant gratification of biological impulses, which, in turn, gives rise to impulsive tendencies. Because of increased ocular armor and underlying anxiety, intellectualization in the form of rationalization is used to justify the expression of any behavior, no matter how inappropriate or destructive. Since emotions are unable to be contained and expressed in an appropriate manner, "letting out one's feelings" and "doing one's own thing," anywhere and at anytime, become socially sanctioned as they are a means of providing immediate relief from inner tension, a form of substitute gratification.

Longing for Freedom, Fearing to Be Free

In today's anti-authoritarian era, people who are neurotic are increasingly unable to express their core feelings because of their anxiety which has been brought on by the weakening of social armor and the resultant eruption of forces from the secondary layer. At the same time, they continue to long for freedom even as they fear being free. They retain freedom as an ideal and are even willing to fight and die to protect it but, for them, it is not something practically attainable. This is because freedom, for the neurotic, often means freedom *from* the responsibilities that go with it.

In contrast, as noted in chapter 3, in the healthy, unarmored individual, freedom and social responsibility go hand in hand. Genuine freedom is accompanied by greater social responsibility, which, in turn, gives rise to more individual freedom.

The capacity for freedom and responsibility is derived from biological orgone energy moving spontaneously, unimpeded by armor. In the unarmored state, the pulsation function alternates between expansion and contraction. Expansion predominates over contraction and there are feelings of pleasurable well-being. However, in the presence of armor, there is a chronic disturbance in pulsation and one function (either expansion or contraction) predominates over the other forming an opposition between freedom and responsibility. The capacity for exercising one component, either freedom or responsibility, then serves a defensive function against the other and this gives rise to the ideological contradiction between liberalism and conservatism. As already noted, the relationship between freedom and responsibility differs depending on the sociopolitical character of the individual. In liberals, freedom serves as a defense against responsibility.

In conservatives, the reverse is true. In both cases, there is a disturbance in and restriction of the ability to be simultaneously free and responsible.

Many aspects of current social turmoil can be understood in terms of people's underlying disturbance in the capacity for living responsibly in freedom. Such disturbance results from the simultaneous expression of the contradictory emotional tendencies found in all armored humans: *the mystical longing for freedom and, at the same time, a very real terror of freedom.* On the one hand, longing for freedom is most evident in people who have had their freedom taken away from them and have been subjugated under Communist or Fascist rule. On the other hand, fear of freedom, manifested as dependency, helplessness, and craving for the authority of and control by a centralized government, is strongest in those living in Western democratic societies who have *not* lost their social and economic freedom. It is a sad commentary on the state of armored humanity that freedom is most valued only when it is taken away.

The contradiction between longing for and fearing freedom can be best grasped by putting together two seemingly contradictory observations. More often than not, there is no country that is more reviled throughout the world than America and, at the same time, there is no country that people from all over the world long to be living in than America. Freedom to live is why people from so many countries keep pouring into America, legally and illegally: They want to be left alone to take advantage of liberty, of work and educational opportunities, and the chance to begin life anew, to raise their children in freedom.

Sexual anxiety, based on armor, underlies the contradiction between humanity's longing for and fear of freedom. This anxiety, which can be clinically recognized by anyone trained in medical orgone therapy, is symptomatic of the *simultaneous expression* of sexual longing and fear of sexual gratification. Armor reduces the capacity to experience all genuine, pleasurable core feelings, especially profound sexual pleasure. Therefore, the capacity to tolerate freedom must also be limited. Armored people cling to their characteristic ways of life, and most really want to have little or nothing at all to do with natural functioning. Emotions are repressed or they are partially expressed through the armor in a distorted fashion. Because discharge is incomplete, there is much associated anxiety, unfulfilled longing and dissatisfaction in life. Frustration accompanied by destructive rage occasionally erupts when unfulfilled sexual longing is particularly strong.

Today's adolescents are not driven as much to rebel against authoritarian society and fight for their sexual freedom as in times past, as they desperately strive to preserve whatever armor they still have in their own structure. Reacting to the breakdown of social structure, particularly the family, adolescents hold on to social armor in whatever way they can. This includes such measures as gang and cult activity. These are, in reality, attempts at retaining some sort of individual or social cohesion through group association. Such attempts can be accompanied by body piercing and other forms of self-mutilation that serve to reduce inner tension. All of these devices are the result of insufficient muscular armor.

An aggravating factor is the media's deliberate arousal of the public's unsatisfied sexual curiosity through visual and verbal stimulation of images evoking horror and pity, emotions which are elicited through the display of carnage and atrocity committed by brutal humans. It is a calculated, unscrupulous exploitation of a mixture of unsatisfied sexual longing, secondary layer emotions, and appropriate compassion in the emotionally crippled masses who crave relief from their inner tension. Since these feelings, once stimulated, cannot be satisfied, they give rise to anxiety and guilt (emotional blocking) and this, in a vicious cycle, lead to people's further need to obtain relief through more substitute activity. As a result, fantasizing, impulsive acting out, and displacement of personal conflicts onto the sociopolitical arena become an ever-increasing part of daily life.

The search for a "politics of meaning," a symptom of the pseudo-liberal's longing for freedom from the restrictions of armor, is an expression of mystical yearning in those for whom religion no longer fills that need. The pseudo-liberal seeks emotional release in the form of restitution of unconscious guilt feelings through political action, but since politics cannot satisfy these needs, political activity becomes increasingly radicalized. The following account of the social nightmare that erupted in the 1960s serves as an illustration.

The Radicalization of the Left and the Breakthrough of the Emotional Plague as Red Fascism

The American leftist movement among the younger generation of the 1960s was the result of the breakthrough of strong impulses of longing, fueled by a desire for sexual gratification. Because they were *biophysically* unprepared to deal responsibly with their sexuality, the longing of American youth for gratification was displaced onto the sociopolitical arena. In the early stages of the movement there was much talk of brotherhood, equality, of humanity's unfulfilled capacities for freedom and love, all expressions of substitute contact. Without reference to a supernatural being, and largely through politics, they proposed to bring their secular vision of the kingdom of God to fruition on Earth.

The result was tragic. Because of their armored structure and the reaction of the armored masses, whose longing for freedom had been squelched in early childhood, they were unable to attain these goals. The emotional yearning for "heaven on Earth" crashed into the harsh reality of their armor and turned to disillusionment. Its benign and peaceful form was aborted and became instead militant and intemperate. This ultimately resulted in a secondary layer breakthrough of unheard-of proportions in America during the 1960s and early 1970s. The most intolerant of freedom were the pseudo-liberal extremists and revolutionaries. Terror of natural genital sensations fueled their intellectual defenses and radical ideology. They displaced their personal Oedipal conflict (primarily revenge against and murder of the father) onto society, reacting with blind rage against all forms of authority: college professors, the police, the military, and so on. Throughout the world, their destructive impulses either were expressed outwardly with sadistic and violent attacks hurled at American authority or were inwardly directed, causing those of the leftist movements of this era to identify masochistically with the "masses of suffering humanity, the victims of American oppression," and with America's political enemies.

As a true expression of the emotional plague, these impulses were rationalized and used by leftist apologists and agitators as a "peace movement" that was directed against U.S. involvement in

Vietnam. The social consequences of this misfired "sexual revolution" (e.g., social chaos and a corresponding rise in contactless and pregenital sexual activity, asceticism, drug use, and mysticism) can all be understood functionally. They are the inevitable result of the contradiction between the younger generation's sexual longing and the inability to fulfill those impulses because of armor: *When core impulses are blocked from natural expression in pleasurable sexual gratification and in work, the results are rage in the form of socially destructive activity and intolerance of freedom.*

Political extremism leading to terrorism can arise from the left and the right. In both, the radicalization of terrorist ideology corresponds to the intensification of pent-up sexual feelings with a corresponding rise in the individual's ocular armor (blind rage). The distortions in inner and outer reality directly lead to ideologically sanctioned, socially destructive behavior. Sociologically, the symptom that ultimately manifests as terrorism from the left appears at a certain point with the breakdown of the authoritarian social order. It is the final result of a prolonged process of de-legitimizing authoritarian society by the political left and is accompanied by a reaction to it from the political right. The social process begins with a group of "true (ideological) believers" who challenge authority long before they become terrorists. They are usually an elite group headed by well-educated middle or upper-class young people, usually college students or drop-outs who are rife with personal guilt, subversive tendencies, rebellion, and a blanket hatred of all authority.

Ehud Spinzak (1998, page 78) has outlined the stages of the process of radicalization of the political left, but his analysis can also be applied to the political right. Each stage, identifying increasing levels of social activation, contains a combination of ideological and behavioral components. As radicalization intensifies, a collective group identity takes over much of the individual identity of the members. At the final terrorist stage, the group identity reaches its peak, and the behavior of the individual terrorist is identical with the ideology of the group.

First Stage: The Crisis of Confidence

This stage involves a loss of confidence (trust) in the existing authoritarian social order. The foundations of the order are not yet challenged. There is only an angry critique of the authorities, who are perceived as being misguided or misled. Although a complete ideological break with the authoritarian social order has yet to occur, there is, nevertheless, a profound conflict with what is perceived as "the Establishment," one that goes far beyond ordinary political opposition. From a behavioral standpoint, there is already an unwillingness to play according to the establishment's social rules. Criticism against the establishment is expressed in ideological terms ("make love not war"), and is accompanied by protests demanding "recognition," demonstrations, and other sociopolitical activity. Early confrontations with society, including the police, consist of small-scale and unplanned, impulsive acts of violence. The relationship between the leftist ideologues and authoritarian society is changed from one of attractive opposition to antagonistic opposition.

Second Stage: Conflict of Legitimacy

This stage is a radicalized continuation of the first. Political activity intensifies as the energy that is contained in the hatred behind the ideology has no outlet for discharge. Criticism of authority changes to questioning the legitimacy of the whole system. Now, the errant rulers are believed to be deliberately leading the people on because the system itself is manipulative, corrosive, and corrupt.[92] This, in turn, leads to the way to get rid of the oppressive rulers: "*transform the system*" altogether; that is, destroy the father. The frustrated energy fueling the ideology now intensifies and seeks more immediate and more extreme forms of discharge in sociopolitical activity. What follows is an ideology of de-legitimating, which calls for a break with the prevailing authoritarian order. At this stage, sociopolitical activity is no longer confined to ideological slogans but now includes a call for greater political action. These range from planned angry protests

---

92. The similarity between this formation of a belief system to the development of a paranoid delusion is based on the fact that both occur because of an intensification of ocular armor. The difference between them is that this belief system is shared by a group, whereas the paranoid delusion is confined to an individual.

(demonstrations and vandalism) to the deliberate use of small-scale violence, all directed against the authoritarian regime. At this point, the movement is now consolidated, and individuals live in a state of intense radicalization: They are consumed by the grandeur of their radical vision. Their language and rhetoric is "revolutionary," and their jargon is full of self-righteous slander and desecrations.

Third Stage: Crisis of Legitimacy

This stage is the logical culmination of the previous two stages. Every person in the movement identifies with the radicalized ideology. Those outside the movement are identified with the stupid, rotten-to-the-core, and soon-to-be destroyed social and political order. They are derogated from the human race and considered to be a form of subhuman species. This mechanism of dehumanization is identical to the psychic defense mechanism known as isolation, in which the emotional charge (affect) behind an idea is withdrawn. Overriding the restraining effects of their armor, the mechanism of dehumanization allows radicals to commit atrocities without a second thought. For them, the world is divided into the sons of light and the sons of darkness.[93] Most importantly, it legitimizes the conflict as true warfare and transforms those radicals who have made it to this stage into accomplished terrorists. Every person who is perceived as belonging to the establishment becomes a potential target for assassination. At this stage, their view of those who belong to the establishment has changed. Words are no longer limited to social or political concepts. They are extended to a language of objects, animals, or "human animals." An indication of the contempt they have for their own sexual feelings, the establishment and their accomplices are now portrayed as "things," "dogs," "pigs," "Nazis," "terrorists," etc. By killing off the "pigs" and "dogs," the terrorists, in effect, are killing off their own frighteningly intolerable sexual feelings. In October 1969, a radical organization, the Weather Men, proclaimed in a leaflet:

---

93. Thomas Sowell's designation of pseudo-liberals as "the anointed" describes these leftists at a later stage of radicalization.

> We move with the people of the world to seize power from those who now rule. We . . . expect their pig lackeys to come down on us. We've got to be ready for that. This is a war we can't resist. We've got to actively fight. We're going to bring the war home to the mother country of imperialism. AMERIKA: THE FINAL FRONT.
>
> (Quoted in Spinzak 1998, page 65.)

At this final stage, the breakthrough of the secondary layer is complete. No longer confined to those outside the chosen group of radicals, the group itself is radicalized. Freed from the yoke of conventional morality, the group engages in all forms of sexual perversity, drug use, and criminal behavior. The boundary between political and personal lawlessness has been totally removed. The political manifestation of this stage is strategic terrorism, and it is marked by the formation of a small, highly integrated underground that attacks the regime and commits a wide range of atrocities. The group constructs a reality of its own and new behavioral and moral standards substitute for the ones that have been renounced. The identity of individual members has been completely submerged with the identity of the group as a whole, so that every individual act has a collective meaning of utmost importance. The behavioral dynamics of the whole unit has now assumed an internally consistent logic.

Today, some of the radicals of the 1960s have renounced their strident militancy but not their radical vision, which is presented in a more cleverly polished form, in a modernized, more acceptable pseudo-liberal ideology. *These well-heeled radicals have successfully infiltrated every area of higher social influence.* The principal organizer and former president of the Students for a Democratic Society (SDS) and 1968 Chicago riot inciter, Tom Hayden, became a Democratic state senator in California; Black Panther Bobby Rush, a Democratic congressman; Todd Gitlin, another former president of SDS, a university professor and frequent op-ed columnist for the *New York Times*.[94]

Although many terrorist organizations undergo all stages of radicalization, they need not do so. The developmental process can be arrested at any time, depending on factors external and

---

94. See David Horowitz. 1997. *Radical Son*. New York: Free Press, page 167.

internal to the group. Furthermore, radical groups with widely different ideological premises (such as communists, fascists, and religious fanatics) may join forces when energy contained within the secondary layer intensifies necessitating discharge. Finally, a terrorist underground cannot sustain itself without nonterrorist support from friends and accomplices who provide information, hideouts, escape routes, money, and supplies. Terrorists only survive with the aid and support of a large number of less committed rear-guardists. Thus, the emotional plague from the left and the right extends itself in a web-like fashion to include the masses of armored humanity who sustain it.

In America today, the emotional plague is becoming increasingly organized and centered on the anti-authoritarian, anti-American ideology of the pseudo-liberal. This drive, which began with the consolidation of the leftist movement of the 1950s and early 1960s, has become highly vocal and structuralized socially. This has come about through the pseudo-liberal's involvement in politics, the media, the cinema, public education, and the legal profession. For example, although radical law professors account for only a minority of faculty in law schools nationwide, they have drawn a disproportionate amount of attention to themselves because they are loud and militant. They wage open warfare over appointments, tenure, selection of deans, the scope of affirmative action, and the imposition of speech codes. They brand those who oppose them as sexist, racist, or fascist. Some professors teach their law students that truth does not exist or, in any event, does not matter. What matters is not an individual's reasoning or academic qualifications but whose side you are on. In universities, Marxists and other socialists, refuted by historical events, are now a dominant force in the tenured establishment of academia, and their assault on American society is expressed in the guise of multiculturalism. These divisive sociopolitical tactics go far to undermine what remains of the cohesive social forces that make America a unified nation and serve to fragment it into multifarious, politicized, quarreling factions. The mission of universities has changed dramatically and is now cast in radical terms of "social transformation." Courses are frequently baldly ideological, and left-wing professors give one-sided presentations of subjects, knowing that students will "learn" and regurgitate their views in papers and on examinations. Students are graded according to their degree of political correctness and are often intimidated, overtly or covertly, from expressing their own perspectives. In the war against terrorism, pseudo-liberal university professors spoke about America's "silent genocide" while students duped by leftist agitators placed placards saying "Stop Your Racist War" in many American college towns.

Despite this clamoring for more freedom of expression, however, most Americans are unable to make full use of the freedom they actually have. An indication of people's intolerance of freedom is that they do not know how to take advantage of opportunities available in a country where personal freedom is almost universally taken for granted. There is no better indication that the masses have become increasingly indifferent to their political freedom than their lost or absent sense of gratitude and appreciation for living in a free country. For example, many Americans favored sending a six-year-old Cuban boy back to live in a Communist country rather than allowing him to grow up with relatives in the United States. It is clear that far too many Americans have lost a sense of their freedom and how important it is to them, an awareness that results from contact with the biological core. These people, including most of their political leaders, do not recognize this critical difference between communist life and life in America. This lack of cognizance is a symptom of the emotionally deadening effect of ocular armor.

Fear, and therefore hatred, of freedom takes many forms. One occurred during the second Iraqi war. As expected, this fear was most intense among specific groups at the extremes of the sociopolitical spectrum. On the left, collectivist activists banded together in world-wide anti-American political demonstrations. They were opposed to American-led forces fighting for the freedom of the Iraqis. However, they were totally unaware that their demonstrations were an attempt to avoid feeling their own fear of freedom and independence. In addition, these rallies provided them with an illusory feeling that they belonged to a worthy cause. On the right, reactionary Iraqis and fundamentalist Muslims unable to tolerate their newfound freedom, and aided by criminal elements in their country, turned their fear of freedom provided by a democratic form of government into violent hatred of America.

The contradiction between longing for and fear of freedom, a phenomenon first described in Reich's *The Mass Psychology of Fascism*, is deeply rooted in the structure of all armored humans. *The longing for freedom from the restrictions of armor and its turning into fear of freedom is seen in every patient undergoing medical orgone therapy when energy has been liberated from the armor to a sufficient degree.* This basic contradiction is also why attempts at social improvement by providing more freedom than the armored masses can tolerate always run into great difficulty.

In removing armor, the medical orgonomist must consider the patient's capacity to tolerate anxiety, as well as other emotions and sensations. As armor is gradually removed, its inhibitory effect is decreased, and the patient routinely experiences anxiety. Flight from therapy and hatred of the therapist may result. The therapist must also consider whether anxiety experienced with the breakdown of armor results from energy mobilized from the destructive secondary layer or from the biological core. The release of the patient's destructive impulses in therapeutic sessions is encouraged and the expression of healthy core impulses in daily life is encouraged as well, provided these do not interfere with the lives of others. The patient's capacity for independent *and* responsible functioning is the most reliable indicator of therapeutic success.

Only at the end stage of therapy, when armor from the upper segments has been largely eliminated, does the patient become able to feel and express genuine feelings of love. These new feelings are unfamiliar and are regularly accompanied by fear of experiencing pleasure and fear of expressing these natural impulses. *Limitations in the patient's capacity to tolerate the deep, pleasurable emotions that come about with the elimination of armor in personal life are identical to the limitations in the capacity of armored people to tolerate freedom when it is made available to them.* These clinical and social phenomena are of the utmost relevance in understanding and dealing with virtually all social problems.

The following case presentation is illustrative.

> A forty-five-year-old patient had been involved in the leftist movement and antiwar demonstrations of the Vietnam War era. At that time, he dropped out of college, having lost interest in his course work. He began smoking marijuana, became a hippie, and associated only with other like-minded ex-students. He decided to form a commune

and the group moved to a remote part of the country and bought a parcel of land. This was done with the idea of having a self-sufficient community wherein each member performed his or her assigned task. He remained in the commune long after it become clear that people were not doing their share of work. When he finally realized that it was up to him to take care of himself, and that he could not rely on others for his survival, he left the commune. Fortunately, while there, he acquired skills enabling him to financially support himself and met a woman who later became his wife.

He entered therapy because of sexual difficulties. In the course of therapy it became clear that these problems came about because of the neurotic manner in which he formed relationships. Therapy proceeded well with systematic removal of armor. However, when he reached the end phase of therapy, he came in touch with deeply repressed longing for his mother, and this was accompanied by deep feelings of sadness and disappointment. These feelings were based on never having been truly loved by his parents, especially his mother. His parents were cold, reserved people who were emotionally incapable of providing him with nurturing and comfort. In his adolescence, he had changed from a well-behaved youngster to a very rebellious young man. With the release of much painful misery over many sessions, he came to realize that all of his social relationships were based on attempts to form emotional ties with others in order to compensate for those he lacked when growing up. He understood that his venture into communal living was nothing more than a way of forming substitute relationships for the ones he never had in childhood. He also realized that the emotion-deadening effect of the marijuana used during adolescence reproduced the same emotional stillness that pervaded his childhood home. He recalled that the only family member who truly loved him was a paternal uncle whose visits he always looked forward to with great anticipation. He felt that if his uncle had been more a part of his life while growing up, he would not have become a rebellious adolescent. He, also, would not have involved himself in leftist causes, and would not have wasted ten years of his life in a marginal existence.

The weakening of muscular armor with its accompanying intensification of ocular armor produces anxiety often manifested as a sense of urgency to be free of the restraints of one's own armor. In leftists, this anxiety appears as a pressing need to bring about social change for any plausible reason and often simply for its own sake. Conservatives, on the other hand, out of their own sense of helplessness, ascribe their unconscious longing (and their biophysical intolerance of social change) onto liberals. They blame them for the continued deterioration of society.

Premature removal of armor, whether intentional or inadvertent, can be disastrous for individuals. If the increased anxiety resulting from the armor removal is displaced onto the social arena, they will shift further to the left or to the right on the sociopolitical spectrum, depending on their preexisting sociopolitical character structure. When the shift is to the left, a typical manifestation of social anxiety is a sense of impending doom and this, in turn, brings about an urgent need to form collectives for social change ("improvement") through political activity, without regard for practicality or consequences ("Better red than dead"). Impending doom can manifest as an irrational fear of terrorist attack resulting in an urge to move to a remote part of the world. These behaviors come about from an intensification of anxiety and guilt, and they covertly fuel the liberal individual's personal neurotic complexes and ideologies. Those on the right shift further in that direction by becoming more mystical or by rigidly maintaining and defending the status quo in every area of social life.[95]

Table 6.1 on the next page summarizes some basic differences between the authoritarian and anti-authoritarian social orders in America. These distinctions intensify as society becomes polarized and individuals shift to the extremes of the sociopolitical spectrum.

Since sexuality and work are two of the core functions of life, different forms of social armor produce different disturbances in these functions. The following chapter will show how sexual and work disturbances in today's anti-authoritarian society differ from those of the past.

---

95. For a more complete discussion, see Baker, E. 1967. *Man in the Trap.*

Authoritarian Society	Anti-Authoritarian Society
Authority considered to reside in local governments	Authority considered to reside in central government
Responsibility valued over freedom	Freedom valued over responsibility
Permanence and tradition valued over change	Change and innovation valued over permanence
Social order, stability	Social disorder, instability
Less social anxiety	More social anxiety
Society's interests considered more important	Individual's interests considered more important
Muscular armor predominates	Ocular armor predominates
Conservatism prevails over liberalism	Liberalism prevails over conservatism

Differences Between the Authoritarian and Anti-Authoritarian Social Order in America

TABLE 6.1

Legal Citations

1. U.S. Constitution, amend. 1.
2. *Abrams v. United States*, 250 US 616 (1919).
3. Quoted in Bork, R.H. 2003. *Coercing Virtue*. Washington D.C.: AEI Press, page 58.
4. *Brandenburg v. Ohio*, 395 U.S. 444 (1969).
5. *Miller v. California*, 413 U.S. 15 (1973).
6. *Cohen v. California*, 403 U.S. 15 (1971).
7. *Lewis v. New Orleans*, 408 U.S. 1913 (1972).
8. *Brown v. Oklahoma*, 408 U.S. 914 (1972).
9. *United States v. Playboy Group, Inc.*, 529 U.S. 802 (2000).
10. Ibid., 826
11. Ibid., 834 (Scala, J., dissenting).
12. Jefferson to Nehemiah Dodge et al., in Albert E. Burgh, ed. 1907. *The Writings of Thomas Jefferson*. (Washington, D.C.: Thomas Jefferson Memorial Association, 16:281-282.
13. *Lee v. Weisman*, 505 U.S. 577 (1992).
14. *Santa Fe Independent School Dist. v. Doe*, 530 U.S. 290 (2000).
15. Ibid., 309.

CHAPTER 7

DISTURBANCES IN SEXUAL AND WORK FUNCTIONS IN ARMORED SOCIETY

Working people who have proved themselves over the years in their profession should determine whether or not the future worker should be a socially potent factor.

—Wilhelm Reich, *The Mass Psychology of Fascism*

In today's anti-authoritarian society, the deleterious effects of individual and social armor are evident in the distortions of the core functions of sexuality and work. In armored individuals, sexual and work functions stem largely from the destructive secondary layer, not from the core. They appear differently in sexually related social problems and in the work disturbances seen in the sociopolitical character types on both the left and the right. Consequently, social attitudes about sexual and work-related matters must remain divided between the two sociopolitical camps.

Confusion with regard to sexual matters is rampant, including programs of the state and federal governments. Sex education, for example, has drawn intense interest from legislators in recent years, with some states passing laws supporting abstinence education and others requiring comprehensive courses in sex education. These measures are designed to deal with the most superficial manifestations of adolescents' sexual problems and therefore serve as evasions. *They serve to obfuscate basic knowledge of the central role of the orgasm function in regulating the energy economy of the individual.* Sexuality is on every adolescent's mind, but it is the "hot potato" that no one in this era of supposed sexual freedom is willing or capable of touching. Specifically, no one wants to own up to the fact that sexual disturbances are at the root of every emotional problem. Related to this evasion is the attitude of liberal-minded mental health professionals that emotionally based psychiatric problems can be treated by those who do not have an expert understanding of and extensive training in the emotional factors that govern life. This attitude, at the very least, betrays a profound ignorance of the importance of basic biological functions. At worst, it is an arrogant expression of contempt for the human condition.

In the past authoritarian era, people were reticent and discrete about discussing sexual matters. Sexual repression was the norm. No one much cared about whether or not an individual was heterosexual or homosexual. It simply did not come up in conversation. Sexuality was not politicized. In fact, it was considered inappropriate and in bad taste to raise the issue of a person's sexual life in public. In other words, there was a clear-cut distinction between public and private life. In today's anti-authoritarian society, things are quite the opposite. According to the morality of political correctness, an individual's sexual orientation should be everyone's business. A manifestation of substitute contact, people discuss the sexual lives of others freely without any comprehension of what they are talking about. They have no idea that the future well-being of humanity depends on the ability to understand and deal with this crucial human function earnestly and rationally.

People on both sides of the sociopolitical spectrum have a distorted and one-sided attitude toward sexuality. Conservatives emphasize the importance of love over sex and rail at the sexual depravity of our times. Liberals view of sex is inclined in the opposite direction. *Not one word is ever spoken about the distinction between natural sexuality and its neurotic counterpart.* Neither group sees that in a healthy relationship between man and woman feelings of love and sexual feelings occurs simultaneously. Conservatives attempt to stem the rising tide of the destructive shift in sexual attitudes by holding on to obsolete moralistic values. Their repressive approach to humanity's sexual misery and condemnation of present-day mores clearly offer no solution. Liberals, while seeming to affirm sexuality—they talk endlessly about sex on radio and television—do not distinguish between natural sexuality originating from the biological core and armored (neurotic) sexuality. As with their attempts to solve other social problems, liberals are incapable of providing adequate solutions to the sexual misery of the masses. In the long run, by considering all forms of sexual behavior equal and "normal" and ignoring the crucial importance of the orgasm function, they only aggravate the problem by generating anxiety and confusion. Articles on "bigger and better orgasms" appearing regularly in *Cosmopolitan* may sell more magazines but will do nothing but obfuscate the problem of the sexual misery of adolescent girls and women. In America today, indiscriminate liberal permissiveness combined with tolerance of every form of neurotic sexual behavior is far more deadly to people's emotional life than conservative repression. By contributing to the already high levels of social anxiety, it has accelerated the disintegrative process. It is an example of the breakthrough of the destructive secondary layer that the old authoritarian order was able to keep in check.

The Effect of Anti-Authoritarianism on the Catholic Church

Until recently, organized religion had been one of the most powerful sociopolitical forces on the right. It was responsible in large part for maintaining the authoritarian social order. The transformation of society has weakened this stabilizing institution. Consider the Catholic Church as an example. By the mid-1960s, young Catholic priests emerged from their near-cloistered seminaries and saw a world changing around them, both inside and out of the Church. The Second Vatican Council, which ended in 1965, suddenly lowered the barriers between the Church and society and between clergy and laypeople. The liturgy went from Latin to English, the altar was turned around, and priests faced the people at mass for the first time in centuries. Laypeople took on leadership roles and priests and nuns joined the antiwar and civil rights movements, rubbing elbows with Protestants and Jews, college students and feminists.

Priests, who once had strict curfews in the rectories where they lived with fellow priests, were suddenly free to come and go as they pleased. Despite being given freedom, they were developmentally somewhere in their adolescence, far below their chronological age. This was a classic case of individuals being given far more freedom than they could responsibly handle. Although they were always supervising alter boys, priests were now taking students on overnight ski trips, supervising teen clubs, and so on. For those with eyes to see, the crisis that later surfaced came as no surprise.[96]

The scandal over the sexual abuse of children by American Catholic priests goes to the heart of the sexual problem of armored society: *the omnipresent lack of understanding of the orgasm function and the failure to make* a *distinction between the primary sexual drives and the perverse secondary drives that must result from the presence of armor.* The Church enforces a policy of celibacy for priests, partly because it attributes all sexual expression outside of marriage to destructive secondary layer sexual impulses (evil) and partly to redirect the sexual drive of the clergy into mystical religious feelings that support the ideological foundation of the Church. To ensure its survival, the Church *must* therefore maintain repression of both primary core and secondary layer sexual impulses. The priest is placed in a most unnatural situation of having to suppress his sexual impulses, natural or neurotic, in order to perform his duties and function according to the moral tenets of the Church. However, the degree to which the sexual drive can be suppressed varies greatly among individuals. Rather than suppress their sexuality, many healthier priests left the Church. Beginning in 1967 and for the next 10 years, priests abandoned their vocation in droves. About 525 priests left in 1968, 675 in 1970, and 575 in 1973.[97] One cannot say if there has been an absolute increase in alcoholism, overt homosexuality, and pedophilia among priests. However, whenever sexual suppression is unsuccessful, people must resort to substitute measures to provide relief from sexual tension. This is

---

96. See "Trial of Pain in Church Crisis Leads to Nearly Every Diocese" by Laurie Goodstein, *The New York Times*, Jan. 12, 2003.

97. Ibid.

why priests who have remained in the Church will always have a strong tendency toward alcoholism and other forms of alternate sexual gratification.[98]

The Sexual Function in Adolescence

The symptoms of unhealthy social relations appear with special clarity in the greatly distorted and disturbed sexual relations of adolescents. Adolescence begins with the second puberty, around age eleven or twelve, and ends with the consolidation of armor at the end of the second decade of life. Adolescence is a stage of maturation, the direct result of emerging sex hormones and a time of profound psychological and physiological change. This should be the time when individuals naturally achieve emotional independence from their parents and find their way to a satisfying sexual life. In our society, however, internalized conflicts combined with the limited capacity of armored individuals to tolerate natural sexuality greatly impair the adolescent's ability to naturally regulate his or her feelings. This is why the issue of adolescent sexuality brings up more emotional charge and more irrational ideas than practically any other sexual topic.

Next to preventing armor in the newborn and young child, the failure to understand the natural sexual function of adolescents stands as the most important problem in the world today. It is a matter of general ignorance that the adolescent's ability to establish a healthy sexual life is central and brings with it maturity and the capacity for satisfaction and self-regulation in adulthood.

In the authoritarian social order of the past as well as in today's anti-authoritarian climate, the natural genital embrace is considered to be off-limits for the adolescent. Yet, the urgency for genital union is greater in adolescence than during any other period in life. If we spent the time and effort addressing and preventing the sexual problems of adolescents, we could prevent many of the neurotic troubles that appear in adult life. Reich estimated that half the adolescent population he studied would have been able to establish satisfying sexual lives if they were provided

98. These manifestations of the emotional plague are not limited to Catholic priests in America, nor are they limited exclusively to sexual abuse. It is a world-wide phenomenon.

with sufficient knowledge and counseling. Because social conditions are worse now than in the past, there are far fewer healthy adolescents today.

In Authoritarian Society

Baker (1967) examined the state of adolescent sexuality in Western authoritarian society. Today, what is of utmost importance is the problem of adolescent sexuality as it exists in authoritarian Islamic fundamentalist countries. *Stifled adolescent sexuality is at the heart of the problem of terrorism. The severe, virtually total sexual repression of Arab adolescents by their authoritarian families, combined with the full support of the mystical teachings of Islamic fundamentalism, provide the fertile ground for jihad.* A power-hungry, hate-mongering, sexually starved Islamic leader needs only to redirect the frustration and rage of these sexually starved adolescents into acts of terrorism.

However, to place the responsibility for terrorism entirely on Islamic leaders is one-sided and erroneous. There is a constant supply of sexually frustrated potential suicide bombers in these countries prepared and willing to blow themselves up for Allah. Clearly, no neurotic adolescent would sacrifice his or her life in this way unless primed through a program of strict, antisexual, mystical indoctrination. It is no coincidence that these highly charged, sexually starved young people literally blow themselves up to achieve relief from unbearable sexual tension. They do this with the promise of virgins for males and handsome and faithful men for females who await them in paradise.

In Anti-Authoritarian Society

Today's adolescents, more than at any other time in the recent history of Western civilization, find it difficult to mature into adulthood without severe obstacles. Despite the pervasive liberal attitude with regard to almost all kinds of superficial social behavior, the importance of and need for *genital* adolescent sexuality is not understood. It is almost never directly dealt with. This evasion leads to the same underlying message as before: sex is wrong and off-limits. This increases adolescents' guilt feelings, intensifies their sexually based misery, and forces them to seek release through substitute forms of gratification, such as drugs and alcohol, pregenital sexual activity, body piercing, or contactless, emotionally sterile sexual intercourse. The expectation and demand for sexual abstinence is directly responsible for the ever-increasing incidence of juvenile delinquency, suicide, criminal (including homicidal) behavior, and social rebellion displaced onto the sociopolitical arena. These are the solutions available to adolescents living in Western societies.

In the former authoritarian society, adolescents were in better touch with their emotions and with their sexual misery and frustration than they are today. In today's anti-authoritarian society, adolescents are constantly bombarded by sexual stimulation but satisfaction is beyond their reach. They are less able to tolerate their feelings than in the past and try to overcome their sexual misery by any means at their disposal such as drug use, impulsive behavior, or flight into homosexuality.

When these behaviors are curbed in the course of medical orgone therapy, the underlying, avoided misery surfaces and can be expressed with resultant clinical improvement. The following case is illustrative.

> A mother brought her seventeen-year-old daughter to therapy because of a conflict the adolescent was having with her parents. She had learned of a homosexual relationship the girl had formed while attending an all-girls boarding school. Her mother found out about the relationship when her daughter quite innocently mentioned it in passing while speaking about an entirely different matter. To the girl's complete surprise, the mother became very upset, demanded the details of the relationship, and pulled her out of the school. The daughter was bewildered by these actions, believing she had done nothing wrong. She reacted to her mother's behavior by becoming oppositional to her parents and developing an even stronger attachment to her girlfriend. It was at this point that the relationship between parents and daughter became so strained that her parents decided the girl needed therapy.
>
> She entered the first session by herself and briefly discussed the situation at home and with her girlfriend. After a period of time, when I had established emotional

contact, I turned my focus to her biophysical appearance. The most prominent feature was her expressionless face. I therefore asked her to move her face. She immediately began to cry softly. She felt relieved, but it was clear we had touched only the most superficial layer of her misery. She left this first session feeling gratitude toward me.

In the second session, she briefly discussed her sexual history. She had been interested in girls since around age eleven. The present relationship was the first involving sexual contact. This was initiated by the patient and consisted of hugging and rubbing together while clothed. She was also interested in boys but did not feel ready to have any kind of relationship with them. In this and following sessions, I continued to have her mobilize her facial armor. She gave in to more crying followed again by feelings of relief. When I spoke with her father after the fourth session, he told me he felt that he was getting his daughter back.

At home, tension over the patient's homosexual interests remained high. She still felt a strong emotional attachment to her girlfriend, while the mother, feeling that she could not trust her daughter to not see her friend, maintained a strict curfew.

In the eighth session, following a discussion of her homosexual relationship, she suddenly burst out crying, and this crying continued for the remainder of the session, after which she exclaimed: "I'm tired of fighting with my mother! I've had enough!" She felt and appeared like a little girl.

In the following session, she told me she felt hurt that her mother did not trust her. She had told her mother that she decided to separate from her girlfriend but felt that her mother was unconvinced. This was followed by deeper crying. Expressing the misery allowed her to feel lighter, more clearheaded, and assertive. She told me she missed the good times she once had with her family and saw herself growing out of her attachment to her girlfriend, but not yet ready to get on with her life. She still needed to resolve her feelings about her mother's moralistic attitude and her own confusion about the issue of homosexuality. Her difficult relationship with her parents remained unresolved.

She stated that her mother was the dominant parent

and that her father played a subordinate role. She wished he would stand up to her mother and be supportive of her, his daughter. The mother, on the other hand, complained that her husband was of no support in this conflict with their daughter. The patient attempted to bring her parents together by reasoning with them. The mother, fearing that her authority was being undermined, responded with an attack accusing her daughter of trying to put the responsibility of the daughter's turning to homosexuality back on her. It was the *moral tone* of her mother's accusation that enraged the patient, and in the sessions that followed, she was able to express rage at her mother's obstinate mistrust. This was followed by the discharge of more misery and she was able to tell me how unhappy she felt.

It became clear that the patient saw her mother's lack of trust as a statement of her moralistic attitude. The patient's ability to feel and express anger toward her mother, in therapy sessions, gradually improved her self-image and also helped her emotional and personal development.

With the ongoing battle between mother and daughter, the mother's moralistic attitude became even clearer. The patient now recalled repeated lectures about "women's safety," which was a thinly disguised way of warning her she had to be careful, since men are "all alike and only after one thing." At this point, the mother accused her of trying to recruit some of her "straight" girlfriends into becoming lesbians, and that she was a "bad seed." This attack under the guise of being "helpful" only further undermined her daughter's self-image, and she began to question her attractiveness and feminine identity. Perhaps she really was homosexual, and this was the real reason why guys were not interested in her. The expression of these thoughts and feelings in sessions was accompanied by deep sobbing.

It was at this point that I arranged a meeting with the parents and directly told the mother to back off in her efforts to control her daughter's life, to take a chance, and see what happened. The mother was able to listen to this advice, which forced her to face and stand her own anxieties. She was able to give her daughter permission to see some of her old girlfriends and this went far to lessen the

> tension between the two, and their relationship began to improve.
>
> Meanwhile, I continued to relieve the patient's armor by direct work on the muscles of her neck and jaw. This led to deep, sustained sobbing. As her relationship with her mother improved, she became interested in dating boys. Her academic success in the new school environment gave her the courage to pursue her art work. Her superior scholastic and artistic abilities led to a full scholarship to a prominent art school. In the last few sessions, she talked excitedly about her art and her relationship with her boyfriend. Therapy lasted for 58 sessions.

In the past authoritarian social order, sexual relations between men and women were not acceptable until marriage, when the individuals somehow became "ready." Today, society accepts and even sanctions sexual relations between members of the opposite sex, even when they first meet, regardless of whether they are emotionally ready. This practice actually prevents couples from forming lasting intimate relationships. Unfortunately, the effect of this permissive attitude toward casual sexual relations on the individuals and on the fabric of society is not recognized.

It is because of the breakdown of social structure that the time-honored traditions of dating and courtship have almost disappeared. As a result, adolescents do not have the opportunity to learn how to handle their intense feelings when they are with someone to whom they are sexually attracted. Therefore, they have to armor against their feelings by being "cool" and must interact mechanically. Referred to as "hooking up," their resultant contactless sexual relations are without true love and actually a way of bypassing anxiety and other intense emotions. Unfortunately, this short-circuiting prevents them from gradually learning to emotionally tolerate being with, and knowing, their mate. It virtually guarantees that a lasting relationship will not develop.

Dr. W.B. Apple, a prominent psychologist on the staff of one of the finest prep schools in the country, says, with regard to the sharp rise in impulsive behavior among adolescents:

With the increase in social anxiety and contactlessness, there has been a rise in impulsive behavior among adolescents that would have seemed bizarre and abhorrent *even to other adolescents*, not to mention their parents, only twenty-five years ago. Today, these behaviors are often not only passively tolerated, but actually socially sanctioned by many in the adolescent culture. Most adults, because adolescents do not talk to them about important issues, do not realize just how commonplace many of these behaviors have become. But if a parent does have an adolescent who tells them of daily goings-on, they will hear stories that are hard to believe. Those therapists who work regularly with adolescents, listen to their misery, and see how contactlessness they are, hear it every day. Here are a few examples.

There is an alarming increase among relative strangers of superficial, exploitative "sexual" encounters—"hooking up"—which range from kissing, to oral sex, to sexual intercourse. No strings are attached—the "partners" may well never speak to each other again. It is all superficial "release," with no sense of obligation or responsibility, and no relationship. Part of this phenomenon has to do with the fact that adolescent sexual behavior has *never* been socially sanctioned. The clearest example of this is that adolescents have nowhere to go to have privacy. What time they do have alone together often must be furtive and secretive, hardly conducive to relaxed, healthy sexual enjoyment. Even with today's increased "freedom," they are largely incapable of taking advantage of such possibilities in a healthy manner. This is due to their neurotic character structure which too often involves a psychopathic component that is quite different from simple rebellion.

At parties or gatherings, the "games" have evolved from the innocent "spin the bottle" of years past (the spinner kisses the person the bottle points to) to "seven minutes in heaven," where the spinner and the "spinnee" go into a closet and do whatever they want for seven minutes. Anything goes.

A female student at a local private school turned down an invitation to the senior prom because it was common knowledge that her prospective date, with whom she had never gone out before, expected sexual involvement as part of the "package." To him, that did not seem unfair at all, since he had paid for the $72 tickets. Later, I saw a photograph taken at that same prom: students sitting around a formally set dinner table, with linen napkins, crystal, and silverware, with their prom dresses and tuxedo pants piled to the left and right of the photographer, who had aimed the camera down at his exposed erect penis, obvious for all to see.

Another reliable female student, a ninth-grader, told a story of coming back to school on a team bus following an athletic event. She was surprised to hear many of the girls on the bus discussing oral sex in casual, but animated, superficial terms. Instead of gossiping about whether or not Susie would be kissing Jimmy on their date, they were contactlessly discussing the pros and cons of giving him "a blow job" when they "hooked up," sharing pointers on how to do it and saying how really great it is. On another occasion, a male student, when asked about his comment about preferring oral sex, stated with a smile that "if it's good enough for the President [Clinton], then it's good enough for me."

My own daughter recently decided not to go to a post-graduation high school party because it was common knowledge that there was going to be skinny dipping at the party. There had evidently been nude swimming at the last party at this particular home. Curious, I wondered if we were talking about a couple or two, and asked how many people were involved. "Lots . . . just about everyone." When I asked where the hosting parents were, she said that they were home but did not check up on how things were going.

Not only are a majority of adolescents now using marijuana, there is an increase in the number of "acceptable" (popular, respected) adolescents who *sell* drugs, rationalizing it as "just a form of capitalism" or "just earning a little pocket money." Those who, in the past, used to be called "pushers" later became "drug dealers," and are now known simply as "entrepreneurs." When most of your peers are using marijuana, how much "pushing" is required?

What adolescents have grown used to, indeed what they read, listen to, and whom they idolize, has changed dramatically as well. For example, in an article entitled "Eminem: The Rapper Is Sadistic, Misogynistic, and Fan-

> tastic,"[99] we learn Eminem's mother was a 15-year-old on drugs and receiving welfare when he was born, and that he never knew his father. This fact qualifies him as "wonderful" and "no fraud." A proponent of the "gangsta rap" tradition, his songs openly honor all that was previously socially unacceptable: "the principles of violence, rape, misogyny, and more violence." On his new album, he literally describes raping his mother, arranging the gang rape of his sister, murdering his wife, and lurking in your backseat to kill you. In one song, he describes murdering his girlfriend and taking his toddler daughter with him to dispose of the body. The last lines of the song are: *"Da-Da made me a nice bed for Mommy at the bottom of the lake. Here you wanna help Da-Da tie a rope around this rock? We'll tie it to her footsie and we'll roll her off the dock, Ready now here we go on the count of free, One . . . two . . . free . . . weee! There goes Mama, splashing in the water, No more fighting with Dad, no more restraining order."* Around this time, Eminem was featured on the cover of *Rolling Stone* magazine. As of June 12, 2000, Eminem's new album was number 1 in the United States, selling 2.5 million copies since its release two weeks earlier.[100]

Heedless permissiveness in sexual matters, within the family and in society as a whole, coupled with lack of parental guidance and inadequate contact with the needs of offspring, has intensified the preexisting neurotic tendencies of children and adolescents. They feel unloved, and this brings about a sense of alienation. Initially, this causes hatred and contempt that at first is limited to the parents, but eventually these feelings extend to all forms of social authority. The result is an increase in mass social anxiety, often accompanied by attitudes of disrespect, disloyalty, and ingratitude for what parents have given to their children. In reaction, this intensifies preexisting sexual repression on the part of grownups. An example of the latter is found in a *New York Times* front-page article, "Sex Education for Young Sees New Virtues in Chastity." Prominently displayed is a photograph of a placard: "Don't be fooled—the only 'safe sex' is abstinence before marriage and fidelity in marriage."

---

99. Taken from the web at http://slate.msn.com/Assessment/00-06-09/Assessment.asp. June 9, 2000.

100. W.B. Apple, Ph.D., personal communication, 2002.

It is during this crucial period of adolescence that parental guidance based on genuine recognition and approval of the importance of genital functioning is so important. If sexual longing is unfulfilled, the adolescent must armor to deaden his or her sexual feelings. If armoring is unsuccessful as it most usually is, the adolescent experiences ever-increasing anxiety and misery. This results in emotional or physical illness, or, to achieve some degree of discharge, the displacement of the sexual impulses onto the sociopolitical arena. Alternatively, anxiety may lead to drug use, contactless and/or pregenital sexual activity, cultism, gang activity, or a tendency to conform to group-defined, "politically correct" behavior. The significance of these behaviors is not commonly recognized as such, but they are all attempts to contain or discharge pent-up sexual energy.

The destructive societal effect of the sociopolitical attitudes toward sex of those on the left and the right is basically the same—to destroy sexual pleasure in general and genital heterosexuality in particular. The attitude on the right overtly blunts sexual feelings through moralistic indoctrination. This produces sexual repression through fear and guilt. Notwithstanding, emotional contact with the forbidden feelings is retained. The attitude of the left numbs sexual excitation in an insidious, covert fashion, while appearing to endorse it by condoning all forms of sexual behavior. The consequence of indiscriminate permissiveness at all levels of development, which promotes pregenital sexuality, promiscuity, pornography, and so on (see, for example, *The Joy of Sex*), produces even more deadening of sexual feelings than the antisexual attitudes of the right. This occurs because permissiveness of this kind desensitizes sexual excitation and divorces it from feelings of true closeness and love.

Sexual attitudes, be they rigid conservative-mystical or liberal-mechanistic, cannot control or address, let alone resolve, mankind's deep-seated sexual problems. In actuality, they only perpetuate them. The sociopolitical pendulum swings continuously from right to left and back again without any lasting, fundamental improvement because what is essential—the natural discharge of sexual tension through satisfying orgasm—is not understood as regulating social behavior and is always avoided.

The transformation of the structure of society from authoritarian to anti-authoritarian came about by overriding the individual's superego; that is, the incorporated, internalized inhibitory forces from the authoritarian environment that were contained in muscular armor. This was accomplished by the upward shift of armor to the ocular segment, which in no small part was manifested in and reinforced by securing the approval of others who shared the same ideological antipathy toward authoritarian society. The material that follows addresses some current social issues that involve sexuality in anti-authoritarian society.

Other Social Issues Involving Sexuality

The rise in the incidence of every kind of overt dysfunctional sexual behavior is a direct consequence of the transformation of society into anti-authoritarianism. Social topics involving sexuality are highly volatile as they trigger intense curiosity and anxiety in the masses. They are therefore fertile soil for the eruption of the emotional plague, including political activism.

Homosexuality, for example, is an issue fraught with confusion. Like genital anesthesia in females, and premature ejaculation in males, homosexuality is a symptom that arises from an underlying disturbance in the orgasm function. (See Introduction and Orientation) Notwithstanding, the American Psychiatric Association, by a simple majority of the one-third of its members who chose to vote, *elected* to remove homosexuality from the diagnostic list of recognized psychiatric disorders (with one exception, ego-dystonic homosexuality, for those unhappy with their sexual orientation). This avowedly political maneuver and intrusion of politics into scientific debate did nothing to clarify a pathological condition. It succeeded in generating controversy and increased public confusion about the sexual function.

Homosexual individuals and organizations on the left selectively ignore decades of scientific clinical observation and claim that homosexuality is biologically determined and hence no different than heterosexuality. It may be true that an individual's level of natural, healthy aggression is biologically determined. Some homosexuals, like heterosexuals, are indeed born with greater or lesser degrees of aggression. However, this is a nonsexual trait based on inborn energy level. They do not determine the gender choice of a sexual partner.[101] As previously stated, character is determined by armor formation in the erogenous zones (ocular, oral, anal, phallic, or genital). As a result of psychosexual developmental factors related to the child's environment, individuals who become homosexual give up their attraction for the opposite sex. Phallic homosexuals, male and female, retain their aggression and impulses to dominate whereas passive-feminine male homosexuals relinquish their aggression in favor of passivity. Homosexuality can be a symptom in any character type. It is not based on genetic factors but is environmentally determined.

Individuals on the left and the right, with no knowledge of the psychosexual factors that determine character armor, cannot comprehend how character armor disturbs sexual and social functioning. Similarly, the controversy and confusion over homosexuality is in greatest part the result of ignorance of the function of character armor and the failure to differentiate between natural (genital) sexuality and sexuality distorted by armor. Adding to the confusion is the rarity of healthy sexual functioning and the all-too-common disturbances in the capacity for sexual satisfaction found in heterosexuals and homosexuals alike.

These confusing attitudes regarding sexuality result from the nearly global and unrecognized terror of experiencing the involuntary orgasmic convulsion and the consequence of that terror—the rejection of genitality (the universal "Don't touch it").

In the past authoritarian society, homosexuality was morally condemned. In today's anti-authoritarian society, homosexuality is viewed as simply an "alternative lifestyle." This politically correct opinion is not supported by clinical observation. The qualitative emotional experience and the quantitative degree of sexual gratification of individuals functioning on a genital level (genital sexuality) are profoundly different from those individuals who function at pregenital levels of development, whether they are homosexual or heterosexual. Furthermore, through medical orgone therapy, armor can be dissolved, and this allows for heterosexual functioning. The reverse development, from a heterosexual to homosexual orientation, never occurs. Finally, on

101. From a historical standpoint, the ideological force behind the gay rights movement in today's anti-authoritarian society is in part a result of the negative reaction to homosexuality found in the past authoritarian social order.

a biological, cellular level, the sperm of all species is attracted to the ovum of the same species. The attraction of sperm to sperm or ova to ova of two organisms never occurs. The gender of an individual is genetically determined by the combination of X and Y chromosomes. The conclusion to be drawn from these observations is that, except for rare cases of hermaphroditism, homosexuality is environmentally determined by early traumatic childhood experiences.[102]

Therapy of homosexuals reveals that in all cases the individual suffers extreme emotional pain in early childhood, primarily the result of profound, continued disappointment of the child's love usually for the parent of the opposite sex. Only after a period of intense inner conflict, much of which is unconscious, does the child give up heterosexual orientation. This results first in extreme anxiety, both conscious and unconscious, then aversion when engaging the opposite sex. In males, this can result in the formation of a passive-feminine character. Such individuals develop intense hatred of women and a reactive expansion (pleasurable sexual feelings) toward males. Thus, homosexual feelings and behavior are reaction formations and examples of substitute contact. When homosexual patients are able to experience and tolerate their warded-off, painful emotions in medical orgone therapy, they spontaneously relinquish their homosexual orientation.

Because it is a symptom of an individual's character armor, homosexuality is not a political issue, nor should it be morally condemned. A person's sexual orientation, regardless of his or her object choice, is a private matter. Homosexuals who are content with their sexual orientation have a right to remain as they prefer.[103] Current anti-authoritarian attitudes coupled with the reduction of overt public censure of homosexuality have caused increased anxiety and levels of contactlessness among all members of society. The issue of homosexuality has therefore become a strong impetus for engaging in political activism, a manifestation of substitute contact, among some homosexuals. The function of

---

102. Research to elucidate the effect of maternal feminizing or androgenizing endocrine hormones on the developing human fetus is essential.

103. Knowing that their sexual orientation is nobody's business but their own, many homosexuals who are characterologically conservative refuse to be caught up in activist programs sponsored by pseudo-liberal characters.

this activism is often an attempt to reduce anxiety by legitimizing homosexuality. Activism for homosexual rights, however, is just one more aspect of the widespread confusion resulting from the failure to distinguish between primary (genital) and secondary (pregenital) sexuality.

An example of this confusion is the agitation of homosexual rights groups to legitimize same-sex marriage. The institution of marriage is a social function that has its roots in the deeper biological domain. A marital relationship consists of both social (less inclusive) and biological (more inclusive) functions. (See chapter 1) Biological functions are those related to procreation and childrearing. On the other hand, functions that are exclusively social include, among other things, property rights and laws protecting these rights. Homosexual rights activists who advocate same-sex marriage confuse these separate domains of life. Whereas property rights are in the domain of *all* people, male and female operating individually, procreation and childrearing require a relationship of two individuals of the opposite sex. This is necessary at all levels of human interaction, from the deepest biological (genital) level of intimacy to the most superficial psychosocial levels of childrearing. Advocates of same-sex marriage confuse the legal relationships of partnership and marriage. Its destructive social consequences are largely ignored. Confounding domains often results in emotional plague behavior. In this situation, doing so serves to weaken and ultimately destroy marriage as a legitimate social institution.

Equating any pregenital sexuality, including homosexuality (which arises from the secondary layer) with genital sexuality (a core function) effectively negates the crucial role of the orgasm function by generating confusion in the public mind as to the distinction between healthy sexuality—genital sexuality—and neurotic, pregenital sexuality. The attempt by liberals to counter conservatives' moralistic sexual attitudes should not blur this distinction between pregenital and genital sexual functioning. Equating the two only perplexes many neurotic adolescents, who are already uncertain and anxious about their sexuality, and this generates identity problems. Holding that all sexual expression is the same ("different strokes for different folks") provides a convenient rationalization for those adolescents not facing their anxiety of making contact with the opposite sex. "If I'm really gay, then I don't have a problem with the opposite sex—I'm just being me." This mindset also facilitates conversion of an individual's ego-alien homoerotic feelings into feelings that are both ego-syntonic and culturally supported in today's society. These politically correct, culturally accepted influences serve to discourage the efforts of youngsters who resist acting on latent homosexual impulses. But for these influences, many with fleeting homosexual feelings, which are not at all uncommon in adolescence, would either repress their secondary layer impulses or seek help for their emotional problems.

What is more, equating pregenital sexuality with genital sexuality promotes emotional plague activity, allowing the displacement of personal emotional problems onto the social arena. This provides a breeding ground for sociopolitical activism. Anyone who takes issue with, or opposes, homosexuality and the sociopolitical agenda of gay-rights activists, for any reason, is labeled homophobic and moralistic. This is a typical emotional plague tactic and it further confounds an already confused public and disarms the effectiveness of any opposition. By evoking guilt and by manipulatively appealing to people's natural tolerance and sense of fair play, it can also provoke emotional plague reactions from the extreme right directed against all homosexuals.

The position held by liberals, that homosexuality is a legitimate alternative lifestyle, not only supports the right of individuals to choose whatever sexual preference they are inclined to, but also the demand that homosexuals have equal social rights as a group ("gay rights"). They insist that there be recognition of homosexuals as a political force; that is, one that shapes and determines social policy. In reality, only individuals have rights. The fight for any form of "group rights" is a manifestation of collectivistic thinking, a form of discrimination. It results from a displacement onto society of underlying feelings of revenge that are originally directed at authority figures in the individual's life, usually the father. At the same time, it is a ploy for gaining political power (substitute gratification) and a tactic to promote public acceptance of homosexuality as equivalent to heterosexuality. This is often done by portraying homosexuals as a victimized, oppressed minority whose low self-esteem and difficulties in coping with life are attributable to societal discrimination, hence the rationale for "gay pride." Anyone who dares criticize or disagree is branded as "homophobic."

Feminism, in its fight for equal rights for women, provides another example of how sexually charged social issues trigger intense anxiety in people and, as a result, are fertile soil for emotional irrationalism and political activism. This is especially so in women who are intellectualized, "up in their heads," and, therefore, have little or no core contact.[104] In reality, feminist political activism allows women to displace their emotional problems and fears onto socially related issues. Anything but feminine, feminists are the female counterpart of the male chauvinist. The function of feminism as a social cause ends up being a negation of the natural biological and social differences between the sexes and a rejection of the importance of heterosexuality in general and of genitality in particular.

Another issue fueling social anxiety and activism is AIDS and AIDS "hysteria" (Harman 1988). Past and current campaigns to educate people about the risk of transmitting human immunodeficiency virus (HIV) and the prevention of AIDS have usually taken a dire, alarmist approach. The message, that everyone who has sex risks death, connects sex with destruction. An understanding of the biology of the sexual function dictates a more responsible use of information and statistics. Information adequate to instruct the public and accomplish the stated goal of prevention could well be provided without fostering needless anxiety and fears of sex, *and increasing sexual stasis*, especially in the young. An understanding of natural sexual functioning might also have dictated a universal rather than an isolated approach to HIV testing. *This would have included mandatory reporting of new cases by physicians to local public health departments for follow-up and tracking of sexual contacts, as is required by law for other, less dangerous communicable diseases.* Instead, we have relied on a symptomatic approach—advocating the use of condoms and abstinence—both of which interfere with pleasure and sex-economic functioning. Thus, we see AIDS "hysteria" used for anti-sexual purposes while responsible social management of a

104. The source of rational authority originates from the biological core and, therefore, rational social authority is not related to gender.

devastating disease is sacrificed to "protect privacy" and to avoid "blaming the victim." The left-oriented media, as usual, has contributed to the problem. They have focused on documenting the unfortunate plight of individual AIDS patients and not on reporting how politicians, physicians, and health departments have abdicated their social and professional responsibilities.

The negation of genital heterosexuality is the core and essential function of the ideology of the left and the right. The energy blockage resulting from this negation is the source of the emotional plague. Both the left and the right use well-rationalized scare tactics to thwart healthy heterosexual activity, the left with its safe-sex movement and the right with its abstinence programs.

Virtually all social turmoil arising from human sexual pathology could be alleviated if the origins of the pathology, first delineated by Reich, were understood (Reich 1983, page 7). Reich went on to point out that, tragically, the prevalent and prevailing attitude of all armored people toward genital sexuality has always been one of avoidance—the universal prohibition "Don't touch it!". The public debate, with its hodgepodge of contradictory information and its predictable, ideologically determined positions on the left and the right, only contributes to the confusion regarding the sexual function. Neither liberal permissiveness and political correctness nor conservative repression and morality get to the root of the sexual misery and the longing for happiness of humanity. When both positions are presented simultaneously, as is currently the case, confusion and social chaos are exacerbated. Sociopolitical solutions, which arise from sex-negative attitudes, are not the answer.

Work

The work function is as much a mystery to everyone as is the sexual function. Neither liberal nor conservative political programs consider that armor disrupts the pulsation of biological energy, the energy that governs all living activities, including work. Neither the left nor the right is able to make a distinction between healthy and neurotic work. Neither has understood the tremendous power in work and in its ability to regulate the energy economy of the individual. Neither recognizes the destructive forces that are unleashed when the work function is blocked and neither understands the relationship between the self-regulating function of work and how it is necessary for healthy economic activity, including the free market.

Several biosocial factors contribute to the development of the work function in humans. Among these are the individual's special innate abilities, play activities experienced in childhood, and learning through observation of the work patterns of parents and other significant authority figures in the child's life.

Emotional problems produce armoring and disturb or arrest development of the child's work function. Disturbed family relationships also have a destructive effect and this routinely occurs when a child is raised in a home where working adults as role models are absent, as is so often the case in extremely wealthy or poor families.

In most armored individuals sexual activity emerges primarily from the destructive secondary layer as sadism, pregenital sexuality, and pornography. In them, the work function is also disturbed and exhibits the characteristics of both the secondary and superficial layers. Examples of work originating from the secondary layer constitute an entire catalogue of human vice. They include criminally-related work activity (as in organized crime), corporate fraud, amassing money for its own sake (greed) or using it for power over others, mechanistic-mystical research in natural science, and underhanded political maneuvering in work situations and organizations. These activities are a manifestation of the emotional plague in the workplace. Other neurosis-based work disturbances will be discussed later.

The acting out of the destructive secondary layer in the workplace, as with criminal behavior, necessitates legal restraints that increase centralized government control, which further cripples a free-market economy. This antisocial activity has always been with us but it has greatly accelerated in today's anti-authoritarian society.[105] Work originating from the superficial and secondary layers is largely cut off from biological core functions but, nevertheless, it often satisfies neurotic needs as a substitute for gen-

105. After a wave of accounting scandals shook the public's trust, the reputation of many of the best-known corporations have continued to decline. See "Corporate Scandals Hit Home," *Wall Street Journal*, Feb. 19, 2004.

uine human activity. Work originating from these layers serves no vital function, either for the individual worker or for society. Examples of work from the superficial layer include "pop" art, high-pressure selling and advertising, manufacturing products such as video games, and much that is marketed as "high-tech" fashion design. These activities serve primarily to satisfy secondary layer needs of people by distracting them from the monotony of armored daily life. *They function to provide substitute contact.* Because of the increased preoccupation with superficialities and trivia, this nonessential substitute market has become an artificially expanding and important part of the world's economy. Work that comes from the secondary and superficial layers cannot provide genuine satisfaction for individuals and, as such, it exacts a tremendous price on people's lives. Table 7.1 describes the sexual and work impulses as expressed from the different layers of the armored bioemotional structure.

Function	Core	Secondary Layer	Superficial Layer
Sexual	Sex as an expression of love	Sex as an expression of revenge (sadism), pregenital sexual activity, pornography	Superficial presention of sexuality in advertisements and other media ("sex sells")
Work	Vitally necessary work in scientific research, medicine, health care, child-rearing, and art expressed from biological core	Criminal work activity, plunder, mechanistic research in natural science	"Pop" art, high-pressure selling and advertising, high-tech fashion design

Source of Biological Impulse

TABLE 7.1

As with the sexual and work functions, true knowledge and understanding are genuine core impulses. They, too, become distorted as they pass through the armor. When the impulse to know passes through the secondary layer (especially the ocular segment with its armored brain), mechanistic and mystical ideas of the world inevitably result. *Knowledge is qualitatively and quantitatively degraded and becomes information.* In today's anti-authoritarian society, ready access to vast amounts of such information on the Internet can appear to instantly turn anyone into an authority on any subject.

In the presence of armoring, natural concepts derived from an individual's contact with his or her core become qualitatively distorted and lose their original meaning. Thus, armored and unarmored individuals view knowledge, work and love quite differently. The significance and value of other things, such as money and material possessions, are similarly rooted in the individual's bioenergetic make-up and are related to his state of emotional health.

The underlying determinants that constitute wealth and poverty continue to remain unclear. An example is an article in *The Wall Street Journal* entitled "Finding a Cure for Joblessness Remains a Riddle."[106] It focused on external factors as the exclusive reason for the problem of poverty and offered as the only remedy the need for federal government assistance to help people find work. The article neglected to mention anything about the underlying source of the problem, the existence of inner biological factors that are always at the heart of all work functions. *Poverty in American society is primarily bioemotionally and biophysically determined, the consequence of a work disturbance. It is not caused by external social factors because, in America, the opportunities for work are present. It arises from a disturbance in the work function, from the presence of individual and social armor.* In America, most people are poor because they are emotionally too sick to improve their standard of living through work. Neither moralizing political speeches and slogans nor thinly disguised socialistically inspired federal programs, such as the "War on Poverty," will help the jobless poor and, as has been documented

106. *Wall Street Journal*, Oct. 13, 2003.

elsewhere (Murray 1984), they actually exacerbate the problems they are supposed to address.

To the degree that individuals are armored, they are unable to enjoy life. As a result, they feel bored and require substitute measures for gratification. They have lost the natural ability to obtain gratification in their personal lives and through their work, are immobilized, and therefore without motivation to find new, more satisfying employment. They feel trapped and they undertake their work with dread, as an endless struggle, and all too often as the bane of their existence. They count down the hours of each work day and live for their time of retirement.

The pleasure that armored people experience in play activities is usually in the form of spectator sports such as watching television, which becomes an escape from a humdrum life and a substitute for satisfying work. Such individuals look forward to winning the lottery so that they can retire and be relieved of the burden of having to work. However, even when idle or retired, virtually all remain incapable of experiencing genuine pleasure and happiness. Many are actually worse off, suffering boredom, anxiety, depression, and physical symptoms. Physical decline and death following retirement is a common occurrence.

Although armored humans may have lost much of their capacity to experience gratification in work, they have nevertheless retained it as an ideal. This longing is often exploited by the advertising industry, which uses the enjoyment and virtue of working in the production of products or providing services (e.g., preparation of food, owning an automobile, medical care) as selling points.

The rise in social anxiety, the result of an inability to tolerate sustained pleasurable core contact, has been accompanied by the shift of the work function from the body (physical labor) to the brain. This change has caused the quality of work requiring manual skills to rapidly deteriorate. Hospitals, for example, are often unable to provide the level of support of medical and nursing care that was considered minimally adequate as recently as a decade ago.

With the development of computers, many people's work function is currently in the midst of a radical transition from physical reality to information. We are living in the age of information.

However, because it is produced and used mechanically, most of this explosion of information is not relevant to people's vital emotional needs. Information has become a poor substitute for real knowledge, knowledge based on true understanding and practical experience. As a result, people get lost in endless detail. They are unable to accurately discern and process what is and is not valuable in this glut of information. There is a numbing effect from information overload and an upward energetic shift to the brain. People are more confused than ever and less capable of recognizing knowledge that is essential to their well-being. They are more likely than ever before to be influenced and manipulated by the emotional plague through the mechanistic-liberal paradigm. For example, within the span of a few short years, the masses have been convinced by the pharmaceutical industry, in collusion with the medical establishment, that psychological-emotional disorders are a product of chemical "imbalances" in the brain.

Disturbances in the biological work function point to yet another source of increased social anxiety: the social problems inherent in excessive financial affluence. When individuals do not have to work to survive, their work function deteriorates. Energy no longer discharged in work gives rise to anxiety, boredom, alienation, a host of neurotic symptoms, and the need to engage in activities for substitute satisfaction. These destructive activities often include neurotic socializing for substitute contact, and drug and alcohol use especially among the affluent young. Because they have so much time on their hands, a significant segment of this population spends much of their lives indulging in endless distractions and diversions. For them, "killing time" is a way of life. For many people, wealthy or not, materialism, in its defensive function, is largely the result of the increased disposable income of individuals who, because of their contactlessness and disturbed self-regulation, are unable to use their financial resources to engage in pleasurable work activity or for other productive use.[107] Most often, they become neurotically caught up with increasing the size of their wealth or the abundance of their material possessions, and this becomes an end in itself.

---

107. Inordinate wealth can be as socially destructive as excessive poverty. By providing a false sense of security, it destroys the individual's core survival instincts and serves to protect the individual's neurotic lifestyle.

Furthermore, stasis of work energy, that is, energy not discharged in work, leads to eruptions from the secondary layer ranging from white collar crime to destructive outbursts of rage (domestic violence) and, when the conditions are right, as explosive terrorist acts. These eruptions occur not simply because of a lack of external restraints or poverty, which are often proposed as justifying rationalizations, but because there has been a damming up of massive quantities of biological energy that need to be discharged in healthy sexuality or productive work.

Work Disturbances in Neurotic Character Types

Individuals who have retained their ability to work, but who do so compulsively and without much pleasure, are as endemic in our anti-authoritarian society as they were in the past authoritarian social order. Since they derive almost no pleasure in their work, such persons cannot focus on the *work process* but only on the financial reward. These individuals, to perform their work, require varying degrees of external social constraints as well as internal constraints that are provided by their armor. This group includes people engaged in mechanical, repetitious (e.g., assembly line) work or other mindless activities who, by the very nature of the activity, cannot make sufficient contact with the work process itself to derive satisfaction. This group also includes individuals commonly referred to as "workaholics," who work excessively but also do so with virtually no real satisfaction. Work provides no gratification because the energy consumed in the process does not reach the periphery of their structure and *without a flow of energy from core to periphery, unimpeded by armor, pleasure cannot be experienced.* Some of these individuals profess to "love" their work. However, on closer inspection, it is clear that, for them, work is their way of avoiding anxiety.

Each individual character type shows a rather specific disturbance in their work function and the type of work disturbance is a reflection of their particular character structure. Since these disturbances are intimately associated with character structure, the medical orgonomist pays careful attention to every patient's work functioning. Below are some typical examples given with the caveat that they describe *qualitative* differences. There is a great deal of quantitative variability in work capacity among the various individual character types.

THE HYSTERIC (GENITALITY WITH ANXIETY)

The hysteric character type is predominantly found in women. She may run from her work into frantic sexual behavior, or run from her sexuality into frenzied work activity, or she may freeze up, inhibited with anxiety. There are various types and varying degrees of flight into or from work. Typically, the hysteric leaves tasks to the last minute or allows situations at work to become problematic, thereby justifying a need to behave in a frantic, "hysterical" manner in order to "get things done." She moves from task to task, often unable to concentrate or patiently develop and execute the work at hand. Her tendency to avoid direct confrontation with co-workers, out of anxiety, gives rise to interpersonal difficulties and problems in completing tasks. Most often, she will complain about these matters to someone other than the individual involved, or if she does directly address the situation, she does so timidly and ineffectually.

With the transformation from an authoritarian to anti-authoritarian social order, the biophysical structure of hysterics has altered. Feeling "liberated" from the shackles of the authoritarian family, many have discarded their traditional role of moralist and developed a phallic façade, using aggression defensively to avoid sexual feelings.

> Because her superior managerial abilities were recognized by her boss, a patient in her early forties was promoted and placed in charge of a small business. She became overly involved in her work to the exclusion of all else, ignoring the needs of her husband and family. The function of this "good" behavior was to please her boss, a father figure. This behavior gave her an enormous amount of substitute gratification while avoiding sexual feelings for her husband. Clearly, her work was being used defensively against facing her genital anxiety. Pointing out the defensive nature of her behavior abruptly and effectively cornered her. Now she was unable to tolerate her underlying sexual anxiety and she responded by viciously lashing out at her therapist. Because she also could not tolerate the intensity of this rage, she ran away from therapy.

THE PHALLIC NARCISSISTIC CHARACTER (GENITAL REVENGE)

The phallic character's work disturbance is related to his heightened sense of self-importance (narcissism) and to his tendency to be overly aggressive. To the degree that narcissistic traits determine their behavior, phallic characters are unable to function cooperatively as part of an integrated social organization. Their phallic structure also prevents them from paying attention to details necessary to accomplishing tasks. They have an overt or covert need to "be the boss." They are driven to direct and control the work process at every turn, even when it is uncalled for. They have a preoccupation with quantity, not quality ("Bigger is better"), and a one-sided (narcissistic) interest in their own particular accomplishments to the exclusion of others, including the well-being of the organization, their customers or the environment. This lack of responsibility based on narcissistic self-interest is the hallmark of the neurotic phallic businessman. Healthier phallic individuals are able to curb their narcissism. By recognizing their own limitations they can cooperate with others. They are the successful entrepreneurs and politicians. More neurotic types have a greater disturbance in their work function. Some are workaholics. Males who are insecure about their erective potency often use their entrepreneurial abilities defensively to perpetually seek greater degrees of success as a form of substitute gratification: They build larger business enterprises or involve themselves in grandiose business schemes. For them, success, financial or otherwise, is equated with sexual prowess. The element of revenge in their business activities is easily recognized in their behavior. To the degree that they are neurotic they will denigrate or ignore the accomplishments of other men who they secretly view as more potent than themselves. Female phallic characters behave in a way similar to their male counterparts in the work place. As a result of the current anti-authoritarian social order, certain female hysterics have developed a phallic façade taking their place alongside men in the business world.[108]

> A hard-driving, middle-aged, phallic narcissistic marketing analyst gave up his job, which he thoroughly

108. This illustrates the reciprocal relationship between individual and social character. Our current anti-authoritarian social order has a destabilizing effect on character formation.

> enjoyed, when he was promoted to a supervisory position. He now had greater prestige and a larger salary, but he soon became bored because this new work was just not as exciting as his previous job. Because of this, his performance suffered and he was dismissed. In therapy, he came to see the importance of enjoying his work and not being overly aggressive, in either his life or his work. He was then able to allow himself more gratification in these principle areas of functioning.

THE MANIC-DEPRESSIVE CHARACTER (GENITAL REVENGE MASKED BY ORAL STRIVINGS)

The manic-depressive, who is a specific type of phallic, is similar to the phallic character in that he too has an inability to focus on detail. In this character type, however, the trait becomes exaggerated and this, in turn, leads to sloppiness and/or poor judgment in every aspect of life, including work. The manic-depressive exhibits a severe pulsatory disturbance swinging, on expansion, between impulsive manic behavior that is often destructive and, with contraction, depression that is marked by harsh, punitive, self-criticism. Caught between expansive impulsiveness and his limiting armor, the manic-depressive typically has difficulty maintaining sustained success. In work, strong drives can propel the manic-depressive to strive to accomplish great feats, but because of his inconsistency, he often sabotages his efforts one way or another and ends up where he started, or worse. This self-destructiveness may be subtle and difficult to identify.

> A talented graphic designer in his early twenties had difficulty maintaining a consistently high work level because of sloppiness and impulsive, sometimes obnoxious, social behavior. These traits combined to sabotage his work whenever he came close to achieving success. Therapy focused on preventing him from behaving self-destructively. When he was brought in touch with his self-destructiveness, he gradually came to be able to tolerate his feelings of deep misery as well as genuine feelings of expansion. He was then able to sustain more consistent satisfaction and success in his life and work.

THE COMPULSIVE CHARACTER (PHALLIC SADISM HELD BY ANAL CAUTION)

Compulsive work habits were the first work disturbance associated with a specific character type described in the psychiatric literature. Although compulsive work habits occur in other character types, they are always found in the compulsive character. He works in a rigid, mechanical, robotic fashion, a reaction formation against the expression of sadistic impulses. Obsessed with meticulous detail and devoid of pleasure in work, the compulsive has a blunted emotional life and pays little attention to the emotional responses of co-workers to his behavior. Depending on the degree of obstinacy, the compulsive's work function may be used to provide sadistic satisfaction in controlling others—making them wait for his services, for example, as do many bureaucrats. The critical faculties of the compulsive are more developed than the creative ones, and the compulsive tends to focus on minutiae to the detriment of the total work product. As a manager, the compulsive may also focus on establishing superficial group "harmony" to avoid painful conflicts, another reaction formation, and as a substitute to compensate for feelings of emptiness.

> A highly efficient, successful city planner in his mid-thirties worked robotically and experienced virtually no pleasure in his life or work. The release through rage of sadistic impulses, in the course of therapy, relieved his affect block and his defensive emotional lameness. As his body softened he began feeling misery. After these long repressed feelings from infancy and childhood were released, he was able to meet a woman with whom he fell deeply in love, married, and was able to experience real gratification in his life and work.

THE PASSIVE FEMININE CHARACTER (PHALLIC SADISM GIVEN UP FOR ANAL SUBMISSION)

Occurring exclusively in males, the passive feminine character has renounced the phallic level and identifies with the mother on an anal level. He feels inadequate and inferior in every aspect of his life, including his work. He may secretly feel contemptuous toward women and harbor fantasies of grandiosity to compensate for his inadequacy.

The work function of the passive feminine corresponds to his character structure in every detail. He views and interacts with the world as a passive observer. A daydreamer, he fantasizes of greatness. He is overly polite, superficially compliant, modest, and retiring. However, underneath this façade, he is sneaky, nasty, and petty. His choice of work can also be a reflection of his passive structure, and his work capacity is reduced in proportion to his lack of capacity for aggression. In contrast to the phallic, who pierces his environment with his work, the passive feminine chooses passive forms of employment: He may become an interior designer (from his feminine identification) or a waiter (from his servility). If he happens to be in a field requiring aggression, such as management, he feels a terrible sense of inadequacy and inferiority. With medical orgone therapy, as aggressive and heterosexual impulses are mobilized, work function improves and work life becomes more satisfying.

> A passive feminine homosexual physician in his early thirties was severely inhibited in his work function, and he knew that it would be better if he were healthier. In therapy, expression of rage gradually gave rise to genital longing for women, accompanied by aggressiveness in all aspects of his life. At the hospital where he worked, he was able to stop behaving submissively toward strong male figures. His new-found aggression was central in his personal life. He eventually gave up homosexual relationships, married and had several children.

THE SCHIZOPHRENIC CHARACTER (OCULAR REPRESSION WITH PANIC AND SPLITTING)

The disturbance in the schizophrenic's work function is primarily related to ocular armor. Depending on the severity of the armor, confusion will impair work function. However, armoring may be so severe as to completely interfere with work ability. Because of the confusion the individual may not know his or her work interest. The inability to have contact with the work process also leads the schizophrenic to use compensatory mechanisms, such as to work compulsively or to be overly aggressive. These compensations may be partially successful in overcoming the effects of the confusion. The schizophrenic's disturbed functioning always clears when the ocular block is eliminated during therapy.

> A paranoid schizophrenic in her early twenties came to therapy very frightened of life in all its aspects. Her fear was so great that she required her husband to accompany her to the first session. She was ambivalent about her marriage, but she had to have her husband near her whenever possible. Reducing the armor in the ocular segment enabled her to become more independent, but, nonetheless, she drifted aimlessly from one menial job to another because of difficulty in knowing what kind of work really interested her. Consistent attention to and dissolution of her ocular armor eliminated her quandary. She became clear about her choice of work and she tolerated not clinging to her husband. She attended graduate school and finished at the top of her class, full of enthusiasm and pride in her accomplishment and profession. No longer confused and secure in her independence, she now derives enormous satisfaction from her work and her life. Dissolving the ocular armor was the key to the successful therapeutic outcome.

THE IMPULSIVE CHARACTER

The true impulsive character is rare, but impulsive traits in the general population are relatively common and are found in people from all walks of life.[109] True impulsive individuals have suffered a defect in the formation of their character armor such that they do not possess a fixed character. They, therefore, often exhibit character traits derived from several different levels of development. Their work function is virtually nonexistent as their disturbance is so great that it forces them to continually resort to substitute activities. These behaviors are drawn from the secondary layer, and include pregenital, criminal, and sociopathic activity. By "conning" and giving the illusion of productive work, the impulsive can assume the role of political leader, social crusader, mystical healer, or guru. In truth, the true impulsive lacks moral integrity. His charm and cleverness make the naïve gullible and the leader-seeking individual easy prey. Because the behavior of the impulsive character quite often has socially destructive consequences, these people can function as emotional plague

---

109. The terms "impulsive character," "psychopath," and "sociopath" for all practical purposes can be used interchangeably.

individuals. However, the precise characteristics that define an emotional plague character extend beyond impulsive behavior. Any character type can exhibit emotional plague behavior.

In treatment, if the therapist is able to successfully curb the impulsive behavior, the patient becomes depressed and quits therapy. Continuation of treatment puts him at risk of developing a serious physical illness. Thus, the true impulsive character is untreatable.

With the anti-authoritarian transformation of American society, true impulsive characters and people with impulsive character traits are increasing. There has been a sharp rise in the incidence of work-related criminal activity.

> An energetic and charming high-level business executive in his early forties demonstrated the ability to work as long as he was working under the wing of the firm's CEO, a strong authority figure. Under this control, the executive was a good soldier and carried out his duties reasonably well, although he performed tasks in response to commands and not from inner motivation. He typically responded to directives with an automatic "Yessir!". I felt, from the beginning of therapy, that he might have difficulty maintaining consistency and responsibility in his work. It was not unexpected, given his impulsivity, that almost every week he became involved in one or another new undertaking. When the CEO suddenly retired, the patient was forced to take charge of the company. At first he performed fairly well, attempting to model himself after his newly departed boss. But gradually his work function deteriorated. He lost his focus, left the organization, dropped out of therapy and became involved with a mystical healer. His work functioning, always precarious, had depended on a dominant authority figure.

Work Disturbances in Sociopolitical Character Types

The discussion so far has focused on the more typical work disturbances associated with neurotic character types. These disturbances largely depend upon how great the impact the environment exerts *on* the individual. The discussion that follows will focus on the individual's neurotic attempts to control the environment *through* his or her work. Such behavior is characteristic of the sociopolitical types already examined. The sociopolitical and the nonpolitical neurotic character types can occur together in any combination.

Regardless of character type, all work disturbances are fueled and maintained by energy stasis. *In sociopolitical characters, the sadistic component of the individual's ideology always contains and expresses genital revenge displaced onto society.* In general, as the ideological component shifts further to the extremes of the left or the right, the work function becomes increasingly disturbed. The following are examples from sociopolitical character types found in our current anti-authoritarian social order.

THE CONSERVATIVE CHARACTER (GENITAL REVENGE HELD IN THE MUSCULATURE)

Since the conservative identifies with the father and openly competes with him, conservatives tend to support individual responsibility and the competitive spirit that is an inherent part of a free market economic system. Since their armor is contained primarily in the musculature, these individuals often choose work that is physical. For example, in the field of medicine, surgeons are usually conservative as compared to psychiatrists who, because of their intellectual orientation, are usually liberal. The extreme conservative is personified by the rugged individualist, who was largely responsible for making America economically great. Healthier individuals of this type have maintained a fair degree of core contact and therefore derive pleasure from their work. As a result, their work develops and grows naturally to the extent that neurotic complexes do not interfere. Their sense of social responsibility is often expressed in specifically targeted philanthropic projects.

In more disturbed individuals of the conservative type, work disturbances are an exaggeration of their innate traits, such as excessive aggressiveness, neurotic independence, and impulsivity. Other pathological manifestations include extreme competitiveness, an inability to cooperate with or a need to control others in the workplace. Such individuals can be reckless in grandiose business schemes, ruthless in business affairs, and greedy in financial matters. When these neurotic manifestations appear in the work function the element of (genital) revenge becomes evident.

Greed is a nonspecific neurotic symptom found in any character type. Based on emotional insecurity, it can appear in those on both sides of the political spectrum. Greedy individuals amass money and material possessions in an attempt to provide themselves with a greater sense of financial security. This behavior is a defense solely for the purpose of avoiding anxiety. Despite espousing contempt for private property, those on the political left can be as greedy and ruthless as people on the right, but they may attempt to assuage their guilt by supporting charitable causes that are in keeping with their leftist ideas.

THE TRUE LIBERAL CHARACTER (GENITAL REVENGE HELD BY THE INTELLECT)

The true liberal, in contrast to the socialist and the pseudo-liberal and like the conservative, is basically decent and reasonable.[110] The reason that most people in the TV and print media, the entertainment industry, education, the "arts," are liberal is that these activities are derived from the social façade, the same layer of the human biopyschic structure that leftist ideas originate. Because they have little emotional depth, liberals usually choose work in intellectual fields.[111] For the same reason, scientists with a liberal structure, or those currently educated according to the tenets of mechanistic materialism in the natural sciences, have great difficulty comprehending the functional energetic basis of biological processes. Similarly, the liberal artist may have difficulty sensing the creative process that stems from work originating from the core. This occurs because in this individual energy is concentrated in the head and artistic expression is intellectualized. Examples include a preference for impressionist and atonal music and art that is derived from the superficial layer of the artist's structure.

---

110. Only by understanding the characterological basis of sociopolitical activity can one avoid damaging, erroneous generalizations (e.g., viewing all liberals as being pro-communist or all conservatives as being pro-fascist).

111. Intellectual functions and the intellect have to be distinguished from the concept of intelligence. The intellect can function either in the service of rational reasoning, in which case it is not in conflict with primary drives, or in the service of defense against core functions. Those on the left on the sociopolitical spectrum use the intellect as defense; those on the right employ muscular defenses. For example, liberals much more than conservatives are likely to act out of guilt or pity, but these are reaction formations and not primary emotions. The liberal's "compassion" serves to block natural aggression and anger.

The current mechanistic approach to natural science, viewing the living organism as if it is a machine, is a prime example of the destructive work function in the armored scientist. Mechanistic thinking and liberal thinking are both derived from the superficial layer. The more neurotic types, socialists and pseudo-liberals, have a greater disturbance in their work function. Full of contempt for the work process and unable to perform productive work, they prefer telling others what they should do. As artists, they often take great delight in shocking audiences by producing provocative material that is often offensive or objectionable.

THE SOCIALIST
(GENITAL REVENGE MASKED BY SOCIAL LONGING)

Those with a socialist structure are severely armored and they, therefore, have a profound work disturbance. Because they have little or no contact with their core, they derive no satisfaction from work. Their opposition to profit in the marketplace is a thinly disguised expression both of their resentment for having to work for a living and their inability to take pleasure in it. Displacement of the Oedipal conflict onto their current social environment is a result of their derisive attitude toward authority and this makes them incapable of assuming an authoritative role when called upon to direct meaningful work. This is the case except when their resentment can be used against the authoritarian establishment (e.g., as when assuming the role of a union boss). Being collectivists, when socialists have to work for a living they are incapable of working independently. Rather they depend on the government or unionized work for employment and security. Feeling that the world owes them a living, they are incapable of emotional independence, genuine self-sufficiency or responsibility. They abhor competition in the workplace and are intolerant of the necessary aggression required in a free market economy. These traits, coupled with a craving to be told what to do, shackle their work function. Their need to be taken care of enables other like-minded individuals, such as union bosses and politicians on both sides of the political spectrum, to assume responsibility for their welfare, wreaking havoc on the free market. Because of their collectivist attitude and sense of entitlement, they believe in the equalization of wealth and have little respect for individual resourcefulness or private property.

Cognitive disturbances, which arise from energy held in the brain, are expressed in their socialist ideals and serve as a powerful defense against therapy. Until the socialist can freely express feelings of revenge against the father or surrogate authority figure, little progress can be expected in therapy. To the degree that this rage is discharged, socialistic longing and ideals dissolve.

THE PSEUDO-LIBERAL OR NEO-COMMUNIST (GENITAL REVENGE MANIFESTED THROUGH THE INTELLECT)

Over and above liberals, pseudo-liberals select work in fields that emphasize braininess, such as the media, journalism, and academia. In the medical profession they are attracted to psychiatry. They do this to make use of their highly developed intellectual defenses so that they can lord it over others who are less intellectually endowed. Pseudo-liberals wield the power of the spoken and written word cleverly and with great effectiveness but, typically, they lack in-depth knowledge of what they speak or write about. This becomes understandable when one realizes that they function exclusively from their façade and secondary layer. Their ideas come out twisted because of armor and because they do not originate from the core.

The pseudo-liberal's use of erudite words and ability to express simple ideas cleverly identifies the brain, and not the feeling body, as the source of thought processes. This cleverness has a peculiar intellectual quality that flaunts their superiority over less intellectual persons and it serves to attract others who are related ideologically. It also is used to ridicule and express contempt for those who are not.[112] Because pseudo-liberals live from their superficial layer, they rarely achieve much of permanence or value, despite their rhetoric and lofty ideals. They are far better at destructively criticizing and tearing others down than performing productive work. The pseudo-liberal obsession with change and social "improvement" belies its underlying function, which has the effect of keeping people confused and immobilized, all the while undermining and destroying true accomplishments and vital knowledge handed down from the past.

112. For example, "lacking intellectual depth" is a pseudo-liberal code phrase that identifies a nonliberal-thinking person.

Despite having little capacity himself for genuine productive work, the pseudo-liberal nevertheless is full of good ideas about what is best for everyone else. In his editorials he simulates concern for the welfare of the world and to this end believes himself certain of what people should and should not do. His involvement in sociopolitics also demonstrates his need to control others. Along with the communist, the pseudo-liberal places little value on personal initiative and resourcefulness in generating wealth. Somehow, he believes, economic wealth simply appears spontaneously. He takes the social benefits that result from wealth for granted. What concerns him most is not how wealth is produced but *how wealth is to be forcibly distributed* from the "haves" to the "have nots." This egalitarian attitude is a direct expression of genital revenge against the father displaced onto authority figures in the social sphere.

The Relationship of Character to Personal Finances

The rational function of money in a free market has been discussed, but character must also be considered in determining an individual's attitude toward both money and private property. In virtually all societies, money is necessary for human survival. For this reason character attitudes greatly influence an individual's relationship to money. Money frequently loses its rational function as a medium of exchange (currency) and is used in the service of neurosis. When used in a *socially destructive* manner, money truly is "the root of all evil."

Nonspecific character attitudes regarding money, such as greed, squander, contempt and envy of others who are "better off" can occur in any unsatisfied character type. Certain characters, however, have a propensity for specific neurotic attitudes concerning money. These attitudes, manifestation of the secondary layer in one's economic functioning, indicate a serious disturbance in the work function and in the ability to self-regulate. Such attitudes and behaviors are highly destructive to the individual and society.[113] Specific neurotic attitudes are often found in phal-

113. The destructive social consequences of secondary layer economic activity cannot be sufficiently emphasized. One of the most harmful effects is that it fuels leftist demands for governmental regulation, which, if enacted, further cripples the free market.

lic narcissistic characters and others with a prominent phallic structure. They also appear in the obsessive-compulsive character and in other character types with a prominent repressed anal block.

For the phallic narcissistic character, the erect phallus is his bulwark of confidence and erective impotence causes him to fall to pieces. His narcissism is directly linked to pride in his erect phallus, and he survives throughout life on his confidence. Neurotic attitudes toward money become evident when his narcissism becomes attached to his financial worth; that is, self-worth and financial worth are seen, emotionally, as identical. Money, including private property, is identified with the male genital (the fantasized erect phallus). For example, for the CEO, having wealth and forming conglomerates assumes the significance of having control and power over others and the environment. The phallic character often uses money in the service of revenge.[114] The relentless drive to accumulate wealth and property is always accompanied by a corresponding loss in the capacity to enjoy work and life.

In the manic-depressive character, a particular type of phallic, the neurotic relationship to money is similar to that of the true phallic character. However, because of poor judgment and lack of self-control, the manic-depressive's defensive use of money is not as effective. He tends to make unrealistic business deals and overspends. Additionally, his neurotic relationship to money is heavily colored by the manic-depressive's mood swings.

The obsessive-compulsive and other characters have a prominent repressed anal block. Their attachment to money is directly related to the degree of spasticity of their musculature, particularly the muscles of the anal sphincter. The spastic musculature gives rise to parsimoniousness in every area of life and these individuals are incapable of giving freely, particularly of their money, but also their emotions. They prefer to collect material possessions and to acquire and hold on to wealth for its own sake.

In summary, healthy sexual and work functioning are central to rational social freedom. Freedom is derived from the individual's unrestricted capacity to develop and only those who are

---

114. Ross Perot entered the presidential race in 1988 as a third-party candidate primarily to make sure that George Bush senior would be defeated.

free or relatively free of armor have both intact work and sexual functioning. For this reason, genuine responsibility and freedom in work cannot be "given" to or forced upon people, as politicians and jurists on the left and the right commonly believe. Government-sponsored work projects or jobs created through *externally* imposed economic policy are limited in their effectiveness and are the result of viewing the biological work function in mechanistic terms. This contrasts with the work-democratic understanding that the organization of work originates spontaneously from *within* the individual and develops along lines that are natural to the work process itself. In such a setting, economic freedom, which is based on freedom in the marketplace, goes hand-in-hand with responsibility for the work performed. Pleasure in sexual relations and in work is retained.

Our well-being requires that we discharge sexual and work energy from the core, relatively unhampered by armor. To bring that desired state to people and society, and to bring to both the benefits of self-regulating freedom, we must begin to remove and also prevent the armor that distorts and debilitates these core impulses. Only through the primary prevention of armor and armor removal, when possible, will destructive social behavior begin to abate.

CHAPTER 8

FUNCTIONAL PERSPECTIVES ON CURRENT SOCIAL PROBLEMS

By molding human psychological structure, social ideology not only reproduces itself in the people. More importantly, it becomes a material force in the form of altered human structure, with its contradictory thinking and acting.
—Wilhelm Reich, *The Mass Psychology of Fascism*

It is not possible to detail all symptoms of the emotional pestilence because, with the breakdown of the authoritarian social structure over the past fifty years, plague behavior has reached into every corner of social life. However, the following social case studies illustrate how armor has devastated individual and social functioning and how humans must now cope with the consequences of this breakdown. The problems themselves, as exemplified by the case discussions, point the way toward solutions and show how a functional perspective can go far to help solve yet other questions. Because these symptoms are so deeply embedded, the improvement of social conditions will be difficult and take patient and persistent effort over many generations. One thing is certain: Any attempt at solving social problems without an understanding of the emotional plague is bound to fail.

The Emotional Plague versus Social Progress

By any conceivable objective measure, the past century in America was unparalleled in bringing about the greatest advances in human history.[115] Table 8.1 on page 315 depicts twenty-four social trends of the twentieth century.

According to the *Wall Street Journal*, real income has doubled since 1960. Some 70 percent of Americans now own their own homes, whereas that symbol of wealth was enjoyed by fewer than 20 percent a century ago. The average home size has doubled in a generation. People can expect to live twice as long as their forebears of 1900.[116] Clearly, according to these objective criteria, living conditions have dramatically improved during the last hundred years.

Yet as William Bennett points out,

> The nation we live in today is more violent and vulgar, coarse and cynical, rude and remorseless, deviant and depressed, than the one we once inhabited. A popular culture that is often brutal, gruesome, and enamored with death robs many children of their innocence. People kill other people, and themselves, more easily. Men and women abandon each other, and their children, more readily. Marriage and the American family are weaker, more unstable and less normative. (Bennett 1999, page 5)

To make sense of this contradiction between quantitative improvement and the qualitative decline of life it is necessary to distinguish between scientific and technological progress. Because of its mechanistic orientation, science is more or less at a dead-end as far as discovering fundamental knowledge about nature that can improve the quality of human life. According to the mechanistic paradigm of science, nature operates like a machine. Therefore, everything is already known at least in principle and Nobel prizes are given for new discoveries that conform to or are extensions of the all-embracing mechanistic world view, never to others that are outside of it. For this reason, Reich's

---

115. See Cato Institute Policy Analysis no. 364, Dec. 15, 1999.

116. *Wall Street Journal*, "The rich are getting richer, but so are others," Dec. 23, 2003.

Trend	Change from the Turn of the Century to Today
Health, Safety, and Population	
Lifespan	Increased 30 years
Infant mortality (per 1,000 live births)	Deaths decreased 93 percent
Infectious disease (deaths per 1,000)	Deaths decreased 14-fold
Heart disease (age-adjusted deaths per 100,000)	Deaths more than cut in half
Air pollution (lead, micrograms/100 cubic meters of air)	97 percent cleaner
U.S. residents	Increased 250 percent
Accidental deaths (per 100,000)	Decreased 61 percent
Wealth	
Per capita GDP (1998 dollars)	Almost 7 times higher
Manufacturing wage (1998 dollars)	Almost 4 times higher
Household assets (1998 dollars)	7 times greater
Poverty rate (percent of households)	Decreased 3 times
Homeownership (percent of households)	Increased 43 percent
Black income (annual per capita, 1997 dollars)	Increased 10-fold
Lifestyle/Quality of Life	
Length of work week	Decreased 30 percent
Number of workers in agriculture	Decreased 93 percent
TV ownership	Almost universal
Electrification (percentage of households)	Increased 10-fold
Telephone calls (annual per capita)	Increased 5,600 percent
Cars (percentage of U.S. households)	Increased 90-fold
Percent of adults completing high school	Increased 4-fold
Women with bachelor's degrees	Increased by half
Productivity and Inventions	
Wheat price (bushels per hours of work)	Decreased 95 percent
Computer speed (millions of instructions/second)	3 million percent faster
Patents granted	Increased 6-fold

Twenty-Four Social Trends of the Twentieth Century

TABLE 8.1

discoveries in natural science, as pivotal as they are to understanding and improving the quality of human life, could never be considered eligible for the recognition associated with a Nobel award.

Since nature is functional and not machine-like, science's mechanical paradigm necessarily limits its understanding of nature. Nevertheless, technological advances continue to abound because the material applications of mechanistic scientific knowledge are practically limitless. This explosion in technological progress, in the form of better television sets and automobiles, gives the illusion that mechanistic science is not at a standstill given its goal of bringing ever-increasing satisfaction for all people. This myth, in turn, perpetuates the illusion that mechanistic science is the answer and that genuine scientific advances will continue and ultimately bring about human happiness.

Although mechanistic science has indeed provided people with considerable material comfort and many conveniences, neither science nor religion has been able to prevent the downward spiral in the *quality* of personal and social life. The qualitative properties of social life are generally included under culture. Mechanistic science is not interested in these qualitative aspects since its primary strength is in its ability to quantify. Quality of human life is relegated to the mystics who are as ill-prepared to deal with it as are the mechanists.

Unfortunately, quality does not necessarily follow from quantity. Bigger and more does not necessarily mean better. This reality is the opposite of the popular misconception that drives today's Western culture and which permeates every area of social life. In our anti-authoritarian and mechanistically oriented society, the importance of the qualitative properties of life has been consistently negated. Most telling is the lack of understanding of the *qualitative* differences between the healthy sexual functioning of the unarmored individual and the disturbed sexual functioning of armored people and the social consequences that these differences have on people's lives. A manifestation of this confusion is the scientific community's glaring ignorance of the orgasm function. (See Introduction and Orientation)

The reasons underlying the declining quality of life are complex and poorly understood by liberals and conservatives alike.

But this lack of knowledge does not deter liberals, pseudo-liberals, and other peddlers of freedom and happiness from concocting make-shift solutions of all varieties while relentlessly attacking American traditions.

Socialism is an application of mechanistic thinking to sociology. Typically, "the rich," "greedy capitalists," and the free market are blamed as the source of social problems. Through well-disguised socialist programs and nostrums, the left promises a better, more just and equal society, and exhorts all to join in the march toward social progress with equality for all. To be sure, the freedom, wealth, and power they promise to redistribute are not put forth as an end in itself but rather as a means to attain greater happiness. Their promises are illusory. What inevitably happens is that wealth and power is expropriated from individuals and become collectivized, further degrading the quality of social conditions. In point of fact, they cannot provide the concrete measures needed for achieving real freedom nor are they capable of doing the actual work necessary to effect genuine social improvement. They are not interested in knowing that redistributing wealth is not an answer but only aggravates social problems. Nor are they capable of seeing that before there can be real improvement in social conditions there first have to be *qualitative* changes in the way people function, particularly in their work and their sexual lives, and that this consideration goes to the heart of their emotional well-being.

In contrast, conservatives are acutely aware of and bemoan the decline in the quality of social conditions, but, aside from blaming the left, they too are unable to understand its origin and are helpless to do anything about it. With functional thinking one can understand that this degradation rapidly accelerated at the time of the transformation of society from authoritarian to anti-authoritarian when destructive impulses from the secondary layer broke through in full force.

What is not recognized by everyone is that the emotional plague stands as the principle reason for the contradiction between quantity and quality of life in America today, between material betterment on the one hand and the decline in contactful gratification experienced in emotional life and in culture on the other. The emotional plague has always been the underlying cause of social deterioration and the greatest impediment to genuine social progress.

As Reich wrote, *"Century after century, the forces of any freedom movement, truthfulness and objectivity, failed to prevail against the effects of the emotional plague. Consequently, no freedom movement has any chance of success unless it opposes the organized emotional plague with truthfulness, and does it clearly and vigorously."* (Reich 1949a, pages 253–54; italics added)

The following sociological case studies are presented to illustrate how the emotional plague's destructiveness is operative in the social afflictions of modern society.

September 11, 2001: The Global Breakthrough of the Emotional Plague as Black Fascism[117]

When a core impulse seeking expression is blocked by armor, it loses its natural, healthy quality and becomes distorted, often violent. Most emotional plague attacks focus on a single individual. Less often, the assault targets a group. Rarely, the outbreak is pandemic. Such an eruption occurred on September 11, 2001 when a highly trained and organized group of Islamic Black Fascists hijacked four American commercial airplanes. Two flew into and demolished the World Trade Center in New York City, one damaged the Pentagon, and another went down in western Pennsylvania.[118] Although the target of the attack was America and the American people, in reality, the attack directly or indirectly involved every nation on Earth.

The nature of the attack is shrouded in confusion. For one thing, it is difficult to pinpoint the onset of the conflict. It has

117. As stated above, "Black Fascism" means fascism on the right, as opposed to "Red Fascism" which is fascism on the left. These terms do not refer to any race, nation, or ethnic group.

118. The emotional plague is more inclusive than terrorism. In the war between the United States and the Islamic fanatics, for example, the emotional plague includes not only terrorist groups, but also individuals and countries that harbor and support terrorism. The list of those who lend their support to the emotional plague extends to life-inimical social institutions (Islamic religious schools that teach Arab children to hate America), Islamic governments that directly and indirectly support terrorism, criminal organizations (drug cartels that finance them), the media that creates confusion, as well as the ongoing destructive acts of the innumerable "little men" throughout the world who simply hate America for whatever reason, and, like the terrorists, want to bring about its destruction. Without an understanding of the emotional plague, it is not possible to fully make sense of terrorism.

been argued that it started with the 1979 Iran hostage crisis, the bombing of the World Trade Center in 1993, the bombing of the U.S. embassies in Africa in 1998, or the U.S.S. Cole incident in 2000. For another, there is uncertainty in some quarters whether or not America is even engaged in an actual war. For these people, simply pulling American troops out of military engagements against terrorists groups would somehow end the hostilities. Lastly, why did the attack against America occur in the first place?

Why America Is Hated

Why did the 9/11 fanatics, who knew none of the people they killed, go to such enormous lengths to commit these heinous acts? To say they hate America and that it threatens their religious beliefs or that they envy the wealth and success of Americans is not sufficient to explain the consuming hatred they harbored. Who are these fanatics and why do they terrorize? Why are they attracted to fundamentalist religion and wherein lies the enormous power of fundamentalism? Are the attackers limited in number and what is their relationship to the rest of the Arab population? Why did they attack America at this time? Conventional thinking cannot provide answers to these questions. *There is no way to effectively answer these questions according to classical psychiatric, political, or social thought. They can only be understood with the knowledge of orgonomic biopsychiatry as an outbreak of the emotional plague on a global scale.*

Without an understanding of the existence and operation of the emotional plague it is impossible to comprehend why America is the object of Islamic fanatic hatred. The relationship between the emotional plague and unfettered life is one of attractive opposition. As long as America is perceived by the world as a symbol of freedom and liberty, the plague must act to destroy it. *America always has been and will always be the primary target of the emotional plague no matter whether it originates from the political right or the left.*

The prevailing idea that murder and other forms of destructive human behavior must be understood from a rational perspective is a serious limitation in current sociological thinking. A criminal act without a motive is considered a "senseless crime" because it defies rational understanding. From this perspective, terrorist acts are senseless crimes because there is no rational explanation for the hatred that terrorists feel toward America and the Free World. Moreover, psychological explanations for the hatred are not sufficient. This is because the emotional *source* driving the criminal behavior originates from the enormous reservoir of pent-up hatred contained in the destructive secondary layer which is from a *deeper, more inclusive biological realm* than the psychological. (See Introduction and Orientation) This is why the psychological approach is useless in understanding and dealing with terrorists and other murderers. Invoking psychology only further obscures the problem of the source of human destructiveness. According to Paul Mathews, a contributing author to the *Journal of Orgonomy*:

> Terrorism is triggered by the rationalizing of the secondary layer so that an individual overrides traditional inhibitions and thus acts out the most monstrous and unprincipled atrocities. These atrocities are typically directed against defenseless, unarmed civilians either as "lessons" to others or in reprisal against a decency which the emotional plague cannot tolerate. Those who design and direct these acts of terror are fully aware of the mechanisms they set in motion, even though they themselves may be incapable of the actual physical act of terror.[119]

A central characteristic of the emotional plague is that the stated reasons justifying its destructive actions are never the real reasons. Some of these alleged explanations for 9/11 are the following: outrage over Western social, political, economic, and military dominance in the world; indignation over U.S. support of Israel; the sense of grievance for the perceived humiliation of the Islamic people at the hands of the West; and the decadence of Western society. Although their hatred in some part was precipitated by fears of Western influence in the Islamic world and the perception of Western society as debauched and immoral, these reasons were not the motive behind their antipathy. Such explanations could have given rise to animosity and irritation toward the West, but not to

119. Matthews, Paul. 1982. On Terrorism. *Journal of Orgonomy* 16 (2): 237.

blind, enduring hatred leading to mass murder.

According to Islamic fundamentalism, Islamic countries are the motherland of the human race and the Islamic people are fighting a holy war against the infidels, against corrupt Western civilization. The *alleged reason* is to reunite warring humanity into one universal family in which each nation takes its proper place under the divine sovereignty of Allah's appointed minister on earth. "Islam" is the Arabic word meaning "submission to God's will," and since a Muslim is "one who submits," individuals are not responsible for determining their life. Everything that happens is Allah's will. Infidels, that is, non-Muslims, are inferior beings who must be made to submit to Allah. This highly mystical ideology and its religious text provide the rationale for and conceal the *true unstated reason*: violent Islamic expansionism and justification for every sort of atrocity in pursuit of *jihad*, or holy war.

In Islam, *jihad* is a religious obligation. It is not simply a "spiritual war" but a real military war of conquest. It is necessary to release the enormous amount of sadism that is barely contained in the secondary layer of Islamists. According to Islam, the world is divided into only two regions: the "domain of Islam" and the "domain of war." *Jihad* forms part of the duties that the true believer must fulfill. It is Islam's normal path to expansion. Those who practice it are above the law of any nation. They have no borders and have no qualms about murdering ordinary citizens. In short, *jihad is an undisguised example of the institutionalization of the emotional plague on a global scale.*

The Koran is a collection of Muhammed's sermons, some of which provide justification for the hateful vengeances. Much of the book is replete with commandments sanctioning secondary layer behavior such as "fight and slay the pagans wherever you find them . . . those who reject our signs we shall soon cast into the fire . . . those who disbelieve, garments of fire will be cut out for them: boiling fluid will be poured down on their heads . . . as to the deviator, they are the fuel of hell." Thus, according to Osama bin Ladin: "Being killed for Allah's cause is a great honor achieved by only those who are the elite of the nation. We love this kind of death for Allah's cause as much as you like to live.

We have nothing to fear. It is something we wish for."[120] "Our work targets world infidels. Our enemy is the Crusader alliance led by America, Britain, and Israel. It is a Crusader-Jewish alliance."[121] To kill the infidel is to fulfill Allah's cause as "submission to the will of God." Thus, murder in the name of God is permitted by God.

This grandiose ranting justifying a death wish is only understandable from a functional perspective. The wish to die for Allah's cause arises out of a masochistic desire, one that seeks death (relief of inner tension) through bursting. Thus, a sadistic act becomes the way to discharge a masochistic wish. This is the only way that one who has been so crippled by armor can surrender to preorgastic feelings and it becomes a literal, actual truth for the individual suicide bomber or terrorist.

However, none of the arguments put forth in defense of *jihad* can account for the persistence and intensity of the Islamic fanatic's hatred. The real reason that they as an organized group are driven to destroy America is their *absolute intolerance of free-flowing, life-positive impulses originating from their biological core.* Despite its many flaws and imperfections, America still inspires the hope of humanity's core impulses throughout the world: the principles of freedom, responsibility, independence, honesty, decency, fairness, generosity, and tolerance of others. These impulses trigger envy and hatred in the pestilent individual who is incapable of experiencing pleasure, blocked as he is from contact with these core impulses. Therefore, America and all that it represents creates an *intolerable*, viscerally-felt longing leading to murderous rage. *This is the root cause and driving force in every Islamic fanatic afflicted with the emotional plague.* Pleasurable longing not experienced and expressed turns inward into self-hatred, which, sooner or later, is then projected outward as *destructive hatred directed against the source of emotional excitation.* Like the serial killer on the national scene, the sex-starved terrorist operating internationally *must* kill freedom-loving Americans and destroy Western ways of life to stop feelings of unbearable longing that torture him to the point of bursting. To accomplish this, the sex-starved fanatic is actively aggres-

120. From a CNN interview, 1997.
121. From a *TIME Magazine* interview, 1998.

sive and, with fantasies of young virgins gifted to him by Allah that are waiting for him in heaven, believes in the certainty of success.

The reason that the attack occurred at the particular period that it did was significant. At this time the social decline and cultural degeneration in America was perceived as a sign of weakness and vulnerability. One of the sites chosen for terrorist destruction was the World Trade Center, the pride and symbol of America's success. Another was the Pentagon. Their goal was, and is, to attack America militarily and destroy the economic system that sustains the lives of hundreds of millions of people. If successful they will paralyze the work function of millions of Americans.

Identifying the Pathogenic Agents

To combat an infectious disease it is mandatory to precisely identify the infectious agent (bacteria or virus), and understand its metabolism, life cycle, pathophysiology and so on. Similarly, to contain and counter an emotional plague attack, it is essential to identify the particular pestilent characters involved, their particular sociopolitical character type (whether they belong on the left or the right), and their mode of operation. It is equally important to understand the specific *relationship that always exists* between the pestilent leader and the fanatic followers.[122]

Leaders come and go, and the elimination of a particular despot, say a bin Laden, only results in replacement by another. On the other hand, the mystical masses require a leader, one who has a high degree of charisma, single-mindedness, and the cleverness to excite them into action. Because they have been crippled emotionally, the masses are essentially helpless, with little or no ability to improve life on their own. This is why they require the excitation of charismatic leaders. Given their plight, they seek relief by mystically and totally placing their hope for a better life in their leaders. The relationship between the Islamic fanatics and their leader is one of simple attractive opposition (Fig. 8.1).

122. The type of relationship between the masses and their leaders is a good indication of the health of any social system.

Masses of Islamic Fanatics →∫← **Fanatic Islamic Leaders**

FIGURE 8.1

The Islamic cult leader can take hold of the mob only if they are willing to identify with, be taken care of, and be led by him. This is so especially in the lower socioeconomic strata of Muslims where religious fixation and authoritarian fixation are identical. The people fall under the leader's sway and develop an emotional attachment to him to the extent that he personifies the religious movement that embodies their mystical feeling. If the leader understands how to arouse a sense of family attachment he also becomes a benevolent authoritarian father figure. He becomes the object of the emotional attachment that the follower, as a child, once had toward the protecting father. The followers believe the cult leader knows everything, much more so than they, and that he "can do it all." This blind trust in the pursuit of protection indeed gives the cult leader the power to do it all and, at the same time, to direct the mass individual to do his bidding.

The more helpless individuals are made by their upbringing, the more strongly they will identify with the cult leader. This identification is the basis of religious narcissism; that is, of self-confidence based on virtually total identification with the *greatness of the religious movement.* It is this identification that allows people to feel and believe that they are defenders of the true religion. Their personal misery and insignificance are drowned out by mystical identification with the great leader. Such individuals constitute the masses of fundamentalist fanatic youths who are prepared and willing to die to do the bidding of the cult leader.[123]

The Anchoring of Mysticism in the Masses

Mysticism in the character structure of the leader but more so in the masses is essential for the acceptance of any Black Fascist ideology. An understanding of Islamic Black Fascism is impossible without knowing its energy source and how mysticism becomes anchored in the individual.

---

123. The deaths of over 3,000 Americans on September 11, 2001 was cause for some Palestinians to dance in the streets, although media coverage of their rejoicing was suppressed.

In the unarmored individual, ideas and feelings about God and sexuality are closely related. This identity is based on undistorted core contact. In primitive religions, religiosity and sexuality are identical: There is no antithesis between the two states of feeling. When society armored, religion became dissociated from and antithetical to sexuality (Reich 1946, page 125). Sexual feelings became repressed and opposed by religious feelings. Once they were separated, religious excitation was distorted into mysticism and assumed the function of a substitute for lost sexual pleasure, a natural, healthy pleasure no longer affirmed by society. *The energy source of religious fervor is repressed sexual excitation.*[124] The structure of the mystical individual is described by Reich as follows:

> Biologically, he is subject to states of sexual tension like any other living being. But, through the assimilation of the sex-negating religious ideas in general and the fear of punishment in particular, he has lost all capacity for natural sexual excitation and gratification. As a result, he suffers from a chronic state of excessive somatic excitation which he is constantly forced to master. Happiness in this world is not only unattainable for him, but it does not even seem desirable to him. Since he expects happiness in the hereafter, he develops a feeling of being incapable of happiness in this world. But, being a biological organism and thus unable to renounce happiness, relaxation and satisfaction, there is only one thing left for him to do: to seek the illusory happiness provided by the religious fore-pleasure excitations, the well-known vegetative currents and excitations in the body.
>
> (Reich 1946, page 125)

The source of the Christian idea of original sin, for example, has its roots in the repression of pleasurable sexual feelings. All forms of mystical experience are based on distorted perceptions of sexual excitation, and sex-negative, moralistic attitudes have made full, natural sexual pleasure unattainable. People must then seek substitute measures for gratification.

---

124. A distinction must be made between religious feeling and mystical feeling. Not all religious experiences are mystical and not all mystical experiences are religious. In the case of fundamentalism, however, religious feelings are mystical.

The major Islamic currents, with their divergent religious views, fall in varying degrees to the right on the sociopolitical spectrum. Proceeding from the center right to the extreme right corresponds to an increase in mysticism.

The fundamentalist Islamic religion and its social institutions are authoritarian and the degree of mysticism, sexual frustration and repression is more severe than any of the orthodox sects of Judeo-Christian societies; hence, the fundamentalist's greater capacity for brutality and violence. In fundamentalist-dominated Islamic societies, men and women do not demonstrate affection in public, nor can they be alone together unless married. However, men are permitted to kiss and hold hands with each other anywhere. Sexual feelings are discharged through the mystical practice of prayer and discussion of Islamic ideology.

Relations between the sexes are not a matter of choice in Islamic societies. Women are unable to make their own life choices and are far from being on an equal footing with men. Throughout the Muslim Middle East, the inferior status of women is integrally bound up with custom and religion. The segregation of boys and girls begins soon after birth. Islamic custom dictates the wearing of the veil and the seclusion of women. Boys are regarded from birth as a capital investment, in the words of the Egyptian sociologist Hammad Ammar, while girls are the fountainhead of shame, valued only because, in due course, they will develop into producers of boys and more capital. Marriage by arrangement and consent of the parents of the prospective bride and groom is required. The choice of the marriage partner is not based on biological attraction and compatibility, but is instead subordinated to the economic and social interests of the families of both parties. The Muslim family is in the hands of an undisputed autocrat, the father, who judges himself fit to assess and extend the collective interest. This relationship is as true of the state as it is of the family. The ruler of the state is viewed as the father of all its members.

Sexual inhibitions and fears in the Muslim masses are the inevitable consequences of the all-pervasive, sex-negative attitudes and restrictive social customs found in Muslim societies. To manage fears of sexual inadequacy and impotence and to provide a substitute feeling of virility, Muslim practice allows "temporary marriage" wherein a man can take a wife for a brief period fixed by contract. He may also practice outright polygamy. (Price-Jones 2002, page 124)

The social consequence of this sexual repression speaks for itself. With the exception of Turkey and Bangladesh, there are no real elections in any Muslim country. Punishment for transgressions of extremist Islamic law is meted out not only by God (as in Judeo-Christianity), but also physically by "protectors" of the state. The latter is a more effective method of repression and instilling on-going terror than awaiting punishment by God in the next world. Two-thirds of the world's political prisoners are held in Muslim countries, which carry out eighty percent of all executions world-wide each year. It can be seen that the capacity to produce terror and armor by fundamentalist Islam is more effective and more incapacitating than any of the Judeo-Christian religions. It is therefore not surprising that acts of terrorism are prevalent among Islamic youth living in fundamentalist nations.

Fanatics, of course, belong to both extremes of the political spectrum—these plague characters are either Black or Red Fascists. People belonging to the fundamentalist religions are on the extreme right, and the further they are to the right, the greater is their sexual repression. Consequently, their mysticism and expression of sadism and brutality is also greater, as evidenced by sex-negative laws and the tendency to engage in religious wars. Islamic fundamentalists are characterologically Black Fascists, and are even further to the right on the sociopolitical spectrum than the most orthodox sects of Judeo-Christianity.[125] Those familiar with school textbooks in most Muslim countries know the twisted view of the world they propagate and the hatred they espouse and promote. Undisguised expressions of the emotional plague, fundamentalists' statements in the media, editorials, articles on the Internet and their sermons in virtually every mosque, including many in the West, are vehemently anti-Western, especially anti-American.[126]

---

125. Most Arab leaders throughout the Middle East were Nazi sympathizers before and during World War II (Price-Jones, page 184).

126. Amir Taheri, "Islam Can't Escape Blame for September 11th," *Wall Street Journal*, Oct. 24, 2001.

The Characterological Basis of Fanaticism

Because Islamic fanatics are Black Fascists, their hatred is held primarily in their muscular armor and not in their intellect. Their intellectual defenses are in the service of rationalizing their hatred and are not as well concealed as in the case of the Red Fascist or communist. For this reason, the irrationalism and destructiveness of Black Fascist ideology is relatively easy to detect. Nevertheless, there is enormous *emotional* power and conviction behind their mystical thinking and actions.

Maintaining racial purity is the foundation of all Black Fascist ideology, including Nazism and Islamic fundamentalism. Race-mingling is viewed as a decline of the "pure race" and of culture. Maintaining racial and cultural purity and spreading Islam throughout the world are central functions of all Muslim fanatics. Muslim fundamentalists see the Islamic world as a monolith and believe that the entire Islamic community should oppose racial contamination from the debased and "inferior" non-Muslim world.

Black Fascism thus combines reactionary (racist) ideology with rebellious emotions. This form of the emotional plague is highly contagious, especially among mystical Islamic youth on the extreme right. Mixing with foreign races is equated with permitting sexual intercourse with those who are racially impure. The ideology of racial and cultural purity is their rationale for maintaining sexual repression.

As stated earlier, unexpressed sexual feelings, the result of the inhibition of natural sexual impulses, is the cause of all sadistic and cruel behavior. The degree of mystical feelings exactly corresponds to the degree of disturbance in the capacity for healthy sexual gratification. As a result of this inhibition there is a constant longing for some form of substitute mystical gratification. This is accompanied by physical sensations of tension in the solar plexus region of the biological core. Since this tension cannot be released sexually, it turns either into masochism with the desire to burst or into sadism that can lead to violent, explosive behavior. Terrorism, the chosen method of the September 11 attack—blowing oneself up with a plane full of people—bespeaks the desire to physically explode. The emotional plague character must destroy the pleasure of others that he himself cannot enjoy.

Like Hitler, all Black Fascists are *repressed ocular characters*. Thus, diagnostically, they belong to the paranoid schizophrenic character type but with a pronounced psychopathic component. They have displaced their paranoid delusional system from their personal lives onto the sociopolitical arena. In their delusional system, Islam is believed to be under siege by the corrupt West, particularly the United States. America's "oppression" of Islam is the alleged reason given to justify their hatred and why they want to destroy the United States.

The *time* of the anchoring of anti-sexual religious ideas in the individual is a crucial factor. The earlier in childhood this indoctrination is carried out, the more likely it is to manifest itself in some way in the young adult.[127] Those indoctrinated in Islamic ideology are taught to view other cultures, particularly those of the West, with suspicion, fear, and hostility. By inducing ocular armor in this way, innocent Muslim children are trained to hate everything that is foreign to what they have been taught. In short, Black Fascist Islamic fundamentalists are being bred to become instruments of destruction. Fueled by their paranoid, mystical ideology, they are programmed to act out their delusional hatred in the real world. Their paranoid thinking provides them with a well-organized and shared, albeit very distorted, perception of reality that usually protects them from becoming overtly psychotic.

The vast majority of the Muslim population living in Islamic countries has undergone severe sexual repression. Added to this, cultural factors intensify preexisting ocular repression and produce greater degrees of mysticism. The custom of women wearing veils is designed to discourage men and women from looking at each other in social situations and to prevent any sexual excitation between them. Muslim boys and girls are kept separate from an early age and males are taught from early childhood not to look at women for fear of becoming sexually aroused. When Islamic males look at women, they usually do so furtively. Even the veil's degree of visual obstruction corresponds to the degree of

---

127. Throughout the Islamic world, "religious" schools, the madrassas, require young boys to memorize the Koran by rote. They are taken away from their families, prevented from having contact with the opposite sex, and indoctrinated to believe that Islam is under attack, and must be defended with one's life.

sexual repression imposed by the particular Islamic culture. In Afghanistan, for example, the very extremist Taliban government required women to wear a full-hooded veil that allowed them to see only through a screened area in front of their eyes (Esposito 1999). Women are permitted very little if any pleasure in life. They cannot sing or dance. They cannot travel alone.

Another factor in the service of ocular repression is the practice of mystical education. Teaching children to accept mystical ideas effectively discourages them from using their eyes, to avoid relying on their own observations, and to become subservient, obedient listeners to the irrational ideas of authoritarian figures.[128] In the absence of a natural way to discharge sexual energy, tension builds, and this leads to nonsexual forms of discharge such as mystical experiences centered on Islam. As such, the religious schools in Islamic countries such as Pakistan and Saudi Arabia not only inculcate Islamic ideology, but they are also the early training ground for future young murderers.

The origin of the fanatics' hatred lies in the mystical elements of the Islamic religion itself. Fundamentalist Islamists also condemn Western culture, which is depicted as hedonistic and morally depraved, composed of dysfunctional families, sexual immorality, drug addicts, meaningless lives, and psychological disorders (Esposito 1999, page 620). All of these alleged "reasons" for their hatred have some truth, *but they are used to cover up the real reason*—the terror of experiencing their own pleasurable genital feelings and their fear of the possibility of freedom that Western life offers. The full fury of both fear and hatred lie just beneath the surface and are why many Muslims become terrorists.

The Emotional Plague and the Attack on America

The conditions leading up to the attack of September 11, 2001 were first set in motion in 1979, when the Soviet Union invaded Afghanistan, turning it into a no man's land that became a fertile breeding ground for Islamic fundamentalists and later for terrorists. Washington, in response, aided Afghan resistance to the Soviets by giving billions of dollars to the opposition fighters. When the Soviets were defeated and withdrew from Afghanistan

128. "Mysticism" is derived from the Greek word *myein*, "to close the eyes."

in 1989, the opposition forces, no longer united by a common enemy, turned on each other, and the country descended into anarchy. The United States and other Western governments did little to aid in rebuilding civil institutions and militant Muslims eagerly stepped in. In 1994, a band of militant students, the Taliban, launched a campaign to restore social stability and order. They established a ruthless Islamic state and instituted a reign of terror. Initially hailed as liberators who secured towns, made the streets safe, and cleaned up corruption and graft, the Taliban and their strict form of Islamic law soon became a source of world-wide concern. They subscribe to a radical, puritanical interpretation of Islam carried out through a policy of strict sexual suppression. They segregated the sexes outside the home, closed girls' schools, required that women be fully covered and veiled in public, and barred them from the workplace. They also banned television, cinema, and music and ordered men to grow beards and obey Muslim religious law by, for example, praying five times a day. They introduced hudud punishment; that is, punishment for certain crimes as prescribed by strict Islamic law. This includes limb amputation for theft, death for murder, and stoning to death for adultery. The social suppression was a double-edged sword. It promoted social order and stability, but it also heightened sexual tension.

This energy, which had no natural outlet, needed only the triggering effect of a highly mystical, hate-mongering fanatic, Osama bin Ladin, to arouse the masses of Arab youth, themselves the product of repressive upbringings in Saudi Arabia, Iraq, and elsewhere, to wage a "holy war" on the infidels.

Like the Taliban militants, bin Ladin is an emotional plague character of the Black Fascist variety. His association with the Taliban, who treated him as an honored guest for his support in defeating the Soviets, was based on the similarity of their character structure. Bin Ladin was active in fighting the Afghan war against the Soviets because he saw them as a rival for the world domination they both sought and because he viewed them as a threat to his religious world order. With the defeat of the Soviets, bin Ladin redirected his hatred toward America.[129]

129. Long before the tragic events of September 11, 2001, it was possible to predict from bin Ladin's behavior that he was an emotional plague character capable of doing serious damage to this country. However, but decisive action to prevent terrorism was not taken.

Osama bin Ladin's desired goal is to unite the Arab world by provoking America to retaliate against Islamic states thereby bringing together Muslims everywhere against the West under the fundamentalist banner. He rationalizes and hides his murderous hatred of unfettered human life and his grandiose scheme for domination of the Arab world with a pious façade and by invoking the mystical cause that he is maintaining his own purity, that of the Islamic holy land, as well as the purity of his race. Because he is a fanatic, he stops at nothing to achieve his ends and eliminates all whom he perceives as a threat. Sadism, brutality, and cunning are the rule. His object, rationalized as a pious duty, is to destroy all races and religious sects other than his own through terror. His strategy is to fragment the Free World in its fight for survival and he does this by exploiting the fear of someone in the West of an aggressive response to terror.

Like all biological systems, societies pulsate: they expand and contract. American society prior to the onset of the war on terrorism was in a state of chronic over-expansion. The peripheral functions of society, especially pleasurable social activity and economic productivity, predominated over central functions, such as local and national defense and intelligence gathering. To the Islamic fanatics, America appeared contemptibly weak, morally bankrupt, riven by political and social polarization, and vulnerable at all levels of social life. Seriously misjudging the situation, the fanatics believed they were in a position to begin the destruction of the United States.

Also, the state of chronic over-expansion helped to bring about the dissociation of many social components. In America, this was the age of the individual, and, as such, people were increasingly at variance with each other. These factors combined to cause cultural disunity and an increase in sociopolitical polarization of the left and the right. The components of American society were now related to each other as variations of antagonistic opposition, antithetical functions that exclude each other. This can be written orgonometrically, where A1 and A2 represent any two social components (Fig. 8.2):

FIGURE 8.2

As a result of this situation, in the United States as well as internationally, the military was seriously compromised in its ability to deal with the provocative acts of terror by Islamic fundamentalists. Understandably, the United States' failure to take a strong stand only reinforced Muslim contempt and confidence.

After the attack of September 11, the United States declared war on terrorists and American society went into a state of acute contraction. *This state of social contraction in response to the attack was vitally necessary for America's survival.* For a brief time, contraction predominated over expansion. Functions related to the center of the social system (the federal government), such as national defense and intelligence gathering, predominated over peripheral social functions. Nations brave enough to oppose the Islamic threat joined America in the fight against international terrorism.

Militarily, with active engagement, the relationship between the United States and the Islamic fundamentalists changed from antagonistic opposition to attractive opposition—that is, to antithetical functions that attract each other (Fig. 8.3):

Free World →(← **International Terrorists**

FIGURE 8.3

However, because of people's emotional sickness, the state of chronic contraction could not be sustained. Most people in America today are not capable of recognizing that the Free World is in a life and death battle for its very survival. There is no question that the Islamic fanatics will regroup and strike again in an even more deadly way. There is no walking away from this war. There is only one way to wage it—head on with overwhelming force.

The Political Enemy Within

The ideology of Islamic fundamentalism can succeed, in the long run, only if it is concordant with the biophysical structure of the average individual in the West. Unfortunately, the political left has greatly hampered the extent of social contraction needed to most effectively mobilize the Free World's defenses socially and militarily against the Islamic fanatics. The liberal character is *biophysically incapable* of the required sustained contraction and, consequently, unable to mobilize sufficient, effective aggression. To make matters even worse, he continues on a daily basis to politically undermine the U.S. war effort by being in league with the pseudo-liberal plague individual. (See chapter 2, the discussion in the section Sociopolitical Characters on the Left)

In the ongoing war against America, the greatest danger comes from the combined effort of groups at the extremes of the sociopolitical spectrum: the Black Fascists (Islamic fundamentalists) on the right and the Red Fascists (pseudo-liberals/communists) with the active support of liberals on the left. Black Fascist terrorists rationalize their hatred and behavior to their fellow Islamic fundamentalists so well that it is accepted as right and necessary for the common good. Their effectiveness is enhanced when they ignite the latent hatred (guilt) of pseudo-liberals throughout the world against America and its war effort. Although the pseudo-liberal and the Black Fascist are at opposite ends of the sociopolitical spectrum, they nonetheless have commonality: Both are emotional plague characters and, despite different reasons, they join forces and support each other in their goal to destroy life in their own countries and also all that America stands for.[130] Without knowledge of the operation of the emotional plague, the active political attraction of individuals who appear to have diametrically opposite ideologies makes no sense.

Because liberals are unable to employ forceful aggression, they take part in trying to bring about America's destruction by colluding with the pseudo-liberal and actively and passively mobilizing "resistance" against America, its allies in the Arab world, and beyond. They are quick to find any fault with American life that can be used to justify moral equivalence between the Islamic fanatics and the United States. This is a form of moral masochism which, in effect, vindicates terrorist atrocities against the West. Because their contact with the biological core is weak or totally absent, such liberals have no strong allegiance to what America stands for, nor can they sense in their gut the enemy's threat and the destructiveness of the emotional plague. Together

---

130. A recent illustration is the alliance being formed between Red Fascist Venezuelan President Hugo Chavez and Black Fascist Iranian President Mahmoud Ahmadinejad, with the blessings of leftist American Senator Chris Dodd and leftist U.S. Congressman Bill Delahunt. See *Wall Street Journal*, "Hugo and Mahmoud," Jan. 17, 2007.

with the pseudo-liberal, their fault-finding with America creates the illusion that both sides have a legitimate point in the conflict. If only America would stop its aggression against the Islamic terrorists, there would then be an end to terrorism and peace on Earth.

While Islamic fundamentalists teach Arab children to admire the so-called "martyrs" and to hate America—Muslim children are told that "dinosaurs were created by Americans to kill Muslims"—many liberal and pseudo-liberal American high school teachers and college professors submit masochistically and tell their students to "understand" why Islamic fundamentalists hate America.

Contrary to popular belief, masochism does not mean the enjoyment of pain. Rather, it is a specific way of functioning that mires a person in a state of chronic suffering. Masochistic behavior develops because the individual cannot feel true anger from the biological core or tolerate healthy aggression.[131]

Dr. Robert Harman has summarized the prominent applicable features of masochism in the social realm:[132]

> Such individuals blame themselves and attempt to appease the attacker, believing that if they are nice enough, the attacker will "understand" and stop. They believe that any proposed solution other than appeasement will lead to disastrous consequences. As a projection of their own inadequacies, they think that any attempt at aggressive defense will be clumsy, stupid, awkward, and doomed to failure . . .
>
> All of these features result from the inability to express aggression. In the masochistic character this incapacity comes from an inability to expand (i.e., to experience pleasure) and blocks all aggressive expression except complaining and spite. The liberal does not suffer from a general state of masochism, but is prone to react masochistically in certain situations, particularly one where authority must be exerted. Because of a tendency to retreat from the body into the head, the liberal's

131. Masochistic symptoms occur both in the individual's personal life as well as in his sociopolitical ideology. The "battered wife" syndrome is a common example of masochism seen in everyday clinical practice.

132. Robert Harman, M.D. 2001. Responding to Terrorism in the Twenty-first Century. *Journal of Orgonomy* 35 (2).

> masochistic reaction is especially strong when the situation requires the exertion of physical force, because the impulse to use physical force comes from deep inside the body. Thus, when his nation is attacked, the liberal is at risk for having the following masochistic reaction:
>
> - He will criticize and blame his own nation.
> - He will develop a guilt-ridden or anxious desire to "solve" the problem by being nicer to those who hate or dislike his country.
> - He will elaborate varied disaster scenarios that he fears will occur if force is used aggressively. Usually the imagined disaster is a variation of "it will only make them hate us even more" or a feared dramatic escalation of violence, which we will not have the will or the strength (so the liberal believes) to handle: "Violence only leads to more violence."
> - He fears that his nation and its leaders (especially if they are not liberals) are stupid and clumsy, and will insist on half-hearted responses which, if they are accepted, actually will be clumsy and ineffective.
>
> This type of masochistic reaction only increases the terrorist's sadism, leading to new attacks which increase the masochistic response, and so on in a vicious cycle. The September 11th attacks were the culmination of a decade of a cycle of sadomasochistic interaction.

Harman concludes that "in the case of the Arab-Israeli conflict . . . the same masochistic dynamics are operative."

The moral sadism of the Islamo-Fascist causes many liberals to feel unconscious sexual excitement in a moral masochistic way. Thus, the liberal masochistically submits to the sadistic Islamo-Fascist. The relationship between the masochistic liberal and the sadistic Islamo-Fascist is one of attractive opposition (Fig. 8.4):

Masochistic Liberal → ← **Sadistic Islamo-Fascist**

FIGURE 8.4

At the same time, the American pseudo-liberal (Red Fascist) harbors covert hatred toward America that is matched only by the overt hatred expressed of the Islamic fanatic (Black Fascist) (Fig. 8.5)[133]:

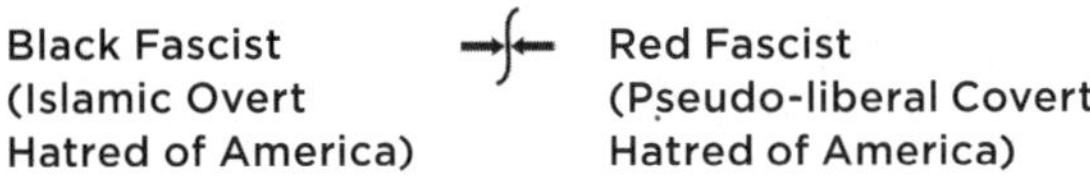

FIGURE 8.5

This equation shows how the extreme left (Red Fascist) and the extreme right (Black Fascist) both hate the biological core functions that America stands for and both function in the service of the emotional plague. Thus, the pseudo-liberal with the help of the politically naïve liberal operate together to level America.

The belief system or ideology of the American left is grounded in the premise that everyone has the right to express their personal point of view regardless of the consequences, and that one person's opinion is as valid as another's. In truth, however, the notion that all social issues are open to debate and that both sides have an equally legitimate point is a highly destructive illusion, one that threatens the well-being of society. It is seen as appeasement and weakness by emotional plague individuals and regarded with contempt. In the battle against the Islamo-Fascist, for example, the American left believe that Hezbollah's cause and that of the other terrorist organizations arrayed against Israel is as legitimate as Israel's. In past wars (except in the case of the Vietnam War), such extreme egalitarian views were not tolerated because the majority of people were in better contact with themselves and, as a result, their survival instincts were more intact. The majority of individuals raised in the past authoritarian era would have had little

133. Many Islamic Black Fascists started out as Red Fascists when it suited their purpose of undermining and destroying stable Arab governments. This happened in Iran when the Shah was in power and in Egypt when Sadat ruled.

difficulty identifying the life-inimical nature of today's Islamic fanatics. Because of severe ocular armor, many people today who have shifted to the left are quite simply unable to recognize the mortal danger to the Free World posed by Islamo-Fascists.

Strongly influenced by the leftist media, an increasing number of people living in the Free World are being blinded to the reality that Arab fanatics with the help of misguided liberals use emotional plague tactics to their advantage as an ideological weapon in their war against America.

The alliance between the pestilence of the political left and the right is being consolidated world-wide at an alarming rate. In a July YouGov poll on the British view of America and Americans, 65 percent of respondents considered Americans "vulgar"; 72 percent think American society is unequal; 52 percent take a negative view of American culture; and 58 percent believe the U.S. is "an essentially imperial power, one that wants to dominate the world by one means or another." Only 12 percent of Britons still have confidence in U. S. leadership.[134] At an Islamic festival London's mayor, Mr. Livingstone, who is a left-wing politician and an Islamic activist declared: "Muslims and the left can come together because we face the same enemies—imperialism, colonialism and racism."[135]

Some of Hezbollah's strongest supporters are in Europe. There, the far left, demoralized by the collapse of Communism, has found new energy, siding with the Islamist militants in Lebanon, in Iraq, and in a wider campaign against what they see as America's influence throughout the world. One astute observer commented: "The sight of Godless Communists in alliance with Islamo-Fascists is one of the wonders of the modern world." This phenomenon is indeed baffling to anyone without knowledge of how the emotional plague organizes and operates.

For leftists, absolute good and evil do not exist. Since there is no good in America and there is no evil in the Islamic world, both worlds are equivalent and everything is relative. According to one Western Islamic expert, "A mass murderer [bin Ladin] seems

---

134. *Wall Street Journal*, "In Britain, the *Jihadi* Is Us," Sep. 5, 2006.

135. Andrew Higgens, "Anti-Americans On the March," *Wall Street Journal*, Dec. 9–10, 2006.

to be winning the fight for the hearts and minds of the Muslim world."[136] The author concludes, "If this public diplomacy debacle persists . . . the U.S. will 'win the battle but lose the war.'"

Consider as one example of the emotional plague the al Jazeera television station in Qatar. It has been the mouthpiece of al Qaeda and claims to have ten million viewers. The alleged platform of this network, accepted by most Western liberals, is that it allows free criticism of Arab leaders where other stations can not. It states that it is the only place where Arabs and Muslims, in general, can debate all issues. In fact, however, following the September 11 attack, al Jazeera's alleged policies changed and were highly biased and destructive to the West. The station never invited Muslims who supported a negotiated peace with Israel, or any who supported the U.S. action in Afghanistan, to speak on air. Although radical Islamists constitute a small, vocal minority in most Arab societies, the network disregarded this fact and gave the impression that all Arabs support radical Islam. In its talk shows it favored radical Islamists and held that the average Arab is deeply anti-Western and especially anti-American. Al Jazeera television skillfully created the impression that the West, particularly the United States, was the cause of all the Arabs' woes, including their own incompetent and corrupt regimes. In effect, the station acted as bin Ladin's private TV channel running documentaries that presented terrorists as heroes of Islam. Such programs were run repeatedly, far exceeding any journalistic justification. Thus, they created the impression, accepted by most leftists, that not only do Islamists dominate Arab politics, but they are also the only ones with a credible program of reform for societies badly in need of change.[137]

---

136. Albert R. Hunt, "An Accelerated Agenda for the Terrorism Threat," *Wall Street Journal*, Oct. 25, 2001.

137. See Amir Taheri, "Bin Ladin's Private TV Channel," *Wall Street Journal*, Dec.28, 2001. To counteract the distortions disseminated by the Islamic world and to expose the true motive of the Islamic fanatics, American broadcasting to the Islamic world must be greatly expanded and intensified as news, not as propaganda. Preposterous charges such as blaming the Israelis for September 11 should not go unanswered. Western news media must be made aware of, and prevented from, disseminating pro-fundamentalist propaganda in America and in other non-Islamic countries. This would not be an interdiction of the Constitution's First Amendment. This information is highly inflammatory, generates confusion and excites those on the political left to agitate for an end to America's defensive efforts. The war against the ideological component of the emotional plague attack against America must be waged as effectively as the military component.

Clarifying the Operation of the Emotional Plague

Jihad is defined as the struggle against the infidel in defense of Islam. Functionally, it is a holy war, *a legitimization of the use of religion in the service of expressing murderous hatred*, against non-Muslims. An undisguised manifestation of the emotional plague, *jihad* operates on two fronts, militarily and politically (ideologically). The goal of *jihad* is not only to oppose democratization of the Islamic world but to spread Islam across the globe. Its mode of operation is to mobilize Muslims throughout the world in every possible way to join in this crusade. Its strategy is to generate confusion, paralysis, and destruction in its wake wherever it can, in the non-Muslim world in general, and in America in particular.

Sanctioned by the Koran, taqiyya is defined as *deception in defense of Islam*. Jihadists, in their training manuals, are taught to *lie* in claiming there is no compulsion in religion, to *fabricate* tales about how their captors have mistreated them, to *conceal* their true mission against the infidels, and so on.

Military *jihad* is carried out in the brutal attacks against military and nonmilitary targets and making use of indoctrinated Muslim youth as weapons of mass destruction. Through intimidation and terrorist attacks, it is aimed at dividing the unity of the forces of the Western world that oppose Islamic fundamentalism. Having America's allies withdraw their support, the U.S. would be isolated politically, militarily, and economically. If successful in their objective, the entire non-Muslim world would then be mobilized against America and her efforts to democratize the Islamic world, becoming in effect and fact an agent of the emotional plague.

On the political front, the forces of *jihad* rely heavily on the support of leftists world-wide and, in particular, those in America, all of whom for whatever reason are opposed to and hate the principles of freedom that America represents. In truth, America is the only viable obstacle to the Islamist's goal of world domination, just as it was the only credible opponent to global Soviet expansion. Significantly, the left has been effective in undermining and crippling America's efforts in combating both of these scourges.

The primary goal of Islamic *jihad* is to destroy America. A major step in the terrorist campaign is to form an unholy (albeit covert) alliance between the Western left and Islamic fundamentalists. If the combined forces of both political extremes succeed in their objective of destroying America, their common enemy, it is certain that the Islamists will then turn on their leftist allies and destroy them as well. There is an old Arab proverb: "The enemy of my enemy is my friend." To that can be added the proviso, "only as long as the common enemy exists."

The strategy of this two-pronged attack on America by the emotional plague is to undermine and paralyze its efforts in the battle between the Islamists and the West: *Whatever America does in its fight against terrorism is wrong.* In the current Iraq war, for example, America is wrong if it prematurely pulls out its military forces since this will undermine the Iraqi people's ability to form a stable government; and America is guilty if it continues to be a military presence since this will mean more military casualties. Paralysis and confusion are telltale signs that the emotional plague is operating and actively in the process of destroying its victim. Incidentally, leftists' feigned concern over military casualties is not only politically motivated to undermine America's efforts, it also elevates them, so they think, to a higher moral plane than those who are in favor of the military intervention.

The Arab-Israeli Conflict

The effects of the emotional plague's global breakthrough have world-wide ramifications. The tactics used by Islamic *jihad* against America are the same as those used against Israel. Without understanding the operation of the Black Fascist form of the emotional plague, there can be no hope of bringing the Israeli-Arab conflict to a satisfactory conclusion—if by this we mean that the Arab and Jewish peoples will be able to coexist in peace. There are only two possible outcomes to the Arab-Israeli conflict: *Either Israel will survive as a democratic nation in the Middle East, in which case the Arab states will eventually be transformed into Western-style democracies, or Israel will be destroyed, in which case the reactionary Arab autocracies will continue to exist into the indefinite future.* No one senses the reality of these alternatives better than the Islamic fundamentalists and the rulers of the Arab states. No one understands them as poorly as Western liberals.

Israel's social life is highly diversified, whereas Islamic societies are fixed in a state of chronic political, economic, and cultural stagnation and religious rigidity. Sociopolitically, Israeli society lies somewhat to the left of center, while the Arab world is to the far right of center. Even apart from religious considerations, the Islamic fundamentalists and the rulers of the Arab states correctly perceive the enormous difference between the two forms of social life as a real threat to their existence, hence their unyielding opposition to the State of Israel. On the other side, Israelis themselves, the hard-liners and the soft-liners, have opposing attitudes how to handle the conflict. From a characterological standpoint, these attitudes correspond respectively to those held by conservatives and by liberals. Neither group has a fully rational perspective and approach to the problem, but the hard-line conservatives have a clearer, intuitive understanding of the reality of the emotional plague. In this regard, the latter's aggressive response to Islamic terrorism has more effectively preserved the State of Israel. Any policy that does not recognize this reality undermines Israel's struggle for survival by encouraging Arabs to believe that Israel's existence as a state is negotiable. However, even the conservatives cannot wage an effective battle because they do not fully understand the existence and methods of the emotional plague that originate from the pseudo-liberals on the left and the Muslim right.

The life-and-death struggle for the survival of the State of Israel is being fought on military and ideological fronts. Both involve fighting the emotional plague.[138] The Palestine Liberation Organization (PLO), Hezbollah and similar radical groups are examples of the organized emotional plague. They are composed of self-appointed Islamic fanatics, allegedly representing the downtrodden Arab masses, who claim to have the right to speak for all Muslims. They challenge Israel's right to sovereignty and existence, and consider

138. The long history of anti-Semitic violence by Islamic radicals began with the 1920 Palestine riots. In 1929, the Grand Mufti of Jerusalem, Amin al-Husayni, the foremost Islamic political and religious leader in Palestine under the British mandate, instigated the massacre of hundreds of Jews and many more hundreds of Arabs who were deemed sympathetic to Jews. In the late 1930s he ordered the extermination of both. The practice of murdering Arabs for their "collaboration" was taken up by Yasser Arafat, who forced as many as 400,000 Palestinians to become political and economic refugees in Europe and America. Thus, the Islamic fanatics succeeded in identifying themselves with mainstream Palestinians. Because of the radicalizing of the Palestinian population, any hope for a Mideast peace in the near future is dim. See Robert Pollack, "Where Have All the Moderate Palestinians Gone?" *Wall Street Journal*, Aug. 13, 2001.

Israelis to be outsiders and Westerners to be alien to the regional religious system. Were they to succeed in their declared goal of reclaiming the entire Palestine region, Israel would cease to exist and Israelis would suffer massacre or expulsion.

One source of the problem is that the entire Muslim Middle East has a long history of being socially dysfunctional and, as a result, highly volatile. This would have been the case even if there had never been an Israel to blame and if an independent State of Palestine had existed all along.

Leftist world governments, politicians, and diplomats have responded in unison to this organized emotional plague in typical fashion: *By siding with the pestilence and openly defending the Islamic fanatics.* For over a quarter of a century, PLO leaders and spokesmen have been received and embraced all over the world. They have addressed the United Nations to standing ovation, been honored at the Vatican by Pope John Paul II, been official guests to delegations in India, Austria, Greece, Japan, China and elsewhere, and established legitimacy thorough diplomatic representation in over a hundred countries. Yasser Arafat was awarded the Nobel Peace Prize for the 1993 Oslo Accords. During the same period, the PLO extended its destructive activity murdering Israelis and its opponents, the vast majority of whom were Palestinians. They also murdered innocent bystanders, including diplomats, and hijacked airplanes, taking innocent people hostage, while claiming to work for peace as they threatened to commit more of these same crimes (Pryce-Jones 2002, page 282). Now, the same kind of support is being offered to Hezbollah in its battle against Israel.

There is no end in sight to the conflict because people are unsure of what is really happening when confronted with the emotional plague's immense destructiveness. The pestilence is highly effective in creating confusion and is therefore successful in paralyzing its victim. Confusion is generated because the statements of the spokesmen for the Islamic fanatics—their desire to peacefully settle political differences between the opposing sides—are not true. The truth is that the fanatics have done and will continue to do everything they possibly can to undermine and destroy Israel because they *cannot tolerate* Israel's freedom. They understand that peace with Israel means their destruction and an end to their pestilent way of life. The energy behind their genital frustration fuels their criminal and sadistic impulses and their only reason to exist is to bring Israel down.

When Arafat was brought secretly to the Soviet Union in order to be trained by the Communists, General Ion Pacepa, the highest-ranking intelligence officer ever to defect from the Soviet bloc, was struck by the ideological similarity between Arafat and the General's own KGB mentor. Arafat declared American "imperial Zionism" to be the "rabid dog of the world," and that there is only one way to deal with a rabid dog: "Kill it!" Many Communist intelligence officers shared this attitude. For example, the chief Soviet intelligence advisor in Romania, General Sakharovsky, who was responsible for killing fifty thousand Romanians, preached that "the bourgeoisie" is "the rabid dog of imperialism," adding that there is "just one way to deal with a rabid dog: Shoot it."[139] The ideology of the Red Fascist is often indistinguishable from that of the Black Fascist.

Arafat made a political career by pretending not to have been involved in his own terrorist acts and he successfully deceived a sufficient number of influential people in the West. However, in 1972, the Kremlin established a "socialist division of labor" for supporting international terrorism. Libya and the PLO were the main clients. A year later, Arafat and his KGB handlers, headed by Arafat's top deputy, Abu Jihad, took American diplomats hostage in Khartoum, Sudan and demanded the release of Sirhan Sirhan, the Palestinian assassin of Robert Kennedy. When President Nixon refused the terrorists demand, the PLO commandos executed three of their hostages, including the American ambassador.

Armed struggle is the only statecraft the Palestinian terrorists know. They seriously and honestly believe in the correctness of their goal to destroy Israel, and they do everything to impose their well-rationalized thinking on young Arabs who are being brainwashed on a daily basis to sacrifice their lives to kill Jews. Retaliatory strikes by Israel always produce anxiety, outrage, and more anti-Western propaganda that is readily disseminated by the liberal-dominated media in the West. The belief that Arafat and the PLO genuinely desired peaceful coexistence with Israel

---

139. *Wall Street Journal*, "The Arafat I Know," Jan. 10, 2002.

is nothing more than wishful thinking on the part of liberals and only serves to give credence to the deceitful propaganda of the Arab fanatics. This is another example of how liberals align themselves with the forces of the emotional plague.

Emotional plague characters have an uncanny ability to recognize the weaknesses and vulnerabilities of their victim, and this ability is essential for their survival.[140] Liberal characters constitute the vulnerable targets of the host organism. For this reason, the social functioning of liberals is the greatest danger to the State of Israel and the Free World. They are the major factor that encourages the Islamic fanatics to feel confident of victory.

As we have seen, liberals are gullible and do not recognize the evil intent of America's enemies. Despite decades of failure with numerous peace plans, liberals *must* continue to place their hopes on a negotiated settlement. This characterologically determined behavior plays directly into the fanatic's tactics: to cultivate the liberal's hope of an agreement through peace conferences.

To make matters even worse, because the liberal is intolerant of physical aggression, sustained force is never an option. Their deeply rooted fear of aggression forces them to go to any length to accommodate Arab demands believing this is the best road to peace. Sensing this fear to act decisively, fanatical Arabs feel emboldened to escalate their demands and increase the military conflict even to the point of risking an all-out war with the West. This liberal attitude has led to a relationship of antagonistic opposition (Fig. 8.6):

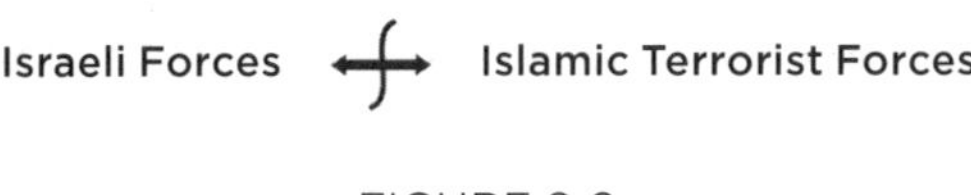

FIGURE 8.6

This situation exactly plays into the hands of the Islamic terrorists. While *pretending* to strive for peace (an emotional plague tactic), they continue their destructive activities and build up their organizations world-wide. This is being done to wear down Israelis' resolve to fight for their country's survival. Since the

140. In this regard, their function is identical to a pathogenic bacteria or virus that is capable of perceiving the specific weakness of the host organism.

Oslo Accords in 1993, in which the Palestinians renounced the use of force and promised to use only political means to achieve their goals, the total number of Israelis killed by Palestinian terrorists has continued to escalate. The victims are predominately innocent civilians including women and children. Meanwhile, Islamic terror groups are proclaiming: "Our struggle with the sons of Israel in Palestine is on civilization, ideology, history, and existence. Our war with them is long and difficult." They call for killing Jews and attacking Americans. Nevertheless many Israelis, because they are predominately liberal, continue to hope that they can make a deal.[141]

In point of fact, from a *military* perspective, it is imperative that a relationship of *attractive* opposition be maintained between Israel and the Islamic terrorist forces. This should consist of swift, preemptive military tactical strikes at Islamic terrorist targets world-wide, accompanied by a public campaign to expose the terrorists as psychopathic criminals. However, from a *political* perspective, a policy of *antagonistic* opposition is necessary. Islamic emotional plague organizations such as the PLO, Hezbollah and Hamas must be sequestered. Former Prime Minister Sharon's doctrine of unilateral separation from these groups is the only way to effectively deal with them.

In addressing the Arab-Israeli conflict, the following points are important to consider:[142]

- "Palestine" is not now, nor has it ever been, a sovereign nation or state. It is incapable of filling the basic functions of governing its own people; i.e., it cannot fulfill even basic functions that any government must discharge. Israel cannot negotiate with Palestine because there is no legitimate entity to negotiate with.

- The only government the Palestinians have at present is the government of Israel, which does make some effective efforts to meet the Palestinians' greatest current need: elimination of the organized emotional plague in Palestine.

---

141. See Daniel Pipes and Steven Emerson, "Rolling Back the Forces of Terror," *Wall Street Journal*, Aug. 13, 2001.

142. Robert Harmon, M.D., personal communication, 2002.

- As long as the terrorists of the PLO, Hamas, and other groups are active, there is no possibility for peace in the Middle East. Through their support, pseudo-liberals and other plague characters in the West and in the Arab world legitimize these emotional plague characters and perpetuate a situation in which the plague thrives world-wide.
- A distinction must be made between the narrower view of anti-Semitism and the broader view of anti-Semitism as a manifestation of the emotional plague. Because anti-Semitism has always been viewed in the narrower context, the true nature of the problem has been consistently obfuscated. It must be recognized that the emotional plague has been, from time immemorial, wreaking havoc on the human race—from individuals to entire social groups. *Anti-Semitism is but one specific manifestation of the emotional plague.* Only if the emotional plague is understood within this context is it possible to eradicate this form of destructiveness, whether directed against the Jewish people or any other nation, ethnic group, or individual.

General Considerations and Recommendations

In order to respond effectively to the evil of the emotional plague, we must recognize it for what it is: *We are dealing with severe social pathology deeply embedded in the biophysical structure of armored humans for countless generations.* Under the best of conditions, it will take many generations to reverse this sickness. Consequently, there can be no quick or simple way to deal with the global breakthrough of the pestilence that led to the September 11 attack. There is no way to quickly or simply put an end to the Arab-Israeli conflict. The key to eventual success will be patience, a clear understanding of how the emotional plague operates, and a willingness to commit to a protracted conflict. *The problem is not only with the Arab fanatics and leaders who are now in power but, more importantly, with the emotionally crippled Arab masses who give them power.*

Except during the Vietnam War, the ideological factor has

never been as important as it is now in America's war against terrorism. Hatred against America, instilled in Islamic children by Islamic fanatics in their so-called "schools," which must be recognized as the breeding ground for future terrorists, must be challenged. These children are being systematically programmed on a daily basis to be the future weapons of mass destruction against the Free World.

There is a basic difference between wars with a strong ideological component (e.g., the Cold War or the war on terrorism) and conventional military warfare. In a conventional war, victory is achieved militarily and perceived as a triumph after the defeat of the enemy. Such conflict has a definite end-point. However, in a successful war on terrorism, because of the strong ideological component, there is no definitive end-point, only the cessation of terrorist activities, which is not experienced psychologically as a victory. There are no victory parades celebrating the end to military activity, only a return to peaceful social life. Yet, in reality, this is a victory nevertheless.

Islamic fanatics are emotional plague individuals. The plague must be seen first for its very existence, and then be recognized as a true *biosocial disease*. Without such recognition, there can only be attempts at symptomatic treatment and it will be impossible to eradicate the roots of terrorism completely. It must be understood, regardless of how painful this realization is, that because of the way people are, there will be ongoing terrorist activity and continuing war against it for the foreseeable future.

Working toward elimination of the Islamo-Fascist plague requires a functional understanding of characterology and can be divided into four tasks of increasing difficulty. Each is part of a stepwise process of eliminating mysticism in Islamic countries and ideological thinking in the West, which are the driving forces behind the emotional plague.

The first task requires identifying emotional plague individuals on the left and the right. It includes exposing, targeting, incarcerating and, when necessary, destroying all individuals who are, either directly or indirectly, a threat to the Free World, as well as those who are responsible for helping them. In the West, this step requires distinguishing between the pseudo-liberal plague individual and the true liberal, who is susceptible to being emotionally infected and becoming a carrier of the plague. *That the true liberal is capable of blindly and mindlessly following the pseudo-liberal's aggressively destructive ideological agenda must be a matter of public recognition.* This step is necessary in order to begin sequestration of the pseudo-liberal plague individual from others belonging on the political left who have not yet been infected. The public must be taught how to make this crucial distinction between these two deceptively similar character types. Education in sociopolitical characterology must be an ongoing process, teaching the masses of humans about the destructive relationship that forms between the true liberal and the pseudo-liberal. (The dynamic relationship between the pseudo-liberal and the true liberal was discussed in chapter 2.)

Islamic terrorists are plague individuals on the political right. They, themselves, have been terrorized into submission early in life. These fanatics and their supporters world-wide must be singled out and made to submit either through sequestration or destruction. This must be done without threatening the masses of peace-loving Muslims. All other Black Fascist regimes supporting terrorism against the United States must also be contained or eliminated. These steps must be the policy goals of the current and future U.S. government administrations.

Given the cunning, mendacity, and sadistic ruthlessness of emotional plague individuals, how does one effectively fight terrorism without turning into a plague individual oneself? The answer: by *sustaining full contact with one's biological core* in order to maintain one's health and decency; all the while, using the methods of the emotional plague itself—clandestine activity, secrecy, wariness, and, as necessary, ruthlessness and assassination. At the same time, the plague must be exposed for what it is whenever possible. These requirements speak to the characterological and biophysical limitations of armored humans, primarily those resulting from the true liberal's devitalized core and hypertrophied intellect. This is why they are biophysically not up to the task of combating the emotional plague.

The second task is to support, wherever possible, the establishment of formal democracies in Islamic countries. This will, over time, break up the tribal systems in the Islamic states. With democracy, women will be emancipated and there will be a shift in male/female relationships. Muslim men and women will then be free to choose their own partners in marriage and their own governments without external coercion from authoritarian family members or totalitarian regimes. However, what is generally not understood is that democracy cannot be forced on society from the outside, just as freedom cannot be imposed on individuals. Most people living in rigidly authoritarian Muslim countries are too armored to tolerate greater freedom than they currently have. Therefore, this process of democratization will, under the most favorable circumstances, take many, many years of painstaking effort, patience and courage. If successful, a stable society will eventually result, one that will not be a threat to the rest of the world.[143] (See the following section)

The third task, which is related to the second, is that Muslims must be able to divest Islamic fundamentalists of their secular power. This applies to Islamic countries such as Syria, Libya, Iran, Saudi Arabia, Sudan, and so on. *A democratic society cannot exist unless religion is separated from the state.*[144]

The fourth and ultimately most important task is not confined to the Muslim world alone but is one that is also focused on addressing the emotional plague globally: To educate younger generations as to the vital need for, and importance of, healthy sexual functioning. Achieving this goal will completely and finally lift the veil of ignorance that enshrouds the Arab people. It will free them from racism, mysticism, ignorance, poverty, and a life of misery. Accomplishing this will ensure that Arab youth, not having been terrorized as infants and children through sex-negative practices and mystical indoctrination, will grow up without the danger of becoming terrorists.

Although presented in degrees of increasing difficulty, these steps cannot happen consecutively. Some, for example the establishment of formal democracy and the separation of religion and state, need to be implemented simultaneously. Unless these steps are implemented, it is not realistic to think the terrorist form of

---

143. The Muslim states are composed of numerous opposing tribal factions. The difficulty lies in being able to determine which groups are genuinely interested in establishing a democratic system of government and which are not.

144. The goal of the Islamic fundamentalists is exactly the opposite: To unite religion and the state, and to make Islam the religion of the entire world.

the emotional plague can be eradicated. Most importantly, until the sexual misery of Arab adolescents is faced head-on, honestly and courageously, young Arabs will be tormented by sexual frustration. Unable to release their inner tension through mystical rituals, they will continue to be duped by pestilent individuals into seeking revenge on nonbelievers and martyr themselves in the name of Allah.

The more far-reaching and ultimately permanent solution to the emotional plague, outside of and within the United States, requires preventing the formation of armor with all its inherent destructive effects. This relationship between armored society and the emotional plague is described here (Fig. 8.7).

FIGURE 8.7

Social destructiveness through emotional contagion defines the emotional plague. Because the destructive component belongs in the social realm and the contagious component belongs in the biological realm, the emotional plague is truly a *biosocial disease.* It exists because this unique and ubiquitous form of human destructiveness continues to remain unrecognized. The approach to it, elimination, is exactly the same as that employed in any infectious medical illness. First of all, that such a disease exists must become common knowledge. The problem here is analogous to that in combating any form of communicable disease. For example, the threat of smallpox as a biological weapon by Islamic fanatics, although of concern and frightening, need not result in disaster because medical science understands the nature of its communicability and how to prevent its spread. In a similar fashion, the global breakthrough of the emotional plague need not be life-threatening, once its true nature is understood and, from that knowledge, the ways to combat it are implemented.

The Democratization of Islam

One thing that people never consider when talking about democracy is the emotional health of the population, which is at the heart of their capacity for independent and responsible functioning. The difficulties inherent in the democratization of Islam are, therefore, no different than those in the ongoing operation of a formal democracy, but on a much larger scale. Because of their emotional sickness, almost all people everywhere on the planet are unable in varying degrees to govern themselves in a rational, self-regulating manner. This is why formal democracy does not work in most countries. People's emotional infirmity is an impediment to their being able to live freely and responsibly in a democratic society. That being said, a formal democracy is infinitely more desirable than the rigid authoritarianism of Islamic societies because democracy allows for the possibility of personal freedom and individual responsibility. Western society permits the freedom necessary for people to grow and develop and this brings out the unique quality of every human being. As a result, people in free societies live longer and are happier than people living in more armored societies.

It is clear that a military victory is not, in itself, a sufficient condition to bring about democracy in Islamic countries. The problem is this: How can a formal democracy be established and maintained in Islamic countries given, on the one hand, the severe repression in Muslim societies where people have never had any experience in self-government and, on the other hand, the widespread social degeneration and sociopolitical in-fighting that Western democracies are currently undergoing? The enormity of these problems in the two widely different and diseased societies is itself a symptom of the emotional plague and a serious obstacle to the democratization process.

Also to be considered are the following realities. The United States has been engaged in a protracted conflict with Muslim terrorists, actually an undeclared war, for over thirty years. All the while, the radical Islamists have been breeding, sheltering, and financing terrorist groups with the blessing of radical Islamic clerics. Meanwhile, Islamic states are themselves being threatened by powerful forces of change that are eroding their ideological foundation. Western ideas, largely through the Internet, are reaching people throughout the Muslim world and are threatening to change the structure of their social, political, economic and educational institutions.

Now, more than ever, knowledge of orgonomic sociology is needed to bring about a favorable outcome. The crucial factors in this struggle are: The degree to which the Islamic people are capable of tolerating the freedom that living in a democratic society affords combined with the determination of America to wage an all-out war against the Islamo-Fascists over an indefinite period of time. It can be predicted that if the current Iraq war does not result in a democracy, that country will become an even more dangerous terrorist state than it was before Saddam Hussein and his government were toppled.

Taking down Hussein's corrupt and despotic regime was the necessary first step in the democratization process. This left Iraq in a state of anarchy since there was no structure to replace the various social and economic institutions that were destroyed and because the Iraqi people were not used to living in a democracy. This void became the fertile breeding ground for the emotional plague where Iraqi insurgency could thrive.

Whether a formal democracy can be established in Iraq or other Islamic nations at this time is uncertain. It depends largely on the interaction of the opposing ideologies at work in both Islamic and Western countries. These forces are a product of the sociopolitical character structure of individual citizens. In Islamic nations, the struggle is between the pro-democratic forces for social progress on the political left and the anti-democratic, reactionary forces on the political right. In Western nations, the conflict is between the pro-democratic, progressive forces on the political right and the anti-democratic, socially regressive forces on the political left.

There are many obstacles in the way of establishing a stable, formal democracy in Islamic countries. Much depends on the degree to which the existing locus of the political center is shifted to the political right, which is an indication of the degree of social rigidity. Most importantly, recognition of the emotional plague's destructiveness and how it can interfere with the democratization process is essential. Without this knowledge, all attempts will be futile.

Can Muslim Societies Be Compatible with Democracy?

When Muhammad died in 632 A.D. he had united almost the entire central and southern portions of the Arabian Peninsula into the Islamic Empire. While the Western world was experiencing the Renaissance and the Age of Enlightenment, Muhammadanism continued to remain in isolation. Moslems rejected Aristotelian logic and reason and held to the concept that man could not control his own destiny. According to the teachings of Islam, *individual responsibility for one's life is not possible* and the fate of the Muslim is in Allah's hands. Islamic religion and the laws derived from it dominate the lives of millions of Arabs and these laws, with their interpretations, have been handed down unchanged from generation to generation. As a result, Islamic societies remain rigidly authoritarian.

Today the majority of Muslim countries continue to be ruled by authoritarian governments buttressed by military and security forces. Few rulers have held elective office as they have mostly been either kings or military officers. Where parliaments and political parties have existed, they have remained subordinate to the ruling government or party (Esposito 1999).

A major hurdle facing Islamic democratic movements is that the leaders in power cannot tolerate open expression of viewpoints different from their own. Their participation in electoral politics is often merely tactical. Once in power, those elected usually impose an intolerant monolithic order, excluding the rights of women and minorities. Another difficulty is the precise manner in which Muslims define democracy and whether that particular definition is compatible with Islam. How democracy is understood varies widely and depends primarily on the individual Muslim's sociopolitical character structure. (See the following section) As a result, it is difficult to arrive at a consensus among Muslims as to the exact meaning of the concept. Muslims who give up responsibility for their lives to Allah lose the ability to govern themselves. It also makes them prone to blame anyone but themselves for their problems.

Raising many rational objections to formal democracy, most Muslims on the political right declare that Islam and democracy are incompatible. King Fahd of Saudi Arabia, long regarded as an autocratic monarch and ally of the West, declared that democracy is a Western institution, foreign to Islam; that Islam has its own form of public participation: "The democratic system prevalent in the world is not appropriate in this region. The election system has no place in the Islamic creed, which calls for a government of advice and consultation, and for the shepherd's openness to his flock, and *holds the ruler fully responsible for his people*" (Esposito 1999; italics added). This sentiment is echoed by fundamentalist Muslims who believe that Islam is entirely self-sufficient, that it is a divinely mandated system based on divine sovereignty and sacred law (sharia), which is incompatible and irreconcilable with notions of popular sovereignty and civil law (Ibid.) Other Muslims differ and accept the concept of democracy built on the well-established Koranic practice of consultation, but these interpretations vary in the degree to which "the people" are allowed to exercise responsibility. They argue, wrongly, that Islam is inherently democratic not only because of the principle of consultation but also because of the concepts of independent reasoning and consensus.

The Sociopolitical Character of Muslims

In order to have a true sense of the underlying determinants of any social process, it is necessary to have a working knowledge of sociopolitical characterology, *the manner in which individuals mold their environment through their ideas and attitudes to fit their personal requirements*. In the case of Muslims, these determinants cut across tribal, sectarian, and ethnic boundaries. While many Muslims have integrated effortlessly into Western society, sizable numbers wonder if they can live as good Muslims in societies dominated by other faiths and laws.

The value of sociopolitical characterology is that it can accurately describe the social behavior of people at any given epoch and in any culture in terms of their *characterologically based* sociopolitical ideas and attitudes. Baker's standardization and classification of these attitudes according to an individual's character structure provide an accurate and complete understanding of social behavior that is *independent of temporal or regional factors*. Since most Muslims belong in varying degrees on the sociopolitical right, we will confine our discussion mostly to the conservative side of the sociopolitical spectrum. Beginning with the conservative Muslim to the immediate right of center, the extreme conservative, the reactionary, and finally the Islamo-Fascist or Black Fascist will be discussed. (See chapter 2, the section on Sociopolitical Characterology) As we proceed from right of center to extreme right, the Muslim individual's personal and social functioning become increasingly disturbed as his ocular armor become more rigid. Correspondingly, his thinking and social behavior become more irrational and destructive, helplessness and irresponsibility increase, and his work and sexual functioning become more disturbed. In general, the ability of the individual to assimilate into Western society is in direct proportion to how close he resides to the sociopolitical center.

THE CONSERVATIVE

The conservative Muslim, like his non-Muslim Western counterpart, has a basic philosophy of "live and let live." Closest to health, he is an independent thinker and regards himself as an individualist. He has little or no group identity as a Muslim. He is rational, honest, self-confident, and has a clear understanding of the distinction between religion and state, believing that religious practice should be restricted to private life. He is able to easily assimilate into Western society and can take advantage of its personal and economic benefits. Having a good amount of contact with his core, he identifies with those who are successful, rather than rebelling against them. When living in the West, he is tolerant of non-Muslim ways of life, is comfortable following traditional Western customs, and adopts the values and laws of that society. For example, he respects Western laws regarding marriage and divorce and the right to accept interest payment. He reacts rationally and appropriately from his feelings to social events. Because he accepts Western laws and customs, he often views himself as liberal. However, his adherence to traditional values and customs such as strong family ties, respect for authority and the authoritarian social order identifies him as a conservative.

THE ENVIRONMENTAL CONSERVATIVE

When the sociopolitical center is shifted to either the left or the right, there are a greater number of people belonging to the side to which the center has been displaced. Many of the sociopolitical ideas and attitudes of individuals are therefore strongly influenced or based strictly on environmental influences. In Muslim societies where the sociopolitical center is far to the right, many seem to be conservative-minded even though their actual sociopolitical character structure is left of center. Forced into silence by the authoritarian regime, these individuals are actually *environmental* conservatives, people with a leftist structure who appear conservative only because they have been raised and are living in a Muslim society. Those in this group who are closer to the center are true liberals by Baker's criteria and, like the true conservative Muslim, are able to assimilate easily into Western life.

It is difficult to identify Muslims with a leftist character structure living in their native country because of their active suppression by the Muslim majority on the right. However, there are telltale signs that identify the Muslim living in the West who is conservative solely by virtue of environmental influences. For these individuals, Islam is not only about rituals and devotion to Allah, but also a matter of their cultural, as distinguished from religious, identity. Like their pseudo-liberal Western cohort, they like to attend leftist political rallies, such as feminist demonstrations, or join anti-American, antiwar movements. They identify with the underdog and view Americans as racists who are biased against Muslims. Their identity is with "victimized" Muslims and not with their adopted Western country. They wear the Islamic veil not so much out of religious conviction but as a sign of protest and as a celebration of their "group identity." They thrive on generating controversy and on debating social and political issues as a way of pulling energy up into their brain.

THE EXTREME CONSERVATIVE

More rigid and authoritarian in attitude and therefore more emotionally defended than the conservative, the extreme conservative favors fundamentalism and expresses a great deal of mysticism in his thinking. He emphasizes a return to Islam and attributes the weakness of the Islamic world primarily to the Westernization of Muslim societies. He is inclined to interpret the Koran literally. Since he has been raised never to question the Koran he feels that it is not his place to denounce those Muslims who "know better." To argue with them is to question the Koran itself, and that is off-limits. For the extreme conservative, the Koran is not like any other scripture: It is the summit of holy books. His religion, in practice and feeling, is more devout in order to counteract the increased hate in his armor. However, his hatred is still able to be contained successfully. Aside from his mystical practices, his other defense is to keep a safe distance from the corrupting influences of Western life. As a result, he has difficulty assimilating, and this failure adversely affects his children who are isolated from the mainstream of Western life and thus more likely to fall prey to Islamic fanatics. His rigid family ties extend to members of the same tribe. Thus, tribal ties are an added impediment to the process of assimilation to Western life. The extreme conservative remains loyal to his native land and even to its despotic leaders from whom he may have had to flee. Upholding the rigid moralistic attitude of the authoritarian social order, he looks upon females as inferior and subservient to males. He is committed to Islamic law, sharia, which is a set of rules that govern daily life of Muslims as the imam, or religious leader of the community, interprets them.

THE REACTIONARY

The reactionary Muslim finds himself further to the right of the extreme conservative and steadfastly resists succumbing to Western influences. The hatred contained in his armor is closer to the surface than that of the extreme conservative and he believes that all nonbelievers will be punished. Although capable of violence, he usually stops short of putting his beliefs into action. The reactionary has less concern for the rights of others, is less rational, less stable in his defenses, and less capable of experiencing satisfaction in life. Unable to regulate his life, he relies on fatwas or rulings passed down by religious leaders in the community or by mullahs on the Internet regarding personal conduct. Mystical thinking permeates every area of his life. Believing that non-Muslims are inherently inferior, he maintains a segregated social life for himself and his family. The reactionary Muslim is an Islamist who believes that the entire world must be made to conform to the teachings of Muhammad, as written in the Koran. He takes the Koran literally, believing in a personal God and the reality of hell. The reactionary believes that it is not Islamic law that must change, but that society must change as it has strayed from God's path.

THE ISLAMO-FASCIST

At the extreme right on the sociopolitical spectrum is the Muslim Fascist (Islamo-Fascist). He is an emotional plague character and stands for absolute authoritarianism. The quintessential "Little Man," he looks up to an exalted father figure such as Muhammad to dictate his life and give him permission to express the brutality and hatred that he is unable to control with his internalized defenses. Rigidly armored, he cannot experience the spontaneous motility of life without lashing out brutally against the living: Natural movement creates within him intolerable sexual longing. An abject pawn to his leader and cause, the Islamo-Fascist stops at nothing in trying to eliminate all those who are perceived as a threat. Because his religious feelings and sexuality originate from his secondary layer, religious ecstasy, sadism, and brutality commingle.

These diverse orientations to social change make it clear that *mainstream Muslim society is shifted far to the right of the socio-political center.* The social significance of this shift is that it is an indication of the severe degree of sexual repression in Muslim societies. Behind this repression there is a great amount of pent-up rage that must be held in check by a rigid authoritarian form of government. In Western society, this shift in the political center corresponds to that part of the sociopolitical spectrum occupied by the reactionary individual. In contrast, and despite the current reaction from the right, the political mainstream in Western societies falls *far to the left of center*—the region occupied by the socialists. This difference in the locus of the political center of these two societies determines, to a large extent, their cultural differences. It is a major factor responsible for the violent collision that is currently happening between them.

These differences in the locus of the political center give rise to fundamental ideological disagreements between Western democracies and Islamic countries. Until these underlying differences are recognized and addressed, there cannot be real hope for a final resolution to the conflict which goes to the heart of humanity's sickness, the omnipresent sexual disturbance.

In order for armored humans to live together there is a need for authoritarian social armor in the form of civil and criminal laws. These laws are necessary to contain the destructive secondary impulses that result from the sexual disturbance. When the authoritarian form of social armor is suddenly removed in a society that is severely sexually repressed, as happened in Iraq following the overthrow of Saddam Hussein, then social chaos in the form of rampant lawlessness or civil war becomes a real possibility.

The different forms of social armor (legal systems) that exist in Western and Islamic cultures are based on differences in the relationship between the authority of religion and the state: separation of these institutions in the West and nonseparation in Islamic societies.

The following table (8.2) highlights the major differences between Western and Islamic societies:

Western Society	Islamic Society
Anti-authoritarian	Rigidly authoritarian
Political center shifted toward the left[145]	Political center shifted toward the right
Freedom and individualism valued over responsibility	Responsibility and social order valued over freedom
State separated from religion	Religion identified with the State
Preservation of the individual valued over society	Preservation of society valued over the individual
Mechanistic orientation to life	Mystical orientation to life

Major Differences Between Western and Islamic Societies

TABLE 8.2

As a result of these differences, the strict authoritarian culture of Islamic societies *must* collide head-on with today's Western anti-authoritarianism.

The following are the conditions necessary to establish and maintain a stable form of democracy in Muslim countries. Each one deals with an aspect of the reactionary character structure

145. The shift to the political left of center is not recognized by Western liberals because they are in their element in an anti-authoritarian society. However, it is recognized by some conservatives.

of the average Muslim. The failure to successfully address any of these factors will interfere with the democratization process.

1. Distinction Between Core and Secondary Layer Functions

It is essential that a clear distinction be made between the core, the biological center from which life-positive impulses originate, and the secondary layer, the origin of the destructive impulses. For example, the concept of the right to free speech and open debate must be distinguished from obscenity, pornography, slander, gossip, and idle chatter, as all of the latter originate from the superficial and secondary layers. The concept of rational authority that is in the service of safeguarding unarmored life must be distinguished from irrational authority that serves to protect neurotic and destructive ways of social life. The concept of responsibly exercised civil rights for women must be distinguished from the tenets of radical feminism. The concept of healthy genital sexuality must be distinguished from neurotic sexual behavior.

Each of the following conditions listed below requires that the crucial distinction between core and secondary layer functions is first made:

2. Lifting Sexual Repression

The rigid authoritarian society of today's Muslim world is anchored in the sexual repression of infants, children, and adolescents. Lifting sexual repression must be done carefully and judiciously, with an understanding of the limits of Islamic youth to tolerate the sudden burst of sexual energy that would accompany it. This is especially so because beneath the rigid authoritarian structure of Islamic society lies a great secondary layer of destructive impulses and terror of freedom. Because of severe repression in these societies, this layer is even more harsh and destructive than that in its Western counterpart. It is the reason that Muslim youth are willing to martyr themselves for Allah. It is why the destructive secondary drives such as promiscuity, pornography, and adultery are strongly defended against with strict taboos and harsh punishments.

One important early social intervention toward the lifting of sexual repression (and the emancipation of women) readily instituted, is to discourage the custom of having Islamic girls and women cover their faces. Wearing the Islamic veil effectively serves to repress the sexual component in being looked at and in looking. The effect of this extreme form of sexual moralism on Islamic males is to produce armoring of the eyes and the opposite impulse, a hunger to look at naked or partially clad women. The result is an ocular unsatisfied block.

3. Parring the Social Forces on the Political Left and Right

In a stable formal democracy there are a fairly equal number of true liberals and conservatives. The opposing attractive forces are equal. Compared to individuals at the sociopolitical extremes (fascists and communists), the ocular functioning of these individuals is fairly healthy. They have the greatest capacity to tolerate freedom. Each social force keeps the other in check and sociopolitical activity is kept at a minimum. An imbalance leads to either excessive repression—more force is employed than is required to keep the secondary layer in check, or too much freedom—more freedom is allowed than the masses can tolerate. The former leads to excessive social rigidity, the latter to social disorganization and chaos. In either situation, social functions are disturbed to varying degrees.

In today's Western societies, an increasing number of people have shifted to the extreme left on the sociopolitical spectrum. This has caused a corresponding political reaction from the right. This condition has brought about increased social anxiety, greater inability of people to govern their personal lives in a rational manner, and an ever increasing tendency to blame the "other side" for their own difficulties. This heightened social anxiety has given rise to sociopolitical activitism and to ideological sloganeering. Presented as journalism, and defended as free speech, these manufactured catchwords created by the leftist-dominated media are all too effective. They result in the weakening of democracy and serve to increase destabilization. An important negative consequence of this is that Western democracy cannot set a positive example for Islamic people to emulate. The breakdown of Western democracy becomes yet another justification for Islamic countries to hold to their regressive customs and traditions, and fundamentalism is reinforced.

4. Jurisdictional Separation of Religious and Secular Law

Religious and political systems can be kept separate in Islamic countries under one condition—that a clear distinction is recognized and made between the core and the secondary layer. Only then can natural core functions be protected under the law and the destructive secondary impulses, that give rise to the emotional plague, be suppressed by law. Muslim clerics are the instructors not only in Islamic theology but also in social and economic conduct. This authority often extends to political ideology. For some clerics, the United States is the "Great Satan."

In strict Islamic countries the law of the land is sharia, which means "the path to follow." Based on the Koran, it embraces a code of Islamic ethics, religious duties, and morality. Justice is administered by a council of religious scholars (the ulema), and by religious courts whose judges are appointed by the ulema. The sharia laws, dating back more than a thousand years, are harsh and punitive. Murder and rape are punishable by beheading, and theft by amputation of the right hand or flogging in public. Adultery demands the death penalty for women, usually by stoning. Needless to say, these forms of punishment serve as a strong deterrent to crime.

There are five pillars of faith for all devout Muslims:

1. Confession of faith: "There is no god but God and Muhammad is the messenger of God"
2. Prayers five times daily while facing Mecca
3. Fasting during daylight hours of the holy month of Ramadan
4. Individual almsgiving
5. Making the hajj or pilgrimage to Mecca

Most of these articles of faith and religious rituals and practices effectively anchor the mystical Muslim religion in the character structure of the Islamic people. They serve as a powerful repressive force largely by inducing mystical feelings. They also make it almost impossible for the devout Muslim to have independent feelings, emotions, thoughts or actions. The phrases most often spoken in Muslim countries are "Allah be praised" and "It's Allah's will."

The consequence of allowing the clergy to have secular authority is that any self-proclaimed imam, or religious leader, can interpret the law arbitrarily, determining what the law will be as he sees fit. Thus, killing innocents in the land of the "infidel" can be justified as they are not citizens of countries sympathetic to "the Arab cause." Moreover, permitting Islamic clerics to have secular authority restricts personal freedom and undermines individual responsibility for the masses of Islamic people. Terrorist organizations, such as Hezbollah, are given legitimacy and are able to wreak havoc because religious leaders belonging to them have secular power.

Traditionally, Western liberals are the ones most strongly opposed to mixing religious and secular practices. Yet, by opposing the current Iraq war and undermining Israel's right to defend itself, these same individuals are effectively interfering with the formation of stable democratic governments in Iraq and in the Middle East.

5. Separation of Religion and Economics

The Koran prohibits certain kinds of economic activity, such as those that involve speculation that can result in profit. This prohibition discourages the potential for economic growth and improvement. The Koran also condemns income generated by interest. Creditors who demand interest are threatened with severe punishment. Those who grow rich in market economies are viewed with suspicion and fear by devout Muslims. These attitudes and practices serve to keep the Muslim multitudes helpless and emotionally dependent on their authoritarian leaders, a condition that is similar to that found in many socialist countries in the West.

6. The Emancipation of Women

According to Wahhabism, a strict form of Islam practiced and flourishing in Saudi Arabia, men are allowed to have up to four wives and are granted instant divorce. Women are kept veiled, completely covered, and socially secluded. Mixed dancing, in the Western sense, is unthinkable. Outside their own family circles, men never mention their wives, although they may have several. Recently, some Saudi hotel pools have been drained to prevent mixed bathing. Dolls have been banished from toy stores as idolatrous. Outside the home, women must be completely veiled and covered by a black robe over their clothes. They are considered the property of men and must be chaperoned by a male member of the family or by one or more women. An unescorted woman seen outside of her home is automatically considered to be a prostitute. If this discrimination is to begin to be eliminated, women must be placed on an equal social and legal status with men and this includes the right to vote. The emancipation of women and universal suffrage will have a dramatic liberalizing effect on Muslim societies.

7. Eliminating Tribalism

From a functional viewpoint, Islamic tribes are extended authoritarian families. Tribalism is endemic in Muslim countries, and it inculcates and fosters reactionary and mystical attitudes. As a step toward democratization, tribal social relationships must eventually be replaced by those that value preserving the nation as a whole. Tribes must put their similarities, their desire for peace and security, over their tribal hatreds. The major obstacle is the tribal members' inability to regulate their individual lives. Clan rulers confer special privileges to tribal members regardless of their personal merit—a sort of affirmative action for family members exercised by the sociopolitical right. As a result, greed and corruption in business are rife and widely accepted in Muslim countries. Under tribal conditions, honest cooperation outside the family is inconceivable. A willingness to trust fellow citizens comes hard to tribal people who are used to only trusting members of the same clan.

In order to introduce tribal Muslims to the idea of becoming fellow citizens, the following factors must be considered. First, the rigid extended family structure is the cohesive unit. Second, it is a patriarchal system where women have no place of authority and where one man sits at the top and controls his family's activities. Finally, Islamic tribal laws and customs are currently inviolable. Consequently, in moving forward, they cannot be placed above the law of the land as established by a constitution drafted by the participating members of Islamic society.

In assessing the readiness of Islamic people for democracy, Turkey might be considered as an instructive example: It has taken Turkey a century to achieve the democratic status it now enjoys, but at the present time its government remains under constant danger of falling into the hands of fundamentalists. Most importantly, the process of democratization occurred from *within* Turkish Islamic society. It was spearheaded by the efforts of a single individual, Kemal Ataturk.

What Will *Not* Bring About a Stable Formal Democracy in Islamic Nations

1. Introducing Western style "pop culture" into Islamic societies.

2. Introducing democratic ideals without the police, military, and intelligence forces necessary to establish and maintain the law, ensure public order, and counteract terrorism.

3. Allowing Muslim tribal groups to become marginalized.

4. Not stopping Islamic "religious leaders" from turning innocent children into weapons of mass destruction.

5. Not exposing the destructiveness (and motives) of the leftist-dominated media in the West in their relentless determination to undermine the efforts of people world-wide to contain the Islamic terrorists and establish democracy in Muslim countries.

6. Not prevailing militarily over the terrorists to show the people of the Middle East, and the entire world, that the Islamic Fascists are criminals that have been completely and unconditionally defeated and humiliated. A peace process that does not have as its goal the complete annihilation of the terrorist forces is bound to result in an interminable struggle.

Terrorists are predestined to self-destruct by blowing themselves up because they have no other outlet for their sexual tension. They are literally time bombs, ready and willing to explode themselves at the bidding of Allah's representative on Earth, an all-powerful father figure, for the sake of Islam. On the most basic level, *the war on terrorism is a conflict between humanity's positive forces of natural sexual life and the life-negative and anti-sexual, mystical forces of Islamo-Fascism aided by pseudo-liberals world-wide.*

What will happen if the democratization of Islamic states like Iraq fails? In the military battle against terrorism, if the American coalition pulls out prematurely, it will allow Muslim countries to degenerate into states with weak central governments, which will then become the breeding ground for future terrorists. At that time there will be a bloodbath, and fundamentalists will seize control of the government and export terrorism throughout the world, as they did in Afghanistan, but with an even stronger foothold. The entire Middle East will become destabilized with devastating consequences. America will lose all credibility as the sole deterrent force against radical Islamic expansion. Terrorists the world over will perceive the weakness of American resolve to defend itself, and they will be emboldened to strike the U.S. homeland. The poison of radical Islamic pestilence will spread far and wide across borders if it can make even a plausible claim to being on the ascendancy, and nothing would reveal that more than a U.S. military retreat. The Free World will become hopelessly divided.

In conclusion, the democratization process will be, under the best possible conditions, a long, hard struggle and take many generations to accomplish. The rigid, authoritarian social order, the severe degree of sexual repression, the religious authority in secular matters, the absence of women's rights, the strong tribal social ties with their racist features, and the lack of a constitutional government all have to be addressed slowly and cautiously. This must be done with an understanding of the limits inherent in the bioemotional structure of the Islamic people to tolerate freedom and independent functioning, and how the emotional plague will attempt to disrupt the democratization process at every turn. Nothing permanent will be accomplished until the crucial distinction between the primary core functions and the destructive secondary layer impulses is understood and this understanding is applied to effect social improvement.

Black/White Race Relations in the United States

Racism is based on the premise that certain groups of people are, by nature, superior to others and that "racial purity" must be safeguarded by avoiding race mingling at all costs. This mystical premise serves to justify cruel and sadistic behavior by those of the "chosen" race toward the "inferior" race. Thus, racism is not confined to any particular race or nation, and it must be seen as nothing more than an undisguised manifestation of the emotional plague.

The overwhelming majority of Americans, regardless of race, have a "live and let live" attitude to the degree to which they can tolerate undistorted contact with themselves and with each other. They are able to enjoy, to a varying extent, the freedom that life in America affords. At the extremes of the sociopolitical spectrum, ocular armor becomes prominent and restricts the ability to tolerate freedom. When this occurs, overt or covert emotional plague reactions in the form of racist behavior appear. Social withdrawal is a manifestation of the repressed type of ocular armoring. In social functioning, these individuals are found on the political right. Those on the left advocate greater control of society by "leaders" in government and seek to enact laws that require compulsory integration, while those on the right react to these measures by segregating themselves from the mainstream of American society and forming self-contained enclaves. An example of this reaction is the Bob Jones University. The tendency of the political right to self-segregate is as prevalent among American blacks as it is among whites. These racial attitudes are in large part characterologically determined. They have nothing to do with being black or white. *They are determined by the individual's sociopolitical character* and are the basis of many social problems that underlie the strained relations that often occur between American blacks and whites.

The social relationship between any two individuals or social groups is written orgonometrically as the simple attractive opposition of two homogeneous variations (Fig. 8.8).

A1 A2

FIGURE 8.8

A1 and A2 represent two entities that function as attractive opposite variations. The interaction is based on the contact between them. The CFP A represents the function (e.g., social contact, work) of the interaction (Fig. 8.9).

FIGURE 8.9

These equations state that in any relationship between two individuals, the energetic attraction between them A is the CFP of the interaction. In the case of two healthy individuals, contact is immediate and undistorted. The interaction is pleasurable, rational, and may have productive consequences. However, when ocular armor is present, contact is always disturbed: Reality is distorted and irrationality and destructiveness characterize social interactions. *Racial problems are the direct result of ocular armor and the consequent disturbance in contact.*

Racial problems in America are complicated because, in large part, ocular disturbances arise from the different layers of armor originating at different periods of individual and social life. The early and most critical period of armor formation occurs in the first four or five years, when the individual character is formed. The later period occurs in late adolescence, when environmental influences produce ocular armor in the form of sociopolitical ideologies.[146]

Historical Background

The history of blacks in America is significantly different from that of blacks in other parts of the New World because many American blacks were cared for and doted on by whites long after

146. Ocular armor can form at any time from birth to the final consolidation of character at the end of adolescence.

they were liberated from slavery. The paternalistic attitude of whites toward blacks did little to provide them with the capacity for independent functioning, whereas most liberated blacks in other countries had to fend for themselves to survive. This accounts for much of the difference in the character of American blacks from other blacks in the New World, and their relationship with whites.

As a result of the Civil War and Reconstruction, the Thirteenth, Fourteenth and Fifteenth Amendments, which abolished slavery and guaranteed civil rights and the suffrage to all Americans, including former slaves, were added to the Constitution. These amendments actually functioned as an additional layer of social armor on top of the preexisting armor of the antebellum South, since neither the blacks nor the whites were capable of embodying these changes from within themselves. Social armor was structuralized in the form of "Jim Crow" law. Whites and blacks lived under conditions of forced segregation.

During the authoritarian era, that is, before *Brown v. Board of Education* (1953) and before the start of the civil rights movement (~1955), only this early period of armor formation affected the social relationships between blacks and whites, particularly in the South. The racist manifestations of the emotional plague came through most clearly from whites on the extreme right, often with undisguised expressions of class consciousness, behind which were psychic manifestations of fear, thinly veiled as paranoid and prejudicial ideas. When among blacks, these whites often exhibited a façade of condescension (masked racism), which was insulting and hurtful to blacks, causing them to feel demeaned and socially isolated.

This situation abruptly changed in the late 1950s and early 60s when the emotional plague, in the person of the pseudo-liberal character, entered the social scene riding on the coattails of the civil rights movement. In 1964, Congress passed the Civil Rights Act outlawing discrimination in all public facilities. The relationship between blacks and whites changed dramatically when race-focused social reforms were offered as "solutions" to social problems. At this time, the pseudo-liberal became politically active, insidiously confusing the underlying issues with a more destructive, malignant ideology. The civil rights movement was radicalized when the central importance of independence and personal responsibility in effective, positive social change was ignored and when lawless behavior and rioting by blacks was supported and defended as "understandable." Urgent demands for immediate changes in the social relationship between whites and blacks were made. Preferential treatment and restitution for past wrongs done to blacks were proposed and forced integration was mandated.

These were indications that a new layer of ocular armor was added. This took hold of susceptible whites, those who were characterological and environmental liberals. The pseudo-liberals' unseeing, collectivist attitude in the civil rights movement was evident in the way blacks were referred to: They did not speak about a particular individual they knew personally and toward whom they felt kinship; they spoke about "blacks." To them, blacks were not seen as individuals in their own right but as a group, representatives of "blackness." A direct manifestation of ocular armor, all blacks were viewed and treated as one and the same, and color was their only differentiating feature—an extremely insulting, condescending, and thinly veiled racist attitude. There was also a feigned attitude of community, of kinship with all blacks, a reaction formation, the effect of which was to impose another artificial barrier between blacks and whites, which blacks rightly resented.

Charles Murray summarizes the shift in social policy that occurred during the Johnson administration as follows: "The economists seemed to have found the secret of lasting prosperity; policy makers and intellectuals[147] discovered structural poverty; the Civil Rights movement moved North, and the original antipoverty programs failed to show the expected results" (Murray 1984, page 24).

The expression "identity politics" crept into the language to describe political messages designed to appeal to voters who identify themselves as members of a certain minority group, such as government employees, Hispanics, or blacks. A racist tactic, it has been used by political and religious demagogues to pit one group against another to achieve power. Many American liberals, out of a sense of guilt for past and present injustices, felt the need to dote on, to feel responsible for, and to "understand" the "victim-

---

147. Pseudo-liberals.

ized" black. Irrational guilt results from an inability to tolerate and emotionally express rational and neurotic anger which then becomes directed inward. *The guilt of liberals is displaced onto social issues.* There is always an ocular (cognitive) component — guilt-ridden ideas that correspond to, and justify, the unexpressed, self-directed rage. These ideas revolve around viewing blacks as victims badly treated by whites under slavery, and after.

By assuming responsibility for the problems of blacks, white liberals attempt to redeem themselves for their past "injustices." Shelby Steele refers to this attitude of white liberals as "redemptive liberalism" (Steele 1998, page 11). This attitude, a more sophisticated form of condescension than that existing prior to the 1960s, had the unfortunate effect of giving an inflated sense of self-importance to those blacks who were susceptible. They were encouraged to feel a sense of entitlement, to believe that they indeed were victims abused by whites, with a right to what the white liberals told them they were owed. Blacks so afflicted were those on the lowest levels of society. They were individuals already dependent on society, with little or no work capacity and those with sociopathic tendencies. These individuals used the pseudo-liberal ideology of entitlement to their political and personal advantage.

To make matters worse, black "leaders" who focus on racial divisions too often continue to be showered with media attention by guilt-ridden white liberals and are given a free pass regarding their demagoguery. For example, recall how 2004 presidential candidate Al Sharpton was handled with kid gloves by other democratic presidential contenders. At the same time, leaders such as Clarence Thomas, J.C. Watts, and even Colin Powell and Condoleezza Rice are often called "sellouts," or worse, for not viewing every issue through a racial prism.

Consider, as another example, the furor that arose when Cornell West, a member of Harvard University's prized Afro-American Studies Department, was offended by Harvard's President Lawrence Summers. During a private, routine review of West's work, Summers voiced his dissatisfaction with West's performance, stating that he should have engaged in scholarly research instead of making a rap CD. West responded by threatening to move to Princeton University and other blacks afflicted by the emotional plague were outraged that Summers made such demands. Jesse Jackson, though never having spoken with West about the matter, charged that West felt "violated." Sharpton, claiming that Summers' chastisement of West could "intimidate" blacks, threatened to sue Harvard. In fact, it was Sharpton and the others who were intimidating Summers and inciting susceptible blacks. The effect of this attack was to produce a feeble, guilt-ridden response by Summers in which he reiterated his commitment to "diversity" at Harvard.

From a characterological viewpoint, blacks at risk for responding as victims belong to the political left. In these individuals, helplessness and an excessive dependency on others is the rule. This ideology, in extreme cases, is identical to the socialistic ideas first promulgated by Red Fascists. Its effect is to produce social anxiety by provoking race hatred.

The pathological symbiotic relationship between the white pseudo-liberal plague character and the entitled black liberal and pseudo-liberal is written as follows (Fig. 8.10).

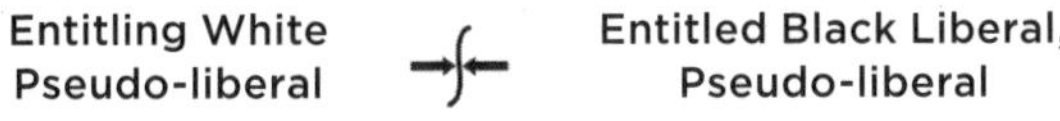

FIGURE 8.10

Steele (1998, page 11) understands this functional relationship correctly. He explains:

> What keeps [the truth] hidden is the symbiosis between whites and blacks by which they agree to let victimization *totally* explain black difficulty. Whites agree to stay on this hook for an illusion of redemption, and blacks agree to keep them there for an illusion of power . . . these investments are illusions . . . whites have no real redemption and blacks have no real power (italics in the original).
>
> When victimization is treated as a totalism, it keeps us from understanding the true nature of our suffering. It leads us to believe that *all* suffering is victimization and that *all* relief comes from the guilty good-heartedness of others. But people can suffer from bad ideas, from ignorance, fear, a poor assessment of reality, and from a

> politics that commits them to the idea of themselves as victims, among other things. When black group authority covers up those other causes of suffering just so whites will feel more responsible—and stay on the hook—then that authority actually encourages helplessness in its own people so that they might be helped by whites. It tries to make black weakness profitable by selling it as the white man's burden. [italics in the original]

Steele is a black conservative who has an intuitive functional grasp of political characterology. He touches on the defensive nature of the ideology of victimization: it prevents contact with the true nature of one's suffering. Being a victim relieves people of responsibility for their own actions. Steele understands that the ideological distinction between liberals and conservatives—black and white—hinges on their view of the black person's relationship to the issue of victimization and therefore on individual responsibility. The liberal looks at black behavior—high crime rates, weak academic performance, illegitimacy, and so on—and believes them to be the *result* of victimizing forces beyond their control. Conservatives do not deny this possibility, but refuse to presume it, holding that blacks are partly responsible for their misfortunes and therefore are capable of improving their lot in life.

To the right of the black conservative on the sociopolitical spectrum are reactionary blacks—individuals who can under certain conditions function as emotional plague characters. Their response to the liberal attitude toward blacks is entirely different but equally irrational. Feeling offended by white liberals' patronizing attitudes and having a greater sense of individuality than black liberals, they segregate themselves socially. To shore up their defenses, they often join fundamentalist religions such as the Black Muslims. When their defenses break down, they often resort to drugs, violence, and other criminal activity. Their contempt for whites is coupled with hatred for American traditions and institutions. Ocular armor prevents them from distinguishing between the sociopolitical attitudes of American whites on both extremes of the sociopolitical spectrum, and the majority of American whites who do not have a patronizing or condescending attitude toward blacks. For reactionary blacks, the white man is an inferior human being. Categorizing him as "whitey," they go to great lengths to prove that black skin is preferred. These racist attitudes result in the antagonistic opposition between reactionary black Americans and all white Americans (Fig. 8.11).

FIGURE 8.11

The Islamic Connection

Of all the varied groups of people who have embraced Islam over the past several decades, by far the largest has been American blacks. It is estimated that anywhere between one and two million American blacks have converted to the Muslim religion (Esposito 1999, page 609). Their conversion came largely through the Nation of Islam, headed by Elijah Muhammad. He taught his followers that whites are devils and that it is Christianity that serves to enslave blacks. His ideas were promulgated by his disciple, Malcolm X, a black reactionary who initially promoted a racist ideology of black supremacy as a reaction to the white supremacist ideology of the Ku Klux Klan. But after a visit to Mecca, he announced that his vision of Islam allowed for cooperation among whites and blacks.

On the surface, American blacks appear to have nothing in common with Islam. Why then have so many blacks living in a predominantly Christian country chosen not to belong to the Christian religion, but to convert to Islam? Four factors must be considered, all of which point to the reactionary character structure of these individuals. First, in their paranoia of and contempt for white America, black American reactionaries choose to identify themselves with a religion that is not indigenous to this country. This is rationalized as a search for an autonomous black American identity. Second, because there has been a breakdown of authoritarian society in the West and an increase in social anxiety, many blacks (like many whites) have turned to mysticism. The *Autobiography of Malcolm X* had a profound impact among American blacks, causing many to convert to the Islamic religion. Third, reactionary blacks have a characterological, sociopolitical affinity with followers of Islam, especially those belonging characterologically on the extreme right. Fourth, in addition to the mystical element, certain reactionary blacks whose armor rendered them unable to function in society, found a much needed external source of armor in Islam, with its religious rituals, social customs, and strict laws and restrictions on the life of the individual. The Islamic religion in its devout form supplies an externally imposed armor—for example, ritualistically praying five times a day, refraining from alcohol consumption, and fasting during the month of Ramadan.

As noted earlier, the Islamic religion is unique in that the overwhelming majority of its members are characterologically, in varying degrees, to the right and extreme right on the sociopolitical spectrum.[148] This puts the sociopolitical center—as represented by the character structure of the average Muslim—to the right as well. For this reason, the sociopolitical left's moderating influence on the right-leaning majority is small, and the potential for the eruption of the emotional plague from the right, given proper conditions, is correspondingly large.

The single most important element in the Muslim character structure that determines the individual's position on the sociopolitical right is his or her degree of mysticism. It is through mysticism that religious practices are anchored in daily living. In extreme cases, mystical attitudes toward life and religion can coincide. This gives rise to an ideology that joins religion and state—the ideology of Islamic fundamentalism. The greater people's shift to the right, the greater their mystical conviction that Islam is the only true religion. At the extreme right is the racist, Black Fascist Muslim, who lashes out with undisguised murderous hatred toward all those living in the West. These Muslims rationalize their behavior as the only way to maintain the purity of their race and bring it to dominance over inferior, "contaminated" races.

In recent decades, Muslims in America from all walks of life have become increasingly aware of the usefulness of political

---

148. Significantly, with an estimated population of some four million Muslims in the U.S., the arena for Muslim higher education is virtually empty. Of the 4,158 accredited colleges and universities in the U.S., there is not one moderate Muslim university.

activism to promote what they see as their common cause.[149] If the ideologies of Black Fascist Arab-American Muslims and Black Fascist American blacks become sufficiently attracted to each other, the groups will organize and increase their destructive forces against Western democracies[150] (Fig. 8.12).

Black Fascist Arab-American Muslims  Black Fascist American Blacks

FIGURE 8.12

Indeed, this association is currently developing. Over the past two decades, these two powerful currents have come together in America. Unless it is recognized and exposed by making it common knowledge, many hardworking, decent blacks and Arab Muslims will be swept up by the confusing rhetoric of Islamic reactionaries and Black Fascist plague characters. It is necessary in this ideological war to wage an educational campaign provid-

149. In 1988, for example, the Muslim Political Action Committee hosted the Reverend Jesse Jackson when he ran for president of the United States. The Arab American Institute was able to raise $700,000 for Jackson's campaign (Esposito 1999, page 637). This interest in political activism has extended to Arab Muslims on the extreme right. The ideology of these individuals is inflammatory and potentially highly destructive to American society. The late Ismail Al-Faruqi, for example, a Palestinian immigrant who founded the International Institute of Islamic Thought, wrote: "Nothing could be greater than this youthful, vigorous, and rich continent (of North America) turning away from its past evil and marching forward under the banner God Is Great. Al-Faruqi's hopes are today shared by educated Muslim leaders. Zaid Shakir, formerly a Muslim chaplain at Yale University, stated that Muslims cannot accept the legitimacy of the American secular system which "Is against the orders and ordainment of Allah. To the contrary, the orientation of the Qur'an pushes us to the exact opposite direction." To Ahmed Newfal, a leader of the Jordanian Muslim Brethren who speaks frequently at American Muslim rallies, "The United States has no thought, no values, and no ideals." He goes on to say if militant Muslims "stand up, with the ideology we possess, it will be very easy for us to preside over the world." (Daniel Pipes, "The Danger Within: Militant Islam in America," *Commentary*, November 2001.)

150. The ultimate dream of the Black Fascist Arab is to infuse the United States with Islamism. According to Shamim Al-Siddiqi, an influential commentator on American Muslim issues, it is the responsibility of American Muslims to bring Islam to power in America. "Every Muslim living in the West will stand in the witness box in the mightiest court of Allah . . . and give evidence that he has fulfilled his responsibility . . . that he left no stone unturned to bring the message of the Qur'an to every nook and corner of the country." These beliefs, manifestations of reactionary and Black Fascist ideology of Islamic Arabs reflect similar ideas of Black Fascist American blacks. Siraj Wahaj, for example, a black convert to Islam and the recipient of some of the American Muslim community's highest honors, stated that if only Muslims were more clever politically, they could take over the United States and replace its constitutional government with a caliphate. "If we were united and strong, we'd elect our own emir [leader] and give allegiance to him. . . . Take my word, if six or eight million Muslims unite in America, the country will come to us." (Ibid.)

ing solid evidence that the Islamic fanatics are infected with this emotional pestilence and that their goal is to destroy not only the United States but also the lives of all honest, decent people, black as well as white, Arab as well as non-Arab, world-wide.

The War on Drugs: America's Second Civil War

The function of the emotional plague is to destroy the healthy life of the individual and, by extension, the life of society, to degrade both to the lowest level of existence. In the United States today, there is no expression of social pathology that is more destructive than drug use. It is one of the principal symptoms of the emotional plague. It therefore follows that the war against drugs is also a war against the emotional plague. Unfortunately, widespread confusion, a result of armor, severely compromises society's ability to wage an effective campaign.

The increased use of illicit drugs has been the single most important factor in the breakdown of the authoritarian social order. Biophysically, drugs increase ocular armor while simultaneously weakening muscular armor in the lower segments. For the individual, the result is dramatic—a reduction in ocular functioning, particularly reducing genuine contact with both the self and the environment in an attempt to deaden painful emotions and sensations. This is the desired effect of all drugs, and it is often accompanied by an induced false sense of well-being, which, in a vicious cycle, necessitates greater dependency and further degradation in personal and social life.

There is currently no real understanding of the underlying cause of drug use and therefore no satisfactory solution. Instead, discussion of the "drug problem" focuses symptomatically on the influx of drugs into the United States and how to prevent it—the so-called "war on drugs." Little or nothing is said about the importance of *why* people are attracted to drugs in the first place. Obviously, without the demand, there would be no drug problem. Therefore, the basic question is why drugs became such a serious problem, with demand rising sharply in the 1960s. Overall drug use rose steadily in the 1970s, reaching a peak of nearly 14 percent of the population in 1979.

The reason for the sharp rise in the demand for illegal drugs was, in part, increased availability, but this is not the whole answer. *The real reason is that prior to around 1960, the authoritarian social order was still intact.* This well-structured social condition functioned effectively to contain the destructive secondary impulses. The rational basis for an authoritarian social order is that, because of armor, people are incapable of living naturally and fully from their core and are therefore unable to regulate themselves. This is why they require authoritarian constraints in the form of external rules and regulations. These serve as an externally applied layer of armor.

When society transformed from an authoritarian to an anti-authoritarian structure in the turbulent 1960s, enormous quantities of pent-up sexual energy broke through the armor of adolescents and young adults, which gave rise to intense longing for sexual fulfillment. Tragically, because armor was still present, their sexual feelings could not be gratified. *Out of frustration, many then turned to drugs to overcome their sexual disappointment.* Thus was originated the rebellious slogan, "sex, drugs, and rock 'n' roll." When this "sexual revolution" did not materialize, many young people were left feeling sexually anxious. The energy behind these feelings turned into destructive rage that was displaced externally onto social authority as provocation and violence. From then on American society became increasingly and hopelessly divided into left and right, and at war with itself.

Thus, the breakdown of the authoritarian social order was fueled largely by the failed sexual revolution of the 1960s. When this happened, adolescents and young adults caught up in it were left feeling emotionally stranded and alienated from their parents. They sought substitute measures to obtain relief from their sexual tension. Some allowed themselves to be duped and were readily enlisted by left-wing activists, becoming involved in anti–Vietnam War and anti-American demonstrations. But for most, political activism was able to discharge only a relatively small amount of pent-up energy. By far the greater amount could be handled only with the use of illicit drugs. This attempt at self-medication was necessary to get relief from unreleased sexual tension or to deaden sensations. The hard rock music that became popular at this time was an attempt both to deaden sexual feelings and to break through the armor and feel more.

The sharp rise in drug consumption during this period was directly related to the breakdown of the constricting effects of authoritarianism and the inability of youth to achieve genital satisfaction. This is the underlying reason why illegal drugs, sexual promiscuity, and defiance of authority became hallmarks of the counterculture. All were part and parcel of the social transformation that was occurring at the time. Thus, illicit drug use was a symptom consisting of two components: it expressed secondary layer impulses in the form of contempt for authority and, at the same time, it defended against the expression of core impulses which could not be satisfied. Without the anti-authoritarian transformation of society, there would have been no serious drug problem in the first place. At the same time, without the drug problem, the social transformation would never have been so harsh and destructive.

The Drug War as Civil War

Approximately one hundred years after the start of the American Civil War, in the 1960s, the United States became embroiled in the drug war. In contrast to the Civil War, which had a definite onset and conclusion, the drug war started insidiously, escalated slowly, and became protracted. After more than forty years, this war still has no end in sight. The Civil War was fought mainly on the battlefield; the drug war is being fought in every area of social life, public and private. The Civil War's casualties were restricted to able-bodied men of military age, whereas drug use destroys people without discrimination, directly or indirectly, at every stage of life. This includes children, infants, and even the unborn. The destructiveness of drugs extends to the very core of life, as they attack both the germinal (genetic) and the somatic protoplasm. Because drugs affect the biological core, they also destroy sexual and work functioning. The Civil War was mainly limited to the use of military weapons, whereas the drug war employs various levels of social engagement, from paramilitary-style battles between drug dealers and law enforcement officers, to ideological battles regarding legalization. There are those who believe that there is nothing wrong with using certain drugs, such as marijuana, and those who believe that all drugs are dangerous. The Civil War extracted a heavy cost on individual and social life, whereas the cost of the drug war, in terms of money spent and its destructiveness to human life, is incalculable. The Civil War resulted from fundamental differences of opinion with regard to basic social issues (the question of the sovereignty of the states and of the legitimacy of slavery), whereas the ideology of the drug war remains vague and confused. In contrast to the limited national scope of the Civil War, the drug war is international. As a result of the Civil War, the nation was preserved as a whole and slavery ended. But drug use has been little affected by the war on drugs. In fact, the war has only helped create a multi-billion-dollar black market.

Yet, from a biosocial standpoint, similarities between the two wars are more significant than their differences. Both resulted from the contradiction between natural core impulses and impulses from the destructive secondary layer. In the case of the Civil War, the core impulse was the biological work function: Armored people (slave owners) forced other armored people (slaves) to perform work. In the case of the drug war, the core impulse is sexual: Armored people who are incapable of experiencing relief of tension through natural sexual gratification turn to illegal drugs as a substitute means of satisfaction.

Slavery and drug abuse, the primary issues of the Civil War and the drug war, are both destructive to human individual and social life. Both are manifestations of the emotional plague. Slavery and slave trading are manifestations from the secondary layer of economic activity. Similarly, drug production and the drug trade also arise from the secondary layer. The outbreak of the Civil War occurred when the slave population increased to the point that it threatened the very existence of the United States. Today, like slavery, drugs have become inimical to the life of our democratic society and a real threat to its existence.

In 1835, deTocqueville accurately described the life-inimical social conditions in the antebellum South that would lead to secession 25 years later. He said:

> The institution of slavery (not geographical or other differences) had created a way of life in the South that was completely different from that in the North. The result of this is that the South was crippled in its development. The South was weaker, poorer, and dependent on the North, and was becoming more so with the passage of time.

He describes the difference between the Slave States and the Free States in the 1830s by contrasting life on the opposite banks of the Ohio River:

> On the two banks of the Ohio, nature has given man an enterprising and energetic character; but on each side of the river, he makes a different use of this common quality.
>
> The white on the right [Northern] bank, obliged to live by his own efforts, has placed in material well-being the principal goal of his existence; and as the country that he inhabits presents inexhaustible resources to his industry and offers ever renewed enticements to his activity, his ardor for acquiring has surpassed the ordinary bounds of human cupidity: tormented by the desire for wealth, one sees him enter boldly onto all paths that fortune opens to him; he becomes indiscriminately a sailor, a pioneer, a manufacturer, a farmer, supporting the work or dangers attached to these different professions with equal constancy; there is something marvelous in the resources of his genius and a sort of heroism in his greed [*avidité*, which means eagerness as well as *greed*] for gain.
>
> The American on the left [Southern] bank scorns not only work, but all the undertakings that work makes successful; living in idle ease, he has the tastes of idle men: money has lost a part of its worth in his eyes; he pursues fortune less than agitation and pleasure, and he applies in this direction the energy that his neighbor deploys elsewhere; he passionately loves hunting and war; he pleases himself with the most violent exercise of the body; the use of arms is familiar to him, and from his childhood he had learned to stake his life in single combat [i.e., dueling]. Slavery, therefore, not only prevents whites from making a fortune; it diverts them from wanting it.
>
> The same causes working in contrary directions continuously for two centuries in the English colonies of northern America have in the end made an enormous difference between the commercial capacity of the southerner and that of the northerner. Today, it is only the North that has ships, manufactures, railroads, and canals. . . . Almost all men in the southernmost states of the Union who engage in commercial undertakes . . . have come from the North." (Tocqueville 2000, pages 333–334; bracketed text, italics added)

In healthy functioning, freedom and responsibility coexist. In the armored, one supersedes the other. In both slavery and drug addiction, freedom is placed over responsibility—freedom to buy, sell and use humans and drugs. Responsibility to do what is right, however, is of no consequence.

The underlying division between the North and the South that led to the Civil War came about as a question of states' rights. The South held that the states had the right to secede from the Union because the Union did not respect their sovereign right to own slaves. The North, on the other hand, held that the states did not have that right because slavery is destructive. The underlying issue of the drug war is whether individuals have the right to use illegal drugs. Do states have the authority to legalize drugs, or is that authority under the jurisdiction of the federal government? These questions a century apart, if answered in favor of slavery and illegal drugs, require the separation of freedom from responsibility on all levels—the nation, society, and the individual.

The biophysical similarity of slaves and those addicted to or abusing drugs is striking. Both groups suffer severe damage in their capacity for independent functioning. As with all human beings, both groups are originally endowed with free will and the capacity for the responsible exercise of freedom. However, severe damage to their core functions leave both poorly prepared to tolerate freedom. It is instructive to see that slaves and drug addicts both are emotionally dependent on a single individual for survival: the slave on the master, the drug addict on the supplier.

Finally, both slave ownership and drug use prevent the individual from functioning with independence and self-sufficiency. The slave owner is dependant on the work of the slave. The drug user is neither independent nor self-sufficient, and he himself is a slave to drugs.

The ideological conflict over the issues of slavery in the antebellum South has parallels to today's debate on illegal drugs. At the outset of the Civil War, most of Lincoln's generals erroneously believed that the war was a battle between two legitimate governments, the Union and the Confederate States. This idea contributed in large part to the military incompetence of the Union forces on the battlefield. Lincoln was one of the few people who correctly saw the war as an insurrection. Not until he ordered

Grant and Sherman to lead the Union Army was this misconception corrected. Similarly, in the case of the drug war, there is much confusion over the nature of the conflict: Is it a legal problem, a medical problem, a psychological problem, or a social problem? Much of this confusion is generated by the pro-drug forces.

These comparisons are not merely metaphorical. The designation of the drug war as a civil war is literally correct.[151] In countries such as Colombia, for example, where narcotic trafficking is a major source of illicit revenue, this civil war exists in a fully developed form; in the United States, the civil war is still in its early stages. Colombia's two most powerful terrorist organizations, FARC and FLN, have been trying for decades to conquer that country and forcibly turn a formal democracy into a Marxist dictatorship. In addition to being funded by the proceeds of drug trafficking, their military power is financed by kidnapping and extortion. The political front of the Colombian guerillas has launched a psychological and judicial war that turns "human rights" into a weapon. To do this, the guerillas use nongovernmental organizations of similar ideological persuasion to attain their objectives. Peasants from rebel strongholds are sent into court to make accusations of human rights violations against military officers. The rebels know that United States policy is to pressure Colombia to relieve of command any officer so accused or risk losing aid. This systematic dismantling of that country's most capable military leadership at the behest of the United States has been a big blow to military morale and has done great damage to Colombia's defenses.[152]

As the wealthiest nation in the world, the United States is the prime target of drug traffickers. Slavery and drugs can destroy a society as effectively as can military conflict. In fact, the United States is more vulnerable to the destructiveness of drugs than to an overt military conflict because the gravity of the threat remains unrecognized. For this reason, effective defensive forces cannot be mobilized. Even when the existence of a drug war is acknowledged, the "war" is viewed only as a figure of speech. This

151. The money that fuels the *jihad* revolutionaries in several countries in Central Asia, including Uzbekistan, comes largely from the opium trade, mainly from the Arabian Gulf states, in particular Saudi Arabia. (See Rashid 2002).

152. See Mary Anastasia O'Grady, "Does Colombia Count in the War on Terror?," *Wall Street Journal*, Feb. 14, 2003.

confusion is at the heart of the drug war.[153] Also, part of the reason for the confusion is that no circumscribed social groups can be identified in the conflict. Drug addiction, use, and abuse cut across all social and economic boundaries.

The drug war is a true civil war because it is an insurrection, a rising against civil authority on a national scale. As in the case of the first American Civil War, the battle of the drug war is over legalizing a product solely for its use to satisfy a secondary layer need. The war pits two opposing forces against each other, those for and those against legalizing drugs. It will ultimately destroy America if the drug cartels and those who support drug use prevail.

The Origins of the Drug War

Illegal drug trafficking is a prime example of the biological work function originating from the destructive secondary layer. The anti-authoritarian transformation of Western society and the concomitant rise in social anxiety, especially among the younger generation, has largely contributed to a dissociation of society into two groups: those who continue to identify with the old social order (primarily conservative characters) and those who now identify with the anti-authoritarian counterculture (primarily liberal and pseudo-liberal characters). Many young people in the counterculture began to use illegal drugs to alleviate their sexual anxiety and also as an act of revenge directed against the hated father.[154] Through this mechanism, rage was displaced onto the social realm as anti-authoritarianism.

This gave rise to conflict between the two groups. The relationship between them is defined orgonometrically as the attractive opposition of two homogeneous variations (groups or classes of individuals). When the hostility intensified, the opposing forces came into armed conflict (Fig. 8.13).

---

153. See Gary Fields, "Move to Link Drug, Terror Wars Draws Flak," *Wall Street Journal*, April 1, 2002.

154. As drug use and its adverse consequence extend to younger adolescents, there is a decrease in muscular armor and an increase in ocular armor, with all of its dire consequences. For example, the reduction in muscular armor and natural aggression accompanying marijuana use has had a feminizing effect on men and this is responsible in large part for the general decline in masculinity in the adult male population.

Anti-Drug Forces (police, nonaddicts)	→⟆←	Pro-Drug Forces (growers, suppliers, dealers, users/addicts)

FIGURE 8.13

The drug user is included on the side of the pro-drug forces in Figure 8.13 because *the consumer is the driving force behind the drug war.* The need for drugs by people who are emotionally sick creates value for the illicit substances. The drug user is the one who supports the drug dealer and indirectly the whole chain of suppliers leading back to the drug producers and the foreign governments that protect them.

The state of attractive opposition between users and nonusers exists solely because of those who oppose drug use. Marijuana users especially and a large percentage of liberals prefer a state of antagonistic opposition. To the extent possible, drug users have seceded from the United States and created their own "nation" in the form of their so-called counterculture.

One clear example of this attempt at secession is the action of Hollywood moviemakers who actively portray marijuana use as a normal and positive part of teenage life. This happens to a lesser degree and in more subtle ways on television, but in films it is quite blatant. Essentially, such moviemakers want to create a new nation, separate from the United States, where drug use is not merely tolerated but is considered natural and something that should be encouraged. As is well known, Hollywood is largely populated by liberals, many of whom live in their own world of unreality and are drug users themselves.

Pseudo-liberals with their philosophy of multiculturalism in effect encourage various groups—blacks, Hispanics, Muslims, women—to secede from society, to live in their own culture. Drug use among minorities is particularly destructive because it usually leads to withdrawal from society whereas, in itself, being part of a minority group does not. Because the ideology of secession is easily rationalized as a form of tolerance, the American tradition of "live and let live," it becomes acceptable to the population in general and to true liberals in particular.

A similar relationship of simple opposition occurred during the first Civil War between Union and Confederate forces (Fig. 8.14).

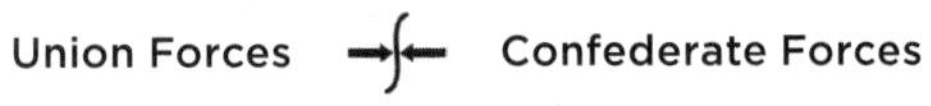

Union Forces →⨍← **Confederate Forces**

FIGURE 8.14

If the South had won the Civil War and slavery had remained legal, the functional relationship between the North and South would have become one of antagonistic opposition (Fig. 8.15).

North ←⨍→ **South**

FIGURE 8.15

Both governments would have had essentially identical constitutions with the exception of the status of slavery.

Similarly, the legalization of drugs would change the relationship between the two forces from simple opposition to antagonistic opposition, bringing about antithetical functions that exclude each other. If this situation prevailed it would inevitably result in the eventual disintegration of American society (Fig. 8.16).

Anti-Drug Forces ←⨍→ **Pro-Drug Forces**

FIGURE 8.16

Orgonometrically, Figures 8.14 to 8.17 state that the anti-drug forces in the drug war are functionally identical to the Union forces in the Civil War. Both serve to preserve the United States as a unified system of government. If the Southern forces had been victorious in the Civil War, the common functioning principle the United States of America would have ceased to exist as a national system. Lincoln was aware of this, and for this reason would not compromise with the South on the issue of slavery. He understood the consequences of doing otherwise. In the case of the drug war, legalization would also split the nation, erode society, and quite possibly bring about its ultimate collapse. This outcome is fully consistent with the sociopolitical agenda of the pseudo-liberal character whose unstated goal is to undermine the authority of America both nationally and internationally.

The current understanding of the drug war does not consider the significance of the functional relationship between drug user and drug supplier. This relationship is one of simple attractive opposition (Fig. 8.17).

Drug User →⨍← **Drug Supplier**

FIGURE 8.17

This equation states that both drug user and drug supplier are necessary for a drug war. *By economically supporting the seller, the drug user is as criminally responsible for maintaining the drug war as those on the supply side of the relationship and must be held as accountable.* Evasion of this fact turns the drug war into an insoluble, muddled conflict in which narcotics officers are placed in the awkward, untenable position *between* the drug buyer and the seller.

The drug war, however, involves every citizen and all aspects of society. The toll on the personal and economic life of the non-user population is astronomical. It includes taxing the public to support the battle, degradation of the workplace and the social environment, and the emotional and financial cost to friends and relatives of drug addicts and abusers, and so on.

There can be only two outcomes to this war. Either the drug cartels are destroyed or, sooner or later, life as we now know it in the United States will vanish. The cause will not be the drug suppliers per se but rather mankind's underlying sexual disturbance that drives the insatiable need. Personal and social anxiety as well as irresponsibility will continue to rise with the breakdown of society. This can only leave an increasing number of people prone to seek relief through the use of illegal drugs. The danger lies in the imperceptibly gradual rise in the demand for illegal drugs from the increasingly anxious younger generations. Between 1992 and 1999, rates of drug use, defined as once a month or more, increased 15 percent. Rates of marijuana use increased 11 percent. The situation was far worse among children: Use of illegal drugs increased 37 percent among eighth-graders and 55 percent among tenth-graders. More than one-quarter of high school seniors use illegal drugs. The rate of drug use among high school seniors increased 86 percent between 1992 and 1999.[155]

The widespread increase in drug use, with all its personal, social, and economic consequences, can be traced back to the emotional plague. Armored humanity, unable to sustain contact and experience emotions and organ sensations, remains terrified, falls victim to the plague, and turns to drugs. *Only when people can tolerate experiencing and expressing their deepest feelings—including love with sexual satisfaction—will drug use cease to be a problem. The drug problem is symptomatic of the inability of armored, orgastically impotent humans to regulate themselves.*

Accordingly, there are two effective approaches to the drug problem. The first is to address the present-day problem and offer short-term solutions: effective public education that focuses on the personal and social harmfulness of drugs and emphasizes the importance of maintaining their illegal status with vigorously enforced laws. The second approach is long-term and requires the prevention of underlying character pathology in individuals: It must be understood that emotionally healthy people have no need to take drugs. This goal can only be achieved by raising healthier children and thereby reducing armor in future generations. (See chapter 9)

Confusion resulting from ignorance needs to be distinguished from confusion originating from limitations of understanding due to the individual's character. The former can be addressed by the presentation of facts and by education, whereas the latter cannot. Confusion about the drug war falls into several categories. Those having to do with the harmfulness of various substances can be addressed using the information available to the public and there is general agreement regarding the destructive effects of narcotics, cocaine, LSD, and other "hard drugs." There is, therefore, no possibility that these drugs will ever be legalized. Marijuana, however, is another matter entirely because there is great confusion and controversy with regard to its destructive-

155. See William J. Bennett. "The Drug War Worked Once. It Can Work Again," *Wall Street Journal*, May 15, 2001.

ness and whether it should be legalized.[156]

The legalization of marijuana is the ideological battleground of the drug war and this issue positively defines it as a civil war, a conflict between those for and against its use and legalization. These forces are in simple opposition (see Fig. 8.14). In addition to its inherent danger, many susceptible individuals who try marijuana start down a slippery slope and become addicted to or abuse hard drugs. The marijuana issue is like a Trojan horse in the drug war.

Despite the overwhelming documentation of the destructiveness of marijuana, articles supporting the harmlessness of marijuana continue to be published in the media and in the medical literature. Their conclusions are necessarily flawed as these reports do not have or include a bioenergetic perspective. They only fuel the widespread confusion regarding the dangers of marijuana use. In fact, in an important way, marijuana is even more dangerous than hard drugs because it insidiously attacks the individual's perceptual apparatus, destroying the capacity for emotional contact with self and with the environment, and all this occurs without the individual's awareness. Unlike moderate consumption of alcohol, a single use of marijuana often has a long-lasting, debilitating effect on an individual's emotional responsiveness to both inner and external stimuli.[157] Marijuana puts the person out of touch with the very things he needs to feel in order to know that he has a problem. After the initial intoxication subsides, it still compromises one's ability to function, although its destructive effects are often too subtle to be recognized by most observers. This has given rise to the mistaken notion that the drug is benign. In both liberal characters and marijuana users, emotions are dulled while sensations are heightened[158] and natural aggression is weakened. The net social effect of legalizing marijuana will be to reduce the capacity for

---

156. For those who believe that marijuana is a harmless substance, I suggest reading W.B. Apple Ph.D. 1999. Marijuana's Role in Inducing Social and Individual Chaos: an Orgonomic Perspective. *Journal of Orgonomy*, 33 (1, 2).

157. This is particularly obvious in ocular characters, in whom a single exposure to marijuana can induce a psychotic episode.

158. Robert Harman, M.D. 1999. Effects of Adolescent Marijuana Use: A Case History. *Journal of Orgonomy* 33 (1,2): 95–113,

independent thought, increasing people's passivity and susceptibility to indoctrination by leftist ideologues.

Moderate use of alcohol usually has no negative effect on social functioning.[159] Even immoderate use of alcohol does not threaten the integrity of America as a nation. Marijuana, even "in moderation," is a real threat to the nation's integrity, just as slavery and secession were. This is why marijuana must be dealt with on the *federal* level. Educational programs that lump alcohol and tobacco together with illegal drugs confuse people, especially the young, and immobilize efforts to curtail the use of all three. For example, the result of the Clinton administration's programs for teenagers was a sharp increase in illegal drug use and often an increase in alcohol consumption and cigarette smoking as well.

To the extent that these areas of confusion can be clarified, it will be possible to relieve some of the paralysis that interferes with truly waging war on illicit drugs. From an orgonometric perspective, the drug war consists of two groups in a relationship of simple opposition. To maintain this relationship it is necessary to keep drugs illegal.

Only two alternatives are possible when the ideological forces behind the pro-drug group increase to a level that threatens social organization. Either the forces continue to remain in simple opposition, in which case the confrontation between them remains permanent, or the relationship changes from simple opposition to one of antagonistic opposition, in which case both groups coexist by way of legalization and try to make their peace with each other. Many people desire to legitimize drug use and, in so doing, they declare that drugs are harmless. Seen from the perspective of character, conservatives, in general, are in favor of maintaining a state of simple opposition, whereas liberals and pseudo-liberals favor changing to a state of antagonistic opposition.

When placed in this perspective, the question of which alternative can better preserve the existing social order becomes apparent: Society can be preserved only by maintaining a state of simple opposition between the two forces. Changing the relationship to one of antagonistic opposition by enacting legislation

---

159. Alcohol metabolizes into water and carbon dioxide and contains none of the complex fat-soluble organic compounds found in marijuana.

to legalize illicit drugs will only further accelerate the continuing deterioration of social order.

Traditionally, the drug war has focused on the role of the supplier. The significance of the user has been misunderstood and not appreciated. It is generally believed that the drug problem can be solved by reducing or eliminating the drug supply. The critical question almost never asked is, "*Why* are *illicit drugs in demand in the first place?*" Focusing on the supplier avoids this essential aspect of the drug war. As noted, there is a close functional relationship between the supplier and the user (see Fig. 8.17). The user is recognized as being part of the drug problem only as a victim who needs treatment, not from the perspective that he or she is as much a criminal and is as responsible as the supplier. Even the staunchest conservative is too "liberal" when it comes to recognizing this point. FARC, Colombia's leftist insurgency, is kept alive by the voracious appetite of American and European drug consumers who crave the coca leaf and other illegal drugs. This demand keeps prices up and the suppliers rolling in cash, weapons, and new recruits.

From the standpoint of therapy, drug addiction or dependency renders an individual a poor candidate for treatment. This is largely because the particular biophysical state of the user is the driving force behind drug use in the first place. The user's armor cannot adequately bind energy, and it is this lack of sufficient armor that results in intolerable feelings that necessitate self-medication, an external means of reducing tension and anxiety. This understanding is central to the physiology of addiction and is the reason why placing users in a therapeutic milieu without their *total* cooperation does not work. Only when the user is made to assume responsibility for his or her addiction and is willing to tolerate and manage the underlying anxiety and other dysphoric feelings without illegal drugs, does therapy have any chance of success.[160]

Falling short of such a development, the supplier *and* user require incarceration. Unfortunately, prison sentences and fines

---

160. The effectiveness of organizations such as Alcoholics Anonymous (AA) and Narcotics Anonymous (NA) depend on alcoholics or addicts assuming full responsibility for their problems.

are usually imposed only on the supplier when, in fact, they must also be levied on the user as well.

Neither the political left nor the political right understands the true function of prison. Since those on the left believe that human nature is essentially good, it follows that, for them, evil is the result of imperfect institutions. They believe that prisons are necessary to maintain social order only because harmful social institutions exist. They believe that if these institutions can be changed, people can be "perfected" and they will then behave rationally, thereby eliminating the need for prisons. Those on the right believe prisons are necessary because evil is part of the general infirmity of human nature. Prisons are viewed as penitentiaries, a place where it is hoped that evil criminals can repent and mend their ways.

Neither the left nor the right views the relationship between prisons and criminals from the functional energetic standpoint. Prisons are necessary for individuals who, because of their insufficient armor, behave criminally. Prisons are a form of *externally imposed armor* for those with insufficient internal armor.[161] Because users have insufficient armor, act criminally, and are not able to care for themselves responsibly, they too require external armor. Imprisoning users is therefore rational from the functional point of view.[162] In armored society, prisons are a necessary condition of social existence. With the rise of anti-authoritarianism and the attendant rise in social anxiety and, with it, impulsive behavior, the use of prison is more necessary than ever before. Removing the user from society is beneficial because it eliminates the addict's social milieu, which often functions to support the drug habit. Incarcerating users also is rational policy because, as consumers of an illegal substance that is highly destructive to both the individual and to society, they are criminals. The freedom they are permitted in society only exacerbates the enor-

---

161. "Gate fever" is a syndrome of heightened anxiety and anxiety-related behavior commonly exhibited by inmates who are about to be released from prison. The phenomenon illustrates the importance of the function of prison in providing an external form of armor to those in whom internal armoring is not effective in curbing socially destructive behavior.

162. The number of individuals needing incarceration would be far fewer than the current number of drug users because the threat of actual imprisonment would be a sufficient deterrent for most users.

mous emotional and economic cost of the drug war. It is directly responsible for supporting the military forces of the international drug cartels, forces opposed to the United States government.[163]

In addition to prison sentences, fines must be imposed on the user. If a person is financially destitute, work can become an acceptable form of payment. The collected fines can go toward building more prisons to house convicted users. Using fines in this manner can give the user a well-needed sense of responsibility for his or her life. Such a functional view of drug addiction removes the issue from the moral sphere of sociopolitics and places it squarely in the realm of social pathology. This functional formulation provides the effective method of dealing with this seemingly complex problem.

At this point, an apparent contradiction arises: How can we advocate the external application of armor when our goal is to remove it? The contradiction can be resolved if we recall that the original function of armor in the infant and young child is to protect the individual against experiencing painful emotions and sensations. At the same time, the life force in the young organism continues to strive to express itself, to grow, and to develop. The continued opposition between these two forces throughout childhood and into adolescence brings to completion the individual's character structure. Character development is the result of a compromise between instinctual forces and those that impinge from the environment. Character, therefore, is made up of both healthy and unhealthy components. In each individual, the quality and quantity of armor needed to oppose impulses from the destructive secondary layer vary. If the destructive impulses can be contained, then armor is successful. If not, then symptoms appear. These can be within the individual (e.g., anxiety, depression) or in the social realm (behavior disorders, drug use, and criminality). Where armor cannot contain secondary layer impulses, external control is required. Psychopharmacological agents can be used for noncriminal neurotic behavior and external constraints (prison) for criminal activity.

With regard to treatment, before armor can be removed to bring about clinical improvement, the discharge of destructive

163. An alternative to prison is "house arrest": using a monitor attached to the ankle that sends a signal to the police when the user leaves the house.

impulses in the individual's social life must first be curbed; that is, the individual must first re-armor. Only then is it possible to systematically remove armor in a therapeutic setting.

It is important to recognize that neither imprisonment nor fines are being prescribed as punishment of the offenders. A functional view of the drug war removes the issue of drugs entirely from the moral realm. We do not want to excuse users and suppliers, as does the liberal, nor do we want to punish them, as does the conservative. Taking the drug war out of the realm of ideological armored thinking is the only way to succeed in this crucial battle. It must be kept in mind that the drug war is but a symptom of pathological social functioning of armored humans. It belongs in the province of the medical and social sciences and it can be understood with functional thinking. Unfortunately, major obstacles to resolving this conflict are to be found in the very people charged with the responsibility of resolving the problem. These include the lawyers, judges, psychiatrists, psychologists, other health care professionals, politicians, and the countless bureaucrats who have a vested economic interest in and personal need to perpetuate this continuing conflict.

CHAPTER 9

CONTAINMENT AND ERADICATION OF THE EMOTIONAL PLAGUE

> We must assume that no freedom movement
> has any chance of success unless it opposes
> the organized emotional plague with truthfulness,
> and does it clearly and vigorously.
> —Wilhelm Reich, *Character Analysis*

It is impossible to completely eradicate the emotional plague, just as it is impossible to totally eliminate human armor. It is possible, however, to prevent some of the plague's destructiveness and to bring a greater degree of peace and security to social life than that which currently exists.

Armored humanity, except for a relatively small number of pestilential people, has always yearned for peace, prosperity, security, freedom, and harmony. Yet, human beings have never been able to achieve these goals. We are fortunate to be living at a time when there is the possibility of harnessing the tremendous power of orgone energy through the application of functional thinking to secure these social conditions for the benefit of all mankind. Why, then, does the practical attainment of these goals remain so remote? Why, century after century, everywhere on Earth, have the forces of every freedom movement, as well as the forces of truthfulness and rationality, failed to prevail? The answer is that *armored people, because of their deep-seated fear of undistorted perception of their own sensations and emotions, are unable to see clearly and act rationally.* As a result, whenever issues of peace and freedom are discussed, they ignore the essential elements that are the natural foundations of peace and freedom. Thus, for example, it is a well-known fact that politics, as it is routinely conducted, greatly interferes with social life and that people are very sick, in the bioemotional psychiatric sense. These obvious facts are never considered in discussions, especially those on how to safeguard peace and freedom. Instead of recognizing biological armor as the root cause of human suffering and irrationality, people continue to flee from this truth, blame each other, and continue to devise one failed thought system after another. Neither liberalism nor conservatism nor any other "-ism" that has been invented by the mind of armored humans has resulted in improvement in the human condition. Some systems, like Red Fascism (Communism) or Black Fascism (Nazism, Islamic fundamentalism), have made matters much worse, and the cost to humanity in terms of lives lost and ruined and resources spent and squandered are incalculable.

Religion and politics are two sacred cows that people can never have a rational discussion about because the third sacred cow, the natural function of human sexuality, is never touched. This "Do not touch it!" was first described by Reich. As a result, armored humans, because of their *biophysical incapacity* to feel truth within themselves and to see their environment objectively, continue to pursue the illusion that there are religious, political, and economic solutions to their personal and social problems. Through this combination of mystical hope and belief, people avoid becoming aware of the legitimate functions of government and *are determined not to take full responsibility for their own lives.*

Psychologists and psychiatrists have described the various defense mechanisms that neurotics use in their thinking. Orgonomic biopsychiatry has shown that these mechanisms result from the effect of armor on the individual's thought processes. These same mechanisms are operative in the case of social armor. Through the protective defense mechanisms of denial, projection, and displacement of personal conflicts onto the social sphere, and through identification with leaders who promise salvation, the masses of people are spared the discomfort and pain of delving within themselves for the source of their problems.

Clinical experience has revealed time and again that it is simply too disturbing and frightening for people to look at and face themselves. Armor, while it protects people from fully experiencing their emotions and sensations, simultaneously restricts the quality of their life in every area. We know, from the case studies of medical orgone therapists, that removal of armor enables individuals to relinquish their neurotic ways of thinking and to think functionally about individual and social problems. Armor removal also enables people to see and combat manifestations of the emotional plague more effectively when they encounter them in their daily lives.

Because he has pulled energy up into his brain, the liberal lives in a world of ideas and idealistic illusions. This inability to see the world realistically puts him and his neighbors in mortal danger when his country is being threatened by a deadly enemy, such as the Islamo-Fascist. He is also an inveterate idealist with all kinds of solutions, some quite detailed, for the problems of the world. Unfortunately, the use of his intellect primarily functions to avoid being in touch with his own secondary layer as well as that of others. Because of his hypertrophied intellect, he is also unable to make contact with deep feelings from the core. As a result, he attempts to solve his personal problems by saving the world, never realizing that his sociopolitical activity is in large measure a defensive action. This results in the quest for and championing of makeshift, substitute solutions which not only complicate and aggravate social problems, they actually *prevent* armored humans from responsibly examining and facing their individual problems. The liberal's longing for freedom is based on his desire to escape from internal restrictions through using his intellect. This longing is projected outward as a social ideal and pursued through freedom movements and other sociopolitical activities. *Just as religion promises salvation to those on the political right, sociopolitics does the same for those on the left. Sociopolitical activity thus is an elaborate evasion and functions as an effective barrier to individual and social responsibility, and to genuine progress.* As people have become more anxious, the infestation of the emotional plague in the form of sociopolitical activism has spread to the political right.

In addition to interfering with social functioning, the avoidance of the essential permeates every area of human life. In medicine, for example, a correct understanding of the true cause of the majority of medical illnesses afflicting people remains a mystery because their fundamental bioemotional basis is not recognized. The mechanistic physician offers the same approach to human disease that the mechanistic liberal politician brings to social disease: Both ignore the underlying origin of the pathological condition and focus instead on the symptom. We are fortunate to have the tool of functional thinking to provide clarity. Reich defined these illnesses of unknown origin as *somatic biopathies*. He found them to be rooted in a disturbance in the emotional life of the individual that, over time, impairs natural pulsation of the plasmatic system.[164] Cancer, atherosclerotic heart disease, diabetes, obesity, and the myriad autoimmune diseases are some examples of somatic biopathies, each with their own constellation of symptoms. Every one of these illnesses involves an underlying sexual disturbance that has, at its basis, disturbed bioenergetic pulsation. Because he does not understand this essential clinical finding, the classically trained physician postulates physical agents in the environment, not at all related to emotion, that with some grain of truth can be plausibly offered as a causative agent. Poor diet, lack of exercise, and tobacco use are but a few examples of the "whipping boys" implicated as the cause of these illnesses.

These factors can exacerbate medical conditions, causing them to appear earlier rather than later in the patient's life, but they are *not* their true origin. The relationship between cancer and cigarette smoking is a good example. From the fact that many smokers develop lung cancer, it is erroneously concluded that cigarette smoking "causes" cancer. Cigarette smoking is a risk factor for cancer in individuals *predisposed to the disease*, but smoking is not the cause of their cancer. The same kind of specious reasoning indicts particular foods or fats as the causative agent in certain other diseases. *Predisposition* is outside the realm of the mechanistic paradigm.

The true cause of these diseases of unknown origin, such as cancer and heart disease, will continue to remain a mystery until

---

164. The plasmatic system is comprised of the autonomic nervous system and the vascular system. A pulsatory disturbance of the plasmatic system can give rise to a somatic biopathy.

there is recognition that individual predisposing factors, not environmental agents, play the determining role in their genesis. In his investigation of the cancer biopathy, for example, Reich found that a severe and chronic sexual disturbance, more specifically, a complete emotional resignation from sexual life and nothing else to replace it with, is the basis for this illness.

With respect to society as a whole, the opposing sociopolitical activities of both the left and the right help to maintain a state of relative social equilibrium, albeit a disturbed one. This is a most important function of social armor. Like religion, sociopolitics provides substitute gratification and substitute solutions for social problems, but sociopolitical activity is less able to provide the social stability that religion does. This is because religion can deal with the problem of human guilt by confining it to the individual's personal life. Religion permits individuals to retain some degree of contact with the self and a strong sense of responsibility for their life. However, when people who have been inculcated with mysticism in their youth renounce religion in adulthood, they no longer have a means of dealing with their personal guilt. Instead they are likely to displace it onto the social sphere and act it out sociopolitically. Guilt is assuaged in zealous support of liberal causes, as in helping the "suffering poor" or colluding with America's enemies. By relinquishing personal responsibility and championing social causes, liberals attempt to assuage their conscience by substituting sociopolitical activity for true social responsibility.

All sociopolitics thus owes its existence to armoring. It is the consequence of the disruption and distortion of rational thinking and a hindrance to genuine social progress. Through the mental straitjacket of religious and political ideology, armored humans, while attempting to address social questions, actually perpetuate and aggravate the very problems they seek to eradicate. Despite the endless clamor for change and progress, social problems continue unchanged, and will continue, from one generation to the next, because people are convinced of the moral superiority of their political and religious viewpoints. The destructive secondary layer impulses found in their armor remain and can only build in intensity, becoming progressively more forceful. What does change is the sophistication and intensity of sociopolitical activity for or against issues and programs thanks to modern marketing, advertising, and public relations techniques. The "New Deal" of the 1930s became the "War on Poverty" of the 1960s[165] and today's social movements with their over-emphasis on collectivization have brought still greater restrictions of individual freedom.

We must recognize the destructive consequences of ever-increasing governmental intrusion into people's lives. Legislation for governmental control is a necessary expedient when secondary layer behavior threatens injury to others, but instituting laws and programs as a *solution* to deal with the social consequences of human irrationality and helplessness is sure to fail in the long run.[166] Such policies are often rigid and one-sided, and the legislation enacted only further secures governmental involvement and diminishes individual initiative and responsibility. Thus, social armor is further entrenched.

Laws against destructive secondary layer behavior are most effective when the authoritarian form of armoring in people is relatively intact; that is, when people are more law-abiding. This was possible much more so in the past authoritarian era, when social order could be maintained through a division of power between the many branches of government and between the local, state, and federal governments. However, the current anti-authoritarian social breakdown has resulted in a weakening of these powers of separation and this, in turn, has necessitated a sharp rise in the powers of the federal government through its various regulatory agencies. In such situations, repressed forces, largely antisocial, that in the past had been held in check by armor, will find a way of getting around the law, or, indeed, with the help of

165. The stated purpose of the "War on Poverty" was to reduce the dependency of "the poor" on the federal government. The actual result was to increase the percentage of people who depended on the government, a direct cause of the decline in individual freedom. When adjusted for inflation, the money spent on this "social war" amounts to almost twice the cost of defeating Nazi Germany and Japan in the Second World War. To date, the "War on Poverty" has cost American taxpayers 5.4 trillion dollars.

166. The pseudo-liberal's reflexive response to the failure or untoward results of governmental intervention is that the program requires "fine tuning," "clearer" thinking, or "more careful" planning. This once again indicates that the pseudo-liberal's contact with living processes is largely through the intellect.

defense lawyers, *will use the law* in their service.[167] Just as individual armor consists of two opposing forces, the destructive and defending impulses, so too, in the case of social armor, every law *against* destructive social behavior originates from the underlying antisocial *impulse* that it is attempting to control. Thus the need for criminal and civil legislation of ever-increasing complexity spontaneously arises with the surfacing of destructive secondary layer behavior.

Although conservatives intuitively understand the limitations of legislation and the dangers of collectivism and centralization, they too resort to lawmaking when it suits their political agenda. An example is their proposed laws banning abortion. Their particular form of sexual disturbance, which pushes them toward mysticism and to their moralistic thinking, is an impediment to genuine understanding. This leads them to prescribe the same old, individualistic precepts: responsibility, traditional values, and moral (sex-negative) education.[168]

Until recently, conservatives did not resort to prescribing political solutions to improve social problems. Being by nature apolitical, they at least remained decent hoping for a return to "the good old days," when things were supposedly better; that is, when the authoritarian form of social armor was more intact. The conservative position has traditionally been to oppose liberal demands for social change, invoking the "tried and true" values of the past as the only alternative. However, because of the anti-authoritarian transformation of social armor and because of the increase in people's anxiety, conservatives have attempted to provide answers of their own. Their efforts also inevitably fail,

---

167. The United States Constitution is under attack by leftists opposed to authority in any form. Although the principles on which the authority of the Constitution is based are in the service of protecting and preserving the life functions of American society, these life functions are not clearly understood. As a result, the position of the defenders of the Constitution, who are mostly on the right, is weakened. Consider, for example, the U.S. Supreme Court's decision in the case of *Ashcroft* v. *The Free Speech Coalition* which held that Congress may not prohibit child pornography made with adult actors who look like minors or by using computer imaging. Justice Kennedy's majority opinion described the Child Pornography Prevention Act of 1996 as "proscribing a significant universe of free speech" that falls "within the First Amendment's vast and privileged sphere." Since such speech is not considered "obscene" under the Court's prior definitions and does not involve real children in its production, the Court found that the government had no constitutionally adequate grounds to suppress it.

168. Although authoritarian moralism is perhaps a rational short-term response to destructive secondary layer behavior, it, too, suppresses the sexual difficulties, problems, and yearning of people, causing untoward consequences.

because they too do not understand what is actually happening. Specifically, they do not recognize the bioemotional structure of armored humans and fail to make the distinction between core impulses, which need protection and support, and the secondary layer impulses which require suppression. When social programs to "help" fail, liberals are quick to rush in with more "finely tuned" programs that impose additional layers of centralized regulation, and more social armor is added. The result is the gradual erosion of personal freedom and its dispossession by government.

A recent example is a new form of socialism in America, corporate socialism, which involves not only the government but private corporations. In the last decades of the twentieth century, partly because of intense pressure from political activists lobbying for insurance companies, the medical profession as a whole gave up its right and obligation to be responsible for patient care, a core function, and private corporations took over large segments of health care, turning medicine into a business. These corporations (HMOs) now effectively control patient care—how medicine is actually practiced. The traditional doctor-patient relationship has been largely destroyed. This private corporate form of socialism is having the same disastrous effect as state-controlled socialization of medicine: The quality of medical care has declined as the physician's responsibility for the patient's care is eliminated. Since corporations have no interest in and are not responsible for the medical care, the patient suffers. What makes corporate socialism in medicine even more destructive than state socialism is that corporations only seek a profit. As business people, they are only concerned with the bottom line and their only interest in the well-being of the patient is how it affects corporate profitability.

Conservatives, caged as they are by muscular armor and being independent by nature, are powerless to oppose this movement toward socialism.[169] They react in many different ways. Some shift further to the right under the influence of extreme conservatives. Others offer centralized political solutions that are really no different from those presented by the left. Anti-abortion legislation is an example. Still others, who cannot accept the extreme right,

169. A notable exception is the Association of American Physicians and Surgeons (AAPS). Among the principal objectives of this organization is to uphold the right of the physician to practice medicine and to treat human illness as the practitioner deems best, while maintaining the highest respect for the dignity of the patient.

may become disillusioned and shift to the left. Political reaction leads to polarization of both the right and the left, and, on both sides, to militancy, and sometimes to overt social violence. These reactions, apparently diverse, can all be understood when seen for what they are: the breakthrough of social irrationalism as a result of the failure of social armor.

Political reaction is thus but another manifestation of the emotional plague that appears with the failure of authoritarian social armor. In the 1996 bombing of the Federal Courthouse in Oklahoma City, Oklahoma, the attack came from the right and led to a marked increase in social anxiety and to calls from the left to control right-wing aggression. This social polarization and similar situations increase social unrest and cause bewilderment and confusion.

Despite all efforts at social improvement, nothing really changes, and humanity is no better off. We must find the way out of this conundrum, a functional approach to social problems that is not centered on sociopolitical activity—one that is beyond opposing political actions and irrationality, the result of the polarization of the left and the right. To do this, we must first recognize and then limit the destructiveness of the emotional plague.

Compulsory (Moral) Regulation versus Self-Regulation

Human beings are the most regimented creatures on Earth. At birth, they are largely free of armor and endowed with the capacity for self regulation, but from that moment on they are subjected to a regimen that allows them little self-expression and practically no opportunity to regulate their lives. Children are told to behave because they must or because they ought to, which makes for mechanical obedience and armor formation. Individual and social armor curb destructive secondary layer impulses and maintain a stable, albeit disturbed and rigid equilibrium as well as social harmony and order. However, they exert their influence at a price, at the expense of restricting individual liveliness and sense of responsibility. People are clueless as to the importance that self-regulation plays in determining social life and that in the absence of such regulation, a moral code must be imposed. Because armored people are *structurally* incapable of personal, social, and economic self-regulation, there is a very real and rational necessity for external control. In the case of social armor this takes the form of state and federal regulation.[170]

Figure 9.1 depicts the functional relationship between destructive social behavior, the result of armoring, and the restrictive, regulatory function of government.

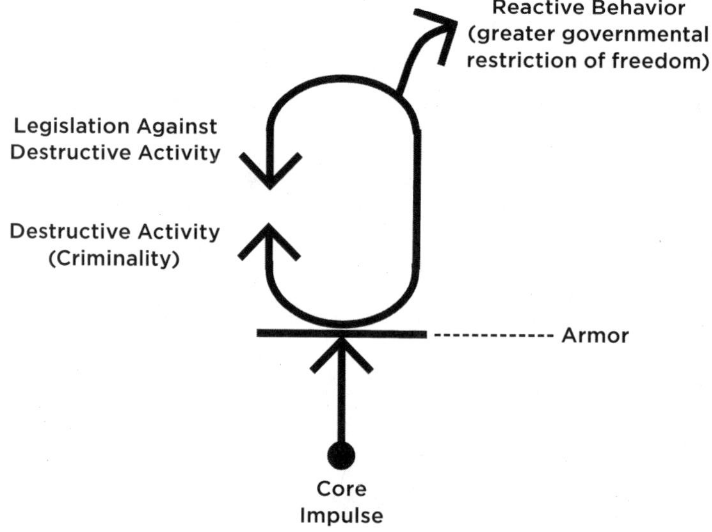

FIGURE 9.1

Although not practically or readily applicable in armored society, self-regulation, not regulation by laws or imposed moral codes, is the *only* long-term rational solution to the antithesis between social license and compulsive governmental control. *A self-regulating society requires that the majority of its individuals be relatively free of armor. In such a society, individuals are capable of being simultaneously free and responsible*; that is, they are able to regulate themselves without external governmental control. Such a society can be expected to thrive and live on. Societies that are not self-regulating must sooner or later perish.

The health of any society can be evaluated according to the degree to which its members are able to regulate themselves and,

170. For example, following the torrent of corporate fraud disclosures, a new corporate fraud chapter in the federal criminal code was created designating a category of crime for any "scheme or artifice" to defraud stock shareholders.

therefore, where social armor is not necessary. In a formal democracy, social armor is at its least crippling. However, because of people's intolerance of freedom, democracies are in constant danger of deteriorating into socialist states. Many European nations are examples of democracies that are in various stages of decline into socialism. In a socialist state or a dictatorship, where social armor is more rigid, the people are less able to tolerate or exercise freedom and responsibility. This is why such states, given appropriate conditions, become unstable and degenerate further into Black or Red Fascism. Many European countries are rapidly approaching this stage of decline.

Fascist states are the most extreme form of armored social organization. They are highly unstable and in constant danger of being toppled. The few dissidents living within them, who have retained enough health and therefore are able to tolerate a degree of freedom, are a constant threat to their survival. In order to survive, these highly armored societies must expend tremendous amounts of energy to not only continually suppress life in the masses, but also to expand militarily; otherwise, they sooner or later fall. They are a constant threat to the rest of the world. Iran and North Korea are current examples.

Today, in America, the armored masses are ideologically polarized, not just sociopolitically but, on a deeper level, in relation to the paired functions of work and sexuality. The political left ignores the importance of personal responsibility and independence in work and favors tacit or overt governmental control of the economy. This is achieved through regulation and tax-and-spend programs, in addition to well-intentioned social service programs in the name of "humanism," "social progress," and "altruism." For the left, virtually every type of secondary layer sexual activity is condoned. They fail to consider the personal, social, or environmental consequences of such tolerance. They emphasize freedom of expression but make no distinction between primary core and neurotic secondary layer sexual drives. The political right ignores natural biological sexuality altogether, while exclusively focusing on the virtues of work. They emphasize the importance of work and of competition in a free market but overlook the distinction between work activity originating from the core and the secondary layer. To illustrate, the relationship between supply and demand, the cornerstone of a free economic system, can pertain to a primary core function (the need for food), to a secondary layer function derived from a substitute need ("sex shops," illegal drugs, control of the market, and so on), or to a need arising from the superficial layer (video games). Conservatism fails to make this crucial distinction when it upholds the virtues of free market capitalism while ignoring the fact that the secondary layer is in operation on a daily basis to destroy the freedom of the marketplace. Maintaining a free market economy is a necessary, but not a sufficient, safeguard for economic health.

Neither those on the left nor the right really understand the importance of self-regulation. Nor do they understand that because of the destructive effects of armor on individual and social life, *compulsory* regulatory measures have to be employed. When social issues as diverse as business practices, poverty, criminality, drugs, and sex are politicized, liberals and conservatives take opposing positions, always based on whether there is the necessity for mandatory regulation. These characterologically biased, partisan views are a symptom of armored (one-sided, mechanistic) thinking and continue to promote social divisiveness and conflict. The result is that the underlying source of the social problem is consistently evaded.

In certain cases, liberals promote centralized controls while conservatives oppose them. Yet in others, the ideological battle lines are reversed. For example, abortion is seen as a matter of choice by liberals, whereas conservatives demand the enactment of restrictive laws. Liberals insist on protecting free speech as an inviolate First Amendment right, whereas conservatives favor censorship of its more flagrant abuses. On issues of environmental protection, liberals are in favor of governmental regulation, while conservatives favor a governmental laissez-faire attitude. Laws against certain types of criminal activity (e.g., physical violence) are more important to conservatives, whereas laws against other crimes (e.g., business corruption) are more important to liberals. Regardless of which political group is promoting governmental control, *freedom and responsibility are always shifted away from the individual onto government. Social armor increases.*

This ideologically driven and always symptomatic approach to social problems only worsens the situation: Government welfare and social programs simply increase human helplessness and create further dependency on social agencies (Murray 1984, pages 45–191). For example, gun control does nothing to strike at the heart of the crime problem, which originates from the murderous impulses that occasionally break through from the secondary layer of armored humans. Gun control only disarms the law-abiding citizen since the criminal can always find a way to get weapons. Making drugs illegal has brought about a thriving black market while the central question of why people need to use them is avoided. Accepting all forms of sexual behavior as normal only serves to fragment society and undermines efforts to educate the public regarding the crucial importance of the orgasm function in regulating human life. The attempt to eliminate racism against blacks by treating them preferentially has helped create a white backlash and increased racism (Ibid., page 221).[171] Mandatory high school sex education programs for adolescents further alienates them from themselves, their parents, and from society since they are uncomfortably aware of the emotionally sterile and mechanical way in which the subject is treated. Governmental protection of the environment often undermines the economic system that sustains our society, the free market, and greatly reduces the possibility for responsible preservation—and so on.[172] These examples of the destructive effects of the evasion of the essential and the application of mechanical solutions are characteristic of armored thinking. As social armor by way of government intrusion increases, personal freedom and the possibility of rational social intervention declines.

From a functional energetic perspective, the biophysical structure and the behavior of the American people, from the country's inception at the end of the eighteenth century to the present at

---

171. "My proposal for dealing with the racial issue in social welfare is to repeal every bit of legislation and reverse every court decision that in any way requires, recommends, or awards differential treatment according to race, and thereby put us back onto the track that we left in 1965. We may argue about the appropriate limits of government intervention in trying to enforce the ideal, but at least it should be possible to identify the ideal: Race is not a morally admissible reason for treating one person differently from another, period." (Murray 1984, page 223)

172. The collapse of the Soviet Union has revealed the disastrous disregard for the environment that was shown by governments and government-controlled industries in countries behind the Iron Curtain. In America, many private, nonpolitical organizations (e.g., The Nature Conservancy) have developed expertise in bringing disparate groups together in the interest of preserving natural habitats.

the beginning of the twenty-first, can be characterized by a gradual bioenergetic shift from the body to the brain, accompanied by a concomitant rise in the use of the intellect as a defense against core feelings. This shift has resulted in a weakening and, in some cases, a loss of core contact with the self, with others and with the environment. Alexis de Tocqueville predicted this resultant decline in social conditions in *Democracy in America* with frightening accuracy. As early in America's history as 1835, he could write:

> I think . . . that the kind of oppression with which democratic peoples are threatened will resemble nothing that has preceded it in the world . . . I myself seek in vain an expression that exactly reproduces the idea that I form of it for myself and that contains it; the old words despotism and tyranny are not suitable. The thing is new . . .
>
> I see an innumerable crowd of like and equal men who revolve on themselves without repose, procuring the small and vulgar pleasures with which they fill their souls. Each of them, withdrawn and apart, is like a stranger to the destiny of all the others: his children and his particular friends form the whole species for him; as for dwelling with his fellow citizens, he is beside them, but he does not see them; he touches them and does not feel them; he exists only in himself and for himself alone, and if a family still remains for him, one can at least say that he no longer has a native country.
>
> Above these an immense tutelary power is elevated, which alone takes charge of assuring their enjoyments and watching over their fate. It is absolute, detailed, regular, far-seeing, and mild. It would resemble paternal power if, like that, it had for its object to prepare men for manhood; but on the contrary, it seeks only to keep them fixed irrevocably in childhood; it likes citizens to enjoy themselves provided that they think only of enjoying themselves. It willingly works for their happiness, but it wants to be the unique agent and sole arbiter of that; it provides for their security, foresees and secures their needs, facilitates their pleasures, conducts their principal affairs, directs their industry, regulates their estates, divides their inheritances; can it not take away from them entirely the trouble of thinking and the pain of living?

> So it is that every day it renders the employment of free will less useful and more rare; it confines the action of the will in a smaller space and little by little steals the very use of it from each citizen. Equality has prepared men for all these things: it has disposed them to tolerate them and often even to regard them as benefits.
>
> Thus, after taking each individual by turns in its powerful hands and kneading him as it likes, the sovereign extends its arms over society as a whole; it covers its surface with a network of small, complicated, painstaking, uniform rules through which the most original minds and the most vigorous souls cannot clear a way to surpass the crowd; it does not break wills, but it softens them, bends them, and directs them; it rarely forces one to act, but it constantly opposes itself to one's acting; it does not destroy, it prevents things from being born; it does not tyrannize, it hinders, compromises, enervates, extinguishes, dazes, and finally reduces each nation to being nothing more than a herd of timid and industrious animals of which the government is the shepherd.
>
> (Tocqueville 2000, page 662)

The degradation that he saw in 1835 is immeasurably worse in today's American society and, in all likelihood, will become even worse in the future. Today, the only self-regulation left is the extent to which social processes are still governed by core work and sexual functions. Everyone, including those on the political left and the right, continues to be unaware of the critical difference between primary core impulses of sexuality and work that require protection and the destructive secondary layer drives that require containment. Without making this crucial distinction, it is not possible to determine whether specific legislation will rationally address any given social problem.

The ability to self-regulate requires a certain level of emotional and economic independence. This, in turn, necessitates a relatively healthy work capacity, the knowledge of which is also foreign to most people, including politicians and bureaucrats who see as their life's mission being caretaker of the masses. This approach only increases people's helplessness and dependency on the state.[173] Without an awareness of the need to identify and protect the core functions of life and the close functional relationship between freedom and responsibility, laws cannot be effectively instituted that will safeguard those who strive for healthy living safe from the destructive forces of the emotional plague.

Beyond Mechanistic Sociology and Mystical Religion

Just as the social sciences must be separated from their mechanistic trappings, so too does religion have to be separated from its mystical overlay. Both sociological knowledge and religious feeling are core expressions. We know that sensation and emotion are the two energy sources from which thoughts originate.[174] All science, including sociology, consists of ideas originating from sensation, from ideas that are initiated by sensory processes, while religion involves ideas originating from emotionally based thought processes. We have shown that, in health, sensational and emotional ideas are in harmony. This relationship leads to functional thinking. In armored humans, they are in contradiction. (See chapter 2, the section on Sociopolitical Characterology)

A prime example of the latter way of thinking was the Communist experiment in Russia, which commencing some ninety years ago was touted by the left as a solution to the immense social problems of humanity. This "solution," a product of mechanistic thinking, was the public face of the Bolsheviks, a ruthless force of the emotional plague, led by the emotional plague character V.I. Lenin who introduced daily terror as a tool of governance. Inevitably, Soviet Communism, a deadly combination of mechanistic thinking and the organized emotional plague, was for the very same reasons an abysmal failure, far worse than the

173. Alarmed by the sharp drop in food stamp rolls following the 1990s reform in the U.S. welfare system which, in part, required that unemployed, able-bodied people find work, lawmakers from both political parties rushed to "remedy" the situation. The solution was to include *more* low-income families and to make it *easier* to collect food stamps. See "Drop in Food Stamp Rolls Is Mysterious and Worrisome," *Wall Street Journal*, Aug. 2, 1999. Despite the conclusion of politicians, the statistics do not, by definition, indicate that children were going hungry. This example is typical of how leftist politicians use statistical "data" to justify their self-serving political agenda, which in this case is to *undermine* people's attempts to take care of themselves.

174. Konia, C. 2001. The Biophysical Basis of Sociopolitical Thought. *Journal of Orgonomy* 35(1).

old czarist regime that it replaced.[175] Inimical to life, the Soviet Communists killed tens of millions of its citizens and, in large measure, destroyed the capacity for productive work and pleasure in those who survived.

After the fall of the Soviet Union, and with it the elimination of Soviet Red Fascism, a new outbreak of the emotional plague from the extreme right appeared, apparently out of nowhere—the Black Fascism of Islamic fundamentalism. This outbreak with its pseudo-religious façade poses an even greater threat to humanity than Red Fascism because the hatred behind it is a more virulent form of the plague on because it has joined forces with the emotional plague on the political left. *It is therefore imperative that the emotional plague be brought to public awareness.*

The same concerted effort directed against epidemic diseases in the field of medicine is now needed to eliminate these sociological and religious eruptions of the emotional plague. The problem of eradicating the emotional plague, if it is seen for what it is, would then be possible. Regarding the threat of a global pandemic of severe acute respiratory syndrome (SARS), for example, Donald Burke, professor of international health and epidemiology at Johns Hopkins University,[176] writes:

> Epidemic-control efforts should not simply be maintained, but doubled, and redoubled again. New diagnostic tests should be mass-produced and made freely available around the globe. Epidemiological teams should investigate every possible case, even in the poorest communities. Face-saving politicians who hide local epidemics must be cajoled, or more forcefully convinced, to cooperate. Special efforts must be made to detect and quench new outbreaks in the Southern Hemisphere. With skill, determination and luck, we might be able to break all the chains of transmission before the onset of winter offers the virus a chance to spread more rapidly again.

We still know little about the biological laws that govern a society that is relatively armor-free. One thing is certain: An honest

175. Reich, W. 1946. *The Mass Psychology of Fascism*. See section on the Masses and the State.

176. *Wall Street Journal*, "Six Months to Act," April 25, 2003.

evaluation of social issues must include a clear understanding of the essential aspects of healthy biosocial functioning, freedom and responsibility, and their respective neurotic distortions: *license* and *compulsive regulation.* An honest evaluation must also be free from the petty "Little Man" concerns and reactions that are bound to arise from each person's own neurotic structure. Furthermore, here in America, still the land of opportunity, *social helplessness and poverty must be recognized for what they really are—the results of the crippling effects of individual and social armor on man's biological work function.* In America, human impoverishment, not economic factors, is the root cause of poverty.

The expectation that politicians and government programs will eventually take care of social problems is a dangerous illusion and evidence of human blindness, apathy, and feelings of impotence when dealing with vital social issues. Politicians and religious leaders must stop championing "the poor" and railing against "the rich" to gain the popular vote and religious power. This will come about only when enough people are able to *see through* the quack remedies, lies, and hypocrisy of power politicians and clergy. *This is an ocular problem.* (See chapter 2, page 71, The Ocular Stage)

Although legislation and liturgy are now too often necessary expedients to curb human destructiveness, a basic understanding of bioemotional functions governing health must be a prerequisite for anyone working in the medical, legal and social fields. This knowledge and the responsibility for its application must reside largely within the medical/psychiatric profession, with those who have acquired the necessary education and experience, and have secured a sufficient degree of personal emotional health.[177] Unfortunately, most physicians and health care professionals today lack such qualifications and have, at best, only a vague and incomplete understanding of emotional functioning from a *bioenergetic* perspective. Additionally, these individuals lack an understanding that healthy sexual and work functions have a fundamental role in life, and that furthermore, these are absolutely essential to maintain emotional well-being.

---

177. The training of health care professionals in orgonomic medicine and sociology is part of the education program of the American College of Orgonomy.

In 1934, psychoanalysts rejected Reich's pivotal findings in psychiatry and sociology that later led to his discovery of the bioenergetic basis of human illness. In so doing, the medical establishment abrogated its responsibility in health care and, as a result, the psychiatric community could not develop an understanding of this critical area of human functioning in a natural scientific manner. One destructive consequence of this tragic decision has been the mechanization of the practice of medicine and the public's increasing disaffection with traditional allopathic (mechanistic) medicine in general, and with psychiatry in particular. The failure of psychiatry to live up to expectation has resulted in the burgeoning popularity of "alternative" therapies. The degradation of psychiatric treatment has been complete: psychiatrists have been reduced to the role of bureaucrat, filling out endless paperwork, and dispensing medication based on the patient's symptoms.

The dissatisfaction with psychiatry as it is now practiced has rationality since conventional treatment with medication addresses only symptoms and not the patient's underlying disease process. The failure of the psychiatric profession to carry out its natural function constitutes the social background that has enabled many to externalize their emotional problems by seeking sociopolitical explanations and solutions.

Fortunately, we now have the knowledge to begin helping humanity find its way out of its trapped existence and to move away from the destructiveness of sociopolitics. We start by distinguishing between *rational politics*, based on the legitimate province of governmental responsibility (e.g., civil governance, the protective function of the police and the military), and *sociopolitical irrationalism*. The latter has to be recognized as a direct consequence of the misguided, misdirected efforts of people and their leaders trying to assume responsibility for their own lives. This different and functional approach to understanding human behavior calls for placing strict limits on the government's proper realm of functioning, so that what is *not* in its legitimate province—that is, all that is pathological—is brought into focus. Those who seek to so curb government's reach will themselves have to resort to rational, deliberate political activity if politics is to be wrested from armored politicians. These leaders and the policymakers in governmental agencies have absolutely no scientific knowledge of the biological functions that regulate life and therefore have no right to be involved in rational individual or social health care.

It will be impossible to completely eliminate sociopolitics since this activity is deeply rooted in fundamental differences in patterns of human armor. However, it is possible to reduce its destructive effects. This can be done through public education and by teaching people how to think functionally; that is, by first making them *aware* of the destructiveness of sociopolitics and then helping people to understand its *defensive function*. This awareness of its function will help contain the ongoing conflict between the political left and the right and help begin building rationally based politics.

Only when people are able to curb their appetite for substitute satisfactions and temporary, expedient solutions to social problems, and when they can curb their sociopolitical activity, will the difficult process of limiting mass irrationalism and eliminating its supporting cast of political hacks begin. This change of behavior will also curb the power of religious gurus and all others who thrive on the inability of people to regulate their own lives. Only when it is recognized that humanity's helplessness is itself *a symptom* of a very real bioemotional disease, and that the primary social goal in every culture must be to raise healthy children who are self-reliant and relatively free of armoring, only then will it be possible to have honest people in government. When this happens, political science will have gained true legitimacy and will be placed on a rational, scientific basis alongside the other social sciences. It will function to preserve the life in society, and be devoted to rational governance and administration of the state.

This is not utopianism. Clearly, there will always be social irrationalism and destructiveness; however what will change is that, because of the knowledge that is now available, for the first time in human history, *the positive forces of life will have a fighting chance against the destructive forces of the emotional plague.* From this perspective, both true conservatives and true liberals can find their rightful place. Conservatives are correct when they say that there will always be social irrationalism and destructiveness. Liberals are right when they say that it is possible for the human condition to improve. What is missing from both viewpoints to make both statements simultaneously true is knowledge of the existence of human characterological and social armor and the operations of the emotional plague.

The heart of all social problems originates from the manner in which *individual character structure* affects others and the real world. For this reason, the *emotional* health of the individual is the critical factor. Emotional health in economic life requires, first of all, the capacity to work independently and responsibly. Second, it demands healthy aggression coupled with an ability to behave honestly, fairly, and decently toward competitors. Third, it requires a respect and a sense of responsibility for the natural environment and an awareness of the need to protect it. These requirements call for emotional and sexual security, without the substitute activities that appear with the appetite for revenge, greed, or personal power. Emotional health also manifests as a desire to give back to the world, in philanthropy and in other ways that promote the well-being of all.

In a constructive economic relationship, the core needs of the individual ("self-interest") and those of society ("the public interest") function as attractive opposites (Fig. 9.2).

FIGURE 9.2

As depicted in Figure 9.2, in a healthy society, the vital interests of the individual and of society are mutually beneficial and, as a consequence, social relationships regulate themselves. Social harmony is the rule. However, in armored societies, self-interest and public interest tend to be at odds with one another; that is, there exists a state of antagonistic opposition with all its destructive consequences to the individual and society. Society fragments and becomes dysfunctional to varying degrees. *Genital frustration, with all its destructive secondary layer manifestations, lies behind dysfunctional social organizations and is the driving force behind every type of sociopolitical ideology.* Whether they know it or not, armored people perpetuate a life of misery and chronic frustration. In an attempt to rid themselves of feelings with which they cannot cope, based on unexpressed rage and sexual longing, many act out in the social arena or seek substitute satisfactions in different ways and degrees of cunning. *There is no skill that armored humans have perfected better than the ability to deceive themselves and others.* What remains to be grasped is that social and political dysfunction is caused by the sexual and work disturbances of armored humans and that before political irrationalism can be permanently reduced, the pathological structure of armored humans must be addressed.

Those who genuinely enjoy productive work originating from their core do not have a need to get involved in sociopolitics. Before people can take true pleasure in their work or accept real social responsibility, work must be freed from its mechanistic and mystical rigidity. This requires a fundamental biophysical restructuring of people, a task that carries profound implications for all sexual and work activity. The process of realigning work so that it corresponds to only what is natural and vitally necessary for both the individual and for society will take generations to accomplish, even under the most ideal conditions.[178]

The question is: In what area of social life can we begin to intervene most effectively? We know that the family is the unit of society and, therefore, it is best to effect social improvement at this level. Troubled people are most likely to be aware of their emotional difficulties when they interfere in family relationships. Some will be inclined to seek professional help and their desire to do so is an indication that, to some degree, such individuals are behaving responsibly. At this point, the availability of *qualified* orgonomically-trained mental health professionals on a large scale will provide them an opportunity for effective bioemotional, biosocial education and treatment.

---

178. The labor union is an example of an armored organization that once held an important function for workers, but is now becoming anachronistic. Workers' unions owe their continued existence to the armored structure of humans, and they prevent people from taking full responsibility for their lives and relinquishing their stereotypical ways of life. Unions are but one way that human armor preserves inefficient social systems. Today, they are being replaced by lobbies and other special-interest groups that control social processes through political action.

Orgonotic Contact

Today, people are farther than ever before from having genuine contact with themselves and the world around them, with most people living their lives in a partial or almost total state of substitute contact. Burdened by their own personal emotional problems, they can hardly conceive of anything beyond meeting their own immediate needs. Securing the future well-being of society is clearly something that is beyond their abilities.

An individual belonging neither to the left nor the right and in whom the instinct for self-preservation is dominated by the instinct to protect the emotional health of other individuals and of society is likely to be regarded as an admirable but startling departure from what is "normal." Wilhelm Reich was such an individual. A nation in which such people are the rule would make eradication of the emotional plague a relatively simple task. But because relatively unarmored people are so very rare, this pestilence passes undiminished from one generation to the next wreaking greater and greater havoc in its wake. Like a deadly virus, it has the ability to "mutate" and readily adapt itself to new conditions so that it can enter, infect, and destroy the life of each succeeding generation.

From time immemorial, the plague and the armor it produces have prevented humans from investigating nature for what it truly is. This is because *armor distorts perception*, and, so long as it is present, clear and deep contact with oneself and the environment remains out of reach. As a result, scientific investigation has necessarily been largely confined to studying the external world. However, since perceptual distortions makes it impossible to arrive at an accurate sense of oneself, there can be no clear understanding of either the outer or inner world.

Because of armor, man's investigation of the external world has been distorted into mechanistic ideas about nature, and his study of the inner world has resulted in mystical ideas. Neither mechanistic nor mystical thinking can grasp the nature of either worlds in general or the emotional plague in particular. Functional thinking, that is, *thinking the way nature functions*, lies outside of armored man's method of thought and, as a result, he has remained forever caught between mystical religion and mechanistic science. This partition between the inner and outer worlds has continued for thousands of years and will remain so until the destructive effect of human armor on thinking is generally recognized. Relegated to the mystics of all denominations, the *scientific* investigation of the inner subjective world has been until recently off-limits.

It was not until Freud's study of the human psyche that people first really attempted to observe themselves in a natural scientific manner. Freud was the first natural scientist to apply functional energetic thinking to his psychological investigations. As a result of this fruitful approach, he discovered the existence of infantile and childhood sexuality and its instinctual energetic underpinning, which he metaphorically called "libido." He understood the psyche as consisting of the dynamic interaction between the instinctual forces of the id and the defensive forces of the ego. However, he lost his energetic orientation and became bogged down in structural concepts of ego psychology. Another limitation was that his investigations penetrated only to the depth of the secondary layer of armored life, the Freudian unconscious. For him, the biological core remained out of reach. He was therefore restricted to the superficial, the psychological realm of human functioning. Without knowledge of the biological core, Freud could not know that there is natural healthy functioning and could not see that there is a real distinction between emotional health and sickness. Given the limits of his understanding, the rational goal of psychoanalysis was to bring the patient into conformity, not with health, but with the standards of the existing authoritarian social order.

When this social order began to crumble around 1960, psychoanalysis had no alternative to offer and found itself more vulnerable than ever to hostile attacks by numerous critics, which now included many of the younger generation swept up in the anti-authoritarianism of the times. Yet, even this limited venture delving into the human psyche was enough to terrify people and turn them away from honestly looking into themselves. Each individual responded to the threat of psychoanalysis according to his or her specific individual and sociopolitical character structure. Significantly, those who reacted most defensively were many of the psychoanalysts themselves. Because they were incapable of grasping the magnitude of Freud's libido theory, many of his followers introduced their own innovations and passed them off as having superseded or refuted Freud. Those psychiatrists outside the psychoanalytic movement continued an active campaign to discredit Freud and his work.

Reich was the only one of Freud's students who fully understood the depth and importance of Freud's work and, because he did, he was able to greatly extend Freud's psychoanalytic discoveries from the psychological (human psyche) into the deeper sociological and biological realms. Because this knowledge was built upon observable bioenergetic functions, Reich provided a physical link between human nature and the natural world, a biologically rooted psychiatry. For the first time in the history of human thought, a genuinely unified view of the universe was made possible. This integrated view rests on Reich's discovery of the orgone, a mass-free universal energy that governs and unifies all realms of nature.

From a cosmological perspective, a practical consequence of this monumental discovery is that it allows humankind to find its place accurately as part of the physical universe. As medical orgonomists, we know that medical orgone therapy provides the patient with a depth of contact into him or herself that was not previously present because of armor. Individuals experience contact with their depths, often to the very foundation of their being, *without mysticism*. These experiences, which are foreign to most armored people, are a reality only open to a few exceptional artists, musicians, and scientists who, by their creations, demonstrate their capacity for deep core contact.

Psychic Contactlessness: The Byproduct of Armor

Contactlessness is a state in which the individual is out of touch with important aspects or events of his or her life. Its manifestations are as varied as they are extensive. If people were aware of the existence and the significance of contactlessness in daily life, many inexplicable social events would become understandable. The contactless state is the reason people remain trapped in their armor, why they are unable to think functionally, and why they cannot grasp the bioenergetic functions that are the basis of life. It is also the reason that people don't and cannot have a clear understanding of what really goes on in the world.

Psychic contactlessness, the absence of contact, can occur in individuals as well as interpersonally. It is a physical condition first described by Reich (1949a, page 316), the result of a dynamic energetic equilibrium between the instinctual forces striving for expression and those opposing them, the defensive forces of armor (see Fig. 9.1). It is an everyday manifestation in our armored society, both in individuals and in social interactions. In individuals, common symptoms include a sense of inner loneliness in spite of frequently ample social relationships; feelings of emotional deadness or of being stuck and aimless; alienation from the world; a chronic sense of boredom; a lack of focused interest in one's life; and chronic indifference, thoughtlessness, or obliviousness in relation to oneself or to significant others. In society, psychic contactlessness is part of every dysfunctional social organization, from troubled marriages to troubled business corporations; from troubles between nations to disturbed relationships and inappropriate behavior between people in everyday life.

Psychic contactlessness is eliminated only when armor giving rise to it is removed and the individual regains touch with himself and the world. Since there is a disturbance of contact in every case of armoring, and since virtually everyone is armored to some degree, society as a whole is armored. All neurotic social activity today contains an element of contactlessness as well as substitute (contactless) attempts to overcome this state.

Currently, one of the most destructive and dangerous manifestations of substitute contact in Western society are mechanistic-mystical ideologies of all kinds including, and especially, sociopolitical activity of the left. We have shown that this behavior has its origin in the displacement onto society of early childhood conflicts with parents, particularly the child's feelings of deep disappointment, covert rebellion, and hatred of the father. These conflicts are not held within oneself as they are in most neurotics but become outwardly directed onto social authority figures in particular and the authoritarian social order in general. The shift of hostility from the father to social institutions and to people in authority is the layer of armor that contains the element of contactlessness: *The individual is unaware that feelings of hatred from personal conflicts are being displaced onto others.*

Individuals who are unusually out of touch in social situations are rather easily recognized by others as being "out of it," "clueless," or "socially inappropriate," especially when emotionally sensitive topics are discussed. The upward rolling of the eyes is a common expression indicating an individual's awareness of the contactlessness state of others. More subtle, but no less pathological, signs can be detected by the trained observer: *The contactless state is immediately revealed in the appearance of the individual's armored eyes and facial expressions.*

Work-related accidents and reduced productivity in the workplace are other destructive consequences of contactlessness. Another commonplace and destructive example is the public's indifference and apathy toward the enormous amount of wastefulness in almost all governmental social programs. A sign of individual irresponsibility, most taxpayers are not concerned or not concerned enough that the taxes on their earnings are being squandered on all kinds of questionable social programs that are never evaluated for their effectiveness.

An indication of substitute contact resulting from the contactless state is an inordinate need for passive entertainment, a need that is often exploited by the media to market not only products but also thinly veiled political ideologies to a benumbed, mesmerized public. The media, on the other hand, has a financial interest in keeping the public "entertained" in this manner. What is popularly called "entertainment" has one main function: It serves as a distraction, diverting people's attention to the lives of others instead of attending to their own. Useful, thus, to the media and its audience, the receptive masses are seduced away from contact with themselves. The advertising and TV industries use every kind of excitatory technique as a lure to attract the attention of an ocularly unsatisfied public: Consider the success of "reality" TV shows. Also, electronically produced visual stimuli, with their ability to simulate reality—called "virtual reality"—have provided yet another, and very deadly, source of substitute contact by keeping people out of touch with the physical world, including their own bodies.

The computer is a tool that has a tremendous potential to be used in constructive or destructive ways. One destructive way is to use e-mail to avoid personal contact, especially when verbal communication is appropriate. College professors now insist on having their students communicate with them by e-mail; in this case, a form of substitute contact. This practice not only avoids necessary and beneficial human contact, but it also encourages people to be more "up in their heads" and out of touch with their bodies than they already are. It also functions to further consolidate the dominance in everyday life of the social façade, the superficial layer, at the expense of the core.

When contact is disturbed, social interactions occur by way of substitute activity from the superficial or secondary layers, never from the biological core. In the armored, an absence of strong, deep, genital sensations results in an inability to establish gratifying heterosexual relationships. Instead, there may be substitute sexual behavior, such as coquettishness, philandering, or the expression of other pregenital or phallic impulses that result from the neurotic need to "conquer," "possess" or "get revenge" on someone of the opposite sex. This substitute social activity is palliative, temporarily relieving anxiety, inner emptiness, or feelings of impotence by, for example, attempting to gain the love of another person. Substitute contact is a flight from, or toward, genuine relationships with the world.

In the world of politics, party politicians also suffer from an underlying state of contactlessness and their attempts to overcome it through substitute political activity.

An example of substitute contact and activity in politics is the relationship between the true liberal and the pseudo-liberal. Because of ideological similarities, the true liberal identifies with and behaves according to the pseudo-liberal's predesigned political program.

The decline of the authoritarian social structure was accompanied by the weakening of muscular armor and an intensification of ocular armor. This shift in the distribution of armor not only resulted in far greater levels of contactlessness in the population than in the past, but also the decline in muscular armor's defensive function, eliminating anxiety and reducing sensation. Both have been responsible for the widespread increase in all manner of substitute social activity.

In addition to the dramatic pervasiveness in sociopolitical activism, there is now an epidemic increase of illicit drug and alcohol use, and a steep rise in the use and misuse of prescribed psychotropic medications, all measures to handle the greater levels of anxiety that people currently experience. (see chapter 7, The War on Drugs: America's Second Civil War) The temporary relief produced by drugs, however, has a price: ocular armor and contactlessness increase even further. In a related matter, the medication-based approach of today's psychiatry—which is diametrically opposed to the functional energetic approach—renders people even more out of touch with their emotions, more contactless, and more at the mercy of destructive external forces than they were before starting treatment.[179] This mind/emotion-numbing approach may be necessary in particular cases, but it most certainly is not curative and should not be used indiscriminately by the medical profession.

Contact is defined as the perception of excitation. It is written orgonometrically as a fusion operation. Two primary biological funcions (perception and excitation) superimpose and fuse to create a single, new function contact. This is shown in the following diagram (Fig. 9.3):

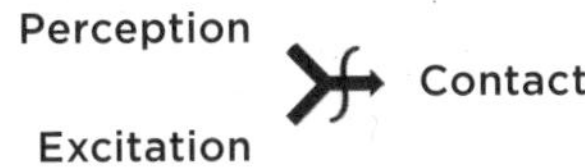

FIGURE 9.3

Contact is at the basis of all biological functions, including social functions.[180] Pathological social interactions always involve a disturbance of contact. In the treatment of social systems, one addresses either the system as a whole or its individual members, depending on the situation. By focusing on their ways of expression and reacting, the therapist first helps the individuals to become *aware* of their contactlessness. For example, does the individual express his or her ideas or hold back from speaking when he or she has something to say? Does he or she speak but not listen to the response? Is the emotional expression of what is said appropriate to its content? Once aware of these behaviors, people gradually become able to recognize *that* they are out

179. The pharmaceutical industry today bypasses the physician's rational authority and addresses its advertising directly to the public. On the surface, this practice appears only as a marketing device to educate the public, which is the pharmaceutical company's stated rationale. However, it is, in fact, blatant commercialism.

180. See Konia, C. 1998. Orgonotic Contact. *Journal of Orgonomy* 32 (1): pages 61–81.

of touch, and this realization can bring awareness of the *consequences* of this state of being. This realization, of being out of touch and its consequences, is usually experienced with shock or amazement, or with feelings of anger or sadness. Addressing the universal phenomenon of individual and social contactlessness in our armored society, that is, *bringing people into better contact with themselves*, will make it possible to gradually effect positive social change on a mass scale.

There are no hard and fast rules as to how to restore contact. In certain cases, a great deal of preparation is required before the individual can become aware of being out of touch. In other situations it may be possible to clear up distorted thinking rather easily. When, for example, defensive sociopolitical ideology or character attitudes are successfully made ego-alien by the therapist, the individual must suppress the underlying intrapsychic conflict. Or, it may be appropriate to address the underlying emotional problem that gave rise to these symptoms. If this intervention is successful, the complex of emotions that had heretofore been displaced onto the social scene is taken out of that context and can then be resolved in the individual's personal life.

Simply recognizing that one is "out of touch" can partially relieve ocular armor and improve contact. Being in contact with one's contactlessness, in turn, can help to inhibit socially destructive behavior in most cases. *This important step does not necessarily require the attention of the physician.* It can be accomplished by qualified nonmedical professionals, such as orgonomically trained psychologists and social workers.

However, the process of armor removal *below the ocular segment* requires the training and experience of a qualified medical orgone therapist. This is necessary because dissolution of armor brings about the release of enormous amounts of energy which must be carefully and systematically dealt with. Such restructuring produces the most beneficial results, as it greatly increases the capacity for independent, socially responsible behavior.[181]

181. The pseudo-liberal's social destructiveness can be stopped if it is exposed to enough people and an alternative way to address social problems is shown. However, exposing the pseudo-liberal character will almost always provoke an attack against those perceived as threatening their belief system. Pseudo-liberals project their deep-seated sadistic attitudes, accusing others of being "reactionary," "fascist," or "paranoid," in ways identical to the methods traditionally used by the pseudo-liberal's communist cohorts.

The following clinical situation illustrates how characteranalytic principles can be applied to eliminate a single layer of ocular armor.

> A patient who lived in another country complained about her government's harsh treatment of captured terrorists. She particularly objected to the policy of placing terrorists in solitary confinement. In her daily life, she ruminated constantly about their terrible fate. I asked her how she would feel if she were placed in solitary confinement and she said she would be afraid of going insane from the lack of human contact. I then told her that since she was not a criminal or a terrorist, she would never be placed in prison. I told her that she was displacing her own fear onto the terrorists and that she would have to tolerate her fear of being alone. By facing this fear in her daily life, she stopped displacing her thoughts and feelings onto the social arena and, as a result, lost her concern for the captured terrorists.

Reestablishing Contact

Because ideas are perceived in the head, it is commonly believed that thoughts originate exclusively in the brain. Although thoughts are sensed in that organ, they are, in fact, derived from the brain's sustained perception of excitation, of emotions and sensations (sensory input) generated throughout the rest of the body, particularly from the erogenous zones. The strength and quality of the belief in an idea is, therefore, determined by the intensity of contact the individual has with the emotional and sensory excitation from the body and perceived in the brain. This is true for internally derived sensations ("feeling is believing") as well as for externally generated sensations from the outer world ("seeing is believing" or "hearing is believing"). The former are associated with the so-called "subjective" component, the latter with the "objective" component of human experience. Examples of the subjective component include sexual ideas that wax and wane with the intensity of sexual excitation, anxious ideas (worries) that wax and wane with the intensity of anxious excitation, and angry ideas that appear and fade away with excitation from muscles containing emotions of anger. Since armor distorts the perception of organ sensations, ideas so derived become irrational.[182]

Reich experimentally demonstrated that the biological functions of perception, sensation, and emotion, as well as their corresponding disturbances, the result of armor, are not merely abstract, psychological concepts, but *physical bioenergetic functions* that can be objectively measured. In his electrophysiological investigation of the sexuality and anxiety functions, Reich studied the relationship between the sensations and emotions *subjectively* experienced by individuals and the excitation he was able to *objectively* measure at their skin surface. The results of these remarkable experiments, which were briefly discussed earlier, provide scientific evidence of the *simultaneous antithesis and identity of the psyche and the soma*. That is, psyche and soma are simultaneously antithetical with respect to each other and identical with respect to their common origin, biological orgone energy. These experiments also show that the emotions of pleasure and anxiety result from the perception of opposite directions of bioenergy movement: outward in pleasure (expansion) and inward in anxiety (contraction). Reich called this pulsatory movement *the basic antithesis of vegetative life*.[183]

To give a clinical example, a patient in medical orgone therapy can be approached through a psychic intervention by speaking to a particular character trait, such as a tight-lipped, stoical expression on the face, or somatically by addressing the muscular armor of the jaw and chin. Armor is both characterological and muscular and is a physical, tangible reality. Its dissolution is accompanied by the expression of emotions and sensations that are bound up in it. During the course of therapy, these expressions are of progressively increasing intensity, from the mildest currents and sensations to deep preorgastic streaming. Overcoming armor restores contact, and, as this is achieved, the patient gradually is

---

182. Normally, ideas arise from organ sensations in the body and are sensed through the ocular segment, which includes the brain. However, in certain pathological states, thoughts originate from the brain and function defensively to avoid painful emotions and sensations.

183. Reich originally thought that bioelectricity provided the basis for his data in these experiments. Later experimentation and observation led to his discovery of a biological energy, which he called orgone, and he concluded that the basic antithesis of vegetative life is a bioenergetic phenomenon (Reich 1982).

able to perceive the movement of orgone energy within his or her body. This movement is perceived as currents and/or streaming. The improved contact with oneself, as experienced with orgone therapy, is accompanied by greater integration. Gradually tolerating these sensations and emotions allows the patient to make stronger contact with energy phenomena within him or herself and in nature. The capacity to fully experience these sensations and emotions produces profound changes not the least of which is the way one thinks and views the world. As armor removal brings about the capacity for functional thinking, mechanistic or mystical thinking naturally recede.

Functional thinking is capable of recognizing and then resolving the irreconcilable contradictions that have arisen from humanity's armored worldview. Political thinking cannot and never will provide solutions to the enormous social problems confronting humanity. Political thinking is essentially either mechanistic or mystical and, as such, is a manifestation of social armor. Both forms of political thinking, left and right, are one-sided and therefore ideological. At best, they are only capable of providing temporary, symptomatic solutions. Genuine solutions to social problems must always remain outside the sphere of ideological, political thinking.

The primary task, therefore, is to find ways to eliminate social armor and, by so doing, bring about rational thinking. This requires the raising of healthy, unarmored children. Reich's hopes for a healthier humanity rested on "the children of the future," on the *prevention of armor* in newborns, infants, and children.[184] Of critical importance is the recognition of the obstacles to this goal. Preventing armor will remain all but impossible until such time as parents are relatively healthy. All those who have the responsibility of caring for children, such as physicians and other health care professionals, must have the medical and orgonomic knowledge to safeguard the biophysical health of infants and children during their critical developmental years.

---

184. See "The Orgonomic Infant Research Center (OIRC)" in Reich (1983). In 1949, Reich organized a group of coworkers to study the healthy child "*to reach the naturally given plasmatic bioenergetic functions of the infant*" (italics in the original). This study was divided into four major categories: prenatal care of healthy pregnant mothers, careful supervision of the delivery and the first few days of the newborn's life, prevention of armoring during the first five or six years, and study of the further development of the children until well after puberty.

Notwithstanding how much this goal requires, Reich believed that it was indeed possible to address the disordered energy functions of people and make inroads into the destructive spread of the emotional plague. The question is this: How does society get from where it is today to where it will be possible to raise relatively healthy children? To the extent that people are clear-headed and can think rationally, they can be educated as to irrational sociopolitical activity. This must stress how adeptly well-meaning public leaders use distorted ideas to influence and gain control of people and to advance their personal agendas in social policy. The public can also be educated about matters relating to emotional well-being so that parents are better able to raise healthier children. Such education must come from a functional perspective, not one that is mechanistic or moralistic.

The first step is for professionals and laypeople alike to have a clear understand of the difference between primary healthy core drives and destructive secondary layer drives that result from armor and must be curbed. The critical importance of personal responsibility must be appreciated, and it must be understood that laws that foster people's dependence on government and private corporations only undermine the basic functions of healthy life. Finally, and possibly most importantly, the distinction between healthy genital sexuality and distorted, pregenital, secondary forms of sexuality must be understood.

Confusion in these areas has not only led to a complete standstill in rationally dealing with virtually all social problems, but has made matters worse. The consequence of the confusion about healthy and secondary layer sexuality, fueled by anti-authoritarianism, has brought about a spiraling degradation in social conditions. This is manifested by the widespread breakthrough of the destructive secondary layer throughout society. One symptom of this deterioration is the public's increasing insensitivity to overt criminal behavior and to the graphic sadism and pornography in film, television programming, music lyrics, and print media. It is not surprising that this tolerance has been accompanied by an alarming rise in all forms of criminality.

When people can understand the distinction between the rational and irrational functions of government and recognize the emotional plague, they will be better able to see how this pestilence *always* interferes with rational politics. The rational elements in our system of government have been able to oppose the effects of the emotional plague only by chance, hampered as they are by a lack of knowledge of its very real existence. However, armed with this understanding, society's battle against the plague will be more successful. For example, having had the opportunity to observe the rise of several fascist movements (Nazism and Islamic fundamentalism on the right and Communism on the left), we know that the way this pestilence can spread globally occurs in two phases. There is an initial excitation of longing for a better society, a better world. This then leads to frustration and social destructiveness when faced with the impossibility of practically attaining these goals. The masses are first stirred emotionally by the idealistic and revolutionary slogans and rhetoric concocted by pestilent individuals. In fact, they are excited beyond their biophysical tolerance into sociopolitical action.[185] Pestilent individuals argue for the need to overthrow the existing social system in order to establish a more equitable, more effective, more glorious, more peaceful society. The pseudo-liberal character on the left and the reactionary on the right expedite this phase through their active involvement in the sociopolitical arena. *They accomplish this task by supporting the destructive efforts and actions of pestilent individuals.* The effect of this activity is to further confuse and paralyze the public at large. They become unable to see the danger; that is, contactlessness becomes more entrenched. Increasingly, the infestation spreads to the masses. When the promised new order fails to materialize, as it must, the carriers of the emotional plague turn their hatred against each other, against like-minded individuals who are perceived as opposing its realization. Ideological slogans excite and trigger violence which, with the help of military or police force, escalate and finally culminate in the destruction of the opposition. This sociopolitical action serves to discharge the pent-up hatred held in the armor.

By counteracting such malignant sociopolitics with functionally based knowledge, we now have the potential to weaken the destructive effects of the emotional plague. We can understand

---

185. Terrorism is the most recent example of political action.

that *armored humans will never be able to be suddenly set free* and that all attempts at social improvement require patience and an in-depth understanding of the limitations of armored humans to tolerate freedom. As in the treatment of individuals, emotional health for an entire society can only be achieved systematically and gradually.

Contrary to what people are led to believe, education is not enough. It must become common knowledge that people are too bioemotionally and biophysically sick to bring about social improvement on their own. Therapeutic social interventions are necessary to deal with the destructive effects of ocular armor. Otherwise, perceptual and cognitive distortions with their destructive consequences will continue.

Rational social interaction is possible only to the extent that ocular functioning and clear perception are intact, free of distortion. This condition provides individuals with the ability to make rational choices based on the facts. Ocular armor always interferes with clear perception and therefore forms the basis of virtually all human irrationality. It will always interfere with natural social processes. Moreover, disturbances of an individual's ocular functioning will cause social armor to intensify. Thus, ocular armor is primary and to eliminate social armor it is crucial to address people's ocular disturbances.

The Orgonometry of Social Pathology

All interactions in nature are governed by a limited number of functional relationships. These were described in chapter 1 (see figures 1.3 through 1.6) and examples are given throughout this book. Orgonometry describes a way of thinking derived from observing how things actually work in nature, not necessarily the way people *think* they work. Traditional sociologists occasionally deal with social problems in terms of these relationships but do so in a hit-or-miss fashion and without realizing their true functional significance. It is essential to view human relationships with the tool of orgonometry if one expects to arrive at an accurate understanding of social processes. The following analysis will point the way to a functional comprehension of the origin of destructive social activity and offer a method to deal with it.

The social relationship between two people can be described as the dynamic interaction of alternating opposite functions. In this interaction, the individuals, designated by the symbols A1 and A2, function alternately in one of two ways, either as *excitant* or as *percipient*.[186] (See Fig. 1.11)

A1	Excitant Percipient	⇄	Percipient Excitant	A2

FIGURE 1.11

The relationship described in this diagram, however, does not tell us anything about whether the social interaction is rational and constructive or neurotic and destructive; that is, whether or not there is *genuine contact between the excitant and percipient* or whether armor is present and interfering with contact.

In a healthy social interaction, the excitant individual communicates and behaves rationally, and the percipient accurately perceives the excitation and responds rationally; that is, appropriately. When a social interaction is not disturbed by armor in either the excitant or the percipient, both excitation and perception are in bioenergetic contact. There is a healthy relationship of attractive opposition between the two individuals. For purposes of analyzing social interactions, healthy or neurotic, each single, paired excitant and percipient interplay as they occur moment to moment is a discrete social event.

The following account of an incident that took place at the Fourth International Orgonomic Conference in Munich, Germany is given as an example to illustrate orgonometrically how an attempted emotional plague attack was aborted.

> On the second day of the meeting, at the start of a lecture on functional childrearing, an individual from the audience stood up at one of the floor microphones and insisted on being given "equal time" to air his views. Members of the lecturing panel were taken by surprise and were placed in a no-win situation. If the person was allowed to speak, a chaotic situation would inevitably follow. If he was not, then the panel members could be, and

186. The economic realm is included in the social realm and the relationship between excitant and percipient applies as well to economic systems.

> indeed later were, accused of employing "fascist tactics" and "suppression of free speech," with the usual false charges and projections that are typical of a plague attack. The correct course of action was clear—to ensure that the lecture be continued without interruption. The conference was never intended to be an open forum. Because of the tremendous amount of information packed into each lecture and the limitations of time, it was necessary to maintain a fairly tight schedule from the start. Obviously, the protester was not interested in hearing the members of the panel, only using the conference to generate controversy and disorder under the pretext of presenting his personal views. Accordingly, the individual was removed from the room by a guard when he refused to give up the microphone. When a second member of the group demanded equal time, he was *brought into contact* by a panel member who reminded him of the fact *that those attending the conference had paid money to hear the scheduled participants* and *that*, if he did not agree with what was being said, *he was free to organize his own conference*. A hearty round of applause from the audience followed, and this forced the dissenter back to his seat and the conference resumed without further interruption.[187]

The reason the agent of the plague attack failed in his attempt to disrupt the meeting was that a panel member *was successful in establishing contact with the agitator through a relationship of attractive opposition*.

The following episode, cited in *Responsibility and Judgment* by Hanna Arendt, is another example of an aborted emotional plague attack. In World War II during the Nazi occupation of Denmark, the Nazis demanded that stateless persons be turned over for deportation; that is, that the German refugees whom they had deprived of their nationality be surrendered to them. The Danes explained that because these refugees were no longer German citizens, the Nazis could not claim them without Danish assent. Under pressure of public opinion, the German officials backed down. They were overpowered by an effective, *rationally expressed response*. In this way, nearly all the Jews on Danish territory, regardless of their origin, whether they were Danish citizens or

---

187. *Journal of Orgonomy*. 1984. Report on the Fourth International Orgonomic Conference 18(2): 252–258.

stateless refugees from Germany, were saved from annihilation. The reason that the emotional plague was effectively counteracted in this case was that *a relationship of attractive opposition with the Nazis was steadfastly maintained by the Danes.*

If these isolated social events, which are the exception in today's world, were to become the rule, the emotional plague could be quickly and effectively exposed and neutralized. This is possible despite the coercive force and cunning of emotional plague characters. These individuals are, in fact, impotent cowards, and they derive their success not from strength but from intimidating and confusing the frightened, helpless masses. If sufficient numbers of people, the *percipients,* were able to recognize the pestilence in its many manifestations and guises for what it is, they would be in a position to oppose the perpetrators, the *excitants,* and expose and effectively neutralize them, their destructive, anti-life actions and their varied, nefarious programs. *Undistorted contact between percipient and excitant is essential if the plague is to be contained.*

Irrational interactions leading to social destructiveness always arise from, and are characterized by, the absence of genuine contact. They are determined by the individuals' particular character. There are two types of irrational or neurotic interaction. Either the irrationalism is reversible, because the percipient individual is capable of reversing the excitant's irrationalism, or it is not. In the latter case, there is always a relationship of antagonistic opposition between percipient and excitant.

There are two other reasons that the destructive social interaction is not reversible. One is that, given the particular social situation, it may not be appropriate for the percipient to address the excitant's irrationality. If such is the case, the individual may choose a later opportunity in private to do so. But, despite his best efforts, the percipient may find it impossible to establish contact with the excitant. An example of this type of interaction occurred between the German physicist Max Plank and Hitler. Plank met with Hitler in an attempt to reason with him about the latter's irrational, destructive behavior. Hitler responded to Plank's entreaties by becoming agitated and then flying into a blind rage, effectively cutting off all contact.

Finally, the most important and common reason that the

pestilent interaction may not be reversible is that *the percipient individual's armored structure thwarts his or her ability to respond effectively to the excitant's irrationality.* The percipient's inaction is often effectively rationalized with excuses such as: "It's not my place to respond"; "Let the leader take care of it"; "He (the excitant) is my senior and a great man, therefore he must be right"; "It's not that important to say"; "It's too obvious to have to explain"; "He's not all wrong"; and so on. These rationalizations are the "Little Man" reactions that every armored person functioning as percipient is capable of presenting.

In effect, the excitant's irrationality excites a neurotic reaction of collusion in the percipient: Excitant and percipient function as co-conspirators of the emotional plague. These interactions may have no particular consequence at all or they can result in the rise to power over the masses of despotic "Little Men" like Hitler, Stalin, Pol Pot, Saddam Hussein, or innumerable other Fuehrers. The only differences are the social situations in which they occur. *These irrational social interactions are directly responsible for the widespread dissemination of the emotional plague, with the result that people are left increasingly confused, out of touch with themselves, and more socially isolated.*

To illustrate, a particularly dangerous social situation always occurs when emotional plague activity is met with an inappropriate response of appeasement on the part of the percipient. Since, for liberals, evil is a meaningless concept, they consistently fail to recognize the existence of the emotional plague. When an individual with a liberal character structure happens to be the leader of a great nation, the consequences of his actions can be disastrous.

A classic example of this occurred in September 1938, just one year before the start of World War II in Europe. When British Prime Minister Neville Chamberlain signed the Munich agreement with Hitler giving Germany the right to annex the Sudetenland of Czechoslovakia, Chamberlain announced to the world that the agreement guaranteed "peace in our time." The prime minister, a liberal character blind to the emotional plague, believed that he could form a relationship (of attractive opposition) with Hitler through rational dialogue. The result was, in reality, a manifestation of *substitute or false contact* that was disastrous for the world. This effort of appeasement played directly into Hitler's hands. It was seen as a sign of weakness and it led Hitler to believe that he was at liberty to pursue his grandiose scheme of world domination.

Another example of blindness to the reality of evil are the public statements of those leftist Europeans and American liberals criticizing President Bush's intuitive, clearsighted characterization of North Korea, Iraq, and Iran as an "Axis of Evil" for, among other things, engaging in the manufacture and sale of weapons of mass destruction. His accurate understanding of their emotional plague activity is contemptuously called by liberals as "simplistic," "absolutist," and "unilateralist overdrive." Former President Jimmy Carter stated that Bush's characterization "seriously jeopardized progress made" and that "it will take years before we can repair the damage done by that statement." Such characterologically based, partisan responses of appeasement and Carter's calling for "understanding the enemy" are highly destructive.[188] If left unchecked, Carter's words will be taken by both Red and Black Fascists as a sign of weakness and an open invitation to escalate their destructive activities. *In dealing with fascist states, it is essential to have* a *relationship of attractive opposition militarily and a relationship of antagonistic opposition politically and socially.* (See chapter 8, the section on the Arab-Israeli Conflict) With disastrous consequences, characterological liberals have it the other way around.

As is the case of exposure to other contagious diseases, a personal encounter with an emotional plague attack, if it is recognized as such, can confer a degree of immunity to the individual. The person becomes emotionally stronger and more capable of effectively dealing with future attacks.

Contact with the self and with the environment is essential not only for healthy functioning, but more importantly for survival. We have shown that armor consists of a dynamic interaction between defensive forces and the underlying impulses from the secondary layer and the biological core resulting in a state of contactlessness.

---

188. Mr. Carter failed to mention that the 1994 agreement he personally negotiated with the North Korean regime to halt their nuclear weapons development program, in exchange for the transfer of peaceful nuclear technology and economic assistance from the United States, was soon violated by the North Koreans, who secretly continued their development program.

Disturbing this equilibrium will always result in the appearance of disquieting emotions and sensations, and sometimes with the ideas related to them.

The way to restore contact in social systems is identical to that in individual characteranalytic treatment. In both cases, the equilibrium of the armor is systematically disturbed. Ocular armor must be addressed at the start, and this takes place in two steps (Reich 1949a). First, individuals are made aware *that* they are behaving defensively.[189] This weakens the defensive forces. Then, they are made aware of *how* they are behaving defensively.

The dynamic interaction between the defended and defending forces is shown in the following diagram (Fig. 9.4):

FIGURE 9.4

When the opposing forces are equal an energetic stalemate occurs, giving rise to an absence of contact. The social consequences of this contactless state are potentially disastrous for both individuals and society. To give an extreme example, when people are in a life-threatening situation and are not in full contact with what is happening, they may well be incapable of a response that ensures their survival.

When one considers the degree of *bioemotional* sickness in the general population, the imperiled world situation is completely understandable. Burdened by immediate problems and life's distractions, most people cannot see beyond securing their imminent physical comforts and material needs. Whether or not they are aware of it, most people spend their lives struggling to survive. Coming into contact with themselves and with the condition of society is far beyond their capacity.

Bearing these considerations in mind, what can those who are orgonomically trained do to alleviate the social effect of human armoring, especially the destructiveness of the emotional

189. Some of the more obvious manifestations of contactlessness, such as difficulty sustaining attention, not listening when spoken to, easy distractibility, and so on, are recognized by general psychiatrists and diagnosed as Attention Deficit Hyperactivity Disorder (ADHD). However, the true incidence of contactlessness is far greater than is generally recognized, and the full extent of its effects is not appreciated.

plague? In contrast to individual armor, social armor involves a dynamic interaction between two or more people. However, it must be understood that social armor, which includes a wide range of pathological human behavior, including sociopolitical ideology and mystical religious beliefs, has a defensive strength as powerful as any intrapsychic defense. It provides hopes and illusions that protect people from coming into contact with inner feelings of insecurity, misery, loneliness, and anxiety. This is why people cling as tenaciously to their religious and political beliefs as they do to the distorted beliefs they have about themselves. This is also why they have no inkling of just how misdirected and destructive these ways of thinking are for their own lives and for those around them.

Because the removal of social armor also liberates large amounts of energy and the conditions for conducting individual therapy are not present, its complete elimination is not possible. Therefore, even though the structure of the armor is the same in both the individual and in society, social armor must be addressed conservatively. How, then, can we approach it?

As in the case of individual therapy, the primary goal is to first improve ocular functioning. In individual therapy, the patient's defenses are quickly activated against the therapist's efforts to help. However, in social situations such as group therapy, these defensive reactions do not usually occur because in these settings, when people openly discuss their feelings and problems, the group members identify with others who, like themselves, are also struggling in their lives. These processes of identification and group tolerance offset defensive reactions in the members. When defenses are not easily activated, the individual members have the opportunity to improve contact with themselves and with others.

True social change requires that the pervasive contactlessness of people be brought to their attention. This enormous task can be accomplished in spite of the fact that people are, to varying degrees, out of touch with themselves. In orgonometric terms, we have seen that accord is reached only if a relationship of antagonistic opposition can be changed into one of attractive opposition. *This change is an indication that energetic contact has been established between the opposing forces.*

Social orgonomy can offer help providing that only the first and second above-mentioned steps of individual armor removal are implemented in a controlled therapeutic setting. The first step is to bring the contactless state to the individual's awareness and the second is to show *how* defensive thinking and behavior are used to provide a false sense of contact and how they actually serve to perpetuate individual pathology. If successful, this step-wise process will partially restore contact and can even improve ocular functioning, thereby withdrawing, to some degree, the energy behind defensive ideas and behaviors. This will enable some people to become introspective; that is, to take a *look inward* at the function of their neurotic behaviors and character attitudes. The third step, which is to bring individuals in contact with and to express their underlying defended impulses, releases large quantities of energy and the removal of deeper layers of armor. This necessarily lies outside the domain of the social orgonomist and requires the expertise of a medical orgonomist.

A highly destructive example of social pathology in international relations is the *false* attractive opposition that has been set up by liberals world-wide between the Israelis and the Palestinians. Both parties are expected to sit at the "peace table" and arrive at a negotiated settlement of their differences. Liberals continue to believe that both parties genuinely desire peace and that it is possible for them to arrive at an agreement, one that will embrace Israel as an accepted nation in the Middle East, including actual recognition of Israel and its right to exist. What is consistently ignored is that the Palestinian forces and many Arab countries have never recognized the State of Israel, and that in fact, by their actions and in their rhetoric, they actively seek her destruction. Therefore, the actual relationship remains one of antagonistic opposition, with no possibility of arriving at an honest, negotiated settlement. Until the Palestinians accept the legitimacy of the State of Israel, all dialogue at the peace table will continue to be a sham. When Israel is finally recognized by the Palestinians, real contact between the two forces will have been established and the relationship will change to one of attractive opposition. What makes maintaining any false attractive opposition relationship particularly dangerous is that it sends a message of weakness to the forces of the emotional plague, leading them to believe that if they continue to pursue their socially destructive activities, they will win.[190]

In Summary

To begin to contain the emotional plague it is first necessary to distinguish between those individuals who, based on their biophysical structure and knowledge of biological orgone energy functions, are capable of improving the human condition, and those who are not. The latter group includes the well-intentioned politicians, educators, traditional psychiatrists, social workers and therapists, and the judiciary. The responsibility for work in the social realm must be in the hands of social scientists and health care workers who are capable of effecting social improvement. One of their primary tasks will be to begin to put an end to sociopolitics as we know it and to place politics on a scientific foundation based on knowledge of human emotional functioning. This will bring about greater independence and genuine responsibility in people and it will inevitably lead to greater individual freedom.

Political science is concerned with the origin, development, and function of the state. From its formal inception with Plato's *Republic*, politics has always been a mixture of rational core functions as well as functions from the secondary layer. From an orgonomic perspective, secondary layer political activity is always irrational and therefore destructive. While not always identical with the emotional plague, it often leads directly to it. This is because the secondary layer is the reservoir of man's irrationality and destructive behavior. As such, it is never concerned with the protection of life's functions, but with the exact opposite: the destruction of natural life and the struggle to maintain power for its own sake. This is accomplished by a handful of individuals afflicted with the pestilence in positions of power.

The rightful province of politics in government is to safeguard natural living functions. Only through a slow process over many generations will people with less armor and clearer perspective

190. The sado-masochistic relationship between the emotional plague individual and the liberal was discussed in the last chapter. (See figure 8.4) It is a typical example of a false attractive opposition relationship based on *substitute contact*.

set rational limits on governmental powers and find ways for the state to function more efficiently.[191]

A return to the old ways of the past authoritarian social order is not possible, nor is it desirable. The genie, in the form of the destructive secondary layer of armored humanity, is out of the bottle. In our current anti-authoritarian social order, the secondary layer in the form of human helplessness and the craving to be led, as well as the many other pathological social behaviors of armored humans, are becoming institutionalized in all sectors of society. It will be impossible to find a way out of this morass without people honestly looking at themselves, at their own damaged character structure. Because the question of why people cannot see themselves for who they are is consistently evaded, an approach to the source of humanity's sickness is now more remote than ever. Instead, superficial self-help solutions are promulgated and marketed extensively to the public, and serve as just another way for people to avoid taking a good look into themselves.

Because ocular armor always distorts perception and thinking and is so pervasive, neither the liberal nor the conservative is able to see that armor exists, let alone that it has enormous adverse social consequences. Neither group, of course, can see that there is such a thing as the emotional plague. As a result of overlooking the plague, the liberal naively clings to the illusion that the human condition can be improved simply by redoubling political efforts and manipulating the environment; whereas the conservative advocates a return to the methods of the past, holding onto the beliefs that human nature cannot be altered and that we can never know enough to effect positive change. These opposing views are clear evidence that people from all walks of life, no matter how well-intentioned, are incapable of dealing with the powerful forces residing below the surface that determine how human beings think and act. Until these forces are recognized, understood functionally and addressed, all political "solutions" are doomed to fail. Through the centuries, all efforts at

191. One method to ensure efficiency is the "sundown" law, which de-funds government departments that cannot justify their existence. However, to date, efforts in the U.S. to reduce unnecessary, ineffective governmental programs have failed because bureaucratic groups, acting out of self-interest, have blocked them.

social reform have not made people less troubled or more satisfied because the emotional pestilence springs into action and turns every attempt at improvement into another tragedy.

Wilhelm Reich concluded from a wealth of personal experience in the field that *all* attempts at a political or economic "solution" to the enormous problems of armored human society, no matter how well-intentioned or how well thought out, are futile. The repeated failure of sociopolitical efforts should make this realization abundantly and painfully clear to everyone.

Fortunately, the sociological legacy given to us by Reich and E.F. Baker has the potential to provide a natural scientific approach that can deal with political and social irrationalism. Should humanity fail to use this knowledge, it is certain that it will repeat the same disastrous mistakes that it has made countless times before and with even greater catastrophic consequences.

The following question arises: Is it possible for individuals with different sociopolitical character structures to see eye-to-eye on social issues and then constructively address them? The answer is that they can *so long as their desire to agree and cooperate is not compromised by intractable ocular armor.*

Only when people finally stop looking to the symptomatic solutions offered by politicians and religious leaders will it first become possible to begin the difficult process of containing the emotional plague. People cling to political "liberators" today as tenaciously as they did to religious saviors in the past. Divesting the masses of the illusion of political solutions to social problems will not be easy. People have to first rid themselves of the mystical expectation of being taken care of in this or the next world. When this process of demystification has begun, people will start looking to themselves and this can lead to more independence and self-sufficiency. They will then have to learn to distinguish between those who have rational authority, authority based on a practical working knowledge of the laws governing life energy functions, and the irrational authority of religious and political leaders.

However, nothing positive will happen until the emotional plague is generally recognized. Therefore, the first task is to increase public awareness of the plague's existence. It will not be easy to bring about recognition primarily because the pestilence survives by being hidden from public awareness. To add to the difficulty of recognition, people today are more out of touch with themselves than ever before. Once this necessary first step—exposing the plague—is achieved, then people will find ways to contain it. *Containment of the emotional plague cannot be accomplished using political tactics.* Forming a cabinet level Office of the Emotional Plague will not work. Since the plague is a medical disease, sequestration and eradication must be accomplished using the weapons of the epidemiologist.

Just as individuals tend to repeat destructive patterns of behavior because of the presence of individual armor, the repetition compulsion, so too does society repeat patterns of destructive behavior because of the presence of social armor. In both cases, despite the repetitive, negative experience, little practical knowledge is gained and nothing improves.

One such example of repetitive, destructive social behavior is the predilection of armored humans to personally attack and destroy those individuals who can observe and speak the truth about subjects that people consistently avoid.

Reich saw Jesus as the supreme example of unarmored life, and he saw the murder of Jesus as the work of the emotional plague. He put the responsibility for Jesus' fate not on Judas, Pontius Pilate, or the Pharisees—not on a man or a group of men—but on the emotional plague, rooted as it is in all who are armored. He saw in the murder of Christ the essence of the emotional plague. He writes:

> The most fantastic, perverted, incredible fact is this: *The murder of Christ through the ages is protected by the people themselves who suffer most from it.* Silence on the part of the multitudes; the people know the truth . . . Why don't they speak up? Open defense of the murderer if and when it happens that a finger is being pointed at him, defense especially by so-called "liberals"; Slandering and persecution of Christ on the part of pestilent little Fuehrers risen from amongst the people. The whole system of procedure in courts and the shaping of public opinion: Silence through the ages about the ways and means of the emotional plague in the books of learning of all ages. Nobody has ever dared to attack the emotional plague as an integral principle of basic human organization.
>
> (Reich 1953a, page 99; italics in the original)

Average men and women flock to Jesus in expectation of a miraculous deliverance from their armor ("sins"). When he cannot rescue them in the way they expect, they turn against him in disappointment. They do not actively kill Christ, but they passively support it, as *they do nothing to prevent the murder.* Thus, the story of Jesus stands as a vivid account of the murder of the living. *This murder goes on continually.* Every newborn has the core attributes of Jesus but these innate qualities are frustrated and smothered right from birth—damaged or destroyed in one way or another by armored people.

In *The Murder of Christ*, Reich uses Jesus' death as an example of how armored humans attack and destroy those who speak for life and the truth. A parallel can be drawn between the mystical distortion of Jesus' teachings shortly after his death and how Reich's discoveries are treated today. Because armored behavior doesn't change, one can predict, as did Reich himself, that the science of orgonomy, for all its truth and potential benefit for humanity, will be resisted, attacked, trivialized, and explained away until it is lifeless and impotent.

Compare the events that occurred in the Roman Empire about one hundred years after Jesus' birth with what is happening now. In 100 A.D., Rome was the greatest power on Earth and the center of Western civilization. It had recently undergone a transition from a republic to an empire, and the Roman emperors had assumed absolute power over the populace, partly because there was widespread social breakdown with the rise of secondary layer behaviors: social destructiveness, diverse sexual practices, and increasing mysticism.

Today, the United States is the greatest world power, but in recent decades, it, too, has undergone a transformation, with power increasingly concentrated in state and federal governments. There has been a sweeping decline in personal responsibility, with a corresponding disintegration in the structure of authoritarian society and of the family as a cohesive social unit. The consequence has been loss of contact, anxiety, discontent, and the destruction of social institutions. Without correction, further social disintegration and chaos are inevitable.

Around 100 A.D., Jesus' life and teachings were already undergoing mystical distortion by his armored admirers. Today, the same is occurring with Reich. The readily available and well-known historical facts of his life and the scientific basis of his work are excluded from centers of learning or ignored. Today, he is even more misunderstood than in his lifetime, and few young people even know of him. What does circulate, the comments one hears, are evidence of the distortion and blatant lies that followed him in his lifetime, after his death, right up to the present. Similarly, Jesus was most reviled by those who were closest to him; it was they who handed him over to the Roman authorities for trial. Reich, too, was vilified by the very psychoanalysts closest to him, the members of Freud's inner circle. It was they who started the vicious character assassination campaign that accused Reich of being crazy, a rumor that continued throughout his life and greatly contributed to his social and scientific isolation.[192]

There were those who mystified Jesus and his teachings or scoffed that he was no better than they. Today, there are idolizers who hold a mystical belief in Reich and in his discoveries. This makes them unable to see both the man and his work realistically. Others misunderstand and trivialize his discoveries, explain them away, and project their own pettiness and limited, distorted view of the world onto Reich. These are what Reich called the "Little Man" reactions of the armored, reactions seen and repeated ad nauseam throughout the ages.

One hundred years after Jesus' birth, cults that practiced an early form of Christianity grew up throughout the Roman world. All but one, the cult of Saint Paul, fell into oblivion. Paul, arguably the most zealous of the early followers of Jesus, succeeded in anchoring his own mystical interpretation of Jesus' teachings in people and it survives to the present day as the central dogma of Christianity. Mystification subverted Jesus' humanistic teachings and this gave the Church enormous power over the populace—pagans and Christians alike. Political maneuverings, especially by the Roman Emperor Constantine, took advantage

192. From personal experience, I know this hate campaign continued into the early 1960s. At that time, during my psychoanalytically oriented psychiatric residency, there were three different instructors, all training analysts, each of whom spent an entire class session slandering and vilifying Reich. These tirades, insolent and filled with rank hatred, were most bizarre, out of keeping with the public persona of these senior psychiatrists. On one occasion, I heard the director of residency training threaten that if any resident even *mentioned* Reich's name, that resident would be dismissed from the program. Incidents like these, although now much less common, still continue to be reported.

of Jesus' influence and helped shape the distorted face of Christianity as we know it today. To achieve this, Constantine came to profess belief in the Christian God, commissioned and financed a new Bible that omitted those gospels that spoke of Christ's human traits and embellished those that made Jesus appear godlike. The earlier gospels were outlawed, gathered up, and burned.

Even before Reich's death, and more so since, self-proclaimed "gurus" have sprung up world-wide to become the leaders of "Reichian" cults. They have done exactly as Reich predicted: They have taken bits and pieces of his body of work and adapted them to their own ends. Because they do not retain the essential—the function of the orgasm in humans and an understanding of the laws governing orgone energy functions in nature—these modifiers and interpreters of Reich move away from thinking functionally in the direction of mechanism or mysticism. They do great damage to the science of orgonomy, all the while exploiting aspects of Reich's discoveries for their own personal or financial gain. Their mechanistic applications of orgonotic functions will turn into dead ends and their mystical interpretations might yet give rise to a new religious faction, one that will take root and hold out the promise of spiritual salvation and social stability; one that extolls a bioenergetic "heaven on Earth" in the name of Reich and orgonomy. Clearly, it is necessary to bring a stop to these distortions and misuse of Reich's discoveries. If this is not done, the science of orgonomy will pass into oblivion.

To prevent such an outcome, it must be recognized that there is a measure of mechanistic thinking and mysticism in everyone, *particularly those who "believe in orgonomy."* To the extent that it exists, people are incapable of living, working, and thinking in accord with the functional energetic principles that govern life.

The distortion and misuse of Reich's discoveries can only be countered by securing in the character structure of enough people the ability to make practical use of the science of orgonomy, the most important part of which today is recognizing and dealing with the emotional plague. If people succeed in this endeavor it will be a first in the history of humanity and it will be evidence that armored people are able to think and act differently in a way to prevent history from endlessly repeating itself. It will mean that people have been able to develop new and healthier forms of social interaction.

Achieving real improvement in personal and social conditions will be extremely difficult and will take many generations to accomplish—there are simply no shortcuts. It is first necessary to fully appreciate the reality of armor, that human beings are literally *trapped* in it and that the most common way the armored protect themselves from being responsible for their life is to blame others for their misfortunes. Their armor protects them through self-deception by leading them to believe that the solution to their problems originates exclusively from outside themselves. A new miracle drug, a better therapy, a more powerful politician or healer is just around the corner. A result of ocular armor, this illusion inevitably provides many with the hope for political and/or religious salvation. At the same time, the survival of the freedom-peddling politician and the salvation-peddling clergy relies on human helplessness and on these leaders' ability to convince the multitudes that they can fulfill people's hopes and dreams better than can their opponents. That these promises have never been and cannot ever be fulfilled has not kept humanity from sustaining this hope.

Nevertheless, there is reason for realistic hope that Reich's discoveries will provide humanity with an exit from its trap. *Reich based this hope primarily on the prevention of chronic armoring in newborns, infants, and children.* Only in this way can people grow up healthier, generation after generation, and humanity's hope for a better world be fulfilled.

These questions remain: When will people stop endlessly seeking distractions, blaming external causes, and face their terror of looking to themselves to deal with the enormity of their personal problems? How much worse do social conditions have to become than they already are before people make a genuine effort to change? History has shown that people will go to any length and expend untold amounts of energy and money on ill-fated social, political, and religious projects, all to avoid contact with their core feelings and their destructive secondary layer impulses. In our current anti-authoritarian era, people are running away more than ever before from the biological core into their superficial layer.

Fortunately, humanity now has access to knowledge that for the first time in its history can help it to break free of an existence that is based on mechanistic thinking, religious illusions, and political ideology. Only when people recognize that they are imprisoned by their armor, that armor results in the emotional plague, and that this scourge interferes with humanity's attempts at self-betterment, will it be possible to begin improvement of the human condition. The humanitarian and technological advances that can be possible when future generations are able to think and behave functionally are beyond the scope of our imagination. This possibility belongs neither to the left nor to the right. It belongs to a future free from the ravages of the emotional plague.

REFERENCES

Adams, Henry. 1889. *History of the United States of America during the First Administration of Thomas Jefferson.* New York: The Library of America, 1986.

Allen, F.L. 1931. *Only Yesterday: An Informal History of the 1920s.* New York: Harper Row, 1964.

Apple, W.B. 1999. Marijuana's Role in Inducing Social and Individual Chaos: An Orgonomic Perspective. *Journal of Orgonomy* 33(1, 2): 68–94.

Baker, E.F. 1967. *Man in the Trap.* New York: Macmillan.

Barnes, C. 1979. Toward a Functional View of Economics. *Journal of Orgonomy* 13(1):124–39.

Bennett, W.J. 1999. *The Index of Leading Cultural Indicators.* Colorado Springs, CO: WaterBrook Press.

Bork, R.H. 1996. *Slouching towards Gomorrah.* New York: HarperCollins.

Bruce, Tammy. 2001. *The New Thought Police.* New York: Random House.

Cato Institute. 1999. Policy analysis no. 364, Dec. 15.

Chan, H.B., et al. 2001. Quantum Mechanical Actuation of Microelectromechanical Systems by the Casimir Force. *Science* 291:1941–44.

Courtois, S., et al. 1999. *The Black Book of Communism.* Cambridge, MA: Harvard University Press.

Esposito, J., ed. 1999. *Oxford History of Islam.* Oxford: Oxford University Press.

Freud, S., and Bullitt, W.C. 1967. *Thomas Woodrow Wilson: A Psychological Study.* Boston: Houghton Mifflin.

Goldberg, M. 1989. Work Energy and the Character of Organizations (II). *Journal of Orgonomy* 23(2):190–209.

Harman, R.A. 1988. The Emotional Plague as Manifested in the AIDS Hysteria. *Journal of Orgonomy* 22(2): 173–95.

Hitchens, P. 1999. *The Abolition of Britain.* San Francisco: Encounter Books.

Johnson, P. 1997. *A History of the American People.* New York: Harper Collins.

Konia, C. 1986a. Cancer and Communism (I). *Journal of Orgonomy* 20(1): 54–66.

______1986b. Cancer and Communism (II). *Journal of Orgonomy* 20(2):195–213.

______1993. Orgone Therapy: Sociopolitical Aspects. *Journal of Orgonomy* 27(1): 61–80.

Lamoreaux, S. 1997. Demonstration of the Casimir Force in the 0.6 to 64m Range. *Physical Review Letters* 78(1): 5–8.

Leo, J. 2001. "The No-Speech Culture." *U.S. News and World Report,* March 19.

Lind, W. 1999. "What is Political Correctness?" *The Schwarz Report,* March.

Marans, S., et al. 1995. The Police-Mental Health Partnership: A Community-Based Response to Urban Violence. New Haven, CT: Yale University Press.

Murray, C. 1984. *Losing Ground: American Social Policy, 1950–1980.* New York: Basic Books.

National Center for Health Statistics. 1998. National Vital Statistics. website: www.cdc.gov/nchs.

Oliver, F.S. 1916. *Ordeal by Battle.* London: Macmillan.

_______1928. *Alexander Hamilton: An Essay on American Union.* New York: G. P. Putnam's Sons.

Pryce-Jones. 2002. *The Closed Circle.* Chicago: Ivan R. Dee.

Rashid, A, 2002. *Jihad: The Rise of Militant Islam in Central Asia.* New Haven, CT: Yale University Press.

Reich, W. 1946. *The Mass Psychology of Fascism.* New York: Orgone Institute Press.

_______1948a. *The Discovery of the Orgone,* vol. 1. New York: Orgone Institute Press.

_______1948b. *Listen Little Man.* New York: Orgone Institute Press.

_______1948c. *The Discovery of the Orgone,* vol. 2. New York: Orgone Institute Press.

_______1949a. *Character Analysis,* New York: Orgone Institute Press.

_______1949b. *Ether, God and Devil.* New York: Orgone Institute Press.

_______1950. Orgonometric Equations: I. General Form. *Orgone Energy Bulletin* 2:169.

_______1953a. *The Murder of Christ.* Rangley, ME: Orgone Institute Press.

_______1953b. *People in Trouble.* Rangley, ME: Orgone Institute Press.

_______1936. Character and Society. *Journal of Orgonomy* 8(12):116–29, 1974.

_______1938. *The Bion Experiments: On the Origin of Life.* New York: Octagon, 1979.

_______1934. *The Bioelectrical Investigation of Sexuality and Anxiety.* New York: Farrar, Straus, and Giroux, 1982.

_______1983. *Children of the Future: On the Prevention of Sexual Pathology.* New York: Farrar, Straus Giroux.

_______1990. Wrong Thinking Kills. *Orgonomic Functionalism* 2:34–43.

Sharaf, M. 1983. *Fury on Earth.* New York: St. Martin's Press.

Sowell, T. 1987. *The Conflict of Visions.* New York: William Morrow Company.

_______1995. *The Vision of the Anointed.* New York: Basic Books.

Sprinzak, Ehud. 1998. In Walter Reich, Ed. *The Psychopolitical Formation of Extreme Left Terrorism in a Democracy: The Case of the Weather Men in The Origin of Terrorism.* Washington, D.C.: The Woodrow Wilson Center Press.

Steele, Shelby 1998. *A Dream Deferred.* New York: HarperCollins.

de Tocqueville, Alexis. 2000. *Democracy in America.* Translated and edited by Harvey C. Mansfield and Debra Winthrop. Chicago: University of Chicago Press.

Toynbee, Arnold. 1946. *A Study of History, Abridged Version.* New York: Oxford University Press.

Von Mises, L. 1949. *Human Action: A Treatise on Economics.* New Haven, CT: Yale University Press.

Wilson, E.O. 1980. *Sociobiology: The Abridged Version.* Cambridge, MA: Belkamp Press of Harvard University Press.

GLOSSARY

anxiety The psychic perception of the organism as it is constricted by a contraction against expansion accompanied by a distressing sense of oppression or a vague, formless worry.

armor The total defense apparatus of the organism consisting of the rigidities of the character and chronic spasms of the musculature. Armor functions essentially as a defense against the breakthrough of emotion—particularly anxiety, rage, and sexual excitation, as well as intolerable sensations. See *character armor* and *muscular armor.*

anti-authoritarianism The social system that is opposed to both neurotic (irrational) and rational authority at every level of social organization.

authoritarianism The social system that operates according to the principle of compulsive moral regulation. Headed by the father, the authoritarian family is reproduced in the authoritarian state.

biological core The autonomic nervous system from which biological excitation arises to maintain the living functions of the organism.

biopathy A pulsatory disturbance of the plasmatic system (which consists of the autonomic nervous system and vascular system) resulting from the presence of armor.

bioenergy The energy in the living organism that provides the ability for functioning. Identical to biological orgone energy.

biopsychiatry Psychiatry from the bioenergetic point of view.

character An individual's particular bioemotional structure; his or her stereotyped manner of acting and reacting. The orgonomic concept of character is functional and biological, not a static, psychological, or moralistic concept.

character analysis The therapeutic technique used to treat the psychic (characterological) aspects of human armor. See *orgone therapy*.

character armor The sum total of typical character attitudes that an individual develops to block against emotional excitations. Character armor is accompanied by rigidity of the body and lack of emotional contact ("deadness"). Functionally identical to muscular armor.

contact The perception of biological excitation.

contactlessness Absence of contact.

core functions The functions of love, work, and knowledge that govern rational human life.

defense mechanisms Specific patterns of psychic action (such as denial, projection, and isolation) that prevent the awareness of any internal or external perception that would be experienced with anxiety or emotional pain.

emotional plague The neurotic character in destructive action on the social scene.

excitation The objective movement of biological orgone energy in the organism. Excitation moves at different velocities in different tissues. Energy moves both within discrete nervous pathways and through the various tissues of the body without respect to structural boundaries.

façade The surface of the armored organism's bioemotional structure from which the individual interacts with the environment. Identical to the superficial layer and the social façade. In health, it is called the "social layer."

formal democracy The distortion of work democracy arising from social armor.

functional thinking Thinking according to the way nature functions. Contrast with *mechanistic thinking*, which is based on viewing nature as if it were a machine, and *mystical thinking*, which is based on viewing nature as if it were unknowable.

genitality The manner of functioning of the unarmored individual. Because there is an absence of sexual stasis, the individual has the capacity for natural self-regulation on the basis of orgastic potency.

ideology A set of ideas based on fixed (i.e., mechanistic or mystical) thinking that produces a social force when it is displaced onto the social realm.

mechanical potential Entropy; the tendency of systems to flow from higher to lower energy levels. See *orgonomic potential.*

mechanistic thinking The prevailing form of thinking in science, mechanistic thinking is based on the assumption that matter and its interactions are the fundamental elements in the universe. Correct when it is used in regard to mechanical systems, mechanistic thinking is highly destructive when applied to the biological realm.

muscular armor The sum total of the muscular attitudes (chronic muscular spasms) that an individual develops as a block against the breakthrough of emotions and sensations, particularly anxiety, rage, and sexual excitation. Functionally identical to character armor.

mystical thinking The belief system based on the idea that nature is unknowable through the physical senses. Mystical thinking has an objective basis in that armor distorts sense impressions and prevents direct contact with nature.

neurotic character The character type that, because of chronic stasis, operates either according to or opposed to the principle of compulsive moral regulation.

orgasm The unitary, involuntary convulsion of the total organism at the acme of the genital embrace. In armored individuals in societies that suppress infantile and adolescent genitality this reflex is blocked by orgasm anxiety.

orgasm anxiety Anxiety produced by final and complete surrender of the organism giving into its involuntary convulsion. Seen in the final stage of medical orgone therapy, orgasm anxiety is behind all armored manifestations. The psychic aspect of armor.

orgastic impotence The absence of orgastic potency, orgastic impotence is the most important characteristic of the average human of today, and—by damming up biological (orgone) energy in the organism—provides the source of energy for all biopathic symptoms and social irrationalism. The somatic aspect of armor.

orgastic potency Essentially, the capacity for complete surrender to the involuntary convulsion of the organism and complete discharge of excitation at the acme of the genital embrace. Orgastic potency is always lacking in neurotic individuals. It presupposes the presence or establishment of genitality; that is, the absence of pathological character armor and muscular armor. Orgastic potency is usually, and erroneously, not distinguished from erective and ejaculative potency, both of which are prerequisites of orgastic potency.

orgone energy Primordial cosmic energy, universally present and demonstrable visually, thermally, electroscopically, and by means of the Geiger-Mueller counter. In the living organism, this type of energy is known as bioenergy, life energy. Discovered by Wilhelm Reich between 1936 and 1940.

orgone therapy. Orgone therapy dissolves muscular and character armoring, mobilizing the individual's biological orgone energy and liberating held-back biophysical emotions with the goal of establishing, if possible, orgastic potency. See *character analysis*.

orgonometry A system of thought that is closely aligned with the natural operation of functions and functional processes. Orgonometry relies on orgonometric notation to convey function processes.

orgonomy The natural science of orgone energy and its functions.

orgonomic functionalism The application of functional thinking to natural processes.

orgonomic potential The movement of orgone energy from lower to higher levels, in contrast to the mechanical potential, which moves in the opposite direction (see *mechanical potential*).

orgonomic sociology The application of orgonomic functionalism to the study of social processes.

orgonotic pulsation The pulsation of orgone energy in living and nonliving orgonotic systems. Measurable by oscillograph, orgonotic pulsation consists of an expansive and convulsive phase.

perception The function of living all systems to be in contact with itself. Armoring interferes with the perceptual function.

political characterology The study of sociopolitical attitudes and behavior from a characterological viewpoint. Identical to sociopolitical characterology.

primary drive The natural expressions of the human organism that originate from the biological core and that are experienced and observable in the absence of armor when there are no enforced inhibitions.

rational politics Political activity that originates from the biological core and serves to protect life.

secondary drives Disturbed expressions of primary drives resulting from the failure of armor to contain destructive impulses.

sex economy The body of knowledge within orgonomy that deals with the economy of biological (orgone) energy in the organism.

social anxiety Anxiety resulting from the breakdown of individual or social armor and manifested in social activity. Not to be confused with the identical term used in the Diagnostic and Statistical Manual of Mental Disorders (DSM-IV).

social armor Any form of social organization that restricts individual freedom and responsibility. It gives rise to the opposing forces of mechanistic and mystical thought that are manifested socially, politically, and economically as ideological forces on the left and the right. The authoritarian form is necessary when people are armored.

sociopolitics Irrational political activity arising from the displacement of intrapsychic conflicts onto the social and political scene.

substitute contact An attempt to make contact when genuine contact is disturbed by armor. Substitute contact, therefore, is stilted and artificial, not genuine.

superficial layer The surface of the human bioemotional structure.

work democracy The functioning of natural and intrinsic rational work relationships among human beings. The concept of work democracy represents the established reality (not the ideology) of these relationships, which, though usually distorted because of prevailing armoring and irrational political ideologies, are nevertheless at the basis of all social achievement.

INDEX